I Feel More
Like I Do Now
Than I Did Yesterday

I Feel More
Like I Do Now
Than I Did Yesterday

[A COLLECTION OF REMEMBERED STORIES]

Brad Terry

ISBN 978-1-329-09957-9

Printed in the United States of America

Book design by Lucia Terry
Cover design by Michael Mahan

For my parents, Arthur and Melinda.

Acknowledgements

December 2014. Bath, Maine

I didn't write this book. Okay... I spent a lot of time collecting the words and arranging them into sentences and then pages of rambling recollections sprinkled as much as possible with facts. But, my 'Big Granny' once said, "When you're telling a story you should never be hampered by facts". I've only tried to be truthful.

Like lots of older people I sometimes repeat the same story. Spell check saved me from my greatest impediment as a writer. And, as Hop Rudd might say, "I type slowly but I sure make a lot of mistakes". I had help, lots of it, sorting this all out.

Many thanks to:

Marylou Terry, my sister-in-law, proofread early on. Her informed and positive slant gave me encouragement to push on with the writing.

Marty Corey for proofreading early on and for saving the e-mails I sent from Poland that make up the Last Diary from Poland. She also took some of the photographs.

Bill Ross, and Rafal and Jesica Zelek for endless support.

Contributors to "Second Stories" and all my friends who have enriched my life so much.

Grand-niece Melinda Holmes for help with formatting and proofreading and creating the timeline, Chapter 19: Brad Terry (So Far), and grand-niece Mary Jewett for help with photo shoots. And others, family and beyond, who urged me on.

Michael Mahan of Mahan Graphics for the book cover design. As Michael says, "I'm not sure I remember how or when we met, seems like I've always known you..." Michael and I met back in the early days of the Maine Festival, and he designed the Jazz logo for a concert poster originally, before I adopted it for my Friends of Jazz logo. There's a picture in the book of the family silkscreening operation in Bowdoinham, with the Jazz t-shirts hanging everywhere.

My cousin Bonnie Trafford who gave me shelter, office space, and dinners in Bridgton when I was stalled at home and couldn't get anything done.

But the real impetus for the completion of this book came from my niece Lucia Terry; even today pushing me to finalize things with the final epilogue and acknowledgements. Without her unflagging support, enthusiasm and input (editing, and formatting, formatting, formatting) this would be a roomful of 137,969 of those little magnetic words people stick on refrigerator doors. I never could have done this alone.

Epilogue One

June 5th, 2010 in Lincoln, Vermont

Almost anyone, given enough time in a studio, can come up with a perfect album. Individual notes can be corrected and timing can be tweaked to within a millisecond. But, in my personal record collection, the live performances captured as they happened, are by far the most exciting and interesting. The same holds for this book. What you will read here is totally honest; the way it happened. I'm sure I could arrange for a dozen qualified proofreaders to fine tune this so every comma is in the right place, everything grammatically perfect, no loose hanging participles, chads or muddled metaphors. But hey... that wouldn't be quite honest. Much to the chagrin of those who have helped me I've only altered things when they told me what I had written was really confusing. Don't look too closely. If it matters to you, you can surely find mistakes. Please just remember who was writing this!

There are more stories to tell and someday I might, or might not get around to putting them down on paper. I've decided, as my seventy-third birthday rapidly approaches, that it's time to finish this project.

My nephew Bern Terry and his companion, partner, and soon to be wife, Katie Shepherd, have graciously given me a place to stay here in Lincoln. Back in April, I invited myself to visit Bern and he introduced me to Jamie Masefield. He told me on the phone that he had a neighbor on the next farm over who played the mandolin. My reaction was pretty much, "Sure, okay, tell me about it, sounds great; really interesting..." I'm sure when he told Jamie he had an uncle in Maine who played the clarinet and whistled, Jamie's reaction was about the same.

Before we actually met, Bern played some of Jamie's CDs for me, and some of my stuff with Lenny Breau for Jamie. When we met in Bern's living room we only played four tunes but the communication was seamless and total. Only a few days later Jamie called me in Maine and told me he had landed us a spot in the

Burlington Discover Jazz Festival, June 7th.

This gave me a perfect excuse to visit here again. The concert in June was a great success but the summer that followed was dismal. I won't go into details except to say I had only three gigs and had little to do. I did acquire a VW Westphalia camper for a dollar and spent all my time and money getting the restoration started.

Now, September 2010, I'm back in Poland, starting a month's tour with Joachim.

And now, back in Bath, Maine. June 18, 2011. The writer's block hit hard. I've done nothing since June 8th 2010. I'm finally at it again and hoping to collect this verbiage and put it into some semblance of order.

Epilogue Two

Hopefully this will be the final attempt to complete this story that seems to get longer as it takes longer. Now, it's November 29th 2011, my mother's 110th birthday.

Back in Poland, with a disappointing lack of concerts, but enjoying the free time. I will enjoy seeing many good friends without being always in a rush to get somewhere.

Epilogue Three

Jazz players often 'vamp', or play a 'tag' to end a tune. "And here comes grandma, swinging on the outhouse door; and here comes grandma . . ." etc., etc. Everybody thinks, hopes, it's the end, but it keeps on going, usually for much too long.

I've been playing a tag on this project much too long. A $75 gig in Danvers gave me an excuse to visit Rafal and Jesica.

It's now Monday July 30th 2012. I'm alone in an empty house with nothing else to do except play the final chord and end this. We'll see.

Craziness… Gift of the artist, Polly K Brown.

Forward

I knew that my uncle Brad was writing a book. He'd been gathering stories and writing and talking about writing for years. We were all like, that's great Brad, sure thing, you do that. I don't know if he was showing it to anyone... I hadn't seen anything.

Then, in the fall and winter of 2011–2012, these emails started coming: Brad's emailed diary entries from Poland, part ship's log, when, where, and how's the water, and part run-on descriptive adventures, so alive for me I couldn't wait for the next installment to pop in. Brad's words fell off the page right into my mind... it was exhilarating! I sent a few notes back saying how much I was loving following his trip through these emails and to keep 'em coming.

A year or so later, when it seemed like a critical mass of material had been reached and Brad was in peril of being overwhelmed by it, I offered to help put the book together. Well, I think I offered to give it a read. Then, touched again by Brad's voice on the page, and reminded of the breadth and depth of the stories he had to tell, I knew I wanted to help.

Now, those emails are compiled as a chapter and added to a set of remembered stories from the multi-facets of Brad's life's work, so far. They're all here, bits compiled from all the adventures over the years... with the music, of course, weaving its way throughout.

We've worked together for a year and a half now, sometimes in great leaps and bounds, our brains on fire, sometimes followed by long dry spells, as our schedules and work loads demanded, mostly mine demanding, and Brad being patient! It is a great joy to share this experience, and to help Brad share his story.

Smooth, as Brad would say. Which I take to mean, good job, well told, time to chill out.

I'm proud of you, Bradski.

Lucia Terry
Bridgton, Maine

Contents

Epilogues

Preface
(1997–present)

Life's a 'take'.
—Red Mitchell

All my life, so my mother told me more than once, I've done things backwards, so to me it makes perfect sense to start with epilogues from a 'now' that keeps going by.

This is a true story about real people and real events. I've used their real names when it made sense to. I have omitted some names. I have forgotten some names and maybe even given names to characters in error. But these are the people and events that had a direct influence on me and the course my life has taken—and helped make me who I am today. I've tried to be as honest and accurate as my memory permits. Because of my ADD (Attention Deficit Disorder) some people, with all the best intentions, treated me badly. I hope the people mentioned in this book are not offended. As I've learned more about ADD I'm gradually realizing that I'm not a bad person—I hold no grudges, only thanks. Some events parallel others. For instance, the Island Camp ran for twenty-five summers with a lot of other things going on the rest of the year. Music seems to be the only glue holding the story of my life together and is present throughout; keeps popping up everywhere. Therefore a resume of musical events and a timeline will be inserted as things move along. Be patient; remember who's writing this. Chapter One starts in Krakow, Poland, sometime between then and now.

—Brad Terry

Never do today something you can let
another man do for you tomorrow.
—Dr. Ritszel

1

Start Here
(1996)

*We don't know, 'Strangers in the Night',
but we know 'Stella by Starlight'...
it has a lot of the same notes in it.*
—Eddie Erickson

Now, it's November I think, of 1996, my fifth trip to Poland. I'm at my desk, in my rented room on the third floor of a home owned by the Zbysezk Zieba family. I'm wearing only socks and a turtleneck sweater over the 5XL T-shirt I use as a nightshirt, four items more than I'd like. My room is its usual mess but warm enough for me to attempt semi-optional clothing, and outside the small, constantly barking dog is back, after a dinner break I guess.

The room, describe the room. About normal size, 14' x 16' give or take a meter, on the top floor of a fairly typical Polish house built in about 1987; a substantial box with a flat roof and balconies on two sides. My two large windows and a glass door that opens to a small balcony, identical to the ones on the floor below, look out over the barking dog's terrain, over the deck of the lower floor, occupied by the family. Their daughter Magda, was with the second group of Polish music students that came to the states and visited Maine. I'll get to Izzy and the Zeleks later. For this part of 'now' I'll stick to the household. Magda is in love, I think, with a very nice, somewhat older law student from Germany. He visits and is more than pleasant with me. Magda is going to visit his family in Germany for Christmas. That makes it serious, I think. Papa Zieba for many years was a highly paid mechanical engineer working for a company that made heavy construction equipment. He was severely injured in a bizarre encounter with a tram. While waiting for the tram to pass before crossing its tracks he was hit from behind by a drunk driver in a large truck. Forced into the tram's path, he and his car were pretty much 'run over,' and he has a partially, but permanently disabled right hand. He went through the understandable depression but courageously tried to re-learn skiing and designed a kayak paddle with special fittings to accommodate his hand. He receives some small pension from the government. He stays home a lot and is always involved simultaneously in dozens of seemingly unrelated projects. One day he'll have a carload of plastic air vent covers that soon disappear. He used to do sophisticated color printing of posters and corporate calendars with dazzling landscapes and mountain scenes. The remains of an elaborate photo lab is now used for storage. Beyond, in a room behind the 'photo lab,' there is a huge machine that I couldn't figure out; had no idea what it was, but it's complicated and looked very expensive. Magda told me it was for making and stuffing a kind of rolled pastry with meat or cheese, a popular item in the more rural northern part of Poland but apparently it didn't catch on here in Krakow. The machine sits idle but takes up a whole room. Back in the photo lab along one wall is a collection of chemical lab equipment with all the Bunsen burners and bell jars and plastic hoses. For a few years this was used as a research lab for a cosmetic line. Most recently, he built elaborate racks in the photo lab for holding bolts of fabrics, and for a while the whole room was full of them and there was a sign on the front of the house telling people about the fabrics; but the fabrics, and soon afterwards the sign, disappeared. This week he is welding some frames to hold metal signs advertising for McDonald's, and I translated a contract from an English marketing firm that wants him to find Polish factories to manufacture some products they want.

Mama Zieba is short-ish, somewhat round and quite pretty. Her round face lights up with an almost constant smile as she barrages me with Polish, oblivious to the fact that I really don't understand her at all. The opener is usually, in a questioning tone of voice and a wide smile, something about "Obiat?" which has to do with "Did ja eat yet?" She seems to cook all the time and enough for an army but there are only four of us; I keep food upstairs and don't eat downstairs all the time. No one except Mama ever washes anything; no one puts anything away. Everybody leaves everything just out; nothing gets covered, rather the uncovered plate with the sliced ham and tomatoes, half an onion and the cheese goes in the fridge, as is. I brought them some zip lock bags but they haven't caught on. Every day she goes to her job at a small shop that specializes in herbal medicine and offers support to cancer patients and the very ill.

I share the upstairs with 700 large boxes of electrical tape of various widths and colors. These are owned by someone and stored, for a fee, by Mr. Zieba. Every week or so, a few rolls or even a whole box disappears. At this rate, the twenty or so boxes in my kitchen, that now make a fine firm base for my new fridge and support homemade plywood countertops on either side of the sink, will be around long enough to become permanent fixtures. There are 80 boxes in the hall and the larger bedroom next to mine is almost full. My room is free of boxes and my view unobstructed, out past the lower deck with its laundry tree to some real trees; trees now naked to face the winter. (Makes no sense; trees cover themselves and spend the hot summer fully clothed, and only when it's really too cold (for me) to be naked do they shed their protective garments to face the winter, naked. (I'd like to be naked all the time, more so now as I approach 60, more than when I was younger; but still not understanding why.) The efficiency of my portable electric radiator is such that I can now shed my turtleneck and get by with just the socks and T-shirt. The plate of spicy hot rice has helped, and I've opened a good, cheap (which makes it better) bottle of wine from Bulgaria, which I bought yesterday at Makro, a huge card-holder's-only 'super store'. I also bought a comfortable chair that swivels so I can observe and try to describe what is outside. Now, there's actually not much to see.

The Polish winter day is over about 4:00 p.m., but I know that beyond the barking dog's domain is a mud hole of a construction site. A substantial apartment complex is underway in what otherwise is a quiet (except for the barking dog) residential neighborhood. Zoning seems not to exist. There are large cranes, backhoes, drilling equipment and crews of men with shovels in action all day. The barking dog takes a long break during working hours and only comes back on line about now. (7:00 p.m. 'til 2:00 a.m. last night.) He quits for a while but starts up again about 4:00 a.m. and continues 'til the workers arrive. My recently purchased CD player, with an automatic shut-off feature, allows me to block out the barking dog with some CDs I brought from home, although last night the background talking of the crowd on the 'live' Bill Evans album was so distracting that I shut it down early and opted for the barking dog.

3

My room is my palace, but I have already accumulated far too much stuff. I have a large trunk that I used to schlep my PA system here last spring. I bought two milk crate file boxes that I've diligently been using to organize mountains of papers that before were just loose in the trunk. The crates hold up one end of Magda's old school desk. I have my new chair, my electric radiator and two red desk lamps, my wine glasses, (more like tumblers) and a plastic bottle of water. (I keep a pan full of water on top of the radiator.) I have some pots and pans and all the silverware and cooking utensils, a new mini refrigerator full of institutional size chunks of cheese, liters of grapefruit juice, mineral water, and Mleko (milk), yogurt, some frozen fish and some ice cream... all this from Makro. I still have here my PA system and a collection of travel cases from previous trips. Each time I come here I bring more things like the new clarinet for Adam Fudali. I met him the year before while on tour with Joachim; he needed a better instrument.

Papa built the house with hired help. In 1987 he was still at his job and had the money to do it. It is all masonry, so the walls are bulletproof. Hanging pictures on the stark white concrete walls is not an option. One whole side of the room is occupied by a blond wooden thing that has shelves like a book case, some drawers, some vertical slots where I keep a few old fashioned vinyl albums with no way to play them. Two thirds of the available space is full of books belonging to the Zieba's. It's hard to even try to explain what kind of books, all Polish of course; some appear to be cook books, some obviously travel books and brochures, and some chemistry text books, in about equal numbers. I suspect a travel agency was a previous venture. There is a Polish translation of Tarzan. The photo illustrations come from the Johnny Weissmuller, Maureen O'Sullivan movie from 1932. I'm sure if I could get any kind of a handle on this crazy language I'd spot some things of interest. Some of the cubbyholes have doors and are full of things that belong to my landlords. My Cannon Starwriter predominantly covers my borrowed student desk leaving room for my lamp, my glass and the bottle, but not much else. There is a sturdy and impossibly uncomfortable L-shaped couch that doesn't fold out but rather re-arranges into a more uncomfortable double bed. I leave it in couch position and sleep on a folding foam mattress which I bought last year from Makro, in anticipation of some kids sleeping over and now use it myself. It's not really long or wide enough, but I can overlap and stretch out. I spread sheets under and over me and, depending on the temperature, pile on the blankets and sleeping bags. The visiting kids do fine on the couch. There is a low table and a square straight chair that somewhat match the 'thing' and wall-to-wall burgundy carpet, indoor-outdoor type I suspect. I bought a rather South Western, U.S.A. looking rug that covers some of it. Finally, covering most of the window, some white curtains with a pattern of orange bouquets; and now, after 2:00 a.m.; no barking dog! Beyond the mud hole is a major intersection with a tram stop for several trams. A small supermarket is on the left of the intersection, on our side off the street. It sells, among other things like food, large quantities of cheap vodka, and the store's front is usually adorned by standing groups of the most recent customers; some grouped sitting, some, the earlier birds, already draped. On the right of the intersection, also on this side of the street, another crane was placing a sign on a new Peugeot dealership now visible through the naked trees.

I knew I would be here for several months and welcomed the time to try and come to grips with my newly diagnosed ADD (Attention Deficit Disorder) and reflect on the journey that got me here.

2

A Friend Indeed
(1995–present)

Two old men are sharing a park bench.
One says, "I think I've forgotten your name."
The other answers, "How soon do you need to know?"
—Jake Stock

Dave Stewart had more than his share of hard times. Somehow his mother found out about the Island Camp; his grandmother provided, and at Camp he was just another 'neat kid'. Since he lived fairly close by in Connecticut I saw him quite a lot before and after Camp and got to know his family pretty well. We enjoyed a real friendship, more than just a camper/camp director relationship. I was teaching at Riverdale, so this was about 1966. In the fall, after his first year at Camp, while riding his bike a car hit him from behind. David was riding exactly where he was supposed to ride. The driver was blinded by the sun and plowed into David's left hip, throwing him over the guide rail and down an embankment. His mother called me at school and I came immediately to the intensive care unit of the Norwalk Hospital; David wanted to see me. His parents were there. I was the only non-family allowed in. He was full of tubes and there were pins through his left knee and right shoulder and arm. He seemed to recognize me but was pretty much out. For quite a few days it was touch and go with the doctors trying to see if they could save his leg, but some amazing surgery was done, skin grafts added, and soon he was out of danger but had a long painful stay in the hospital. I came in almost every day, detouring on my way home from school. I made some supporting braces out of wood from my shop and loaned him my grandfather's huge wooden 'scissors' that could be used to pick up things at a distance. I helped a bit with his schoolwork and told him I didn't care if

7

I had to drag him, carry him on my back all summer, whatever, he was coming back to Camp. All he had to do was convince the doctors. He made it!

Even though we've lost touch for periods of time we have kept the friendship. Toward the end of the summer of 1994 he called and told me that he and one of his sons had been diagnosed with Attention Deficit Disorder (ADD), and could he bring his two boys for a few days of camping out at the Quarry. Of course I said, "of course". I was delighted. He was great and his boys were great. He wanted to expose them to the natural way of things at the quarry, and it didn't take them long to relax and start enjoying the freedom of no clothes. The weather was kind to us. During the course of a few evenings, with the help of a moderate amount of Burgundy, his ADD story unraveled and soon I realized that a lot of what he was telling me sounded like me. He had brought some copies of articles about ADD and suggested a few books to read. After a few days, with the boys' buns only mildly sunburned, we all headed home and I launched in to some serious research. I started with 'The Book', *Driven to Distraction*, by Dr. Ned Hallowell. I was amazed; chapters seemed to have been written about me. I found a wonderful friend, Linda Botto, who ran an ADD support group in Freeport, and I went! I was amazed! There were others like me.

I called another old friend, Dr. Henry Schniewind. He was a classmate from St. Paul's School days and the only one I have kept in touch with. He was the piano player in my first little 'skate house band' (La Rues All-Stars) and has remained a good friend. (I don't know where that name came from.) He was also the only one in the band that made it through SPS. I was insatiably curious and wanted to find out all I could. My plan was to search for all my old school records and retrieve as much information as I could. "Was this a sound idea?" I asked Henry. Henry said if it felt right to me to go ahead with it. After a few phone calls I got in my car and made the rounds. Because of logistics the first stop on the quest was St. Paul's. Henry had called ahead and set up an appointment for me with the records dept. At first they were reluctant to even let me see the files, but I was adamant like Llewellyn the taxi driver in Ogden Nash's story. What I found in the files was to amaze me even more. I had expected to find what I remembered, all the teacher comments, horrendous grades, lowest class ranking, etc., but this was just the beginning—there was much more. There were original hand written letters from my parents, original letters from a clinic in

New Canaan, and correspondence from some doctors there to the doctor and teachers at Saint Paul's. I told them I wanted to take the files with me, and they said absolutely, "no", but grudgingly agreed to let me make some copies of what I wanted. I made some copies, which was taking forever and then insisted again; the files were mine and I would take them; they could have the copies. They still said, "no". Then I did something quite rare for me, even surprised myself. I got angry. I offered them an ultimatum. I told them they could call their lawyers or I would call mine, but I was taking the files, and they fell for the bluff. I came away feeling triumphant. I had won a battle against an institution that had, with all the best intentions, abused and tormented[1] me. My time there had been pretty miserable!

I sat in the car in the parking lot and went through the files carefully. As I read through pages and pages I had vivid recollections of almost all unhappy memories. I became very interested in the 'clinic in New Canaan'. From a pay phone in Concord I telephoned the clinic, Silver Hill, and "Yes", they said. They had 48 microfilm pages of stuff about me! They said they would be happy to give me a copy and I made an appointment to be there in a few days. Bement School in Deerfield, Massachusetts was the next stop where I found all the reports and teacher comments, going back to when I started there, spring term in the 4th grade. Later that day I drove down to Salisbury. They had only one page of some transcripts of dismal grades and a yearbook with the fourth form class picture. I'd been kicked out before the photo shoot; I'm nowhere to be found. That night I stayed with friends in New Canaan. New Canaan Country Day School didn't keep records beyond a few years, so the trail stopped there. I went to Eaton Gate School in London for the first two semesters of the 4th grade where I got routine bare-bottom strappings for not doing my homework. The school was still in existence but records were long since lost. The elementary school I went to in New Canaan is a parking lot. Last stop the clinic, Silver Hill, where I collected the most amazing, upsetting and confusing forty-eight pages of documents. There were transcriptions of conversations and interviews and phone calls, psychiatric test results and comments from doctors that fattened a large manila envelope. As I sat in the parking lot at Silver Hill reading, the anger started.

I brought all my findings to Henry. The first stage, diagnosis, was easy because it was so blatant. I showed Henry what I had found, and he immediately concurred with my suspicions. He was recuperating from surgery and at home. He was confined to his couch, and we spent a long enjoyable afternoon. He was able to dispel some of the clinic's reports as "outdated" and confirm some of the other tests showing "well above-average intelligence" as valid. (Certainly had me fooled!) Henry agreed that I was on to something for sure, and my diagnosis of ADD was accurate from his professional perspective. He recommended Dr. Nagler in Brunswick. I made an appointment for July since I was about to be out the door to return to Poland. Armed with ADD books and envelopes stuffed full of report cards and school records, I left for another few months to a place where I knew I'd be kept busy and felt comfortable. In Poland I kept busy and read and read and learned.

According to 'The Book', (Ned Hallowell's *Driven To Distraction*) I was right on schedule. First, careful accurate diagnosis; be sure. I was sure. Henry was sure. I had read that ADD is sometimes over-diagnosed and used simply as an excuse for various shortcomings. I realized, from reading about myself in 'The Book' that I had mastered the art of finding excuses, honing it to perfection, a real pro. I could justify, rationalize, squirm, and finagle my way in or out of any situation, so I wanted to be really sure that this was not just another lame excuse on my part. All the ADD criteria seemed to fit exactly. First I thought some of the criteria didn't fit. I saw 'risk-taking' and thought, "Nah, I'm pretty careful and cautious." Then I started thinking about some of the cars I've owned and the way I routinely drove them! You'll read later on about the way I rode 'Dumpy' down Cascade Hill, my escapades on bicycles, my brother's wrecked Hillman, then fast motorcycles and several ridiculously fast cars. My A. C. Shelby Cobra, a beast of a car, was the first one of its kind registered in New England. Then the Griffith, even quicker, was for a while the fastest production car in the world!

As I really looked in to the criteria for ADD I had to honestly say yes to all of them except 'compulsive gambling'. All the habits or lack of habits that cause me to malfunction are listed; add to that the endless teacher comments that sound like direct quotes from 'The Book.' Finally, there was all the pain.

No, this ADD thing was not just another lame excuse. I was sure. Right on schedule there was a feeling of relief; some strange inner calm that took over even before I started the medication. Just knowing there was something that had a name, and that I was not alone. The unacceptable behavior was not my fault; I was not in control. I was not a bad person. Things would be okay. I had read about the 'anger stage' and assumed it, too, would pass, but by mid-August I was being consumed by it. I couldn't shake it; I couldn't. I kept going over and over all the negative things that happened to me. It was no one's fault. On the contrary I knew everyone, everywhere, at every step of the way, put in amazing effort to try and help me. In no way do I harbor any grudges or hold anyone to blame. I went to excellent schools with excellent teachers. The schools policies were completely valid at the time. In some English schools corporal punishment, in the form of paddles, straps and canes, applied across bare behinds was still accepted as a way to control behavior.

Most American schools saw punitive extra study halls as the best method. Had anyone known about ADD would I have been diagnosed in second grade or earlier? No one knew; that's the way it was. Back home again, Dr. Nagler, after one visit (armed with all my research and comments from Henry), was also "sure" and prescribed Wellbutrin. It's easier on the pocketbook than some of the other meds and has long-lasting effects; not so much of the roller coaster ups and downs of Ritalin. It's also not as controlled as Ritalin, and I was able to easily get a 6 months' supply to bring to Poland. The Silver Hill files remain the one sore spot that I can't quite alleviate by simply saying, "That's the way it was". The last entry of that forty-eight-page microfilm report is a simple sentence, the summation of their findings. "Brad will have lifelong difficulties with studies." They had come to this conclusion when I was fourteen. I was fifty-seven when I first saw it. Why had no one thought it might be helpful to tell me? The anger still surges when I think of the countless times I made yet another futile attempt to learn to read music, only to fail again, and feel worthless, stupid and terrible again, over and over. I felt like a wooden boat that was launched without a bung plug. I couldn't understand why, as I bailed like crazy, the boat kept sinking. Still, the anger made no sense. If there were someone to blame, a wall to punch, something—it would be much easier. I churned and thought back.

Letter to my brothers from Bath, Maine 1997(?):

> *This has been an amazing time for me as I've gradually become aware and come to grips with the general derailment of my life. I've done more studying and homework in the last two years than in my whole life before and feel I can speak with some authority about ADD; the effect it's had on me and on others. All your input has*

been helpful. I need to follow it through and get ALL the facts. Peter filled in some gaps about my time in Washington. I'm still not at all clear about why I stayed in Beverly with Aunt Ruth, then Wenham with Uncle Brad, and at some point Pittsfield with brother Jim's in-laws, the Cunninghams. I suspect I was driving everybody crazy and only now have any awareness that this was the case. When push came to shove there was sort of emergency support from you. I always sensed the reluctance and a distance. I 'felt the draft' but continued on my way.

Most difficult now is the guilty feeling as the scope of the chaos and turmoil that I caused unfolds. ADD made me do it, but still I did it. It's hard to step away from the guilty feelings. The pros tell me that, however painful, the nitty-gritty is important. I need to know just how bad it was and get on with finishing it. I can deal with the whole picture now. It's not good to find out later that there was more. I've been reluctant to keep in as close touch with you as I would have liked, partially because of my perception of what your perception of all this would be. "Here he goes again". Or maybe, "Here we go again". There is still a lot of uncertainty. Diagnosis, education, medication, direction, and more conscious effort than I ever remember have all helped me put things in perspective. I can start to feel that in spite of everything that has happened I'm not a bad person. This by itself is a big step. It enables me to accept that some of the things I've accomplished have merit and are worthwhile. But. There is no guarantee that I will be able to eliminate these only recently perceived flaws from my behavior. I hope that with my new awareness I can keep things in perspective and exercise some control of my life. I still catch myself, losing it, spacing out, not listening, etc. Medication makes it less of a conscious effort to get back on track, but the problems are still all there. I'm going to do the best I can.

Soon I'm going back to Poland with the usual myriad of schemes I've launched into orbit. This time I have some people, friends in key positions, to help me try and catch a few plans that survive re-entry; still no guarantee. I know I have to do something about accumulating some of the "financial lubricant that enables us to slide through life". (Thanks for the quote, Arthur.) Now, as usual, my cash flow is nearly nil and a constant frustration. I spend too much time just surviving at the expense of pursuing projects. There *have been too many times when a project failed because I was literally unable to pay the phone bill and make the call; or I simply forgot. This has only marginally changed, but at least I don't seem to worry about it as much, and I see some possibilities of significant changes ahead. I'm still feeling pretty shaky and unsure about almost everything. There have been so many failures that stepping out again, every time, scares the stuff out of me. I don't want to fail again. I want the freedom to do the stuff I'm good at and not waste time with the other baggage, the stuff I'm not good at.*

Finally I guess, at least for this chapter, I'm closing in on accepting that my actions were not conscious attempts at rocking the boat and definitely not deliberate. I'll probably always carry some guilt, but you all have made me feel that things are on a better track and have helped me "let bygones be bygones" and get on with things. There's no guarantee that I won't disappoint people again and come up short; I'm nervously hopeful. Please forgive my writing all of you at once, but I'd like this shared with all concerned who have more than shared the burden and now, maybe, some light. You all know how to reach me in Poland. I hope you will.

Back in Poland, David Sobenko came to an informal English class I offered at the music school in Krakow. I invited him to come to the States for the following summer. He returned a year or so later and stayed with me in Bath for his junior year of High School, graduated from George Washington University and now lives and works in New York.

One day visiting David Sobenko's Mom she told me about transcendental meditation. I'm thinking it might be addictive. Can it become something you have to do everyday? She said I should try it, "Just a little bit each day". Scares the stuff out of me! Okay. Just what is 'the state' you reach? I need a complete description, details of exactly where you are if you are successfully meditating. Any ideas? I haven't read anything like this idea in any of 'the books', but Hallowell actually recommends meditation as a possibility. I guess for this reason, if there really is some connection it intrigues me. I can sit stationary, immobilized for hours on end, allowing my coffee to get stone cold, yet I'm wide awake, answering the phone on the first ring. So, was I born with the syndrome 'Uncontrollable Meditation?' Is that part of what (my) ADD really is? Should it be labeled 'UMmm'?

If you can learn to meditate without medication, perhaps there is a way to un-learn it without medication. Of course it's easier to become addicted to something than to kick the habit. I guess I'd characterize myself as being in a state of UMmm for a long time. I want to find out if there are any similarities between ADD and UMmm so I can develop some sort of a 'twould-be-nice corrective ribbon, like the delete function for this machine. UMmm. I really want to control it. Not sure now where to file this but I will wait to finish it after Joachim brings my mail from Krakow.

When I read about "Jim" in Ned Hallowell's book, *Driven to Distraction*, the story reminded me of me, and some friends too. I've written lots down in the two-plus years I've been aware of my ADD. From Bement School, 4th grade on, a clear pattern emerges; year after year the teacher comments read like quotes from 'The Book'. The sigh of relief, knowing there was something, and that I was not alone, came pretty much on schedule. What I was not prepared for were the surges of almost uncontrollable anger. I did go through some really bad shit. Nobody had a clue what to do. It caused major splits in the family. I was being a real asshole at times and was totally oblivious to it. I did a lot of damage and a lot of damage was done to me. I did survive, and I have accomplished some things that I'm proud of in spite of myself. Wow, at times the anger was overwhelming. I think I'm through that now, but it threw me for a loop. Sometimes the emotional churning roller coaster continues even now. The anger makes no sense. Everybody did the best they knew how to help, from my brother who led the opposition against my parents who were seen to be too soft for not sending me to military school, or worse, to the good 'Padre' who, with the best of intentions, wielded the strap in England. I drove everybody crazy, and they all tried so hard!

Linda Botto runs an ADD support group in Freeport. She's good people. Lee, her nine-year-old, has a strong cup of coffee before bed, and he's out like a light. It helps to talk to people who know what you're going through. I'm now on ¼ of my original medication, and I think I'm doing well. I'll have more feedback in January. It's hard for me to know how I really am doing. I find it easy to talk about, and most people seem genuinely interested. There will be changes and difficult things to deal with. The shift is difficult; from blaming myself to accepting that I have ADD and probably did some crazy/regrettable/selfish/stupid things because of it. Try not to blame but accept that this does not make me a bad person. Accept that I am who I am. I will change what I can and try to cope with what I can't change. I'm okay! It's nobody's fault. Etc. It's all there in 'The Book'.

I've finally come to feel that it's okay that I won't ever learn to read music. I'm not stupid or bad. It's the way I am. I've almost stopped beating myself up over the fact that my marriage failed. I think that in eight years of marriage I didn't hear a word Carole said to me, and I was not then, and am still not capable of being in a relationship. I haven't ruled it out, but so far it hasn't worked for me. I don't have to thrash myself over this anymore—I know this, but still, it's easier said than done. I expect to thrash around. I've accepted the notion that I won't be able to learn Polish. Finally, I've come to think that medication by itself does nothing unless you really know what you're trying to medicate; i.e. learning all you can about how you were vs. how you want to be. The meds are very helpful once you know this. For me, it makes things like paying attention less of a conscious effort. I still have to think about it, but I don't exhaust myself trying, and I know what I need to do.

I only drink when I'm alone or when I'm with somebody.
—Bill Ross

i

3

Going Back
(1937–1945)

I have plenty of 'will power',
it's the 'won't power' I don't have much of.
—Red Mitchell

There was a pattern of sorts right from the beginning. I was a pain for sure and was constantly made to pay for my behavior. A lot of these early years are a blur, but I remember some instances vividly.

In kindergarten, first, and second grade at New Canaan Country Day School I was regularly sent to sit in the hall because I wouldn't lie down on a blanket on the floor and take a nap. I couldn't get comfortable, certainly couldn't sleep, and I didn't need, want or plan to take a nap. I also got in trouble because I wouldn't sit on my blanket cross-legged, pretending to be an Indian. It was a stupid game and hurt my knees.

At the other end of the hall was a wooden staircase, dark-varnished with wide worn treads. Looking down between the railings as the stairs doubled back you could see all the way down to the main floor. There were one or two classrooms in the hallway in between the stairs and two more classrooms at either end. Everything was trimmed with dark shiny varnish. My classroom was one on the end.

I met Bill Mather out in the hall. He was a grade ahead of me and probably had some of the same problems because he was sent to the hall almost as much as I was. His classroom was on the other end, and he was supposed to sit on the stairs at his end, me at my end. We always ended up meeting in the middle; how much more trouble would that get us? We became life-long friends. In kindergarten, long before my classmates did, I learned to tell time because I wanted to be sure to be sent to the hall when I knew Bill would be there.

I was also kept in a lot at recess. Outside I would build outrageous structures with some really big wooden playing blocks. They were about 9" x 12" and maybe 2 feet long. I'd pile them up as high as I could, making a platform, stand on them and pile them higher and from time to time I would knock them all over; they'd come crashing down and probably could have really hurt someone. Seemed fine to me. My classmates loved it, but the only way to prevent me from constructing my towers was to keep me inside.

My older brother Jim was at the same school in the 8th grade and during school hours rarely even acknowledged my existence and generally spoke to me only when absolutely necessary. I'm sure his crazy little brother mortified him. One winter day, on the way home from school, he misbehaved on the school bus. I was let off at the usual place, but he had to stay on the bus and got dropped off a few miles away, supposedly to walk home as a punishment. Worried about him, I sat in the snow and waited for him at the bottom of the long hill up to our house; being in the first grade it seemed awfully long. I was cold and a bit scared. It was getting dark, and I didn't know what had happened to my brother. After what seemed like a long time, Mr. Jones, the man who owned Jones's Store and during those war years delivered the groceries himself, came into view in his van. As he turned in our driveway I could see my brother, who had hitched a ride, sitting cozily in the front seat. He looked right at me, or through me and never commented to Mr. Jones who I know would have stopped and given me a ride had he seen me. They continued up the long hill without me; I was in tears and deeply hurt.

One night, Mme. Roger (introduced later) was giving me a bath upstairs. She had turned out the light and I was standing in the tub peering at the stars out the bathroom window while she washed me. We were laughing and pointing to the stars when a substantial portion of the plaster ceiling just detached and came crashing down on me. Amazingly I had only a few small cuts and scratches and a lump on my head. This has nothing to do with ADD except that I remember it. I guess some times shit happened that really wasn't my doing. I remember locking myself in the same bathroom and screaming that I hated the baby sitter. I had a real tantrum. I'm pretty sure I got spanked for that.

On a happier note for me, one day when I was six or seven my brother Jim teased me to the point that I really lost control. I was in a blind rage and with all my strength I hurled a wooden coat hanger at him from across the room. It just missed him, but my father, hearing the commotion, opened the door at that instant. (Jim corrected me on this; it did in fact hit his nose dangerously close to his eye) Pops put the blame on my brother. Being 12 he was responsible for the scene and causing me to lose control, his protests were in vain and much to my delight he got spanked. I begged to watch, but my brother strongly objected and I had to settle for listening with my ear to the door—first to his explanation, then his protests and then the wonderful sound of slaps on bare skin and his accompanying yells. I was gleeful.

My father was working for the Dorr Company, commuting to New York and as I remember, home on weekends. One day he took me to Westport where his boss, Dr. Dorr owned an old mill on the Westport River. Most of the early research for the company's sanitation engineering work was taking place here. After looking at a wonderland of big tanks full of swirling water all being stirred around we went for a walk upstream and toward Dr. Dorr's house. We came to a bend in the river where Dr. Dorr had piled up stones across the river creating a porous dam that backed up enough water to create a bit of a swimming hole. With no ceremony the doctor and my father shed all their clothes and went in the water. I quickly followed suit and was totally at ease. I think it was my first experience skinny dipping—for sure not my last!

Later I learned that John V.N. Dorr, my father's boss, apprenticed with Thomas Edison. He put white stones along the edge of his long dark driveway so he could see better at night. Then he started something that has become universal, internationally. He convinced the town of Westport, Connecticut, that if he bought the paint, they would put a white stripe along the edges of the town roads. Think of that!

Mother started my brothers playing piano but passed them on to Mrs. McFarland for more formal lessons. When I was seven, Mrs. McFarland convinced mother to let her start me off right. After just a few piano lessons, Mrs. McFarland told mother, in front of me of course, that I was, "A hopeless case. No talent; no possibility of playing music at all. Couldn't learn; couldn't be taught. "Un-teachable." She said. I still remember those were her exact words. If she had known, she might have used Louis Armstrong's words. "He has a perfect ear. There's no hole in it." It hadn't taken long for the lessons to become a dreaded affair.

Early on, I asked her to watch how fast I could scramble to nearly the top of a huge maple tree in back of our house. Then I'd spend half the lesson time coming down very slowly. She caught on to this game and vetoed it, so each week I just waited for her up the tree instead. Perched high up, I could see her car coming well down the road. The huge tree, huge to me then, was my special refuge. I could swing up into its branches and disappear, become invisible, invincible, hidden by its leaves, secure in its great heights. I could hurl things down at my enemies and even pee on them if need be. It was like having my own nuclear bomb (which had not yet happened, and I certainly didn't know about). I didn't really plan to use it, but with a small boy's understanding of gravity and of water flowing downhill I had the option, the ultimate weapon. That was enough.

As the seasons changed so did the evolution of structures in the tree. Various platforms and shelters came and went, held in place by salvaged beams lashed together. For a while old bed sheets provided invisibility even from directly below. For a while I had an elaborate tree house, a small portable Hodson playhouse, hauled up and assembled by my brother, Peter. As winter approached this was considered such an eyesore that it was moved to another larger tree in the lot across the driveway and out of sight from the house.

This new tree held the portable house and supported a large deck on two sides. A flimsy white picket snow fence offered only visual sense of security around the deck. I often slept in the tree house. During the move something punctured a small hole all the way through the wall of the house. This proved very convenient on dark nights, and was exactly the right height to pee through when I was seven. There was a spiral staircase that wrapped around the base of the tree and came up through a trap door in the deck. There was a hasp and a padlock! From above, with the trap door shut the world below ceased to exist. My brother, Peter, built most of it with enthusiastic but limited help from me. It had all the trimmings—a young boy's dream, but it always lacked the security, the familiarity, of *my* tree, and I kept spending most of my free time there.

There was one particular spot about 15 feet off the ground in my tree where I could sit on a large branch, quite securely, without holding on. Exactly at the right level for hands, not for peeing, was another skinny branch that was my keyboard. My thumbs would be underneath and my fingers on top, more like a horizontal clarinet (I can see now). I was always barefoot and there was a curly section of bark that exactly fit the ball and big toe of my right foot. This became the foot pedal that controlled the swell, like an organ. The tree was my symphony orchestra. It could also be a piano or an organ, and I spent hours, sometimes whole days, sitting there, playing it with fingers flying up and down the keyboard. The tree sang to me. I really heard it and the possibilities were endless; the entire classical repertoire my brother was practicing mixed with, "My Bonnie Lies Over The Ocean", Stephen Foster, and the hundreds of standards my mother played. WQXR radio was tuned in most mornings and sometimes at night so all those classical selections were mixed in too. Of course, I composed great works that were flawlessly played by my orchestra, its versatility unlimited. The music swelled, surrounded me and comforted me for entire summers.

So piano lessons were a bust and soon the dreaded confrontations with Mrs. McFarland came to a stop along with any attempts to push me toward music. I noodled a lot with a soprano recorder; there was too much competition for our one piano. Perhaps my parents, for a while, agreed with Mrs. McFarland. She was huge and early on I had the picture Marshall Dodge would much later describe of the "Large Lady whose car 'twas all slanted over to the driver's side even when she got out of the car." Maybe he took piano lessons from Mrs. McFarland?

There was always music around. My brothers, one seriously, played the piano and Mother played the great tunes of the 1920s and 1930s, all on the black keys—melody with right thumb and all the right 'changes'. There was singing, not just at Christmastime, but a lot of the time and I pitched in. Other participants, who always seemed older and bigger than me, would be very possessive about 'their note'. If I landed on someone else's 'note' I was quickly in big trouble, maybe even a rap of knuckles across my head, so early on I learned to listen and try and find an acceptable note not already claimed. I got to be pretty good at it! When I was in the third grade, Jim had gone off to St Paul's, and I had a brief and unhappy time in elementary school in the Stamford Public School system. We lived in Stamford but were much closer to the school in New Canaan. For a small tuition I was transferred to the public school in New Canaan. Bus transportation was not included, so I was driven to the top of Cascade Hill where I could board the bus, but often when the weather permitted I rode the three-and-a-half miles each way by bicycle. Sometimes I wore real Dutch wooden shoes brought from Holland by a friend. I had made outlines of my feet on a paper, and they were custom-made with allowance for growing and fit very comfortably. I amazed my classmates by being able to run down the halls and up and down stairs at school in my wooden shoes with out making a sound.

In the fall I picked up some woolly-bear caterpillars on the way to school, mostly to keep me company on the bike ride and to show to my friends. The first few times it was okay, but one day I was told not to bring any more and the ones I brought were confiscated. I kept on bringing them to school but kept them in my socks all day so I could safely put them back where I found them. They'd curl right up and stay still until I put them back. Then after less than a minute they would uncurl and head off to wherever they were going as if nothing had interrupted their trip

I loved Mrs. Lamont, my third grade teacher, but even with her support and understanding I was doing nothing in her class and was transferred to the other third grade class where I was miserable. The rest of the year is pretty much a blur. On the way back from the bathroom I'd pause and press my face against Mrs. Lamont's classroom window and look in until the other teacher would notice I was gone too long and drag me, always in tears, back to her room. Mrs. Lamont knew about the caterpillars in my socks but kept my secret.

My best friend was a black kid who named me something to do with coal, and he was "snowballs," maybe the other way round. His real name was Charlie Nash. He beat up a bigger kid called Dennis Ross who was always picking on me. I had to ride past Dennis's house on my way to school. If he was outside waiting for the bus he'd throw things, rocks or sticks, and really try to hit me and he sometimes did. Sometimes his father would drive him to school. They always roared past me very fast, and I was afraid because sometimes it seemed they came quite close; it was a big fancy car. I hated them both. After school one day Charlie knocked Dennis down and sat on him and invited me to punch him in the face or spit on him. I thought I'd kind of like to pee on him, and I told him so, but I relented and did nothing. Charlie held him down and warned him to leave me alone and to make the point slapped him a few times and rubbed dirt in his face. I watched. Like my brother's spanking, justice was being served. I was gleeful. Dennis was not so aggressive after that. I could have done really nasty things to him but I let him off. He thought it best to ignore me; Charlie was my friend, small, but the toughest kid by far in the third grade.

One of the kids in my class named Bruce (something) was killed in some sort of an accident during Christmas vacation. I liked him and a few times had gone to his house after school on my bike. The accident had to do with a river and thin ice. It was a shock but I didn't understand, really. Martin Finger was another kid who died, I think of Meningitis, but not right then. He lived on the top of Cascade Hill on the New Canaan side of the line. I could ride my bike up there and leave it in his barn and ride the bus to school with Martin. Martin was with me when I loaded my Mack-pedal-truck, "Dumpy", full of rocks from the fancy stonewall of an estate at the top of the hill. I had discovered the "Hill" and delighted in coasting down it in Dumpy. Almost half a mile long Cascade Hill was the challenge in the winter. After the first snow the school bus never attempted it and cars were always getting stuck halfway up. It ran steeply down, pretty straight to a crest, and then a short, very steep part to a sharp right-left S-turn, to a hollow at the bottom. I'd push the pedal-truck to the top and come flying down. After a while I felt I wasn't going fast enough so I loaded the truck with stones from the wall at the top. With the extra weight I could really careen down. The pedals were going much too fast; my feet had to be outboard. I really went fast. At the bottom, not about to lug the rocks back up the hill, I'd dump my load and push the truck up the hill, reload it with rocks and come hurtling down, again and again. It took my brother Jim a day to rebuild the substantial section of wall I had removed. Once Martin and I played doctor in his barn. In an empty horse stall we took turns taking each other's temperature. Our mothers had done it with a slippery thermometer but with small sticks it hurt quite a lot and we decided it was not a good game. After I heard he had died, for a while I was afraid he might have died from that. We had a green 1941 Ford Station wagon, a wonderful light green. The license was HG763. Mother was a really good driver. Even though gas was rationed I remember her taking it to 55 on the Merritt Parkway, and on slippery, wintry days she'd negotiate Cascade Rd., fishtailing through the corners using the gas pedal and almost never moving the wheel at all. Later, right after the war, cars were hard to come by in Holland, and in 1946 HG763 was exported and became the Dorr Company car in The Hague. I think it had a fatal encounter with a tram. We also had a black 41 Ford convertible that eventually would become my first car.

I remember saying goodbye to Madame Roger, the French governess who had been with us for years in Holland. She was from

Alsace and it was obviously dangerous for her to return home in 1939, so my parents sponsored her and she immigrated to The States. She accompanied my brother Jim, age eight, and me at the age of two on the last trip the Normandy made before the war, but she was put off on Ellis Island. Jim had to cope getting me organized and off the boat to be met by an uncle. Eventually she found her way to us in Stamford. I have only sketchy memories of her. She was kind and nurturing; soft blue-grey eyes and friendly glasses, her grey hair neatly up in a bun. When she left I didn't understand the situation at all. We couldn't possibly pay her a fraction of what she could earn being a "nanny" for well-to-do New Yorkers. I had no idea about economics; I just thought she should be "there" forever. She stood on the big stone front step saying goodbye and had on a big black hat. I watched from my upstairs window and cried and cried; she'd been there all my life.

My father's mother, 'Big' Granny, would come out from New York and play the piano and guitar. I usually went to sleep under the piano listening to music. She was big and always smiley and friendly and unthreatening. I went to New York to visit her when she was very sick, and she died before I got to know her at all well.

My mother's mother, 'Little Granny', scolded me when I tested the tea water with my finger and insisted I pour it all out and boil up a new batch. I disappeared into the kitchen and pretended to do it but brought back the same water. Even so she lived to be ninety-nine. She was hard of hearing, and sometimes she walked with quick little steps, and with each step she'd pass gas and make these little pftt-pftt-pftt noises that she couldn't hear. One day Leila—you'll hear more about her later—was there and heard it. We tried to be quiet but almost died laughing. From the Silver Hill microfilms I learned 'Little Granny' told our family doctor she "actively disliked me". I felt the draft.

Summers were busy with a Victory Garden of considerable proportions. My brothers all helped. We had pigs and a lot of chickens. I only watched once as my brother stuck a chicken headfirst into a kind of inverted funnel, and, when it stuck its head out he lopped it off with a knife. I only watched once when Mr. Thornton stood directly in front of one of the pigs and, with a silver bullet from his 22 shot it between the eyes and then, before it toppled over, slit its throat. I couldn't deal with any of this at all. I spent my time loading smelly apples in Dumpy delivering them somewhere and would pick up something else and deliver it. I did nothing that in anyway was connected to the farming activities surrounding me. I played in the huge maple tree that was my special hideaway and place of comfort, my tree. My beloved Dumpy finally completely rusted apart. I sat crying when the scrap metal man took Dumpy away. I couldn't bear to watch, but I had to. Dumpy, now in several pieces, was unceremoniously piled onto the junkman's truck with other rusted bits of once-loved bicycles and express wagons, all mixed in with old water heaters and car parts. I hadn't yet been to a funeral, but this was worse than a funeral. Long after this I would wake up at night at the slightest sound, jump up and peer out the window to see if someone had brought Dumpy back. I'd be very excited; sure I'd heard something. I'd look out all the windows and sometimes even go outside to see, I'd be so sure. Then tears would well up like a signal telling me to go back to bed. It wasn't there. My brother Peter made me a wonderful wooden replacement vehicle, which I definitely appreciated but it wasn't the same.

I know we went to Maine for part of every summer. We took the sleeper train from Stamford to Boston, stayed over night with the Boyden cousins in Beverly then another sleeper to Rockland and woke up as the train stopped at every crossing in Maine, dropping off the morning papers and mail. (I had to have gone right by my Willow St. property) I'd watch out the window all the way. I shared the bed with Jim, our heads at opposite ends, his feet kept poking me; they were cold. We'd be met in Rockland by Mr. Roakes, who was the taxi company. A short drive took us to the dock and the *JO*, a 38-foot passenger boat that looked a little like a lobster boat. Jim Brown the builder/owner and skipper brought us across to Vinalhaven and, if the tide was right, landed us on our own float. Once at summer's end Mr. Roakes was hired to drive my grandmother and me back to New York. We stopped somewhere for lunch, and I left my teddy bear, 'Nou-nous' behind. All the fur was long since worn away and it was patched and stitched together, looking more like Frankenstein than a kid's toy, but I was devastated. Mr. Roakes picked it up on his way home and mailed it back to me.

I don't remember much of those summers in Maine. A few times my big brothers, Peter and Arthur, took me by my arms and held me between them as they ran across the granite ledges on Calm Island. Every now and then my feet would touch down; I'd push off and go flying again. I loved it. I was into flying! My brothers and older cousins were much older, and my younger cousins, younger by only two or three years, seemed much younger. Most of the time I was alone

My grandfather was very formal. We all had to wear a jacket, and he greeted us each with a handshake at the bottom of the stairs promptly at 8:00 a.m. for breakfast. I have heard that he was kind and generous but my most vivid memory of him was being sent from the dinner table in disgrace for interrupting him while he was talking. I never recovered from the hurt of that experience. I didn't want to open my mouth in his presence again and certainly never thought I'd have anything I wanted to say to him: a small incident perhaps, but for me, a major wound that never healed.

I lost touch with Charlie Nash after 1944 when business took my parents, with me in tow, to Washington D.C. I don't remember when during the year this happened, but I was enrolled in a public school near our house, near DuPont Circle, picking up somewhere in third grade. I don't have any memories of the school. I went with an elderly cousin to the Washington Zoo and was fascinated when we forded streams in the car, somewhere in a park. At one point my father was headed to Europe and wanted to make a quick trip to New York to visit his mother. I chose this day to stray on my way home from school and ended up at a black friend's house in a questionable neighborhood. I didn't think to call home to tell anybody and nonchalantly stayed for supper. Oblivious to the lateness or the dangers, I came home well after dark. A police car was parked in front of our house. My father had called them and also had canceled his New York trip to help look for me. When the police had left he quietly, but oh so firmly, took me by the arm and brought me upstairs into the bathroom. There was none of the gleefulness of hearing my brother's yells and protest this time; I knew what was coming! I soon was over his knee, my pants around my ankles, my arms and legs immobilized in a grip of iron. He whacked my behind with a leather moccasin for what seemed like an eternity. I cried and yelled and pleaded to no avail. He never raised his voice or lost control and I guess only stopped when he thought I'd had enough. I missed the next day of school. I really couldn't sit down. The rest of Washington is a blur. I remember sitting in the bathtub and hearing on the radio that FDR had died. My parents were scheduled to have lunch with him and Eleanor the following week. We went to England soon after that.

The war was over in Europe but the Bomb had not yet been dropped on Japan. The North Atlantic was considered safe from U-boats, and we boarded the *Acaroa* in New Port News, Virginia. I kept a diary on the trip, long since lost but the events were etched in my mind. The *Acaroa* was a medium-sized, very slow New Zealand freighter that usually took about 35 to 40 passengers plus the freight. Every recreation space, every closet and even some of the stairwells were packed full with boxes of mostly meat products for England. The small swimming pool was filled with cases of canned bacon. Mother and Daddy had a small stateroom on an upper deck and I had a tiny space in the crew's quarters. It was well below the waterline in a corner near the stern where things got very narrow. My bunk took up more than half the compartment. In fact my bunk was too short and narrow for an adult and got even narrower at its foot where the bunk and compartment tapered to a point; perfect for me. There were some interesting mechanical noises and my whole compartment vibrated enough so that all my loose parts jiggled a bit as I lay in the bunk. It felt nice and was funny to watch. Always curious I lifted up my mattress and the boards under it and to my amazement found a huge shiny spinning propeller shaft about a foot below my bunk! I loved it. I slept so well there. Early each morning a steward, who could barely squeeze into my cubby hole, woke me and gave me a cup of tea with exactly the right amount of sugar and just enough milk so I could drink it right down. Then I'd jiggle back to sleep for an hour before waking up again, feeling refreshed and wonderful and looking forward to joining my parents, top sides, for breakfast. There was a shower across the companionway from my parents' stateroom with always-limited fresh water.

The passengers were mostly military and State Department people and a few dependents like my mother and myself. I was the only kid, youngest on board by at least forty years I guess. I made friends with Dame Noel Streatfield, the famous author of children's books. I spent a lot of time talking with her, and I shared with her the daily entries in my journal. I didn't mingle much with the other passengers who all seemed to be rather stuffy and too busy to talk with a kid. There was one man, rather large and very pompous, who scowled at me every time he saw me and led me to think he really didn't like my being there at all; I tried to avoid him. Every day most of the men, the least stuffy ones, my father and I assembled on the stern cargo hatch. We'd all strip naked and climb into a big cargo net. The net was attached to a crane and we were all hoisted over the side and lowered into the water, huge ocean waves crashing completely over us. Like a fish in a fish net, I couldn't possibly fall out but it was scary and I hung on tight. One moment we'd be high and dry; time to take a deep breath. Then a wave would crash into us and we'd be completely submerged. It was great fun until the day we got out of the Gulf Stream and got dunked in really icy cold water. Everybody started yelling but the noise of the engine driving the crane covered our cries. The crane operator probably thought we were having our usual noisy fun and the usual 10 minutes overboard became an endurance test! I don't remember ever being colder; still it was fun. Later that day we saw an iceberg. Did the crane operator know?

For several days we were tossed around by a big storm. The waves broke some windows in the passengers lounge, only one deck below the bridge. Water cascaded down the stairs, and we had to slow way down to ride out the storm. It was a quite dangerous storm and lots of people got sick, but I loved it. I'd wait, poised at the bottom of a flight of stairs as the ship rose up and up on a wave. As it started down I'd make my leap. Almost weightless I could easily make it up to the top of one flight and sometimes, if the ship was still dropping, I could grab the rail, whip myself around 180 degrees, and be halfway up the second flight before it hit the bottom of the trough and started coming up again. More wonderful flying! We couldn't go out on deck for several days but I still had great fun helping the army of stewards mop up water and go flying up the stairs. On very big waves the stern lifted so high the propeller cleared the water and would spin very fast, violently shaking my compartment. I thought it was great but was told it was unsafe and for two nights lugged my mattress up to my parents' stateroom and slept on the floor. When the weather cleared I was glad to get back to my compartment and resume some of my activities on deck.

One of my favorite pastimes was to climb up the ladder on the crane and crawl out on to the boom. I'd lie down, legs dangling, straddling the boom and slide on my belly way out to its end where there was a big pulley and cables to hold onto. It was very high off the deck. The boom was usually not tightly secured, except during the storm, and the end where I liked to lie would swing way out over the water. It was very dangerous but my favorite perch; being the only kid on board no one really noticed. One afternoon, lying way out on the end, I pushed myself up to a sitting position, and I really crushed my balls in the process. It hurt like nothing I had even imagined and completely took my breath away. I didn't dare move. I sat there for quite a while trying to understand what happened to create such pain. I was pretty sure I couldn't get off the boom without getting on my stomach again and was terrified I'd crush them again. I tried to lift myself and somehow lie back down, and I crushed them again! I was painfully aware of that part of my anatomy for the first, and for a long, time.

When we finally arrived in Southampton after 14 days, I watched from on deck as they unloaded cargo with the same crane that took us swimming and crushed my balls. They loaded a new Cadillac that belonged to the large man who hated me, into our swimming net. As they hoisted it over the side something in the net parted and the Caddy made a near perfect nose dive from about forty feet to the concrete dock below. It made a great sound and retained a definite banana shape even after it landed. Justice again! Not too secretly, I was gleeful.

He's a revolving SOB, which means he's a
SOB no matter which way you look at him.
— Helen Handley

4

London: Cold and Dark Winter
(1945–1946)

With World War II barely over, the fall and winter of 1945-46 in London were pretty bleak. School started soon after we arrived. If left to my own devices I thrived, enjoyed, and learned from life; my natural curiosity propelled me, but if I was confined, controlled by a school with guidelines and programs, I could not function regardless of the consequences. In London the consequences started to get serious and soon, very uncomfortable. We lived in a flat owned by my father's firm, the Dorr Company, at 25 Jermyn St. right in central London, only about a block from Piccadilly Circus. My father was working long hours and traveling to the continent often as he tried to rebuild the company after the war. Mother often traveled with him and I was on my own; a latchkey kid long before it was the norm. If they were not traveling they went out a lot; mostly entertaining various Dorr Company people from the continent.

A big part of my father's success was that Mother could deal with the wives and was always there to be a most gracious hostess. Diplomacy was essential and Mother was good at it! In London, even before the war, the theatres started relatively early so my parents usually came home at nighttime to see me off to bed, or if I was already asleep they would come in and say goodnight. Almost everything was rationed; I went the whole year without a glass of milk. The powdered substitute was healthy but tasted terrible. There was no meat and the cases of canned meat that came across on the *Acaroa* went to schools and hospitals and didn't come near our stores. Eric Moseman, the Dorr Company's manager from Switzerland and a close friend of my parents, brought me a can of Nestles Hot Chocolate and some white chocolate. I would lick my finger and poke the chocolate powder and lick it off. I couldn't imagine taking spoonfuls to make a drink! I had to make it last! A few times Andrue's, a restaurant, a block or two down Jermyn Street, featured whale steak, and once we braved the long queue and tried it. For me it wasn't worth the wait. I already hated standing in line.

Large parts of London were in ruins with many streets still filled with rubble and impassable. Shells of buildings, some bombed flat or gutted by fire, were everywhere. Unexploded V2 bombs had a curious way of going off randomly but mostly at night. I'd hear the terrific thump and soon the sirens would start. I never got used to it. Unless it was very far away I always woke up and sometimes got up to look out my window for a while.

Soon after securing my route to school I started going on my own, taking a number 19 or 21 bus from Piccadilly to Sloan Square. I walked the few blocks to school from there. Coming home there were the same buses but I had a choice: I could stay on the bus all the way to Piccadilly Circus and have a short two-block walk to the flat or I could get off a stop sooner and have a considerably longer walk down Jermyn St. After dark, Jermyn St. was scary with its fair share of ruined buildings. For its whole length there was only one lonely street light that worked, and then only when the power was on, two hours in the morning and two hours at night. The schedule for power was staggered, so I never knew. The real advantage of Jermyn Street was a wonderful toy store at the end near the bus stop. I'd always stop and look and look and look at the ever-changing window display; sometimes I went in but never could buy anything. They had the most marvelous truck with a big crane on it. It had two front axels and countless tires. There were trains and little wind-up Shuco cars with gears you could shift and a steering wheel that worked. Things like that would have to wait for a birthday or Christmas. Looking at these things gave me courage, I guess, to walk, trying not to run, to our end of the street. Immediately next to 25 Jermyn Street on the left was a burned-out shell of a building similar to ours. It took up the other half of the block and there were no fences or boards or anything covering its gaping windows and doors. It must have had several ground floor shops, now all glassless and staring out at me. It was the scariest of all the buildings on the street. I tried not to but always ended up running past that one. During the Blitz the building took a direct hit and was completely burned and gutted. Its roof was gone but its walls were pretty much intact. Local theory had it that another V2 had buried itself down the airshaft but didn't go off.

Life in London was great. I got along pretty well at school at the start and absorbed some good-natured kidding about the way I held my fork and knife. Our system of cutting one way and shifting utensils from hand to hand to put the morsel in your mouth and then shift back again did seem awkward. I soon learned their way and still use it. This was an easy lesson to learn. We had cold canned corned beef quite often for lunch, perhaps from the *Acaroa*? The academic picture didn't get any worse because it never got started. I had never had homework before and couldn't deal with it; just could not get it done. The first two weeks of school went by and I had done no work. I assume my parents were told this but it was by now an already familiar story to them and nothing changed or was said at home.

On Friday of the second week of school I was given a three-by-five card with the names of my five teachers and a small box for each school day of that week. Only a few other boys got cards. I presented my card to each teacher and as the day went on there were more and more check marks in boxes. This was to tally up the assignments given that I had not done, meaning all of them. After school the cardholders were told to go to the headmaster's office where we were lined up in alphabetical order. There were five or six of us. The first boy in line was called up and presented his card to the headmaster. He had six boxes checked. The headmaster then took him by the arm and made him stand next to a big chair. He was told to pull his pants and underpants down to his ankles. Some sort of wooden block on the floor kept his heels from moving. A coach who was assisting grabbed him and forced him to bend forward over the arm of the chair, pulled his shirt and school sweater up over his head effectively pinning his out stretched arms and held him down while the headmaster administered six resounding smacks with a wide leather strap across the boy's bare behind. Large red marks appeared instantly and the shirt pulled over his head muffled the boy's screams. When it was done the boy shuffled, sobbing, back to his place in line. When the procedure started again with the second boy in line I started to understand what was happening and realized it would soon be me. I had twelve boxes checked. I was really scared and with two or three boys still lined up ahead of me I started to cry. When it came my turn I added to my own humiliation by thoroughly wetting myself before my pants were even down. I had experienced some similar pain at the hands of my father but nothing as severe as this, and this was in public, so to speak, by a stranger in front of my peers. We had to stand in our place in line, sobbing and sniffling, to wait and watch 'till the last blow landed on the last culprit.

Under normal circumstances with normal kids, I suppose educators assumed an experience like this would have some effect, create some inducement to do the work and probably would have to happen to a boy only once. A week went by. I had been given a clean slate; a chance to start over, but again accomplished nothing. On Friday, the end of the second week, the three-by-five cards were handed out again. I now understood this was school policy and would happen every two weeks unless I handed in my homework. This knowledge and fearful anticipation of the strap had no effect on my ability or induced me in any way to complete my work. As those alternate Fridays drew near I'd desperately try to do something, but hours of sitting at my table never produced anything. I knew sitting there was pointless so I'd detour and visit the toyshop instead.

The dreaded Fridays came and went. Every now and then, instead of the headmaster, the football coach who was also a 'Padre' complete with a backwards collar and a Sacred Studies class, would wield the strap. The first time this happened some of the other kids were whimpering before the session started because, as I soon found out, he hit us much harder than the headmaster. What ever happened to forgiving our sins? At first I'd stand on the toilet at home and inspect the damage in the bathroom mirror; little blue lines lasted all week but it got boring. It looked about the same and the strapping became routine. Back home Martin Finger had to go once a week to the doctor for a shot. He told me it hurt a lot and showed me the little mark it left. But he said he "got used to it". I never got 'used to' the strap, but I learned I could endure the pain. I knew the rule. I'd get a whack each time I didn't do my work. I never was able to do my work and sustained a lot of whacks. I don't remember even telling my parents, out of shame, embarrassment, perhaps, or that I just felt I was getting something I deserved. I knew the rule and really didn't think to question it.

Almost every day except when it was raining I'd dawdle past the toyshop or make other much longer detours on my way home from school. Mother would sometimes be there but if she was not home I'd find Patrick, the bus boy/bellhop/maintenance man of our building, and spend some time with him. It was Patrick who had the theory about the V2 bomb next door. I was sure he was right. Patrick was the youngest of 23 children. He was always fixing things. I liked it best when there were problems with the lift. He'd have me crawl around, under it and over it. There were places in the motor room where I could fit and he couldn't, so I was really able to help him at times. I'd crawl and squirm into tiny places guided by a pinpoint of light from Paddy's flashlight. He'd hand me a screwdriver or wrench and tell me which clutch band to tighten or which relay to "give it a whack". I learned a lot about how things work. Sometimes someone would use the lift and it would come to life while I was inside. It always startled me, but I was fascinated by the sight and sound of the big gears and drums turning and being so close to them. The relays made huge sparks and gave off a wonderful lightning smell. The gears smelled nice, too.

Mrs. Kelley, who ran the switchboard, was my other great friend. Often she would greet me with a message from mother with instructions about dinner or changes of plans. Often the message was that I'd have supper with Mrs. Kelley, which always suited me. She taught me some math by showing me how to figure out that Patrick's mother had to have been pregnant a little over seventeen years. Twenty-three kids, times nine months, divided by 12 = 17.25 years. I never could get that straight in school.

After delaying homecoming as long as possible and after supper with mother or Mrs. Kelley I'd try and sit at my table in my room staring at, but never doing, the homework. All of London was outside my window, all the sounds all the excitement. How could I study Latin? There was so much to see and do. Weekends, during the day I'd wander; it was safe for a nine-year-old to be out on the town. At night my parents often took me to the theater, which I loved. I saw *Ten Little Indians*. I saw Edith Sitwell in something, and we saw Ruth Draper do an evening of monologues. I was fascinated and could really *see* all the characters in *The English Garden Party*. All the people touring the cathedral were there! I insisted we go backstage and she remembered my father as a kid from Camp Merriweather, where she was a counselor. We went to the symphony several times. It inspired me to buy colored clay from the toyshop and construct a clay model of the orchestra with about fifty musicians, all with instruments.

One Saturday, on my own, I went to Madame Tussaud's Wax Museum on the far side of Hyde Park. Again I was fascinated. I took a peek behind the black curtain that bore a sign saying, "NOT FOR CHILDREN". There was a beautiful naked lady. She was bent over backwards with her arms tied behind her, her head and feet dangling down. She was suspended by a giant hook, put sideways through her stomach! She was all bloody. There were other ghastly things in the Chamber of Horrors, all "NOT FOR CHILDREN", and I saw them all. But nothing was as great as that lady.

I saw the 'Changing of the Guard', the choir at Westminster Cathedral, Stonehenge and the miracle of St Paul's Cathedral surviving the Blitz and the phenomenon of hearing a whisper in the dome. This is what I learned out of school. And then there was the bomb next door! Late one night the V2 in the airshaft of the burned-out building next door went off. The sound and simultaneous shock in our flat was incredible. Everything flew off the shelves, pictures came off the walls, and my mother was tossed out of bed. The wall of my parent's room was the outer wall of our building immediately adjacent to the building next door. My clay orchestra was thrown off the dresser, landing upside down on the floor; glass and broken dishes were everywhere in the kitchen. There were clouds of dust everywhere, which at first I took to be smoke. I raced to my parents' room. Mother was sitting on the floor still completely wrapped in her old skunk skin fur coat which she slept in to keep warm; father calm and quiet, sitting naked on the edge of bed comforting her and surveying the damage. The sirens came right then and there. Right outside my window were all the fire trucks, ambulances, and police cars, flashing lights, men in hats; the works; everything a kid could ask for! As scared and literally shaken as I was, I stayed glued to the window until the last truck left. The whole parade came right down my street. The show of a lifetime! The next morning there was a pile of rubble where the five-story shell had been. Rubble piled high over the sidewalk and spilled out nearly across the street. There was no damage to our building but the bricks from the shell had completely peeled away, exposing the outer brick wall of #25. It did cross my mind that I could have been walking on that sidewalk. I did everyday.

We spent Christmas vacation visiting my two older brothers who were studying in Switzerland. They were playing hockey with a Swiss team, and I remember going to a game in an alpine town called Lobersant. Mother and I shared a tiny room with a tiny bed in a really grubby hotel. The only access to the room was through a small door behind the bar. I don't remember much except we got there from the station by horse-drawn sleigh, and the men's room was so foul that in the middle of the night I had to come back, through the bar, to get my boots. I remember my brothers getting in a big fight during the hockey game. Their apartment in Geneva was on the 5th floor and had a funny elevator they rode up on a huge shaft, like an old-fashioned automobile lift. For some reason we were not supposed to ride it down but I did anyway.

After Christmas and back in London, school started. I made a stage out of a cardboard box complete with several levels for my orchestra. I decorated it using crayons for organ pipes and it became almost a substitute for my beloved tree. I could sit and stare at this and really hear the entire orchestra. I could isolate the instruments. By looking at them I could hear them separately. The orchestra, like my tree back home, had unlimited performance skills and could envelop me in its sounds for hours on end.

I don't remember much more about school either. After Christmas it became known at school that I was returning to the States before the end of the year, and the strappings stopped. I think they sort of gave up on me and left me alone. I learned much more from my own explorations and associations with Patrick and Kelley than at school. At school I only remember learning how to use a fork and knife efficiently. I do remember tearful goodbyes to Paddy, as I called Patrick, and Kelley; I had dropped the 'Mrs.' early on. I had no school friends except an older boy named Daniel who I only knew because he got strapped almost every time I did.

The trip home on the *America* was like stepping into another world. A world of plenty! No limits. The first meal was served in the palatial dining room. Spotless starched white tablecloths, sparkling silverware, gleaming glassware and plates, all with the ship's logo engraved, etched or stamped somewhere in gold. There was a small plate with real butter and on the menu I saw MILK. The waiter brought some to me in a tall glass... tall, cold, and full, with just a hint of foam on top. It was the best thing I had ever tasted and I made it last through the whole meal. I nearly went into shock when the waiter offered me another glass. After a dish of real ice cream I asked for a third glass of milk. The *America* was new and quite different from the old *Acaroa*. It went very fast and much too soon we were back home and back to Stamford. My parents would have to continue traveling extensively for business. I had fallen far behind in school and the experts put the blame on too much moving around, too many different schools and environments, no stability, not enough structure, etc. Bement School, a small boarding school in Deerfield, Mass. was chosen and would be my place. My freedom to explore and investigate on my own would be confined to school vacations for the next ten years.

5

Reining Me In
(1946 – 1950)

According to the report cards I collected, I started at Bement, a small K-8th grade boarding school in Deerfield, Massachusetts, in the spring term of my fourth grade year. There must have been some miserable transcripts sent from London. I had accomplished nothing in school there. At Bement's request, a Stanford-Binet intelligence test was done and I had an I.Q. of 139 (obtained).

Mathematical Reasoning at "Year Average Adult Level" (Thanks, Kelly.) Reasoning at "Superior Adult Level". *"His Perceptual Speed seems to be excellent."* I was (Willingness) *"normal attitude"*, (Self-confidence) *"Rather self-confident"*, (Social confidence) *"Perfectly assured in personal contacts."* (Attention), a written comment, *"Tires easily or gets bored"*.

I was allowed to continue in fourth grade and not be put back. The very first report, with teacher comments, shouts "ADD!"

From the Headmistress:

> *"Brad is a lovable, agreeable, happy and completely unmotivated member of the group. All his oral work, except spelling, is very good and all of his written work exceptionally poor. I have put the pressure on and Brad has done the minimum amount of work necessary. He has never sulked and has done it after hours very often. His sportsmanship is excellent and his callousness to group pressure amazing. Up to date, he shows little pride in a job well done, but does show pride in a finished task, however haphazardly accomplished. Brad comprehends easily and is mature and fluent in group discussions. Arithmetic is to him most unpleasant, but he actually knows his fundamentals well and is mature in his reasoning."* (Thanks again, Kelly!) *"Inaccuracy through carelessness alone, is his greatest weakness in this subject. There is certainly a mountain to be moved as far as lack of concentration in*

written work is concerned."

And, Social Studies:

"Brad is a quick little boy, incredibly destitute of concentration powers. Despite his lack of effort he has managed to do well enough in map location work to pass the course, (I had been to most of the places, why not?) *but it's a shame to see so much ability wasted. He is easily capable of achieving top grades if he decided to apply himself."*

These reports loaded with ADD buzzwords continue in the same vein throughout.

My father, with Mother close by and a real ally, were working non-stop to rebuild the Dorr Company's European offices. They did their best to be home for vacations and as much of the summer as possible.

Disappointed but understanding, I'd be at boarding school from now on.

More, Fifth Grade:

".... any respectable written composition is still almost impossible" "... has yet to settle down and do the work of which he is capable." "He is inaccurate due to lack of drill in the past and due to poor concentration..."

Yet amazingly I had started doing a little better academically. Every Saturday morning I sat in study hall for two hours and was stuck in constant extra study halls where I was supposed do my work. There was no physical punishment except once, early that first spring term; and not for academic failures; but actually, for me, a funny situation.

George Withington, two other boys and I shared a room in the Barn, as the boy's dorm was called. It had been a barn; half converted to dorm rooms and the other half a small general purpose gymnasium/assembly hall and sometime movie theater. Our room was square; institutional linoleum tiles on the floor, cool for bare feet in the spring; cold in the winter. The sheetrock walls were painted light institutional green (or yellow) and were easily damaged by collisions with rough-housers. An occasional careless foot or a deliberate fist would easily make a hole, and we'd be made to pay for the damages, which seemed unfair since the walls were really pretty flimsy. The institutional white sheet rock ceiling had a single overhead light in the center with a square glass dish for a shade that we were constantly breaking and paying for. The door to the room was flimsy too. It was made of 1 x 6 pine boards with a large 'Z' from top to bottom that held the slats together. It hung in a standard, mass-produced frame and had a noisy latch with a thumb on one side and a hook on the other. Across the hall were tall curtain-covered closets, one for each boy with some hanging space and shelves for clothes. We each had a small bureau in the room. Large old-fashioned multi-light windows let in a lot of light, and we looked out over the small lawn and the girl's dorm. The windows had uncertain curtains and very secure roll-down shades. God forbid the girls might see us! We slept in two institutional wooden double-decker bunk beds. The guy below could poke your mattress through the wire lattice, or pushing with his feet could give you quite a ride or even debunk you onto the floor. All these things were done. George and I had the top bunks and one night got to talking and giggling. We couldn't stop. It was way past lights out. Ruth Fisher was the dorm mother and on duty that night. It seemed to me she was always huffy, a term we used to describe people who were angry about something. That night she was definitely huffy and with good reason. She had been in and out of our room and warned us to be quiet half a dozen times. Finally she came in wielding a fifteen-inch wooden ruler. She was really huffy, more like furious. I was the new boy and George had been at school longer, so he was first. She made him get up on his hands and knees on his bunk with his head on his pillow and his behind in the air. She pulled down his pajamas and started whacking his behind. He yelled and squirmed around and after eight or ten red stripes appeared she stopped and turned to me. With my face in my pillow and my bare behind in the air she started in, and I started to giggle. The more she hit me the more I laughed. It hurt but compared to the strap in England this was a cool breeze. She couldn't make me cry and eventually gave up and went storming away. George decided it would be best to keep quiet.

Later on that term, one sweltering night toward the end of May, I was trying to sleep. I only had rather heavy flannel pajamas from London. I had stripped them off and gone to sleep, lying naked and cool on top of my sheets. Ruth peered in, making her usual rounds, saw this, came in, woke me up and insisted I put my pajamas back on. As soon as she left the room I took them off again and went back to sleep. She came back later and woke me again. This was repeated a few more times but finally she must have gone to sleep herself or again, just given up. Initially I did it because I was uncomfortably hot but later I did it just to be stubborn; they wanted me in pajamas; I wanted out. I'd manage to lose them a lot or forget to collect them to go to the laundry. I won in the end. I've kept the habit and still like sleeping that way.

After a flurry of moderate success the grades began to slip and the "lovable, agreeable" little boy started being "aggressive and disruptive".

Later in fifth grade:

"... can easily do work at a B level but he fails to do his daily work. Brad has failed almost every review test. His daily work assigned in class is seldom completed accurately or on time".

"Unless he is willing to work harder he should repeat this year in spelling."

"Brad is a likable little boy who tries to solve all his problems with a smile and a promise, which he immediately forgets."

"He is careless in his work and very untidy in dress and care of his clothes. He is extremely slow in all dormitory life. Brad's attitude is poor in respect to his room and his personal belongings."

"Nothing seems to concern him or have an effect on him. His whole attitude appears to be indifference".

My parents were entertaining Dorr Company directors of foreign subsidiaries on a regular basis and I was always included and delighted with this parade of interesting people. Most are a blur of faces and familiar sounding names and all had to have been when I was home from Bement on vacation. One morning I woke up and headed for the bathroom. Lying on the floor in my room was a man with the blackest skin I had ever seen. He was flat on his back with his face and feet sticking out from under the sheet covering the rest of him. His arms were folded across his chest and his head was supported by two or three books. I simply stepped over him and continued on my way, totally unfazed and thought nothing more about it. But I do remember it.

At Bement in the 5th grade there was music. I was in the choir and remember really getting excited about singing multi-fold 'Amens'. A 'one-fold Amen' was just 'Amen'. The most we got to was a seven-fold that I really liked. There was singing in music class, which mostly bored me. Only a few of the other kids could sing in tune, most could not. This amazed me because it seemed so natural. Why couldn't they hear the pitch? Also most of the music was old to me. Once in a while we'd learn something that was new to me and that was fun but I was bored by the lack of repertoire. Same old songs, it seemed, over and over.

I played my recorder a lot and struggled with reading notes. All through baseball practice I played the recorder instead of paying any attention to baseball. I kept losing sight of the ball and got beaned a few too many times and never managed to actually hit the ball, so I usually sat, center field, with my back to the play, making the smallest possible target and played my recorder. The coach must have given up on me because I was allowed to stay out there in center field even when my team was 'up'. Is that what they call it? I don't remember what I was playing but I could keep it up for hours.

Sixth grade things keep slipping, the comments about the same, with catch phrases like, "doesn't apply himself", "lacks self-discipline", "doesn't concentrate", etc.

At home during spring vacation and quite by accident I discovered masturbation. I had heard the older boys at school talk about 'the feeling' and obviously was curious to know what they were talking about. I was in bed one morning, naked, already a habit, and quite erect, which was not new, and it did feel nice to massage myself. I started feeling the urge to pee, or so I thought, and continued to massage as I trotted into the bathroom. Then it happened! 'The Feeling!' "This must be it"! I panicked because it wouldn't stop. My previously well toilet-trained little member was out of control. I really thought it would never stop and it scared me so much I didn't try or experiment with it again until the summer when it soon became part of my regime.

I was cast as Peter Pan in the spring play. We did the real, uncut version, complete with flying. Marianna, the dorm mistress at the girls' dorm and in my mind another generally huffy person, made a harness that went around my chest and shoulders. Like a life jacket, it had two straps between my legs that sort of scrunched things but would support my weight reasonably comfortably from one little hook in the back. The hook was strategically placed so when a thin piano wire was attached I could be lifted and dangle almost upright instead of face down. By arching my back and bending my knees a bit I could fly! The wire went up and attached to a rope from a block and tackle, in turn attached to hook high in the ceiling. Tony, the maintenance man and to me a bit of a giant, was 'flight control'. He held the rope effortlessly with one hand and swung me around with the other. The harness chaffed and hurt a bit but I still had great fun practicing this. I could leap from the floor to the mantelpiece and fly from chair to chair. I learned the entire script; my part, everyone else's part, stage directions and lighting cues. There were original songs. I don't remember ever studying the script.

At the same time my English teacher assigned a sixteen-line poem by Edna St. Vincent Millet. I was to memorize it and recite it at the Friday assembly. The first time I thought I had it, but less than halfway through, in front of the whole school I fumbled, lost it, forgot it completely. Dissolving in tears I went back to my seat. George Withington, who by then had become quite a baseball jock, giggled at me. I was hurt and furious and I hated him. It seems Fridays would continue to be my nemesis, something I had to endure. I was made to repeat this, week after week. I never did get through it; always I'd falter, start crying and face the humiliation of defeat. The eighth graders placed bets on how far I'd get, this time. They'd stand at the back of the gym all smirking and giggling at me. I thought about punching holes in the walls but knew it was expensive and probably wouldn't really make me feel better.

The only bright spots were the glorious unsupervised bike rides to Memorial Hall for Peter Pan rehearsals and flying practice with Tony. The play was a smash. The flying scene, kept very secret, was a total surprise and brought gasps from the parents. John and Wendy flew, too, but their wires were attached to a connecting beam that kept them about four feet apart and they had to fly together at the same time. I was alone on my wire and made daring sorties out over the audience. Tony had been patient and tireless; we made a great team. My flying was spectacular. After the play I felt sad and longed to keep flying. I spent what spare time I had, often sneaking out of study halls, visiting with Tony, somewhat comforted by knowing the term was nearly over and summer was coming. I started sprouting a few little hairs under my arms, the first place they showed up. The comments continued. The rest of school continued to crumble. With lots of pushing I just managed again to make it through sixth and in to seventh grade.

My family and I all spent the summer of 1950 in Holland. We stayed in Wassenaar at an estate called Duinrel. The Van Zuylen Family owned a castle there, and we stayed at what had been the carriage house, which was huge. My parents had known the family before the war and had helped the Van Zuylen kids with college in the States. The use of this house was the 'thank you.' I had a borrowed bike, and was responsible for taking care of Rex, a large and friendly German Shepherd. We were inseparable. I'd ride endlessly on wonderful paved bicycle paths that criss-crossed and swooped over and around the dunes that surrounded the house. I didn't have anything else I had to do to all summer. I found a book of photographs that was quite a turn-on, and it was also fun to find isolated places in the dunes to amuse myself. The summer ended much too soon!

The comments from the seventh grade became voluminous as the situation deteriorated more. More hair was showing up in different places and after my summer experiments I became increasingly aware of the changes and a bit more self-conscious about my body. I don't remember thinking one way or another in group shower-room situations except for some curiosity about the various shape and sizes of my dorm mates. I derived great physical pleasure and comfort from solo sex whenever I could, but this pleasant activity was severely curtailed; there was rarely any privacy. The classes were small and I sat off by myself, rarely next to any of the boys in the class and as far away as possible from any girls. Primarily, I didn't want to be called on to answer a question or read something out loud. I wanted to be left alone and often fantasized about how nice it would be to be invisible; just disappear.

I imagined myself in a transparent indestructible flying egg. I controlled it with a small curlicue of bark that exactly fit the ball of my foot and my big toe. I could feel it! It was capable of instantaneous transitions between wherever I imagined I was and wherever I imagined I wanted to be. I could swoop down and pick up a friend but nothing could reach in to hurt me. I made incredible rescues and foiled armed bank robbers, drifted over snowy fields and could travel to London, visit the lady at Mme. Tussaud's or the toy shop, chat with Kelley and Patrick and then be back to my beloved tree at Woodbine Road in a heartbeat. Traveling alone, I floated through class, life and everything else at school. In spite of this drifting and isolation, at some point I noticed Julie Russell. Julie was a year older and I was sure she would never talk to me. She was very pretty, very smart and very athletic. In fact she could ski faster, kick a soccer ball further, slam a baseball harder than any of the boys; she could beat up any one of us.

Well, she did speak to me. We started hanging out, which meant we tried to sit together at meals and ride bikes on Saturday as soon as I got out of the Saturday morning study hall. We stood together in the choir and in the gym, Saturday nights we'd sit together and actually hold hands. Not the whole hand but enough to get pretty sweaty. We'd sit close to the noisy projector and watch the movie at first, but as the reel got close to the end we'd watch the projector so we could unclasp before it ended and the lights went back on. We kissed a few times behind the old schoolhouse after a particularly sweaty movie. I didn't like it much. It felt sort of wet and tasted of second-hand double-mint gum, which seemed nasty to me. I think we went skinny swimming once with a few other kids in a pond hardly bigger than a large puddle. I say "think" because this might be something I imagined at the time, but it could have happened; I like to think it did because I can visualize it pretty clearly. Julie, definitely beginning to look like a young woman, and me, a long year behind, still just barely and self-consciously sprouting a few hairs, doubting I'd ever grow. There were 6th graders in every way bigger and more grown-up looking than me! One of my roommates, a kid my age, was shaving!

Meanwhile, back to the grind. On to 8th grade, more comments:

" ...fails conspicuously because of his unwillingness to work"

"...does not take the time to carry out his basic ideas which are generally good" "

"...Will not make a consistent effort."

"... vocabulary is excellent but so far his period of concentration is of so short a span that little is accomplished before day dreaming and frustration take over."

"Makes no effort to do any sort of real work."

"Unwillingness to conform to the group..."

"... still not applying himself."

"Continues to fail grammar chiefly through lack of effort..."

"... the holes for unfinished work are still enormous."

"... strong compulsion to be different"

"... must be convinced often of the necessity of doing daily tasks of all sorts."

"... has done nothing all year."

"...would not spend the required amount of time..."

" Unfortunately it remains the same story of incomplete assignments and half-known facts."

"Brad tries for a short period and then gives up."

At Benny Goodman's suggestion during spring vacation my parents bought me my first clarinet from the Connecticut Music Exchange in Stamford. It came with three free lessons from the owner, Ray Taranto. Back at school I learned to play some basic things pretty quickly on my own but had no success reading my 'part' in the little 'band'. Barbra Best the music teacher was pretty nice to me but got angry when I made up my part rather than try to read it. I tried to play every chance I had but as I remember the clarinet was taken away from time to time as incentive to make me get my schoolwork done.

I was denied the annual school ski trips. Roller-skating Sundays was out too. I missed a lot of Saturday night movies. I'd have to stay in my room, lights off, while the movie was being shown in the gym right next to my dorm room in the barn. I could hear the louder music and almost make out some of the words. I was made to skip lunch. While the other kids were eating I would be sent to a small office adjacent to the dining room and next to the kitchen. I had to sit at a big table with nothing on it but my homework and a glass of water. Sometimes the cook would sneak me a plate of whatever she could. I was in every Saturday morning study hall and spent the time staring out the window at the other kids riding their bikes or just playing outside. I remember wishing they would just give me a few whacks and let me go. I would have preferred that to sitting for two hours. Incentives didn't work, nothing did. They hadn't worked in England, either.

March 24, 1952, much of the family managed to get to Paris for my brother Arthur's wedding to Perrine Chan. Stories should be told about that but not from me. Her mother Louisette Bertholle co-authored Julia Child's famous cookbook. I remember lots of good food. I remember the feeling of panic as I performed Danny Boy with Ken Smith in front of the gathered wedding guests on my new 'Conn' clarinet, generally hanging on wondering if I could hit the high note. Ken Smith, (Kenneth Leslie Smith) was a close friend of my parents and grandparents and part of the family. He was a well-known English composer and wonderful piano player.

And I remember deer hunting with Perrine's father Henri Chan at some friend's estate in a fancy open car. The manicured forest had straight roads intersecting other straight roads. At one intersection we stopped because at the next intersection was a large beautiful buck. My brother Peter, on leave from Korea, leapt out of the car first and stood in front of the other hunters, blocking them. He aimed and fired and I saw a little puff of dirt inches behind the back foot of the buck, who bolted away to live another day. Peter gave me a sly wink and a smile as he sheepishly apologized for missing the shot.

After another terrible year at Bement I did manage to graduate, finishing the eighth grade; I had no idea that I would make it through. Thinking somehow maybe it was educational, they refused to tell me if I had passed and kept me in the dark up to the last minute. At graduation I got up on stage to receive my diploma, and the principal handed me the document. Only then did she whisper to me that it was signed.

That's the way things were. I longed for my tree.

I'd be shipped off to St. Paul's School in Concord, NH in the fall.

6

The Reins Tighten
(1950–1955)

Our (football) team may not be big but they sure are slow.
— Hop Rudd

Within days of arriving at St Paul's, now in the ninth grade or 'third form' and before any academic failures with subsequent restrictions on my time took place, I started choir practice with Dr. Channing Lefebvre. He became my best friend and mentor although even he couldn't extricate me later from my endless punitive study halls. My brother Jim had made a friend of 'Doc' a few years earlier. He had been a strong tenor and also played the organ well. His musical reputation opened the first door with Doc for me. We all auditioned. I had a pretty strong tenor voice and could sing in tune, but because I was a lowly third former I was supposed to be an alto and sing falsetto so the older boys could fill the tenor and bass spots. Fortunately for me the other older tenors were not very strong and Doc put me in with them because I could hold the section together. We sang some complicated anthems; I particularly liked Vaughn Williams's *100th Psalm*, which, like everything else, I learned by ear. I could hear and sing all the parts, not just mine, but I couldn't understand why I was getting nowhere with reading music. I could see the notes going up and down on the paper but kept getting lost, I couldn't even follow the words; I had to learn everything by ear.

There were no clarinet lessons available, at least not for me. Perhaps it was policy for third form, but I think a request had been made and probably it had been decided not to add anything 'extra' to my schedule. I played my clarinet in my room from time to time but really didn't get much encouragement. I met Henry Schniewind who played the piano and had the highest academic ranking in the form. We became friends. We rounded up a drummer, a tuba player and a trombone player and formed "La Rue's All Stars". (I have no idea where the name came from.)

We got permission to use an empty room in the old Skate house for our band room and lugged in two derelict upright pianos. It did have heat and I robbed enough parts from one piano to keep most of the notes going on the other one most of the time. We sounded pretty awful but had a lot of fun and tried to rehearse regularly.

Soon I was in so much academic trouble and was being sent to so many extra study halls that I could only rarely get time off to play. Doc managed to talk the authorities into letting me stay in the choir but couldn't convince them about "La Rue's" which, if I was lucky, became once a week only. A few times I snuck out of study halls, but one day got caught and was put on a special list telling the study hall monitors to watch me more closely; I couldn't get away with that again. The choir and Doc's non-judgmental support saved my life. I missed the band. All of the study hall time was a waste. I sat at a desk with nothing but music and a million thoughts whirling through my head.

Back in my room I'd often cry myself to sleep worrying about the mountains of incomplete or un-started work due the next day, dreading the cold stares and verbal scolding from my teachers and the derision of my classmates. But I had discovered that masturbation not only was fun but also a great sleep aid so I comforted myself quite often; and quite often fell asleep thinking of being in my tree.

There was a set of shelves with glass doors in the common room. Various trophies and some sports memorabilia were on display and posted next to it was a list of all the third formers and their class ranking. There I was. The first thing I saw going out the door in the morning and last thing I saw headed for bed was that I was 103 out of 103, positive proof I was the dumbest kid in the class. Positive reinforcement?

On the midyear Latin exam I got a 14% out of 100. I promised to try really hard for the rest of the year and endured every possible extra study hall; I got a 7% on the finals.

Somehow, without Latin and the possibility of a Latin Diploma, I got through the year but only with promises of successful summer tutoring in French and Algebra would I be allowed back in the fall. Why, for God's sake?

Summer of Madness

Early in the summer of 1952 after a dismal first year at St Paul's, word came from brother Peter and Marylou that their border collie Tamper was not doing well in the heat at Fort Sill where they were stationed. I happily volunteered to take her on and in a week or so she arrived at Woodbine Road in a crate. After days of confinement she was filthy and very distrusting of everybody including me. She nipped me often as I tried to get her cleaned up. She would growl and snap at me if I got anywhere near her food. I countered by making her eat her dinner out of my hand and in the beginning I had to muzzle her if other people were around. My parents had brought me a Raleigh bicycle from England; four speed, beautiful British racing green. I attached a milk crate to the rack on the back and soon Tamper was happy riding in it. She became much less aggressive and I didn't need the muzzle. To put her to the test I decided a long bike trip was in order.

I packed some camping gear and headed up Rt. 7 into Vermont and then over to New Hampshire staying a few nights at Camp Red Fox Run by Kay and Gug from Bement. From there, on to Rockland and Vinalhaven. I don't remember how long I stayed there but do remember I was running out of summer. I peddled to Boston and, to avoid rough roads for biking and meet my deadline to get back to school, we checked in at South Station

As a last-ditch effort for me to be exposed to something other than riding my bike or spending days on end in my tree (which was still my favorite refuge even at 15) I found myself being directed towards some dancing classes, which led up to a Cotillion. According to some of the letters I uncovered on my ADD quest, arrangements had also been made for two tutors to work on me for the summer, one for French, one for Algebra. I spent my summer going back and forth between them and home by bicycle, and going to Silver Hill, being tested and evaluated. I was playing my clarinet quite a lot on my own. I did some playing for a summer youth theater group musical where I learned tunes like "Chicago" and "Nice Work if You Can Get It" and "They All Laughed". I was meeting kids my age and had developed very strong legs and a firm muscular ass from all the biking, which the girls and football coaches alike seemed to approve of. Nonetheless I always felt very insecure with girls. I played Sebastian in an amateur summer production of Twelfth Night, in Westport, I think, and somehow I was persuaded to attend the formal Cotillion at the New Canaan Country

Club. "La-de-da and humpty-dory-bee-bob." (Lester Young quote; I like it.) My parents had been Country Club members years before it became exclusive and snooty, but we were still on their mailing list.

Dressed in one of my father's old tuxedos I felt really foolish and uncomfortable, and I was sure everybody thought I looked goofy; they all looked pretty goofy to me. Pete Wells, a guy about my age, was standing near the band listening to "Big Chief" Russell Moore, who was fronting the Lester Lanin Society Band. Pete looked equally uncomfortable and probably feeling about the same way I did about the whole affair. We said hello and soon discovered that we both had musical interests; he was a trumpet player and a junior at Darien High School. We agreed to get together. Later I met a few of his friends who also played some Jazz, and although not much happened that summer we stayed in touch.

At Silver Hill I was an outpatient of sorts although I did spend about 3 weeks there, and the recorded interviews of that time and subsequent visits to Dr. Scanlon were part of what I found on my ADD quest.

When I got back to St Paul's in the fall, study halls started up almost immediately. I failed both the special make-up exams for Algebra and French, the proof of my summer's labor. I felt enormous pressure and simply sat for two hours without answering a single question. Unknown, but running rampant, my ADD took over completely. I just stared at the exams without even putting my name on the paper. In spite of this, I was allowed to continue at school and tried to make up the summer's incomplete work. Thanks to Doc Lefebvre I was allowed to stay in the choir and found some unrestricted time to meet with "La Rue's" twice a week. We even played at some school functions and once in a while, after dinner, played in the dining room lobby. Matt Warren, the new headmaster, played society-style piano pretty well and helped and encouraged us to a point. But, as always, academics were supposed to come first, and he had to enforce that philosophy; at least he let me do some playing.

I soon was failing just about everything and hated sports, so I didn't do anything there either.

Along with all my classes I was being prepared for Confirmation. I tried to pay attention but did no better than in any other classes. I did manage to do some thinking on my own, and on the Sunday morning of my confirmation ceremony I decided not to go through with it. I was

With Tamper at
South Station,
Boston.

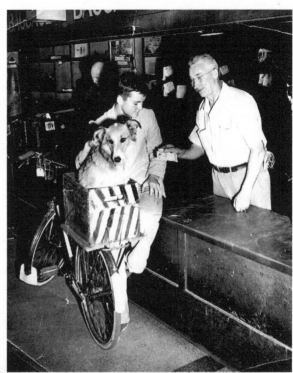

With Tamper,
Ted Mather,
and Lambretta.

practically assaulted by Mr. Warren and three 'padres' from the Sacred Studies Department who were more than a little upset. They pleaded, begged, cajoled, and then got angry and shouted. I sat there like a lump and flatly refused.

My reasoning then was simple: if the doctrine I had been spoon-fed all year was 100% true, the real, the only, the way things were, the whole truth and nothing but the truth, then the fifty-two bazillion people in India who liked Buddha were wrong; so were all the Jews and the Muslims. I wasn't feeling smart enough to say the Episcopal doctrine was right, therefore they were all wrong. I didn't like the idea of a God I was supposed to be fearful of and was supposed to get on my knees before when I wanted to talk to him. I've thought for years that there is no way to be closer to what ever you believe to be your creator than to be naked, outside, exposing yourself completely to the sun, the air, the rain. Why do we need to put on all our best clothes and huddle inside some building when "his/her" nature is all of outdoors?

I wasn't sure of all the questions, but I didn't like the answers I'd been getting. I still can't accept any of the organized religions. I just don't know. I didn't feel like joining the club. This certainly went on my overall scorecard as negative numbers.

I was living in the old Middle House dormitory on the third floor. I was assigned a single room probably to prevent the distraction of someone to talk to— no roommate; but that afforded me some enjoyed privacy too.

Right outside my window was a fire escape that practically intersected the path Doc used, to walk from his house to the chapel. A few times well after lights-out I heard him walking along with his dog, Digby. I'd call out to him and we'd talk, he holding the straining setter and me hanging half way out my window. One night, quite late, I heard a banging on the fire escape. I got out of bed, looked out and saw Doc. "Come on!" he said in a loud whisper, so I scrambled into some clothes and went down the escape to meet him. I was pretty sure he'd had a drink or two, but I went with him anyway. Soon we were in the organ loft and he played and played, all stops open. It was magnificent. I got back to the dorm just in time to "wake up", take a shower and get to breakfast without getting caught. These escapes soon became routine. Once, sometimes even twice, a week I'd hear the knocking on the fire escape and get dressed quickly. The fire escape was nothing compared to my tree and I had real incentive to scramble down it quickly.

Doc and I walked without speaking; keeping silent as though anticipating the colossal sounds that would surround us soon. Digby's clicking toenails was the only sound as we tried to creep silently into the chapel through the locked door of the choir room and up the tiny spiral stairs to the organ loft.

Once there, with the door to the rest of the world securely locked, we started to breathe normally again. Digby would curl up in a corner and go to sleep. Doc would switch on the power to the blower. This created wonderful wheezing sounds, amazing creaking and groaning as all the air chambers gradually filled up. It reminded me of an eager horse getting ready to really go for a run. The whole instrument seemed to be stretching and loosening up for the exercise about to follow, and exercise it did! Doc always surprised me.

Sometimes he'd wedge a pencil under a key so it would sustain the note forever. He'd pull out one stop of some tiny, far-away pipe and it would start. He would harmonize and re-harmonize using the single note as a center. He'd drop it an octave and find ten more ways to harmonize it. Down again, double octaves, and soon the organ would be at full volume, all stops out. The only light came from a tiny lamp over the music rack. I knew the chapel was there but it was only a black hole. It was like standing on the rim of the Grand Canyon at night. It seemed that our little light and Doc's one little note had become the center of the universe. The whole chapel reverberated and seemed reluctant to let go of that last echoing great chord, lingering long after he took his slender fingers off the keyboard and finished playing. Sometimes he'd ask me to turn pages. He'd nod vigorously when to turn because he knew about my problems reading music. I got to be able to follow the bass lines, sometimes. Mostly he would improvise; just start out playing and letting the ideas flow and carry the music. After our ever-so-cautious tiptoe entry into the chapel I was always amazed at his abandon and the volume of sound. Occasionally we'd sample a bit of Communion wine; I was sure we'd get caught but we never did.

When the snow started in the late Fall these wonderful escapes became less frequent, The path would get slippery as it got much colder, but almost every week I could expect at least one clanging signal on the fire escape, right up until I got kicked out of school. Part of my demise at St Paul's was caused by lack of sleep and the ADD did the rest. Under ideal conditions I couldn't focus in class and routinely fell asleep anyway. Those mornings after, particularly those mornings after those very cold nights when we had helped ourselves to a sip, or three, of Communion wine, I didn't have a chance.

During the Thanksgiving break I contacted Pete Wells and we made plans to do some playing over Christmas vacation. Things were going even worse at St Paul's and I was eager to get home for Christmas. Pete and I immediately went to work putting together a combo playing pretty much Dixieland tunes. We landed a New Year's Eve gig, the first for any of us, at a private party and we knew twelve songs. We played the same twelve songs but at different tempos, made a few into waltzes and made it through the night. The adults played "Pin the Brassiere on the Hostess," a game I'd never seen before. Pete and I were both fifteen and my brother had to pick us up as we didn't have our licenses. Mickey Earnshaw and Doug McLaughlin, our drummer and bass player, were about that same age too. Fred Fischer, our piano player, was twelve. This was the start of a career?

Back at St. Paul's after Christmas vacation I lasted only a few months. I was doing dismally. I was miserable.

As everything spiraled down and out of control my father made a special trip to visit me at school and I'm guessing to discuss my imminent and unavoidable departure.

Hockey was the winter sport. I was assigned to the lowest team in the form, couldn't keep my ankles straight, could hardly skate at all, and was a miserable failure on the rink too, as everything scholastic was crashing simultaneously. The rinks were all on natural ice. The boards were held in place by L-shaped braces made of 4x4 posts; the ends stuck out like fingers around the out side of the rink. Pops was a superb hockey player but had a gimpy leg due to several back operations. As I tried to keep my ankles off the ice and once in a while make contact with the puck, Pops skated like he was on a scooter, pushing with his good leg. With deadly accuracy he shot the puck and hit every post end; never missed, as he went round and round the outside of the rink. The visit must have been hugely disappointing for him, to see me failing everything. But he never showed anything but love and support for me.

Doc lobbied hard and I was allowed to stay in the choir 'til the end. Three of the guys in "La Rue's" had been kicked out of school. Henry, the only survivor, remained and we played occasionally until I left for good.

There were only a few more meetings with Doc. During the last one, only a day or two before I left, we didn't speak. He played quietly and I cried quietly 'til dawn. For sure the hardest part of leaving St. Paul's was not being able to share more time with Doc. I learned so much.

A few weeks before spring break I was "withdrawn". I would find out it was a kinder, gentler way of saying "axed," "expelled," or "kicked out". My parents were in Europe so I was summarily collected by my "Uncle Monk" Terry who had made arrangements to transfer me to Salisbury. He was well known as a member of the Independent School Headmasters' Association and knew every headmaster. He somehow convinced George Langdon at Salisbury to take me on. Uncle Monk was also headmaster of Middlesex School but certainly didn't want me there.

St. Paul's had a policy that I could not visit the campus until my class had graduated. Doc died before I ever got back to see him again.

That organ loft was his refuge, his special place, complete with spiral stairs and a lock at the top. He created musical masterpieces that he shared with me. He let me share his magic tree.

Salisbury (Why, for God's sake?)

Transferring to Salisbury was just another bad idea. I was destined for failure from the start but of course no one recognized that. My uncle Monk deposited me at Salisbury, starting the spring term. It, too, was an Episcopal school with chapel every day, but they didn't attempt to recruit me. I don't remember if I was even in the choir. With special tutoring I was eeking by and for the first time started with real music lessons. Frank Pouillat was a piano teacher, but he took me on and tried to get me reading music. I spent a full week trying to figure out the first line of the Mozart Clarinet Quintet and realized it was hopeless. The lines and spaces I knew, were 'FACE' and "Every Good Boy Does Fine". (Where had I heard that before?) I knew this, but was unable to recognize it or carry it through from day-to-day. I might recognize one or even two notes on the staff one day, but by the next day I'd have to go back to counting the lines and spaces. I couldn't understand why, was terribly frustrated and angry at myself. What I was able to play by reading was so elementary compared to what I could play by ear. And what I could play by ear was nothing compared to what I could hear in my head. I had no idea how to get these three skills even connected, much less get them closer to being on equal levels. I felt frustrated and stupid about not being able to read, and more frustrated by not having the technique to find the notes I heard and wanted to play. How did Benny play so fast, so clean? An impossible, frustrating dream.

I had to play one movement of the Mozart to get a passing grade in music. This was my first real music class. I wanted it badly and had to find a way. Since it was early in the term, grades had not been posted and I wasn't yet being restricted. I was still allowed off campus, and on a trip to town I discovered in a small music shop an album of Benny Goodman playing the Mozart. What wonderful luck! I bought it and in a few days learned the part I needed to play by ear. I made a 'mono' record player using a large whiskey barrel. It had a 12" speaker poking out through the bottom, an amp on a shelf with extended tuning knobs poking out in the middle and a turntable suspended by screen door springs at the top. The top came off and there it was. I listened and listened to Benny. Punitive study halls started up almost immediately. At the spring recital I played it well enough to get a passing grade. I put the music in front of me so people would think I was reading but halfway through I realized I was playing with my eyes shut. I still passed. Meanwhile, another teacher was sharing his musical 'tree' with me. "Hop" Rudd, was the hockey and football coach and a long-time family friend from New Canaan days. His son Roswell Rudd is an acclaimed trombone player. During the years before WWII when we were in Holland, the Rudds rented our house in Stamford. Hop and his wife both taught at the New Canaan Country Day School. There were lots of connections from when I was very young and now their son, Ben, was in my class at Salisbury. Hop Rudd was Director of Athletics. He was famous for his comment about his football team, "They may not be big but they sure are slow".

I was put in the dorm that Hop supervised so at least as a new boy, coming in late in the year, I'd be near someone I knew a little. My room was at the end of the hall and right next to his living room. Even though I was nothing of an athlete it didn't take long for our musical relationship to develop. He had his drums permanently set up in his living room and he knew I was starting to play a little Jazz. Just after "lights out" he'd crank up a Benny Goodman trio record. That was my cue. As soon as I heard it through the wall I'd get on some clothes and without even knocking come into his apartment, clarinet in hand, and we'd both play along with Benny, Teddy and Gene, full blast. He had an ancient drum set. The Hi Hat was loose at its base and this caused the cymbals for some curious reason to wander around sort of in orbit. They were never in exactly the same place so when we played duos the time tended to be a little that way, too. Hop more than made up for this with his gusto, exuberant spirit, and total joy. Such passion, and with Benny, Teddy and Gene to guide us, we swung like crazy. His drum set was his special 'tree.' Like his 'hi-hat', the music went round and round 'till very late at night. Consequently, I slept through a lot of classes. Sound familiar?

My brother Jim got married in Vicksburg, Mississippi, April 23, 1955. I was able to go to the wedding as I was home from Salisbury on spring vacation. My father had bought a white Ford sedan nicknamed "the Ghost" to replace his black 1941 Ford convertible, which became my first real car. Soon afterwards Dorr-Oliver insisted the execs be given a company car in lieu of increased salary. Pops objected, some because he wanted the salary, but more, he didn't want to drive around in a fancy Lincoln or Cadillac and was happy with his unpretentious Ford. As a compromise, the company delivered a Mercury to him.

The Ghost was offered to Jim for his honeymoon. Han Andre de la Porte, a close family friend, and I were volunteered to drive the Ghost from Stamford to Vicksburg. Han was funny, brilliant, multi-lingual, and a fourth brother to me. He delighted everyone with his ability to superimpose the accent of any of six or seven languages to any other language. We were in a booth in a roadside restaurant somewhere in the Smoky Mountains and Han was reading the menu in English with a strong German accent, almost unintelligible. Directly behind him was a young waitress was looking at me, wide eyed; I was trying not to laugh without much success. The waitress ventured around into sight and asked if we were ready to order. Han answered in perfect English with a slight British twist. The waitress was really confused and I completely lost it.

Going through the mountains Han told me when you go down the hill use the same gear you'd use to go up it; or you lose your brakes. That important tip probably saved my life more than once.

Back at school, spring term, I was being tutored in algebra by Mr. Carr. He was ancient and had come out of retirement to tutor me. I sort of never knew if he'd make it to the next day but he was a good teacher and did his best. He gave me one bit of advice that has stuck with me. He told me about the guy who ate a bushel of bad apples. He bought a barrel of apples. There were a few bad ones on top so, not wanting to waste anything, he ate the ones that were almost spoiled. The next day there were three or four more bad ones and he ate those and eventually ate a barrel of bad apples. To me that translated to: "Don't put up with something bad or mediocre; go for the good stuff."

In spite of his help everything academic spiraled down; report cards were dismal. Mozart gave me my only passing grade, and for reasons unknown, I was told I could return in the fall without tutors! Again I was relieved to get home and be free for the summer.

Woodbine Road, Fast Cars,
and the Neighborhood Gang
(1929–1979)

My parents bought a small parcel of land with a small house and small separate garage on Woodbine Road in North Stamford, Connecticut. The road paralleled the river that connected the two Stamford reservoirs. My parents had been living in New York and my father still worked there, but he sold all his stock and used most of his savings to buy the place. "Moving away from New York?" "Away from both sets of parents?" "So far out in the country?" "The long commute?" everybody asked, and told him he was nuts. It was April 1929. A year or so later they'd be in Holland, with the house rented and secure. His stock would have been worth nothing. Crazy? Like a fox.

The driveway to the house was a dirt road coming uphill from Woodbine Road, running pretty much east to west. A sharp left turn through a narrow opening in the stone wall, up a slight grade and you were there. The low farmhouse was on the left and the gambrel-roofed garage on the right. We had about five acres, starting at Woodbine Road and continuing past the buildings, a hundred feet of field to another stonewall along the property line on the west. Behind us, south, beyond another stonewall was a strip of our land and then acres of yet-to-be developed woods.

Mr. Delafield, who sold them the property, had promised my parents first refusal on the land west and beyond the stone wall, but during their nine-year absence in Holland he had widened the bottom part of our drive way and now it was called Pinewood Road. He had extended the road past our property and a large house had been built in the next parcel just over the wall. My parents were really upset by this new house, but Nancy Lounsbury now lived next door in the new house and we became life-long friends. I'd have to say she was my first girlfriend, although at five (she was six) she was really just a girl friend. I even let her ride around with me in my treasured Dumpy. I'd pedal and Nancy, sitting backwards in the dump part of Dumpy, would push from behind; 'four-wheel drive', long before we knew what that meant. She was definitely 'one of the boys'.

One spring, on vacation from Bement, I was riding my bike along Woodbine Road. I rode everywhere and constantly; so glad to be away from all those study halls and other constraints of school. Up ahead I saw another kid on a bike heading my way. It was Bill Mather, my great friend from hall-detention days at New Canaan Country School. We fell on each other. He had moved in only a few hundred yards away; my best friend now was my neighbor. His mother, Helen, became a second mom and soon a soul mate of my mother's; best of friends. She also was famous for her 'wall-to-wall' welcome mat especially for the neighborhood kids. I was parked there often for meals and to spend the night if my parents were busy. Helen was everybody's second mom.

Bill told me he had recently lost his father, Bud Mather to a fast-moving cancer and that his mom was well along pregnant with their fourth child. Bill had an older sister Marianna and a little brother. Ted, "Edward my son" his mother called him, was about seven and really alone. Twelve-and-thirteen-year-old boys really don't need a seven-year-old hanging around, but Ted spent the bulk of that summer riding on the handlebars of my bike and was one of the original six Hurricane Island campers.

Summers away from school were glorious times. There were a few other kids in the gang, Chris, 'Kippy', and Mike Clark. Kippy was a year or two older than me; Mike a year younger. Ron Chappell moved in, adopted by neighbors. His mother, Dickie Chapelle was a photojournalist for *Life* magazine during WWII. (She was killed in action in Vietnam in 1965.)

We all rode bikes, furiously, everywhere. We had elaborate trails crisscrossing through the woods connecting everybody's house. Bill, Ted, his sister Marianna and I, Nancy, too, I think, often went skinny swimming in the water company's river. Some of us also snuck into the actual reservoirs for a swim in the daytime and sometimes at night, too. It was scary but fun too; sneaking through an opening in the chain link fence, hoping the warden, Billy Botts, wouldn't spot us and catch us or chase us away without our clothes, or find our clothes, take them and leave us naked and stranded. He'd spot us coming out of the woods, riding our bikes with dripping wet hair obviously just returning from a swim, but he never could catch us in the act. There were usually other kids with us too. Kippy's mother, Mrs. Clark, valiantly tried to start a Cub Scout group. She thought it would be a helpful 'taming' experience for Kip and Mike who were both pretty wild, and she rounded up me and a few neighborhood kids. I went a few times and even bought a little blue Cub Scout cap and yellow scarf but gave up pretty quickly. I couldn't remember the pledge and it seemed to me we spent much too much time on stuff that reminded me painfully of school. I just couldn't remember how to tie a damned square knot.

Kippy and I remained friends for a long time even after he got me in serious trouble. He stole some cigarettes from his mom and being two years older (I was about 11) pretty easily convinced me to go down to the straw barn across the street to give smoking a try. A straw barn— really! Not being the cleverest place to experiment lighting cigarettes, we managed to start a small fire. The barn didn't burn down but Bob Smith, the tenant farmer, saw us come running out of the smoking barn. Kippy ran like hell and got away but Mr. Smith caught me, first dealt with the fire and then dealt with me. He dragged me by the arm into his pick up truck and roughly took me up to the horse barn. He secured my feet in a feeding trough, bent me over the stall wall, pulled my pants and underwear down around my ankles and went after me with a bridle 'till I was bleeding. He then telephoned my father in New York. When Pops got home from work he came up to my room all set to spank me some more. He pulled me out of bed and hauled me over his lap only to find there was no undamaged area left to spank. Kippy's mom wouldn't allow him to be spanked; he got off scot free. For a while I hated him for that, but I never touched another cigarette; an important lesson well learned.

One summer as we were approaching adolescence we started noticing and talking about our physical changes, but our swimming, camping and crazy bike riding were not diminished. Then I remember the terrible day when Nancy's mother told her, "No more running around topless in just shorts and sneakers like the guys". Now she had to wear a T-shirt when she was outside playing. It cast a pall over the whole neighborhood.

Gradually we drifted apart, sort of growing up and going different ways. I've recently seen Nancy in Maine, and Bill, who is in Los Angeles, Ron in Albuquerque; haven't seen the others in years.

Exactly one month to the day after my sixteenth birthday, in accordance with Connecticut state law, I got my driver's license. July twelfth, three days later, I totally demolished my brother Peter's Hillman Minx convertible. It happened on Wire Mill Road in North Stamford about nine at night. With the top down, I was driving like I was Juan Fangio, the famous Argentine racecar driver, except I did everything wrong. There was a bridge covered with wooden planks that I hit at about sixty. I got airborne, turned into the turn instead of letting it drift out and slammed on the brakes. Wrong, wrong, wrong! The car came down nose first on the right front wheel, which was turned hard left. The tire disappeared and the rim caught the wooden planks and stopped right there. The rest of the car went end over end and landed on the driver's side in the shallow stream just beyond the bridge.

Pete Lombardo, a Stamford cop, had seen us (Kippy was with me) head into Wire Mill much too fast and had started out after us. With lights flashing he was the first on the scene. Kippy was unhurt, without a scratch, but he had recently been in some minor trouble with the police. He stayed with me to be sure I was all right until he saw the approaching flashing lights; then he took off running through the woods. I'd been thrown out of the car and was bruised, lost considerable skin on my butt and one knee but nothing was broken. I sort of remember Kip telling me he was okay and running away. Pete Lombardo would later tell me that when he found me, I was in the car, sitting at the wheel in the drivers seat on my side, the car on its side, in about a foot of water. I was trying to start the car explaining I had to get it home before my parents found out.

As a precaution, Pete and his partner took me to the hospital. I guess I looked worse than I was. By the time we got there, the raspberry on my right butt cheek, through a plate-sized hole in my jeans, had oozed and glued me to the seat. Pete, I guess, had seen the damage and figured out why I couldn't move. He grabbed me by the hair and gave my face a slap, which startled me and unstuck me. Nothing was seriously damaged except my pride but I really howled when they applied disinfectant green soap and picked bits of tar out of my behind. The hospital people thought it was quite funny, took their sweet time; probably thought I deserved it and seemed to enjoy making me scream.

I was banged up enough to have to lay low, and a few days later

Kip came to the house to see me. He had a big bandage on his forehead and two black eyes. I knew he was unscratched from the accident. Running from the scene in the dark he'd collided with a tree. Maybe that made up for his not getting that thrashing for smoking in the barn. I vowed that I would learn to drive. The car was totaled. It had no windshield and one door was gone but it was still running so I bought the wreckage back from the insurance company.

Behind our house was about a hundred acres still owned but not yet developed by Mr. Delafield. It was mostly woods but had horse trails, maybe old logging roads, some steep hills and some open spaces. I found it to be a wonderful place to drive like hell in the wrecked Hillman. Stonewalls were no obstacle; I'd move a rock or two or just drive over them. I roared around corners, broad sliding in any open spaces, spinning out, getting sideways and backwards, even tipping over from time to time. I'd just hop out, right the car and as soon as the gas refilled the carburetor go at it again. I spent the rest of the summer driving under almost rally conditions, always full speed and learned a lot about what to do and what not to do. No vehicle would stand up to that abuse without a lot of repair work; that summer I also learned a lot about fixing cars.

After a series of rollover experiments in Bill Mather's driveway the Hillman finally deteriorated beyond my abilities to keep it running. In the fall before returning to St Paul's, like my Dumpy had been, the Hillman was unceremoniously hauled off to the junkyard. I would soon be driving my father's 1941 black Ford convertible that had been promised for the next summer. Years later, during my time at Pitney Bowes and at Riverdale the small apartment over the garage became my home. It had a small kitchen. I made it seem larger by cutting a hole in the wall between the narrow kitchen area and the main room and adding a big slab of oak as a counter. There was a shower and a john next to the kitchen and the bedroom/living room was ample and had closets tucked in either end under the eves. Access was via an outside staircase.

A shop had been added across the whole back of the building. It had a flat roof, which soon became the floor for a second room upstairs with a big picture window facing south towards the woods. For a while a piano was there, and we used the room for making music, usually well into the night. The original windows at the end of the building were transformed, one into a narrow door to the new space and the other simply removed for light and access.

Early on friends nicknamed it the "Emporium", and there was lots of partying going on, always wall-to-wall kids. In 1964 word got out about my Cobra and the local hot-rodders appeared as if by magic. Weekends almost always saw a variety of visitors, some by day, some over night; always an interesting mix. We often gathered to watch the N.Y. Giants on TV. On the Sundays they played at home the New York TV stations were blocked but by getting up on the roof we could turn the antenna to pick up a snowy signal from New Haven. The weekend also spawned at least one beer run to The Vista Market on Rt. 136 just over the NY state line where the legal age was 18 not 21. We had a carefully crafted operation so as to avoid the Connecticut State cop who always parked just over his side of the line looking for kids like us. We went in two cars, parked and went in the store. One group would buy a case or two of sodas and soft drinks, get in their car and head home on the highway almost always getting pulled over. As soon as that went down and the cop was distracted, the group in the second car with the beer scooted directly across 137 to a maze of small roads, some not even paved, that eventually led back to the Emporium. It worked for years. If the Giants were losing at half time there usually was a pick up game in the field.

Word spread. I did have some smarts about diagnosing and fixing car problems. Old campers showed up from time-to-time and some runaways discovered it was a safe place to stay a night or two. Sometimes I'd come home from teaching at Riverdale to find some strange kid sleeping on my sofa. I'd talk to the kid, contact the parents and usually deliver the boy home the next day. Word got out. I could fix those problems, too.

Once a kid in his twenties who I'd known casually for a few years showed up in the middle of the night in a stolen U-Haul truck full of stolen TV sets. There was a thirteen-state-alarm out for him. We hid the truck behind the house. We talked 'til morning and I finally convinced him he had to give it up. I called my old friend Pete Lombardo, the cop who had rescued me from the river. He happened to be on duty and I explained the situation. Pete went home, changed into his civilian clothes and came to get the kid in his own car so as not to embarrass him with a cruiser. I drove the U-Haul to be impounded and Pete gave me a ride home. The kid did some time but this act of kindness and consideration from 'The Law' helped turn him around and he stayed

Cobra
mug
shots.

Griffith mug shots.

out of trouble.

I bought an old blue METRO Van, converted it into a camper and used it to lug kids and equipment up to Camp in the summer. Some of the letters had fallen off the front so it only said –T- O but I made a 'G' out of heavy aluminum foil to put in front. In those days, a 'G T O' was very cool. I put a wide white racing stripe up the middle but it was still only a METRO van and looked kind of like a blue skunk.

I've been fascinated with vehicles ever since hurtling down Cascade Hill in Dumpy, loaded with rocks for speed. The Green Bitch band station wagon ended up with all sorts of modifications including a huge V8 engine salvaged out of a wrecked state police car. For fun I bought an Alfa Romeo Sprint special and had a ball driving it as fast as I could. It had a tender transmission; too complicated for me and really expensive to repair. Mixed in there I built up two VW beetles with 356 Porsche Super 90 engines, one with complete Porsche running gear.

Thanksgiving break I took a group of campers to NYC for the auto show, saw a Shelby Cobra and fell in love. A brief talk with Jack Griffith and the deal was made. The Alfa was registered in my father's name. He was in Europe but had given me permission. His scrawl of a signature was easy to copy and soon I owned the first Cobra registered in New England. It was a high maintenance beast. 0 to 60 in 4.2 seconds, way too much fun but I needed something affordable and found a split window VW: 0-59 in a minute and 49 seconds. At one point the clutch linkage broke and I drove the Cobra from home to Jack Griffith's dealership in Syosset, Long Island, with no clutch; a trick I'd learned rescuing Meyerhoff school buses.

Jack was experimenting putting Cobra running gear in a much smaller TVR. I fell in love again. The soon to go into production 'Griffith' prototype was much faster than the Cobra and soon was mine; for a long time the fastest production car in the world. I still did most of my own maintenance.

The Emporium evolved. For several years the garage area was a Mecca for all sorts of budding hot-rodders, but eventually the space was converted into a downstairs living room and the shop and room with the big window were eventually torn down. The foundation and concrete floor of the shop became a fenced-in private sunning terrace. A two-car carport was added, and then, a year or two later one port became the new kitchen and an inside stair was installed.

As word got around about my crazy cars, I was asked to be Adult

Advisor to a hot rod club called "The Road Gents". We had a small garage next to the firehouse in New Canaan, rent donated by the Town, and I was on hand to help the kids work on various cars. Aside from trying to keep the kids safe on the streets the club had another mission. Anytime a club member came across a motorist in distress they volunteered to help. Sometimes they could fix the problem or go for help and often just gave the people a lift home. They didn't ask for money but simply handed them a club card. Again word got out and some donations came in. A new firehouse was built and we lost our space but while it lasted we had fun at the drag races, legally.

8

Setting the Stage
(1950–present)

*Playing jazz is the most fun you can have
with your clothes on.*
—Herb Pomeroy

Back at Salisbury in the fall, the general picture faded with grades in the basement right from the start. I was moved from the dorm to a guest room at the headmaster's house, I suppose to give me fewer distractions but I continued to accomplish nothing academically. (Sound familiar?)

Hop Rudd tried to get me interested in sports. I had athletic potential but zero desire. My potential had been evaluated during the first interview at SPS, but I didn't realize it until it was evaluated later at Salisbury. In each school there was someone at the interview who represented the athletic department. I remember being grabbed and squeezed by various football and soccer coaches at SPS and didn't understand the significance. At Salisbury, a coach, not Hop Rudd, grabbed me by the shoulders and shook them, nodding approvingly, and then reached around and took a handful of my left cheek, squeezed quite hard and grinning said to the admissions director, "This kid's linebacker material". I was a 'thing' with a firm muscular ass, useful for knocking people down.

I was dismal in athletics; hated Hockey, hated Soccer, really hated Football; Baseball was the worst. I was pretty strong and well built for my age. I didn't have to worry about being bullied, but if forced to participate in a sport I shied away from any contact and was a klutz. I rarely worked up a sweat. I was in no way a jock. I felt very strange just wearing one, clutching my front and exposing my behind. I was moderately endowed, but for the first time I started being self-conscious in the group showers after practices because I was sure the others were staring at me to discover why I was such a wimp. I just didn't like getting hit or hitting people. Even then I was afraid of getting a fat lip or hurting my hands, and I just hated sports. I don't remember if I made it through to the spring vacation, but at some point, well before the end of the year, my parents were asked that I be "withdrawn"; again the kinder, gentler, way of saying, "kicked out".

My parents were in Wiesbaden, Germany, for an extended business visit, actually staying at a resort hotel in Schlengenbad, an easy commute to the office for Pops. As my departure from Salisbury became imminent a few cables were exchanged with my parents, and I made arrangements to fly and meet them in Wiesbaden. This must have been the first week of June 1955. I turned eighteen on the ninth of June, got my international license and a new Lambretta motor scooter in Wiesbaden that day. Old friend Ken Smith joined my parents on long over-due vacation at the Schloss Siegartstein, a small castle just outside Salzburg, Austria, It was a long drive; we were in no hurry and took several days. I followed on my scooter, behind my parents driving the company-owned Opel. Often, if the scenery was particularly interesting, mother would ride with me on the scooter allowing a slower and better look. We all stayed at the Schloss, owned and operated as a guesthouse by the Palfe family. I made friends with the kids in the family and soon I was giving their friends in the neighborhood almost daily rides on the scooter. I also made my first serious attempt to learn to read music at the Mozarteum in Salzburg, but from day one to the next I couldn't remember anything I had learned... zero progress. I gave it up after only a few weeks. Meanwhile, my parents and Ken had returned to Wiesbaden, and I was supposed to visit old family friends in Arnhem, Holland.

I headed west at a roaring top speed of 80km. I had memorized the street name and number of the friends, the Van Bootselaars, and practiced my limited Dutch all the way. After a long, long ride I arrived in Arnhem and spotted a large, very Dutch-looking policeman directing traffic from a little pedestal in the center of a 'rondo'. I approached him and asked in my carefully rehearsed Dutch for directions. He smiled and answered in perfect English. So much for trying to learn languages.

After, I revisited the Van Zuylen's at Duinrel where I had spent that glorious summer when I was 13. Eventually I took the channel boat to England and found my way to 20 Carlisle Square, Ken Smith's flat in London.

I lived with Ken in his rented flat and played in a Dixieland band once a week at a small club down King's Road. I was not supposed to be earning any money but this was kept quiet and the income was very helpful. Ken helped me enroll in a music reading class at the London Conservatory in attempt #2 to learn to read music. Again I got nowhere with the reading music project and gave it up after only a few weeks.

I had considerable free time and did a lot of exploring on my own, buzzing around London on my scooter. I'm not sure of the details of how Claire Massy came to be in Vinalhaven to help with the house and tutor me in French. I'm also not sure why I needed tutoring in French. But she had moved to England and married a man who owned a castle that had been in his family since forever and I decided to find her. I've now forgotten his name and the name of the castle or town and just think it was south of London and not too long a scoot.

The castle was impressive. A long driveway lined with trees opened out to a circle paved with cobblestones. Wide stairs went up to large oak doors and the entrance of the castle, all stone with leaded windows. It wasn't fortified or old enough to have a moat but obviously had been around a while and made pretty luxurious quarters. Downstairs there was the kitchen, dining room, a formal parlor and several sitting rooms, one of them a man-cave-office with a fireplace, massive leather chairs and walls lined with old leather-bound books. A large central staircase lead up to four or five bedrooms including mine, which was on one end of the wide hallway. The hallway had a polished wood floor and a blood-red carpet running its length. There were several complete suits of armor. It was dark and windowless. Even in the daytime it felt a bit spooky. The only plumbing on that floor was about three quarters of the way down the hall from my room, just past the top of the stairs.

Over dinner Claire and her husband filled me in on the history of the castle and told me that some ancestor had been axed for some misdeed and that for years his head had been stored in a crypt in the cellar. After a lot of talk and some probably fancy brandy I headed for bed.

Like most of the castle my bedroom had finely detailed leaded glass windows, which overlooked a substantial lawn studded with apple trees. I hopped into the huge four-poster bed, lots of big pillows and fluffy quilt, and slept.

Nature called. The moonlight was flooding in though the windows and I could see the tops of the trees moving with the wind. The scene was a perfect set up of the scary story Mother used to read called *Moonlight Sonata*. In the story an old woman seemed to be doing needlepoint in the moonlight but was actually one by one, plucking grey hairs from the head of the man she had killed! I remembered the story in detail.

Sleeping as I always did without clothes I felt no need to put anything on for the trek to the bathroom, but as soon as I stepped out in the hall I felt spooked. I tried not to look at the empty armor of soldiers past and kept moving deliberately toward the bathroom. As I passed one imposing door with soldiers on either side the hall suddenly got much colder, sending chills through me—really a jolt. I dashed to the bathroom, fortunately found the light. After doing what I came to do I contemplated my return and eventually literally streaked back to my warm bed. Claire, over breakfast, told me that what I had experienced was quite normal. The head was still looking for the rest of him.

During the week, Ken and I would often take day trips out of London on the scooter; a funny sight because he was quite large and the scooter quite small. The two of us probably outweighed the Lambretta. He would direct me to amazing little pubs in tiny villages along roads not much wider than the scooter. He knew every turn in the road, amazing for someone who didn't drive. More amazing was that he seemed to know every barkeep in every pub.

Ken was very modest about his accomplishments and never really talked about himself at all. My father once told me of going with Ken to play golf at an exclusive London club. We knew Ken played golf; my father didn't play at all but went along to keep Ken company. Dad was impressed because the ball seemed to go in the right place but really didn't follow the game. After watching Ken play a round of eighteen holes Pops went into the clubhouse for a drink while Ken changed. Along the wall was plaque after plaque, year after year, "Kenneth Leslie Smith, Club Champion", literally dozens of them. Ken was also an authority on many levels of spiritualism, faith healing, clairvoyance, etc. He learned Italian at a very late age in order to translate an Italian doctor's writing, which he found interesting. I was interested but didn't know much about it. However there was one event, which stands out and still baffles me.

One afternoon we hopped on the scooter and drove to the other side of town. We had been invited to tea with a woman who Ken told me was clairvoyant. She was quite elderly and beautifully dressed with perfect white hair and wore a striking emerald brooch.

Her flat was full of old, and I'm sure valuable, furniture, just what I'd expect in the home of someone as really elegant as she was. Tea was, well, tea. There was small talk and some pleasantries exchanged, weather discussed, various 'goodies' passed around, and Ken related some of our scooter adventures in the country, all very polite and rather formal. As we were leaving the lady told me that I had a pinched nerve in my neck, third vertebrae, that was why I was feeling tired all the time and I should see a chiropractor right away. I was somewhat stunned because except for shaking her hand we had never been closer than across the room, several feet away. I'd never mentioned being tired or anything else. Ken made an appointment with a chiropractic friend, and after one visit I felt better almost immediately.

I was living with Ken in London. This was long before e-mail, and even airmail from the States took a week to ten days. About two weeks later Ken and I went to tea again, pretty much a repeat of the first visit except upon arriving the first thing she said was, "I'm so glad to see you're feeling better". Then as we were leaving she said very casually, "I had a lovely visit with your mother last fortnight". I tried to take it in but really didn't get it. My mother was in Stamford, Connecticut. When we got back to the flat there was a letter from home postmarked about ten days earlier. In the letter my mother filled me in on all the news and towards the end of the letter she wrote that she had woken up in the middle of the night to find an elegantly dressed, elderly lady sitting in the rocker in the bedroom and went on to describe the lady in detail right down to the emerald brooch.

I stayed on with Ken and finally, uncertain about possibly imminent looming induction in the Army, headed for home. My father had given me a letter of credit I could use to buy my ticket. I packed up my belongings and 'scootered' to the coast, took the Dover-Calais boat and drove to Amsterdam over a lot of cobblestones to catch my boat home only to find that the port of departure had been changed; it was leaving in thirty-six hours from Le Havre. Now really in a hurry, I really bounced over the cobblestones. To sustain myself I bought a big bag of cherries because I could eat them on the fly. To stay awake I learned how to tie the stems in a knot in my mouth with my tongue. With very little time to spare I got myself and the scooter safely loaded on board.

The scooter came home with me and was, for a while, my only transportation. I looked for work and quite soon found a job with Pitney Bowes in the Service Annex. It started well and got more interesting. At first I learned how to recondition their TIC machines that printed consecutive numbers on tickets for theaters. (This was long before computers would do it.)

The machines came in pretty ratty-looking, and we'd disassemble them and install new bearings, any worn and all rubber parts were replaced, the covers repainted and they were shipped back to the customer, looking and operating like new. This was interesting to a point, and I was able to stick at it. I got along well with my co-workers and started getting a few weekend gigs with the Yale band.

After about six months at Pitney Bowes I was told it was my time to report for my six months' active duty with the Army. Pitney Bowes guaranteed my job when I got back, so Feb 4, 1956 I boarded a train in Stamford bound for Ft. Knox, Kentucky.

9

A Piece of Meat
(1957–1959... 180 days)

A verbal contract is worth the paper it's written on.
—Francis Ross

At eighteen I had been given a choice (the only one ever in the Army) to be drafted for two years and be sent, with no say-so from me, God knows where; or I could enlist in a special highly recommended six-month program. "Normal basic and secondary school and a commitment to a reserve unit for weekly meetings and a two week summer camp. 180 days of active duty." I was just starting to get some playing gigs in New York and really didn't want to be away for two years. I opted for the shorter active duty time.

From day one I hated the Army. All personality, individuality, was literally stripped away, starting with the first haircut and going downhill from there. I remember standing in a long row with 30 other guys, naked, with our underwear in our hands. We were all told to bend over and spread our cheeks. I watched down the line as one by one a nearly shaved head would rise up showing part of a face and then would suddenly jerk up higher with an accompanying grunt. Without knowing what to expect I watched the chain of reaction. My immediate neighbor flinched and then his head jerked up and he let out a loud groan followed by a hissing intake of breath; now my turn.

I flinched as a glob of Vaseline was applied to the spot with a tongue depressor and sucked in air with a hiss as a finger in a rubber glove was forced in and roughly probed around. There was no warning and no time to relax. It hurt a lot. We had to maintain this spread and exposed position as various doctors walked behind us and inspected us until the last guy in the line was done. Then we were marched, still clutching our skivvies, to another room where simultaneously one needle was jabbed in our arm and another in our butt. We were standing, muscles tensed, and the shot in the butt really hurt. We were then told to put on our skivvies (Army issue boxers, 'swing easies'), which felt really nasty since we were still all greasy from the Vaseline.

Basic was not as harsh as I expected, but I resented being yelled at and objected to the overall stupidity of the people in charge. The recruits were all about my age, but some 'turkey' also about our age, because he been a sergeant in his reserve unit at home, was given almost total power over the rest of us 24/7. He paraded us around doing stupid marching drills and made me, at least, feel like a total fool. Lots of push-ups and P.E. The guy was really a jerk. Harsh? Nah, not really, more like advanced boy scouts but definitely stupid. I got pretty good with the M-1 rifle and even earned a few little marksmanship doodles to hang on my uniform. But every time, after a day on the firing range, I would be totally deaf for about 24 hours. I could hear whispers but nothing else and had a hell of a time doing our daily company drills. I absolutely couldn't hear "company halt!" or anything else. (Firing the M-1 without ear protection did permanent damage to my hearing. I've lost the whole top octave of the piano, can hear the percussive sound but not the pitch, and I have a constant ringing in my ears. Thanks, Uncle Sam.)

We learned some rudimentary hand-to-hand combat stuff which was kind of fun, but I really didn't like boxing. One day out in the field the group stood around in a big circle, and we were paired off more or less by weight. Gloves put on, we were forced to fight each other. I really didn't want to do it and didn't attempt to hit my opponent, just kept my gloves up and protected myself. I thought this was okay, and we'd get by if we just jostled each other and not really hit each other. My adversary had different ideas and seemed hell-bent to hurt me. I was upset by his savagery but refused to hit him back and was able to hold him off for the first round, nothing really hurt but my pride. After a short break we were instructed to go at it again. Apparently this spectacle would continue indefinitely. The two of us would have to stay in the ring until someone got knocked down. I guess I let my guard down. In an instant he had landed a really painful hit to my nose, which really hurt me for the first time. I stood still, bleeding from my nose with my hands by my sides. Then from somewhere behind me, I think, propelled by my rage, my right hand came up and out and caught him square on the jaw. He crumpled to the ground and flopped like a fish. The sergeant threw some water on him to wake him up; the recruits cheered, but I was horrified by what I had done. Back at the barracks I was treated with considerably more respect. Even though my victim seemed okay with it all I felt I had lost control and couldn't justify what I had done.

The total lack of privacy was a bit difficult, but I had no problems with crowded group showers and was unfazed when, on the way back from a long march with full field gear, the whole company stopped at a stream for a nude swim. I soon realized I was not supposed to be anything except a 'thing' that did what it was told. I was not supposed to think. I belonged to the Army. They could inspect me, force needles or fingers into me, anywhere, anytime. I was more valuable than a Jeep, but for a tank I was expendable.

What finally did it for me, as far as my seeking a career in the military was concerned, was the Carbine Range. The carbine automatic rifle fires something ridiculous like 750 rounds a minute. We were introduced to the weapon somewhere out in the field and then, after the usual terrible field lunch, were marched several miles to a special range. It was set up to look like a European village; the 'course' was a street with mock houses on either side. We were supposed to walk up the street with our carbine cocked on our hip. Then from a window, a target, a big white circle with a white 'X' would appear for only a second or two, the object being to see how many rounds we could get in the target before it disappeared. This was kind of fun and I blasted away filling my targets. Then, about two-thirds of the way up the street, a very realistic dummy with a small target on its chest popped out of a doorway. My reaction was to empty my clip into the side of the house and violently loose my lunch. Suddenly it dawned on me: they really were training me to become some sort of machine that without thought or conscience would kill any person who got in my way. From that moment on I did everything I could, short of breaking the law, to get out of the Army. I froze in Fort Knox during basic and sweltered at Fort Sill during my secondary school. The only time it got below 100 degrees in the barracks was during a tornado alert, and we were evacuated and made to stand outside in the sun in our dress khakis. In keeping with my plot to get out ASAP, I volunteered for radio repair school, knowing there were no radios in my artillery reserve unit. The nearest unit that needed my particular radio technician M.O.S. was in New Haven and would be ruled out as being too far away; I had done my homework!

Somehow I managed not to get court-martialed for almost flunking Radio Tech School. It was really difficult for me, lots of memorizing ohms and resistance and the difference between voltage and amperage, RF vs. normal electric current, etc. Some of the guys wired a plastic fly to the RF output of a field radio and put it in a urinal. Some poor bastard would come along and, obviously seeing the fly would pee on it only to get short-circuited with 12,000 volts of RF current through his pecker. (They practically flew backwards across the room.) Everybody delighted in hot-wiring something on a neighbor's workstation, sitting back and watching the fun. I also took a civilian TV repair class that was interesting and got me off the base, but I didn't learn much. I got some extra-duty pay riding 'shotgun' with the MPs. We'd ride around Lawton in a Jeep and help break up bar fights or pick up stragglers and give them a ride home. I got to know most of the MPs.

I was also the proud owner of a 1936 Plymouth sedan. It was registered but pretty much a wreck, and I kept it at the base garage. The troops could work on their cars there and get expert help from some motor pool mechanics. Even when I started racing the car at the local dirt track they helped me keep the car going. There were strict standards about personal vehicles allowed on base, but my MP friends let me slip through the gate regardless of what pieces might be dangling off my car. The rear seats were replaced by an old mattress in case I couldn't make it home.

One night after a fun night of these grown-up bumper cars I came back to base as usual, barely slowing down at the gate. There was a new lieutenant on duty who wasn't pleased that I hadn't slowed down and that both of my headlights were missing as was most of my windshield. Almost safe at the garage he caught up with me. I got an "Article 15", "Restriction to company quarters," for two weeks. I couldn't even go to the garage to work on the car, had to stay put. By the following Saturday I had reached an "I don't give a fuck" attitude, got the car and went to the races. I had a great night and, for the first time ever, won a 3rd place in one of the early races. The other two place winners and I all posed for the cameras. The tiny photo in the base paper Sunday unfortunately was spotted by the CO and by lunch time I had gotten another two weeks' restriction to quarters, lost my recently acquired PFC stripe and slight pay raise that went with it: back to a lowly Private

A Piece of Meat

E2, my rank 'til I was discharged.

I returned home from Ft. Sill, Oklahoma in my old Plymouth sedan August 7th, 1957. It was still pockmarked and dented from the weekly stock car races. I knew Carl Terrwilliger because he was alphabetically one ahead of me in line. He lived in New Jersey and made the trip home with me. Soon after leaving the base he got really sick. As we drove through the outskirts of Oklahoma City we saw a house with a sign that said "Doctor So-So" and a pointing finger pointing to his "Office". We stopped and knocked on the door. The doctor, at first reluctant to treat Carl, gave him a massive shot in the butt and suggested we really should go back to Fort Sill and get medical attention at the base. "No way," we both agreed, never going back there! Carl laid low in the back of the car. The seats were gone but the mattress was still there and he managed to sleep as I drove all the way. After dropping him off in New Jersey I drove the rest of the way home, total elapsed time non-stop from Fort Sill to Stamford, Connecticut: 56 hours! I still had to go to weekly reserve meetings in Stamford and a two-week summer 'camp' at Camp Drum in Waterville, N.Y.

At my reserve unit I did everything I could to be a pain in the ass. I'd show up five minutes late. "Just back from New York, the traffic was terrible," I'd tell them. I'd show up in my fatigues the night I was supposed to be in dress uniform, or visa versa; or I'd be missing one button or my belt buckle would be tarnished, shoes unpolished; nothing serious but just enough to be constantly getting written up with minor gigs (not the musical kind) and therefore on the top of the list to be transferred to 'control group' meaning pretty much getting out. The brass really wanted to get rid of me; that was my plan!

At Camp Drum during summer camp I volunteered to stay at the barracks and take care of the three coal-fired hot water furnaces. Volunteering for that sounded crazy, but I was already unpopular with the brass; they were delighted to stick me with this unpleasant chore. Mopping the barracks, peeling potatoes, K.P. and general latrine duty was carried out by other grunts as punishment for various screw-ups. My job was great. I didn't have to hike miles out to the field every day carrying a heavy pack, hear artillery shells zoom over my head and eat a lousy field kitchen lunch. I didn't have to get up at 5:30 a.m. and march around the parade ground doing stupid drills in formation. I didn't have to sit through hideously boring training movies or listen to endless recitations of various field manuals by instructors who had trouble reading. I'd sleep late in the morning. About noon I'd go downtown and get a good lunch. At 4:00 I'd be back and stoke the furnaces. It took about forty-five minutes' work to ensure lots of hot water for the 'grunts' when they hiked in from the field. About 7:00 I'd head back to town with clarinet in hand. I'd found a nice place to play with some pretty good musicians. I'd have dinner and play 'till closing time. Then back to the base about 4:00 a.m., stoke the furnaces and hit the sack. I even finagled a staff room, so the noisy, early-rising, showering, grumbling 'grunts' didn't disturb my routine. After two summers of tending the boilers and about a year of weekly meetings the brass was only too happy to send me to 'control group'. I was out. I got my discharge acknowledging my 180 days of active duty and honorable service to my country. Years later I would find out that to qualify for any V.A benefits like a low interest loan I needed 181 days of active duty.

10

Making Music
(1950–present)

Within a few weeks of returning from active duty in Oklahoma I went back to work at Pitney Bowes, and as soon as school started in September the gigs with the Yale band picked up. Everything was going well at Pitney Bowes. I traded in what was left of the Plymouth and with my first, second, third and fourth paychecks put a down payment on a 1954 Ford station wagon.

After high school Pete Wells had gone to Yale and gave my name to Mike Mallory (of battery fame) and Pete Elebash, co-leaders of The Yale Bull-Pups. Soon I got a call. Their regular clarinet player couldn't make a gig, they asked me to fill in, and I got the gig permanently! I was never sure if it was because of my clarinet playing or my reliable station wagon. Soon I was making as much money with the band as I was at Pitney Bowes.

My recently purchased three-year-old Ford station wagon had a V8, standard 'three-on-the-tree' transmission with overdrive: the perfect band vehicle. It was a dark metallic green and had the real wood strips along the sides and back. It was in pretty good shape, and I started learning how to keep it going, doing all the mechanical work myself. At one point, however, the real wood did what real wood does and started to rot and flake away. I decided the only thing to do was to remove all the wood. When the wood came off I was left with 56-nickel size holes that had to be plugged, sanded, primed; then I had to get the whole car ready to paint. I was working at Pitney Bowes all week; commuted on the scooter when I could but still needed the car for band duty every weekend; this would be a long process. The first trip out with the band, with some but not all of the holes plugged, I discovered that at about 60 miles an hour the car started letting an unholy whistling, no, more like a howling, wailing noise. It was really loud. On the Merritt Parkway people ahead of us were pulling over to let us pass.

After many thousands of hard miles the original engine was burning lots of oil, making ominous amounts of black smoke and eventually gave up. At Sears I bought a 'short block' and in a few evenings during the week switched engines and was up and running by the weekend for the trip to Florida. Not too far along the trip, south of Washington D.C., one of the pistons developed a hole. It would run okay on 7 cylinders, but every so often the right fuel mixture would leak into the crankcase and cause it to fire. We were spewing out clouds of oil and smoke. The explosions destroyed both valve cover gaskets and sent the dipstick and oil filler cap into orbit. Our bass player, Joe del Princepe was following us. He wouldn't go ahead and insisted on following close behind because he was paranoid about getting lost. His quite pretty, pristine Mercury was coated with oil. There was nothing I could do. We had to go on because we had confirmed gigs in Florida. Like Sherman scorching the countryside we forged ahead. In Miami Sears honored the warrantee and replaced the piston, but the engine never lived up to my expectations; just too small for the job of lugging six guys with instruments countless miles at above average speeds.

Back home after Florida through some hot rod friends I found a huge Ford V8 engine out of a wrecked state police car in a junkyard in New Haven. My friends told me it would fit. I borrowed a bay at a gas station and in two days had made the swap. Now, with well over 300hp, the car was formidable; blew the doors off almost anything on the road. Body work finally completed I had repainted it a strange sort of soft pea-green color made up of a mixture of leftovers, canceled orders of green paint from the paint store, certainly one of a kind. It looked stock but didn't sound quite right for stock. We nicknamed it "The Green Bitch".

My job had evolved into customizing the Tickometers to print on all sorts of weird things like plastic bags; items they were not designed to handle. There was lots of designing, improvising and testing, pretty good fun. I remember one trial run. The machine completely shredded about two hundred plastic bags of panty hose into confetti and sent it flying all over the shop before we could shut it down. Everybody was in hysterics.

Frank Liberty, the Vice President in charge of Personnel, made it a policy to invite every new employee to lunch with him in the executive dining room. Around Thanksgiving time it was my turn, and we had a nice talk, mostly my answering his questions. Over dessert he told me either I could quit my job and go back to school or he would fire me. I was surprised because I felt at last I was really able to contribute, be of value to the company, and I enjoyed my job. Frank Liberty cared more about me and my future than he did about gaining an employee for Pitney Bowes. I owe him a lot; it changed a lot for me. Faced with this I left Pitney Bowes, found a tutoring school in Somers, New York, and started full time the first of December cramming one and a half years of high school credits into six months. One-on-one with a tutor I'd study one subject. As soon as I could squeak a 60% on the New York State Regents Exam on that subject I'd move onto the next one. I was still playing a lot with the Yale band.

The Yale band continued all winter with wild and woolly weekend jaunts all over New England, mostly college gigs. After its final engine transplant, beefed-up suspension and snow tires all around, the Green Bitch performed flawlessly, loaded to overflowing, high speeds, rough roads, and overnighters through blizzards; no problems. There are many stories but one stands out.

We played a Friday night gig at Colby College in Maine. As we got there it started to snow and was coming down pretty fast when we were through. We had motel rooms nearby but had to be at Rensselaer Polytechnic Institute in Troy, N.Y. Saturday. We canceled the rooms and headed out. This was before the Maine Turnpike, I-95, or the Mass Pike; back roads were the only roads. It was still snowing and dark when we arrived in Troy; visibility almost zero. Coming down the main street at an intersection was a cop car and we asked directions to the fraternity we were headed for. "Second left," he said, "About half a mile; you'll see a bright light." We turned at the second left and the road seemed rough even for the G.B. but in the distance was a light. Very soon the light seemed to be getting larger, fast, and instinctively I turned sharp left sliding down a bank and landing on a parallel road. At the top of the bank the light went rumbling by, attached to the first of three N. Y. Central locomotives pulling a long freight train. We got to the gig on time.

I don't remember anything I studied and only remember my math teacher, Mr. Appelhagen. I passed Algebra II in spite of him because he spent most of the time telling me wonderful stories. He had been in the German Army in WWII and captured by the Russians. Even though he was a college level mathematics professor they put him to work as a waiter at an officers club. He told me that one night while serving dinner, he had placed a platter with eight pieces of Wiener schnitzel on the table. There were seven officers who each took a piece. Suddenly the lights went off. There was a scuffling sound and then a loud scream. When the lights came back on the commandant's hand was on the remaining schnitzel and there were four or five forks sticking out of it!

I finished school on my twenty-first birthday in June. Fred Fischer came to play at my graduation. There would be a busy summer with the Newport Jazz Festival and Army Reserve summer camp plus the first summer of Camp on Hurricane Island. Eli's Chosen Six, our rival band, asked me to spend a week at the Newport Jazz Festival. George Avakian and Bert Stern were filming what would be an award-winning documentary, *Jazz On a Summer's Day*. We were supposed to provide some comic relief and were filmed riding around in an old car. (In the opening segment check out the kid with the clarinet wearing a straw hat.) Originally they had planned to use recorded music for these segments but thanks to my association with Benny Goodman they recorded us, and we're on the sound track. The festival flew by.

One day we were asked to accompany S. I. Hayakawa during his lecture on the "Semantics of the Blues". Apparently there were some problems with the music union and we got the gig since we were just a college band and not union. It was pretty intimidating because the gallery included practically every jazz icon I'd ever heard of. Jimmy Rushing, the famous "Mr. Five-by-Five" (big hit tune with the Andrews Sisters) was featured with us, and taught us "A Fine Romance" on the spot, live, in front of that audience!

I had never heard anyone sing so far behind the beat and swing so hard. Backstage some of the other musicians were kidding him about his size; he was huge. Someone asked him, "Jimmy, when was the last time you saw your pecker?" Without dropping a beat he answered, "I have a picture of it in my wallet".

I had to leave the festival a day early. I was supposed to go to Camp Drum for the two weeks' summer camp, and the Army refused to let me stay even an extra day. I offered to drive up to Camp Drum myself and be there in time Monday morning, but they insisted I had to be on the bus in Stamford at 4:00 a.m. Sunday morning. We'd had very little sleep and I was exhausted but made the trek home safely thanks to Benny's daughter, Rachel. As I remember she dropped me off at the bus. At least I could sleep the ten hours it took to get to Camp Drum. Later that summer I took the first group of Boy Scout dropouts to Maine for what would be the start of the Island Camp. In the fall I would also meet Buddy Tate. I honestly believe had it not been for my friendship with Buddy Tate, his support and mentoring, that I probably would never have gotten beyond being a weekend Dixieland player.

Some time in fall after Newport I ventured into New York and went to the Metropole. Long before it became a strip club it offered an ever-changing lineup of some of the best straight ahead jazz players in town including people like Lionel Hampton, Dizzy, Virgil Jones, Roland Hanna, and Pepper Adams to name just a few.

I went that night to hear and hopefully sit in with Sol Yaged. I'd heard he sounded very much like Benny Goodman and I was intrigued. During a break I introduced myself even telling him that I knew Benny and was there at his suggestion. Sol wasted no time to brush me off.

As I remember, it was a few months later that Benny asked me to bring Rachel in from Connecticut to go to a concert in the city. After the concert Rachel, Benny, Duke Ellington and I had dinner and then went to the Metropole. Sol practically fell to his knees and almost begged me to play; I politely refused.

I also remember going to the Metropole to hear Coleman Hawkins; I don't remember who else was in the band.

Metropole was long and narrow. The bandstand was a small platform behind the bar that made it necessary for all the musicians to line up in a straight line. There were mirrors along the entire opposite wall providing the only way the musicians could see each other.

Single file the band assembled and started in with one of Hawkins' wonderful 'heads'. Right then, a totally gorgeous young woman stepped up to the bar directly in front of Hawkins. He looked at her and soon there was a noticeable bulge. The other players of course also saw it in the mirror and were cracking up. Hawkins closed his eyes and played about a 15 min. solo of sheer brilliance and then, after just that one tune, sidestepped off the bandstand and disappeared into the back room with the lovely lady.

Coleman Hawkins was definitely in his prime that day.

In 1956–57 my status with the Yale band as a ringer was secure. We were pretty busy doing a lot of traveling, mostly weekends to colleges all over northern New England. Spring break we made the oil-soaked trek to Florida and had a rather strange gig at a small club called the

Stut & Tut. The audiences were small but appreciative and the music went well. Slightly distracting was a very large fish tank in the center of the floor. Swimming around inside all night was a quite attractive young lady adorned with nothing except a clear plastic breathing tube. Periodically she would press her more fleshy parts up against the glass. We tried to get used to it. Across the street at a much larger club Kai Winding was playing with his famous Septet, four trombones and a rhythm section. Wayne Andre, Dick Lieb and Carl Fontana were the other horn players, and I met Mainer Roy Frazee who was playing piano. I don't remember the bass player and drummer, Tom Montgomery and Kenny O'Brian, but do remember we were invited to sit in with the Septet playing until closing one Saturday night. We were all somewhat 'impaired' and decided to stay put and sleep in the car outside the club. Bright and early, certainly before 8:00 a.m., Carl Fontana appeared with a pitcher of warm beer and started shaking the car to wake us up. He had scheduled a softball game with the local coast guard reserve unit for 9:00 a.m. Sunday morning. Our team was made up of the surviving band members and bartenders from the two clubs.

Blinded by the dawn's early light we struggled to see the ball (and the game). Carl, our pitcher/manager/coach and beverage comptroller kept things moving. Every so often, not necessarily after a stunning defensive play, he would call those of us who could walk to assemble at the pitcher's mound where he encouraged us by pulling out a substantial flask and passing it around. I don't know if there was a score. Two weeks gave us a lot of sun and limited sleep.

Our last Friday we had booked a double header in Miami, and I had spent the day under my station wagon replacing a cracked front A-frame. The first gig was from 8:00–12:00 p.m., the second, 1:00–4:00 a.m. We packed up, drove furiously and just made it on time for a 9:00–1:00 p.m. gig in Atlanta. The Yale contingent had to be back for classes Monday morning, so we left immediately after the gig and drove straight through. Even though I was thoroughly exhausted, after dropping off the Yalies I drove back home, showered and continued on to my school. I was still trying to finish a year and a half of high school at that very expensive tutoring school. I felt lousy all day and felt really lousy when I got home. About 6:00 or so I contacted our family doctor who happened to be doing his rounds at the Stamford Hospital. In less than an hour I was poked, probed and prepped and my appendix was coming out; close call. In those days this meant a week in the hospital, but I had things to do. We had a big concert in New Haven that Friday night and were booked to appear on Sam Levinson's TV show *Two For The Money* in New York, Saturday. I wasn't going to miss any of that. As the guys waited below with clothes from home I painfully came down the fire escape with my ass hanging out of one of those flimsy hospital johnnies. I was full of stitches and didn't play many high notes. I snuck back in Sunday afternoon, stitches came out Monday morning, and I rode my Lambretta scooter to my tutoring school in the afternoon. I wasn't supposed to drive anything for a month.

Gigs with the band continued. We played almost every weekend, mostly at colleges throughout New England and New York; lots of traveling, lots of adventures.

Summer of 1958 and the Yale Bull Pups are now run by the only Yalie left, Chuck Folds. He took the Pups to Europe for a tour. Steve Swallow on bass; drummer, Charlie Kiel; and trumpet player, Pat Williams made us a quintet.

We got free passage by providing music on the *Grote Beer*, a Holland-America student ship. The ship had been converted to a troop ship during WWll and was left that way so students with shallow pockets could sleep in canvas bunks stacked three layers high—but travel cheap.

We played every afternoon and evening in the lounge and I remember the feeling that our music was directly responsible for the forward movement of the ship. The fourteen days seemed shorter due partially to unlimited supplies of Heinekens for five cents a bottle.

We arrived in Rotterdam and the band cooled their heels for a few days while I went by train to Paris to pick up a car. I'd never been on a train like that before. It ran smooth as silk, very fast and exactly on time. The plan: My father had planned to buy a new Peugeot Combi for the Dorr Company and made arrangements for me to pick it up early so we could use it that summer for our tour.

I arrived in Paris before the Peugeot agency had finished getting the car ready and things started to get rough. I got a serious bout of the runs and the facilities at the agency were nasty. One of those bathroom fixtures that serve all... footrests, drop trow, back in and do your best; pants around your ankles, grasping handles with both hands to keep from falling in—now what? I stayed there 'til closing. The car would be ready by noon the next day and I found a cheap hotel near the agency and eventually felt better. After long drawn out paperwork was completed I was all licensed and insured and headed out fast to join up with the band in Holland.

The car was smooth and great fun to drive. The roads were mostly in remarkably good shape and I could go quite fast except for the many small towns where I had to really slow down; narrow, narrow streets with houses pressed right up to the road; practically no sidewalks. About an hour out of Paris going slowly through such a town I heard something but never saw the chicken that popped out of a doorway and under my right rear wheel. I stopped and looked back as a small boy popped out of the same doorway, grabbed the totally limp chicken and took it inside. Then a large man appeared. With sign language only I was made to understand I was to get out of the car and follow him into the house. I thought, "This is it. Young American kid driving a fancy brand new Peugeot running over the man's chicken....?"

On the other side of the door everything opened up into a large court yard with neatly trimmed grass, espaliered apple trees and a cozy house with bright white curtains, window boxes of flowers, a well maintained barn, a few sheep and some of the victims relatives casually pecking at things in the grass, picture book stuff.

I was prompted to sit down at a table with a bright-checkered tablecloth; some other probably family members assembled and the grilling began. One of the girls spoke some English and combined with signs and gestures I managed to explain my story starting out with how sorry I was. No one seemed very angry. Soon some wine in a carafe came out, then some fresh bread; more talking, signing, explaining, more wine, more bread, some cheese and pate and after quite a while plates with vegetables and then, the chicken!

I eventually found out that the small boy had been chasing the chicken so as to have it for dinner. The door to the street was ajar and I had saved them the bother of killing it themselves. I played my clarinet for them and they sent me off with a basket of garden fresh vegetables, some cheese, and a bottle of home-made wine.

That summer tour is another story. We played in several private homes and spent two weeks in a club in Frankfort. We had jam sessions with students in Heidelberg and went to one of the outlawed fencing matches, workshops with students in Mainz, and visited family friends of mine in Holland.

We were in Paris for two weeks at The Blue Note opposite Chet Baker. We stayed at the private home of organist Pierre Cochereau and were invited to the organ loft at Notre Dame on Ascension Day. Pierre had the largest privately owned organ in Europe at his home; it took up the whole center of the house, three stories high.

Ghana-um-Bow had a stone drum with a fish-skin head and sat in with bands all over Paris. Inside the drum he also had small bags of super weed from Nigeria that he sold for very little. We knew we weren't going to risk bringing it home and certainly didn't want to throw it overboard—only one thing to do!

The ship was very slow and as we landed in Hoboken it seemed to reach its peak speed and took out a substantial chunk of the pier we were landing at.

I managed to smuggle some seeds that started a lovely garden at Woodbine Road. Busy summer, happy days!

The same weekend the Yale band appeared on "Two for the Money," we got a chance to play at Eddie Condon's in NYC. Eddy Condon said we were by far the best college-level band he had ever heard and for the first time, I heard live—Wild Bill Davidson. I had heard him before on the classic Condon recording, *Jam Session Coast to Coast*, which first gave us the idea of adding extra guest players to our band.

Through an agency in New York we contacted some players from the City who were willing, for pretty good $$, to spend Sunday afternoon jamming with some college kids. One of the first to sign up was Wild Bill Davidson. He played some gigs with us, several at Yale, and one, which especially stands out, a benefit for the Bedford Village, NY Fire Department.

I'm fuzzy about who got the gig or who else was on it but clearly remember Bill. I'm guessing it was June, a warm night and we set up in the parking area in front of and facing the firehouse. Bill was well known for imbibing and for pretty bad behavior. As the evening wore on he lived up to his reputation but still played with skill and gusto.

At one point he went to the firehouse, wobbling a bit to use the john. On his way back he picked up a coat hanger, straightened it out and was using it to lift up skirts of some of the dancers—crude but really funny. A bit later he got up and again wobbling a bit, went across the parking lot with his hanger and lifted a skirt. The woman, startled, turned around and it was Bill's wife. Not at all chagrined he said, "At least I'm consistent".

This idea of adding players lead to my lasting friendship with

Buddy Tate. Our agent rounded up some players and, as official driver I went into the city to the corner of Lex and 125th St. and picked up Buck Clayton, Dickie Wells, Rex Stewart, Jo Jones and Buddy Tate. They were very friendly and mostly told stories about other Basie alumnae whom I didn't know. The trip went quickly but as we set up I could tell they were a bit nervous about what they were getting into; far too many blue blazers, white kids, button-down white shirts, and Yale ties. They seemed even more nervous when a blues was suggested as the first tune. However, Steve Swallow was our bass player. Steve, about eighteen I think, was draped around his acoustic bass and started playing with a sound as big as a barn. The whole front row spun around with big grins on their faces. The concert went well. Buddy and the others all enthusiastically agreed to come back. We did two more similar concerts with a few personnel changes; Buck Clayton and Buddy were the regulars. On one of the return trips to New York we stopped at my parents house for a quick visit/pit stop. Buck and Buddy for sure were there; probably Dickie Wells, maybe Sadik Hakim. Leila was in charge of the kitchen.

Leila knew exactly who Buck and Buddy and the other distinguished musicians were and presented her special ham with sweet potato pie and was the queen of the kitchen, serving us all as we crowded into the tiny breakfast nook. My father provided ample good booze and it was a raucous time as we had our fill.

After this very happy stop I continued into New York City and dropped Buck and Buddy at the Celebrity Club on 125th Street. Buddy told me to come on in and instructed me to double-park my Ford wagon in front of the club with the keys in the ignition! I didn't feel in any position to argue. We went down a very long stairs to a huge hall with several hundred people. Some were standing; some sitting at big round tables around the perimeter of the room. I think I was the only white face in the place. I remember the bouncer, a huge man who occasionally would grab one of the big round tables by the rim and casually pick it up to move it! Buddy hustled me up to the bandstand and said, "Play your horn motherf___r." Fortunately I had learned from our three road trips that this was the extreme compliment. Buck Clayton was a regular and Dickey Wells was there most of the nights just sitting in. Buddy's other regulars were Pat Jenkins (trumpet), Eli Robinson (trombone), Rudy Rutherford (sax and clarinet), and Bobby Pratt (drums). Bobby was a huge man and used to play on the kick-off team of the New York Giants; he was as friendly as he was huge and would come in usually a bit late, usually all beat up and disheveled looking. Sadik Hakim was the piano player and we later played a lot of gigs together. Major Holly was often there playing bass. I'd see him again playing with Eddie Thompson. Subbing might be Osie Johnson (drums), Wendall Marshall (bass), or George Tucker (bass).

This was the defining moment of my musical life. Most of the tunes were either blues-oriented or "I Got Rhythm"-type things. My ear was sharp enough to pick up on the forms and chord changes pretty fast and for some reason I was able to remember them. Four hours of amazing musical stimulation flew by being kicked around by that Basie style rhythm section and hangin' on to Buck and Buddy's solos. I had no thoughts about my illegally parked car on 125th St. When we were through playing and going up the stairs I suddenly panicked but across the street, keys still in the ignition and headed the other way, sat my car, safe and sound!

At first these Sunday visits to the Celebrity Club were monthly, but soon they became a weekly habit. Buddy seemed to be the unofficial mayor of Harlem. He seemed to know everybody; everybody seemed to know him. I traveled with a sleeping bag and pillow in my car and very often ended up sleeping on the kitchen floor in his apartment. As I remember it was on Amsterdam Ave. about 128th St. Further uptown we'd check in at Basie's, and when Shirley Scott was there we'd listen to her play the organ. Buddy liked to lean on the railing directly behind her. He liked to "watch her legs," he told me.

Uptown there were a lot of small clubs with the traditional Organ Trios, like Shirley Scott's and Jimmy Smith's; a Hammond organ player providing the bass lines with his feet, usually a drummer with just a snare and hi hat, and a tenor player. Of course Buddy knew them all, so if the group playing at Basie's was not our thing we'd head to one of the smaller clubs. Buddy would delight in pushing me through the door ahead of him into these small, smoky rooms. I was sort of skinny and very white and the looks I got were interesting at least. Then Buddy, the mayor of Harlem, would appear in the doorway behind me; smiles and applause would immediately break out and the tension would be gone. He would usually go right up to the leader and ask if I could sit in. Sometimes he'd play too. Again, I could rely on my ear to get me through tunes I'd never heard before, and I think Buddy got a kick out of exposing me, watching me struggle and cope with new material and eventually come through. I could and did swing with enough conviction to keep getting asked back. Buddy liked some of the younger players of the time but commented that some of them who took things so seriously and were so intense were "too hip to be happy." I kept in touch with Buddy even after the Celebrity Club closed down.

Years later he and Buck Clayton came up to the Sugar Bush Inn in Vermont where I had a trio gig with Don Coates (piano) and Howard Kadison (drums). We hired a bass player, Joe Davis, for the week. Buck and Buddy were there. The music was fantastic and another educational experience for me.

One night we invited a few other players from the area in to have a jam session. A young tenor player who played at a nearby club asked to sit in. (He obviously had no idea who Buddy Tate was; that he was standing next to the man who was the powerhouse lead tenor sax player with the Count Basie Band for 12 years.) He sort of bulldozed his way into the first solo and went on and on and on... forever. Finally when he got through I whispered to Buddy that I would take only one chorus and then he should go. I played my very short solo and when Buddy took over I'm sure the bar at the back of the room moved back about six feet. It was not just volume or massive sound. It was not a lot of notes; it was the authority and his total control of the situation. He was saying, make no mistake, "You sound nice, kid. Now look out, 'cause here is what it's all about!" Buck Clayton and I exchanged winks and glances as we watched the reaction of the kid who at least had sense enough not to play again that night; actually we didn't see too much of him the rest of the season.

Years later Buddy visited us in Maine and played several concerts with Roy Frazee (piano), John Lockwood (bass), and Steve Grover (drums). Buddy stayed at our chaotic house; we spent a wonderful week together. My last visit with Buddy was about six months before he died. Of course I'd kept in touch by phone and occasional postcards from Poland. He had long since stopped playing and was living in the family home in Massapequa. I had called him and sort of invited myself to visit. I was proud of the brand new CD of my Polish kids, *Triology*, and really wanted him to hear some of it. His son greeted me at the door, ushered me into a small back room, and in a few minutes Buddy walked in. He was in pajamas and a robe. His hair, now totally white, was wispy and a bit unkempt. He looked thin and frail but the twinkle in his eye and his smile were as fresh as at our first meeting. We talked for a while. I told him about discovering the Polish kids and played a cut from the CD. He listened intently, tapping his foot and grinning at every little nuance, every bit of interplay, totally concentrating on the music. After a few cuts I asked him if he was tired, had heard enough, maybe wanted to take a rest but he insisted, "No, no, no," he said. "Play some more." I played the whole CD, and he never faded or lost interest even for a moment. After listening to it all we talked and reminisced some more. He told me again a wonderful story he had told me many years earlier about times with the Basie band. They would be playing somewhere and someone in the band would spot maybe a Mafia character or worse or someone from the union, standing in the doorway. He'd nudge the guy next to him and say, "I feel a draft." Finally he admitted he was a bit tired and wanted to have a rest. There were tearful hugs as I said goodbye. He thanked me for coming to see him and sharing the music. He stood in the doorway, watching me as I went to my car. Again, the twinkle in his eyes and his smile were as fresh as the day we met. Buddy's influence on me was monumental; I won't forget.

Backing up. In the fall, after meeting Buddy Tate and about halfway through the semester at Yale, Steve Swallow decided enough was enough and made plans to move to New York and pursue music full-time. I decided to move with him. Several students who had been involved and recently expelled in a widely publicized sex scandal were leaving the campus the same day. As we were packing up Steve's stuff into the old Green Bitch we got a lot of strange looks.

> *Some young be-bop musicians are too hip to be happy.*
> —Buddy Tate

11

New York, New York
(1958–1960)

Steve Swallow, Hank Breedenberg and I moved to the big city in the fall of 1958 and found a cheap place to live: a loft. 28 Broad St. was on the corner of Exchange St., way downtown. (Hank had been the trombone player in the Yale band with Steve and me. He had worked his way through Yale and Yale Law School playing trombone.)

The space was on the third floor and had been a carpentry shop, and along the back wall was a pretty substantial pile of scrap wood, old pallets, etc. Other than the leftover junk from the carpentry business it was empty, and we busied ourselves scrounging for furniture and appliances. Access from Broad Street was up a long flight of stairs to a room-sized landing, then another stair with a door at the top, our level. Our bathroom was on the second level. There was a door in the landing leading to the hallway. This hall went to a stairwell leading down to the side street and ran along the full length of Nemo's studio, which was directly below our space.

After the co-leaders graduated, Steve and I had pretty much taken over the Bull Pups, playing quite a lot, sort of maintaining the Yale connection but using more and more ringers from New York, so living in the city made sense. At the end The Yale Bull Pups ceased to have anything to do with the University. Charlie Folds, the piano player, was the last Yalie in the band and moved to New York himself after graduation.

As soon as we got our phone connected we started being in the 'music business' and managed to get some work. One memorable gig was a private party way out on the end of Long Island. The only reason we got the gig was that our rivals, Eli's Chosen Six, had been seriously late three years in a row. We were determined to be on time. This was before most of the expressways were built.

Trouble started right away. In the confusion of moving beds and clothes in multiple trips to and from Connecticut I had left my clarinet at my parents house in Stamford. We were still okay with time. I called my old friend Bill Mather who scooped up my horn and raced on his motorcycle to meet us on the Long Island side of the Whitestone Bridge. The pick-up was made and we were still okay. We went from there to an address in Queens to pick up a piano player Buddy Blacklock, an older guy and new to us. We found his apartment but as soon as he got into the car we could tell he was in terrible shape. His first words were mumbled before even saying hello, "Has anybody got some Tums?" Still okay for time we headed east but about every fifteen minutes or so Buddy would make uncomfortable noises and have to find a bathroom; he'd disappear, lose whatever he was losing, and come mumbling out and we'd go on.

After several of these stops we'd run out of our comfortable cushion of time. Buddy took an exceptionally long time at the last stop. I used the time to call our hosts and explained our piano player was deathly ill and we were doing our best; they were very nice and understanding. At least I had called. Finally, concerned about our new friend taking so long, I went in the bathroom to look for him. I was feeling uncomfortable about my checking up on him. I found him on his hands and knees fishing around the bowl looking for his false teeth.

We got to the gig late of course but played way overtime and everybody was happy. Upon arrival Buddy had a quick couple shots of gin and was fine the rest of the night.

Back on Broad Street, our downstairs neighbor Nemo was becoming less and less neighborly. We were invited in his space once early on, but after that the welcome faded fast. His studio was filled with expensive-looking modern furniture and Persian carpets. Real or not, they weren't what I expected in the pad of a struggling artist. Along one wall was a stack of huge canvases probably six feet by eight feet. He'd lean one against the end wall and paint it black with a roller. Then he'd take a sponge dipped in red paint and throw it at the black canvas. That was it! Another huge canvas painted black; another sponge hit with red paint, again and again. If we were playing upstairs he'd bang on the radiator pipes and demand silence while he contemplated the next throw. Then he'd lay the finished product flat on the floor and let it dry overnight.

Soon we ignored these demands of silence, and he retaliated by refusing to unlock the door to his hall and our bathroom (really only a toilet and a sink). After his busy day creating his masterpieces he'd head to his uptown apartment and leave us locked out with no access to our toilet. The damned bathroom was six feet on the other side of the door, but we had to go downstairs, out to Broad Street, north around the corner to the entrance on Exchange St. up the stairs and down the long hall to the john. Meanwhile we were doing what we could afford, bit by bit, in the way of home improvements. We had a sink with cold water. I hooked up a water heater, and standing in front of the sink we could wash with washcloths, what we called 'Chinese showers'.

Our next-door neighbor, at number 26, was my old friend Roswell Rudd. He had a working shower and gave us a key. Still, going to the 'John' was problematic after sponge-throwing quitting-time. While moving some plumbing things around, next to the sink drain I discovered what seemed to be a sewer pipe pointing across the room. Following that sight line there was a hole in the floor covered by a flattened #10 tin can. I pried up a corner and discovered a four-inch sewer pipe 90-degree 'L'. Following in the direction it was pointing there was another squashed # 10 can and under that, just below floor level, was the end of a straight-up sewer connection. I wasted no time going out to the Stamford House Wrecking Company and buying a toilet, complete and ready to go. We installed it and with considerable fanfare and some invited guests, gave it it's maiden flush. Everything gurgled successfully away, the tank started refilling nicely and then we heard shouts and screams from downstairs. Somewhere between the sink and our newly installed toilet there was something missing. A substantial chunk of the flimsy plaster ceiling mixed with an assortment of things like mouse skeletons and debris was covering Nemo's latest creation drying on the floor. He was furious, really upset, hysterical I'd say. Roswell with his art critic/connoisseur's look on his face and stroking his chin commented that his new work seemed to have, "so much more substance, body, and texture." Nemo must have had some pull with the landlord; maybe he owned the building? Anyway we were evicted shortly thereafter. One night Wayne Wright who often played trios with Steve and me called me up sounding very excited. "This amazing guitar player, Wes Montgomery, is playing at the Half Note tonight. You gotta hear him."

As I remember the Half Note had sort of a horseshoe-shaped bar with the bandstand in the center. Bartenders worked the space between the bandstand and the bar and customers sat on stools in a semi circle around the bar. Anyone at the bar had a front row seat. Just as the band came on stage guitarist Kenny Burrell took the stool next to me. Of course I recognized him but respected his privacy and didn't introduce myself. The music started and Wes started his solo with his usual wonderful melodic lines, then to the octaves and finally to several choruses of his already well-known trademark chord solos. About midway during the chord solo a somewhat overwhelmed Kenny Burrell took a big swig of his beer and said, "Shee-it," and walked out.

I heard some crazy music at the Five Spot, most of which zoomed over my head: Monk, Ornet Coleman, Coltrane, Eri Dolphy and Pepper Adams, to name just a few. Bass player Ahmed Abdul-Malik, who I would play with later, was with Monk's quartet.

A story was circulated about an uptown guy who came in with his hip friend; they were listening to Monk. Chorus after chorus, with rhythm section burning Monk sat motionless, hunched over the keyboard not playing a note. When he finally straightened up the crowd went wild. "What was that?" the up-town guy asked, "He didn't play a note." His friend responded, "Yeah, but just imagine what he was thinking."

Steve and I moved to another loft on 6th Ave, over Bernie Koral's hardware store and continued trying to get gigs. Steve was already in demand and still playing acoustic bass with Jim Hall and Art Farmer; I was struggling. Who needed a clarinet player who only played by ear and didn't read music? The graffiti was on the wall. We landed a gig with the whole band at a girls' college in New Jersey, and I encountered my first rock & roll band. We were to alternate sets with three guys who were getting as much money as the six of us. Charlie Folds literally had to tune the guitar for the lead player; he didn't know how! They played the same three to four tunes with two to three chords each set; we had a 'book' of hundreds of tunes. This was more than graffiti. For me it was a career death knell. Within weeks my phone stopped ringing and I gave up, went home and started driving school busses for the Meyerhoff Brothers. I was not quite 21 and had to fudge a few numbers to get my P.U.C. bus driver's license.

12

Bucky Johnson
(1960)

School buses are fun to drive. I was given a fifty-four-passenger bus on a Ford F750 chassis with a pretty strong V8 engine and a standard four-speed transmission. I was assigned an early morning high school run, a junior high school run and an elementary. In the afternoon the order was reversed.

I'd been told that my junior high school run had really bad kids who cut up bus seats and vandalized the buses, etc.; nobody wanted to drive for them. Since I was the new guy...

My first day, I made a point of being friendly, greeting the kids as they got on the bus and introducing myself. I told them my name and asked for theirs. My friendly greeting put them off, no one had ever treated them with respect. I had no problems at all. There were all sorts of conversations going. I could drive and apparently be constantly looking in the rear view mirror at the same time; I was always making eye contact and talking to everyone; we had a ball.

Halloween rolled around and the kids asked if they could decorate the bus, bring confetti and wear costumes. This was totally against school policy but I said, "Sure, why not?" Before my first pickup I stopped at a donut shop and picked up 14 dozen donuts, five gallons of cider and paper cups to go around; enough for all the kids on all three runs. The high school group was delighted with the snacks. Then Jr. High kids went wild decorating the bus. Each kid or group of kids at each stop brought more stuff to stick on the windows or tape to the ceiling. It was wonderful to watch these 'bad' kids opening up and really having fun. The elementary kids of course were delighted with the goodies and the decorations. In the afternoon runs the high school kids thought it was cool, and the junior high kids were having a ball all the way home. I dropped the last three kids off at the last stop, and they asked me to wait a minute. They ran over to the garage of the nearest house and came back with brooms and a trashcan and swept and cleaned up the whole bus.

Later one of the kids showed me some really interesting cartoons he had drawn. I suggested he put them up on the bulkhead over the driver's seat and soon the whole front half of the ceiling was covered with his wonderful drawings. One week I announced that I was going to Simonize the whole bus at the bus yard Saturday morning. About twenty kids, some from each run showed up, a lot with their parents who wanted to meet this crazy bus driver. The bus sparkled and I never had to deal with a slashed seat or a square inch of graffiti.

I usually had a short break between the Jr. High run and the Elementary run. I'd stop to get a coffee to go and park the bus off the road about 100 feet short of the intersection that was my first elementary pick-up spot. I'd wait there until a small boy, Bucky Johnson, appeared. I'd roll up to the intersection and let him on. We still had to wait a few minutes to start the run so we'd chat and soon became friends. On cold mornings I'd bring hot chocolate for him and he'd sit on the big bus heater next to me to get warm while we waited. When the time was right we'd start the run. Sometimes when the weather was bad and after determining that I could turn the bus around I'd drive into the narrow private road he lived on and drop him off right at his house. One afternoon as he was getting off the bus he very casually said, "My mother wants you to come to dinner tonight, can you make it?" I was flabbergasted. This was not at all what I was expecting; I mean you usually just don't ask your bus driver to dinner. I accepted with pleasure.

My parents were on an extended business trip to India, and an invitation to dinner was special to say the least. I was keeping the bus at home at night so I went home, showered, changed and went back to 96 Eagle Drive.

It was a sprawling house nestled into to the woods. The living room was L- shaped and "dog and children colored" as Jimmy, Bucky's mom, described it. Bucky was not an only child; there were four others. All great kids and it wasn't long before I became a regular for dinner. I watched Mimi, the oldest sister graduate from high school. I recruited older brother Tom for Camp the first year at Mills Farm and continued to drive Sarah and Bucky to school. Christie, the youngest, was five or six. I was invited to Thanksgiving and since my parents were still away, for Christmas too. Tom's father was, shall we say, not very supportive of his sons, and Jimmy and I went to watch Tom play football in the fall, hockey in the winter. I taught him to drive and helped his mom pick out his first car. We surprised him with it on his birthday. For many years to follow I was there once a week for dinners, and almost every year Thanksgiving and Christmas. After about a year of bus driving, another summer of Camp, and then back at it in the fall, I fell in love—with an Alfa Romeo Jullietta Sprint Special. I still had the Green Bitch and used it on weekends for the band and also for taking kids camping, lugging them and gear to Vinalhaven for Camp, etc. It wouldn't quit. But I thought it would be nice to have something small that handled well.

The Alfa was great fun and I drove it with gusto, but it was mechanically pretty hi-tech. I had to get pros to work on it so it cost a fortune to maintain. A year later, during Thanksgiving break, I took some of the early campers on a trip to New York, primarily to see the automobile show at the Coliseum. I ogled all the new stuff and then saw a mustard-colored Shelby Cobra and stopped breathing. I certainly stopped any reasonable thinking. Jack Griffith was a Chevy dealer in Westbrook Long Island and was handling the Cobras for Carroll Shelby. We talked and they agreed to take the Alfa in trade and I signed up.

Dealing a bit underhandedly, I consulted with my father who was in Europe. He did say okay but his signature was on the Alfa's paperwork and was needed to make the transfer. Fortunately his signature was a bit of a scrawl and nobody noticed. I don't have to tell you about the Cobra—volumes have been written about it.

After a busy fall of activity with McTerry, (the tree service I ran during these years) I was due, at least in my mind, for a vacation and decided to head for Florida. My goal was to try and find Dr. William Scanlon who was the psychiatrist at Silver Hill and who I considered to be a friend. He'd retired in Jacksonville, Florida. (This was many years before discovering my ADD, but I had burning questions I wanted to ask him.) The trip started without incident. The back room of the Emporium was now the office of McTerry, and we even had a part-time secretary so I'd be able to check my messages. I visited a cousin in Washington and continued south, enjoying the Cobra's amazing speed and handling and somehow avoiding the law until one afternoon in Georgia. The road was fairly wide and smooth with drainage ditches on either side and straight for miles and miles. There were occasional intersections and I'd slow down to eighty or so. As I zipped by one intersection, a state trooper pulled out from behind a billboard. This was Georgia, just after the Selma church massacre and I had been told nightmare stories about people being thrown in jail for days and days for speeding. I was in one of the most exotic cars in the world, sporting Connecticut 'Yankee' license plates. I had just seen a sign advertising, "Stuckey's 7 miles, Last Texaco gas in Georgia". The roadside mile markers told me I was eight miles from the border. I downshifted to third, red lined and then into fourth, pedal to the floor. In my rear view mirror the flashing lights got smaller and smaller and finally disappeared. I passed Stuckey's and crossed the state line at 155 miles an hour. The specs in the brochure about the Cobra didn't lie. I located Dr. Scanlon in Jacksonville and made arrangements with his daughter (I think) to see him. He had been retired for a long time and really wasn't able to tell me much of anything. He was dear and friendly but pretty well along with some sort of dementia I guess. I wasn't sure if he really knew who I was. My quest had hit a dead end. Not really knowing what to do I checked for messages back home. There had been a call from Hank Breedenberg, now teaching and living in Detroit. He had a gig Saturday night, could I make it? I called him, "Sure," I said. It was already late Friday night in Jacksonville. I put the Cobra to the test and made the slightly over one thousand miles in just over twelve hours. That night, after the gig, I decided it was time to go home. About one a.m. I headed across the bridge to Canada and pushed as fast as I dared toward Niagara Falls. The road was empty and I could go fast. The night was balmy—I had the top down. I was in my dream car with my faithful shepherd Duchess curled up on the seat next to me. There was an uninterrupted Andres Segovia recital coming through my ear phones and then, to my left, a display of the Northern Lights that made the front page of the New York Times the next day. I made it home by lunchtime Sunday.

This was one of several times I felt that if, at that moment, I'd been run over by a bus, it would have been okay.

That winter, I found a job at Bob's Sports installing ski bindings in their shop in Stamford. The job was tedious, the only perk being a substantial discount on ski equipment and rentals.

Christmas vacation I got asked by neighbors of the Johnsons if I would take a load of furniture up to their new condo at Sugarbush in Vermont. Bucky and Tom could come with me and help load and unload. We could stay at the condo and they'd pay for gas and skiing for me. Sounded like a plan. We stuffed the van and unloaded everything with no damage. We were too late to ski but went looking for dinner. On the way back the kids were already asleep in the van, and I saw a sign at the Sugarbush Inn saying something about "Live Jazz" Monday through Saturday, 9:00 to 1:00. I parked the van in the parking lot, kids sound asleep inside. I grabbed my clarinet and went to investigate. The room was called The Wild Boar. There was a nice trio playing good tunes so I waited 'til their break and asked if I could sit in. I played the rest of the night and had a ball. Jim Herman, the owner of the inn, happened to be there that night. He had just flown in from the Bahamas on his jet that afternoon and came to the inn for dinner because his larder at home was empty. He spoke to me saying he loved the clarinet and would I consider playing the room for the rest of the season. I told him I was pretty sure I could, had to check with Bob's Sports, make a few adjustments and basically said, "Yes". By the first week of January I was back in Vermont playing six nights a week at the Sugarbush Inn. The money was pretty good, free room and board and free skiing were the added perks. The gig was fun and the discipline of playing that much was good for me; the season was over much too soon but I returned home with a wad of money in my pocket. Spring was spent working on the Emporium and getting kids lined up for another summer on the island. The Camp took all my time in the summer, McTerry in the spring and fall, and I played at Sugarbush for three more winters.

The second winter I was hired back as the leader. The bass player/leader had run up enormous bills and credit card debts at multiple local stores in town and several more in nearby Montpelier, had returned to his home in Canada and I guess wasn't planning to come back. Jim Herman called me and offered me the gig. I hired a wonderful musician, Howard Kadison, who was recently back from the road, from playing drums with the trio backing up Barbra Streisand and had had enough. I hired an unknown piano player from New York who had some serious personality baggage that made sharing a house more than uncomfortable and I was about to ask him to go, when he totaled my VW.

It was considerably more than just a VW. It was a white 1954 convertible; I bought it cheap. It was in great shape and had those little flippers for turn signals; great, but it had no engine. I had learned from my hot rod friends that Porsche running gear would fit a VW. I found a fairly new wrecked Porsche in a junkyard and installed all the parts I could in the VW—chassis; engine, transmission, front suspension, and therefore big Porsche brakes all around; even Porsche seats. It was a 'sleeper', a normal-looking old VW convertible that went 120 mph. Then one night our ill-fated piano player asked to drive home early after the gig. We were happy to let him go and not invite him to hang with us for a few drinks. About an hour later the State Police showed up and told me the guy had slammed into an illegally parked car halfway down the mountain and totaled the car. He'd banged up his face and broken his nose and had cracked a bone in his foot. He took to blaming me for the poorly designed defroster and not the illegally parked car or the driver who should have seen it. I was able to strongly suggest that he go home and not try to do the gig with a broken foot, and he agreed so I didn't actually have to fire him. The engine block/transmission was cracked and everything was twisted and ruined! $5,000 worth of sparkling running gear ruined, but I only got a token from the insurance company of the illegal 'park-ee'. $800 for a totaled 1954 VW.

I had played some with a wonderful piano player, Don Coates, also from New York. He was a friend of Howard's and he agreed to come up. We still stayed in the 'band house' provided by the inn.

Both Howard and Don had irrepressible senses of humor; together they were relentless. One night, a slow one at the Boar, we got to doing what musicians sometimes do. The few but generous patrons had plied us with way too many drinks. I had four or five glasses of Tanqueray on the rocks, the rocks in varying degrees of decomposition, number five fresh, number one clear liquid. The music was getting sloppy. (This also sometimes has been known to happen)

One of our patrons asked for "Strangers in the Night," perhaps my least favorite tune. We started in and not too far into the melody I reached for a high note but screeched it instead. Don, his head on his arms collapsed on the keyboard and Howard pitched forward sort of through his drum set into a heap on the floor. We were laughing and out of control and quit early. Later we made a recording complete with the sound of glasses clinking and general bar sounds including a noisy guy trying to pick up a girl. While I paraphrased the melody Don played bad changes and Howard randomly launched into furious drum solos. Way too much fun—the tape disappeared... too bad.

Several campers came to visit for some skiing, and I had a

recruiting poster for Camp in the game room at the inn. One day on the slopes (I tried to ski every day) I was waiting in line and a call for a 'single' went out. If you were skiing alone they wanted you to share a chair with another single skier to speed things up. A young boy who I immediately determined to be the right size and shape for Camp was the next single in line. On the trip up the mountain I wasted no time telling him all I could, in six minutes, about the Camp. We parted at the top but he said he'd bring his parents to the inn that night. We met, talked and quickly signed the forms for the boy and his younger brother.

Arne and Allen Gronningsater both came to Camp the following summer; great kids. It was an easy summer. I had purchased a 54-passenger school bus from my old bosses the Meyerhoff brothers. I got it pretty well equipped for camping and brought it to Vermont for season #3. Don Coates and I decided that rather than live in the rented house paid for by the inn we'd live in the bus and pocket some extra dollars. We parked it in the lee of the pro shack at the golf course. The maintenance people from the inn plowed, we had ample heat, a cook stove and went to the sauna/showers at the inn or visited friends to wash. Don soon asked his wife to join him so he moved to another place; I can't say I blame him. I too had found a friend. We met as singles on the chair lift; she was a much better skier than me. We skied like bandits, had dinners together and she showed up regularly at the gig. Very often I'd go to her house for dinner, but sometimes pass on that and snooze in the bus for an hour or two before the gig; all very loose and informal but we spent a lot of good times together and I was thinking about getting more serious. New Year's Day we skied with wild abandon all day and I decided, with a long New Year's 'special' that night, I'd opt for a nap instead of dinner with her. We agreed to meet later.

When I got to the room there were 40–50 people there, all dressed up, some already with party hats, ready to go. The bartender motioned me over, poured me a drink and then told me that my friend had choked to death on a steak bone during dinner. I don't know how I got through the night. I did finish the season but skiing wasn't the same; my life wasn't either.

A strange 'inner vibe' of some sort often came over me during my stint at the Sugarbush Inn. It was the complete opposite of 'feeling the draft' which I was all too familiar with. Somehow, without any signals from the bartender or any conscious effort of counting heads or the number of drinks ordered, I sort of knew when the register had reached the point where the room was paid for: "the 'nut' had been made".

Without counting heads in an auditorium I can still sort of sense when the presenter has reached the breakeven point. I can't explain it. I just sort of know.

The Gronningsater boys were at Camp again for their second year that summer, and following that, I had my third winter at Sugarbush. When the season ended sometime that spring the boys invited me to visit them in New York for dinner and to spend the night; I was glad to accept. I knew by then that their father was connected with a school and was happy to accept an invitation to visit Riverdale the next day. I was given a tour that included a glimpse of a seventh grade swimming class, all boys, all naked, in the Olympic-sized swimming pool. No wonder Arne and Allen were so at ease at the quarry. The tour ended in the head master's office and I was introduced to Johnny Jones. We exchanged pleasantries and then like a bomb they offered me a job. Dr. Gronningsater was more than just involved at the school; he was Dean of Faculty and head of the English department. He liked what he'd seen happen with his two sons at my Camp and wanted me on board. I protested. "I'm a high school drop-out. I can't teach, I don't know anything." Dr. G. (Arne) said he'd put me in the English department and offered me $3,500 for the year. He said I could think about it and I could start in the fall. I grinned all the way home.

In the mail that day was the new contract from Jim Herman at Sugarbush offering me four times the Riverdale offer for sixteen weeks of work compared to a year at the school. I spent a long night thinking about it and talking with my parents and came to the conclusion that the Sugarbush gig was great but completely self-serving. I was playing for people who didn't need anything and other than creating a good time for myself I wasn't doing anything for another human being. I had arrived at some of these same conclusions about my life before and The Island Camp had been born from that soul searching. Here was a chance to do more of the same.

That night I called Jim Herman suggesting Don Coates should have the gig. Then I called Dr. G to tell him I'd be there in the fall.

13

Riverdale
(1966–1970)

The last time I played 'Stella by Starlight,' I lost.
—Eddie Thompson

September 1969, after another smooth, fun summer at Camp, I started my new gig at Riverdale. Past summers I had experienced serious 'empty nest' letdown when the Camp ended and all the kids went home. There I'd be with nothing to do. Okay, there was Sugarbush and a few other music things but so much had dried up; I was really alone and really depressed. Those next two summers I ran double sessions of Camp and I'd come home and in about twenty-four hours start up at school. I needed a few days and going back to the single session was about right. Camp would close and as soon as I got my breath I was in up to my neck with kids who seemed to like me and benefit from what I could give them. It worked. I had a ball!

My four-and-a-half year teaching stint at Riverdale, with the exception of the long stretch of the Island Camp, not really a job... proved to be my longest steady employment and kept my interest longer than anything except music. I knew I got along well with kids and appreciated the confidence and support from dean of faculty and head of the English Department, Dr. Gronningsater. Wilson Alling, also in the English department was a faculty advisor and wonderful mentor to kids. He also made it possible for me to handle my two seventh grade English classes by making a copy of his lesson plan that I'd find in my mailbox every Monday morning.

I immediately liked the kids, and it helped that Allen, Arne and Kenny Gronningsater, all campers, had spread the word about this crazy English teacher who commuted in a 180 mph Griffith, insisted on being called "Brad" instead of "Mister," and was someone who was unflappable and nonjudgmental; you could tell him anything.

I was assigned two sections of great kids, about ten in each. Soon we started forging ahead with the boring grammar and exercises early in the week so we could spend the rest of the time with writing and mostly pretty animated discussions about almost anything. In a small "Do not erase" box on the black board was the standing homework assignment: "Write something". And they did! Almost everyday they'd turn in something and I tried to keep up and write pithy comments on every paper. I know the comments were being read because they came back with my spelling corrected—they were delighted that I couldn't spell.

Wilson gave me an outline for the mid-year exam but told me to write it myself. As a bonus extra credit question I told the kids there were three misspelled words in the text; they all found five. They tested me. One boy (trying to shock me?) wrote a rather silly story using almost all the four letter words he knew. I told him that after a stint in the army and thirty plus years on the bandstand I'd heard them all and, not being shocked at all, made him read his work out loud to the class. Another teacher might have reported him, kicked him out of class, given him a detention, who knows. I handled it then and there in the classroom; that solved that. Another boy simply refused to "write something" to the point that Wilson suggested I threaten him with a failing grade. That did it, and he finally, reluctantly, wrote a quite good piece about a sailboat race. Since I knew a bit about sailing I wrote a long 'answer', correcting a few technical errors to which he responded with a longer rebuttal. For the rest of the year this 'non-writer' and I corresponded about all sorts of stuff. After I left Riverdale I heard he was the editor of the school newspaper.

I was having a ball. Dr. G. had arranged for me to have access to all the kids' records and I was soon knee-deep with my kind of off-the-wall guidance. I knew everything that was going on. Kids felt comfortable telling me things they couldn't tell their teachers, their parents, and some kids, even their shrinks. If I didn't have an answer I was pretty apt to be able to find it. Before school I was giving swimming lessons to some kids who were not good swimmers and felt really uncomfortable with the nude swimming classes with 70 classmates. The nude part not the issue; they stood out in the group because they were poor swimmers. I worked out with the wrestling team. The heavyweights had no one to train with, so I'd just try and be an immovable lump. Usually they just sweat but couldn't move me. I had kids with all kinds of problems. I testified at a custody hearing for two brothers who wanted to be with their Dad, extracted an unhappy kid from swimming class because he felt abused by the coach; it goes on and on. With complete access to student files I could gather information about a kid before I even met him. Once, a name was given to me and I had no idea who the kid was. In his file there was picture, and I was able to spot him in the lunchroom. Now all I had to do was to figure out a way to approach him. I couldn't just go up to him and say, "Mrs. So and so says you have problems; we have to talk." I waited 'til he came by with his tray, stuck my foot out and tripped him; his food went flying. I apologized, bought him a new lunch and the interview started. (After two summers attending camp I told him how we met.)

Almost immediately, as part of my deal with Dr. G., I started working on a few empty dorm rooms to establish some sort of a woodworking shop. With the help of Allen and Arne I started classes and had the kids tear down a few walls to make a reasonable space to put some shop tools. The news about tearing down walls in shop class spread like crazy, and soon there were kids there all the time, some watching but most participating, some skipping study halls to find out what was going on. I'd dust myself off to do my two English classes and then the rest of my day, pretty much hang out in the shop. There were some assigned students for shop class but also kids would get excused from study halls or get out of lunch early and just wander in. Some would ask to do some special project, some just wanted to hang out. Kids were curious about this guy who wanted everybody to call him by his first name, let the kids knock down walls and taught English but couldn't spell. Arne and Allen's explanation of why they didn't have any tan lines also got kids curious and well before Thanksgiving I had nearly a full crew signed up for Camp.

The shop developed and the school came up with a modest budget to buy some tools. The space was cramped but it worked, and the kids were really proud of their efforts. Routinely, when parents came to school they'd get dragged in to see what we had done. One of my campers, a star soccer player, came into the shop complaining that he'd gotten hit hard in soccer practice and was hurting. The school nurse had checked him out and sent him back to class, but he skipped and came to see me. I knew him well, and knew that he was in no way a quitter. I found something padded for him to lie on and stretched him out on a workbench. We called his parents, and right after school I took him to his parents who immediately took him to the doctor. He had two broken ribs.

We eventually were able to move the shop into the old bus garage. Most of the maintenance was being farmed out, so we got the space. We acquired some better power tools and embarked on more projects; some you might not expect to see at an upscale private school. I had a good stereo and brought my collection of good jazz records, which I played constantly. We rebuilt a derelict couch and some chairs all salvaged off the street. The kids could pop in, make something or not, do homework, listen to music or take a snooze on the couch. It became a much more popular place to hang out than the assigned student lounge in the main building.

Kids could make almost anything out of wood, from kitchen islands, one with a tiled top, to bookshelves and even salad bowls. I started a Go-Kart club, found funding to buy 5 cars in kit form and had about 30 kids involved in 5 teams, all of them driving, all working as pit crew and all learning how to rebuild the cars after each race. One older boy (now, Dr. David Jablons), brought in an almost wrecked Karmen Ghia, rebuilt and installed a new engine and restored the car. We built a canoe from a kit I purchased for Camp. One weekend with the builders, mostly Camp alumnae, we gave it its sea trial in the school pool. After a ceremonious launching we gingerly lowered ourselves into the canoe one at a time from the diving board to see how many it would hold before sinking. The head of the Athletic Department, who had no sense of humor, chanced in about then and was quite upset, not by ten naked kids in the canoe but by the canoe. I had to convince him that since it was brand new it was not going to hurt his pool. His anger got all the way to Dr. Gronningsater who thought it was hysterical. His sons, Allen and Arne, were among the builders.

Wilson Alling, my mentor at Riverdale, became a close friend. On snow days when school was closed I'd drive in anyway. I had a Ford Bronco, Wilson, a Jeep. We'd meet at school and usually open the pool. Local day students and some of the boarders would show up for impromptu water polo and roughhousing. Then we'd take as many kids as we could fit in the two 4x4s out to lunch, go sliding around, and generally play in the snow. Several spring weekends we rounded up carloads of kids and went to Wilson's family place near South Hampton. The house had some beds but not enough for the whole crew, so we brought sleeping bags and 'camped out.' Part of the fun was roaring around on the beaches in our four-wheel-drive rigs. The kids loved it, so did I.

I stayed at Riverdale for four wonderful years and got more and more involved. I gave Jazz concerts at school with Fred Fischer and Dave Bargeron. I met and started playing with the incomparable Eddie Thompson and recorded some of the Eddie and Me album, live, in the auditorium. I was faculty advisor, splitting the one hundred seventh grade kids with Wilson, but as word got out, I was solving problems for kids from all the grades. Camp was going well and I was really happy with everything I was doing.

Riverdale came to a close for me, spring vacation, my fifth year. That September a new headmaster had taken over from retiring Johnny Jones. I kept up with all my activities but mid-year got the disturbing news: The new guy had looked at all the faculty resumes and saw simply "Brad Terry", with no letters, numbers, or mention of any degrees. Who was this guy who seemed to be everywhere, into everything, with apparently no credentials? Dr. Gronningsater tried to explain why I was there. Wilson Alling, now head of the middle school, and Larry Ransom, head of the upper school, wrote a joint letter explaining my tenure and the contributions I'd been making to the school. It fell on deaf ears; the new guy was very rigid. No more access to student records, therefore no more guidance, no more English classes. He offered me the shop teacher's position, period. Salad bowls this week, then saltshakers, give grades and take attendance. Nothing more. I had agonizing talks with Dr. G. and Wilson. I had a group meeting with all my seventh grade advisees and the older kids who had been to Camp and painfully explained my decision to leave.

During Christmas vacation I had visited The Village School in New Gloucester, Maine. It was a small alternative school; I immediately liked it and they offered me a job.

In my letter of resignation to Riverdale I explained that clipping my wings this way would negate everything I thought I could contribute to the kids, and I'd be not really be helping anyone. I gave them thirty days and left at spring break. In my letter I misspelled "New Gloucester".

I learned recently that on October 5th, 2012, Wilson died suddenly of a massive heart attack.

I tried the 'Thirty Day Diet' and lost three days last month.
—(?)

14

The Island Camp
(1958–1981)

I got married when I was 43 and I was much too young.
—WBT

In August 1955 the band station wagon was pressed into service during the terrible flood along the Saugatuck River in Connecticut. I volunteered to collect food and with help from the scouts went door-to-door, mostly in Danbury. As soon as I had a full load I took off over roads closed by mudslides and washouts to Red Cross collection points on the outskirts of Torrington. We were loaded down with only enough room for one kid to squeeze in the front seat to help unload—then turn around and do it again, non-stop for several days. We got almost no sleep but there was always an eager group of kids waiting to load up again and take turns riding shotgun with me. This got me thinking these pretty young kids could cope easily under trying circumstances.

In the fall of 1957, fresh out of the Army and not yet twenty-one, I was asked to be an assistant scoutmaster at the local North Stamford Boy Scout Troop #26. After only a few weeks I discovered an interesting slightly older group of boys who, if they came in, caused trouble and were summarily kicked out; nonetheless, they showed up every week just to hang around outside. The kids inside were happy in their uniforms, forming ranks, saluting and getting their feet tenderized. They really didn't need me, and I was totally fed up with any semblance of military uniformity. No one was paying any attention to the crew outside, so I started having my own meetings.

Early on I started taking my 'drop-outs' camping on weekends. My grandparents gave me permission to camp on their small, gentleman's farm in Newtown, Connecticut. At first we parked the band station wagon at the farmhouse and used a donated Model 'T' tractor to haul ourselves and our camping gear up the hill to the campsite. Soon, the station wagon, considerably modified and with snow tires all around, easily negotiated the road, more like a streambed, and bounced our way from the farmhouse to the big overgrown fields on the top of the hill; affectionately called, "The Mountain". We lugged one of the portable chicken houses from Woodbine Road and enjoyed camping well into the fall. Later I bought an ancient Dodge surplus ¾ ton army ammunition carrier which became the first official Camp vehicle.

The following summer I rounded up six of these boy scout dropouts and took them to Hurricane Island for three weeks. The island lay eleven miles out to sea from Rockland, Maine, and years later would become the headquarters of Outward Bound. We hitched a ride out to the island with Mitch Gratwick, then headmaster of Horace Mann School in New York and an old friend of my uncle, Brad Trafford, who came along for the ride. We were left on the island with two leaky tents, some tarpaulins and assorted cooking supplies; we borrowed a leaky dory from the local fish plant owner, Clyde Bickford. It rained most of the time.

It was a two-and-a-half mile row to Claudine Dyer's store at Dog Town Harbor on Vinalhaven, easier going than returning. Going, we could hoist a blanket lashed to two oars and take advantage of the prevailing southwest wind. Claudine welcomed us and filled us with homemade chocolate chip cookies and only chuckled and handed out towels when the kids nonchalantly stripped and put all their wet clothes near her stove to dry. We'd get dry and warm, pack up supplies and make the long row to windward and home.

At one time Hurricane Island had supported a substantial community of quarry workers and their families. There were two thousand people living there then. The cellar holes of many houses, several stores, a school and a church were still clearly visible. We swam at one end of the abandoned quarry and filled our leister bag with drinking water at the other. No one had to be warned not to pee in the quarry. We established camp in a small cluster of trees at the extreme southern tip on the Island. We made a driftwood table and lugged rocks to use as chairs. There was a huge millstone, abandoned, just sitting there, maybe eight feet across with a two-foot hole in its center.

It became our camp kitchen fire pit. We were invisible to the occasional expeditions of visitors. If we kept quiet they would walk within ten feet of our tents and not see us.

One of our games was to follow people around without being observed, and we got pretty good at it. As rent to the owner we cleared some paths and spent time exploring, swimming and scrambling up the cliffs. There were huge granite blocks from the quarry that had been discarded and dumped in piles, helter-skelter, which left endless spaces to crawl through under the blocks. Sound traveled very strangely and we'd spend hours deep under the pile trying to find each other by following the voices. We explored most of the island and scaled the cliffs where Outward Bound now has their ropes course, only we were without ropes and usually without clothes, just sneakers.

We invented another wonderful game. We'd all get naked and row the dory out off the seaward side of the island, and when we got a hundred yards offshore we'd pull out the bung plug. The brutally cold water would start rushing in. The idea was to ride the big swells and by paddling furiously try to get back to shore before the dory filled with freezing water and became dead in the water, leaving us with a long, cold swim. Even with perfect timing we'd have to go overboard near shore to pull up the boat. Then we'd streak across the narrow spit of land that separated the quarry from the ocean and leap into the quarry that had seemed so cold earlier and felt like a bath now.

Even at this early beginning stage I thought things out very carefully; there were specific reasons behind every concept. Most of the ideas put forward were culled from my own experiences. There was definitely a method to my madness. With the help of this first crew I had established three rules that were to remain for the life of the Camp.

Rule one: "No boats or swimming without permission."

Rule two: "Do what you're told."

Rule three: "No smoking."

Given the situation these seemed pretty obvious. There was nobody on the island except us, and I was justifiably paranoid about fire. Before we left home we discussed how to handle discipline. We were all pretty physical; there was a lot of roughhousing and wrestling, and all agreed that breaking these rules would result in something physical. Someone suggested, "How about a paddling?" Everyone concurred.

In spite of lousy weather things were going smoothly, and we all were having a good time. There were patches of sunshine allowing us to get things somewhat dried out, and our time was spent clearing the path from the landing around the southern tip of the island to the quarry. Lots of time was spent quarry swimming and taking boat expeditions when the fog lifted.

Every few days we'd make the trip to Claudine's. We managed to rent a small skiff with an outboard. It was too small for all of us but we could all go 'yachting' if we towed the dory. We visited all the neighboring islands in this mini flotilla, landing, exploring, swimming, racing around, sometimes playing serious games of hide and seek. We washed and rinsed clothes in quarry water and dried them on the rocks when we had a glimpse of sun. We swam every day regardless of the weather so our bodies were clean if our clothes were not! We used the fire pit for most cooking and had a campfire every night. We also had a Coleman stove and Coleman lantern.

One day two of the boys asked to camp by themselves out on a small island, connected to us at low tide but a separate island at high tide. I gave them permission and helped them, as they quickly got busy to get their tent set up before dark. I knew these boys pretty well, and even though I had specifically warned them again about not smoking, and the consequences, I suspected they would try something. They had miscalculated and thought the tide was coming up and therefore would isolate them and insure their privacy. But the tide was mid-way, going down, not up, and in about half an hour my path was dry. I went across to check up on them and my suspicions were confirmed. They were quite surprised when I stuck my head into their smoke-filled tent. I decided to let them wait; I'd deal with them in the morning. I confiscated the cigarettes and matches and left them to contemplate their fate. They knew what was coming. In the morning I found an appropriate piece of driftwood for a paddle and they got their ten each, leaning over a log, side by side. There were no other problems.

The three weeks flew by all too soon. For all of us it was time to head home. We hitched a ride back to the mainland on the *Kingfisher*, a 90-foot bait boat owned by Clyde Bickford (owner of the leaking dory and mini skiff) and skippered by Captain Hartland Small who also played the drums in the town band. He picked us up early in the morning with a promise to get us to Rockland before dark. In return for our passage to Rockland we were to be his crew. We had to help Hartland deliver tons of foul-smelling bait to numerous lobster pounds around Vinalhaven and spent all day with pitchforks, shoveling dead, smelly fish from the hold of the *Kingfisher* into barrels or down to the waiting 'lobster cars'.

Kids being kids, the bait ended up everywhere, detouring into people's shirts and down their shorts. At first the stench was overwhelming, but soon we got used to it and didn't notice anymore; we all smelled the same. Late in the afternoon we were dropped off at the fish plant in Rockland and packed ourselves into my station wagon, really like sardines, for the seven-hour drive home. We smelled much worse than sardines. We smelled so bad that we were not allowed in the Howard Johnson's on the Maine turnpike.

We drove all night, getting to my house in Stamford early morning. Everybody showered and washed clothes and slept 'til noon before we even called parents to say we were home.

After a year off because of a musical tour of Europe I decided to run the Camp again. Hurricane Island was not available, and I had had some serious thoughts about the isolation of the island. I had experienced feeling sick and just making it home for an emergency appendectomy on the way home from that spring vacation trip to Florida with the band. I was scared by the thought of something like that happening or someone getting hurt and being so totally out of touch. I liked the isolation, but the weight of the responsibility prevailed. I made an arrangement to camp on Mill's Farm on Vinalhaven, property owned by the Rheinlander family and farmed and maintained by Hollis Burgess and his family.

Mills Farm

The decision to move to the Mills Farm was definite. Phil Rheinlander, the owner and an old friend of the family, agreed to fund our food and traveling expenses and allow us to camp on a peninsula jutting out into Mill River. In return we were to clear away all the slag and junk wood left over from a very sloppy logging operation years before. I had acquired an ancient four-wheel drive Dodge Ammunition truck with a wooden flat bed and a powerful winch on the front. Hoops and canvas covered the back and we loaded up and left from Stamford with seven kids. After we arrived on Vinalhaven it took us a few days to actually reach the campsite.

The road into the campsite, inspected and dry and hard as a board in the fall, quickly, magnificently, mired the truck up to its belly in mud in June. The winch could do nothing. We off-loaded and hacked a path toward the proposed campsite on the point. Then we lugged in the two 14-man army tents that I bought at an Army surplus place in Philadelphia; at 160lbs each it took most of a day and help with a front-end loader, on loan from Mr. Burgess, just to get them where we wanted. We did get them set up in the first small area we had managed to clear of brush. Some large unmovable stumps now inside the tents provided cot-side tables, and soon we were cooking over a fireplace enhanced by an old stovetop from the dump, complete with an oven. We had the same leister bag from Hurricane for drinking water and made a new driftwood picnic table with logs for seats. Our larder was a large wooden 'field kitchen' that kept things dry and bug-proof. We had a Coleman lantern hanging on a rope and a few flashlights. The crapper was a deep hole we dug under a fallen tree that provided us a slightly slanted but smooth, splinter-free toilet seat 30 feet wide.

Even after un-sticking the truck, which took several days with help from Hollis Burgess and the farm tractor, the road remained so wet that we had to park in the field and lug in everything. For most of the summer we trudged the 3/4-mile trail carrying water and all our supplies.

We'd start the day with a swim. There were great tidal rapids just off the point, and we made it a habit to take a quick dunk there before breakfast. If the tide was going down the rapids ran faster and the water was warmer; tide coming in, it was brutally cold, but we did it anyway. At low tide there were mudflats that got warmed up in the sun and proved to be great fun. After funny, frantic mud fights we could always go slightly down toward the inlet and rinse off in clean, very cold ocean water. After the swim and some breakfast we usually put in a few hours of work, cutting anything we could with handsaws, stacking brush and collecting piles of wood for our own use. Grimy and sweaty we'd hike out to where we parked the truck, carrying empty water bottles, and head first for the Quarry. Shame, shame, we used soap to wash our clothes and ourselves. Little did we know then about the ecological damage to the quarry and little did we know that you could get badly sunburned on an overcast day. We found out the hard way.

We swam naked, of course, and washing clothes on the granite ledges required getting down on hands and knees to kneed the clothes on the ledge, with our tender buns pointing straight up at what seemed

The Green Bitch makes it to the top of the hill at Newtown...

with help from this tractor.

First tent at first Island Camp site on Vinalhaven: Mills Farm.

With John Howard and the GTO van.

$10 1951 Ford F100 from Meyerhoff Bus Co.
At Hopkins Farm, pre-A-frame.
Thinkers, John Doscher and John Howard on the
hood, and Rick Magner, standing.

Bucky Johnson: Army tent at Hopkins Farm,
pre-A-Frame.

Island Camp-style, Hopkins Farm, pre-A-Frame.

The Blue Lunch and crew.

like no sun. I managed a painful trip to town to buy quantities of Noxzema. We were all so badly burned we had to stay at Camp; most of us couldn't wear pants for several days. We learned! One day after a swim we were downstreet doing some shopping and encountered my grandmother who, amazingly enough, invited us for tea. Happily surprised, I accepted. I wanted the boys to see the Big House my grandparents had built in 1916.

We arrived at the specified time and were greeted by Anna Whittier in a kitchen smelling divinely of chocolate chip cookies. Anna had worked for years as a housekeeper and was best friend to my Boyden cousins. She was cooking for my grandmother that summer and, knowing boys, had made bushels of her famous cookies. While I tried to visit with Grandma the boys inhaled Anna's wonderful cookies. Jokingly she asked, "Why! Doesn't Brad feed you at Camp?" "Oh no," someone answered, and they all launched into tales of deprivation and abuse. "We have only saltines for breakfast!" "We try and catch fish sometimes!" "We had some cold soup yesterday." It went on and on as they demolished all the cookies. Anna took the bait and thought it all to be true.

The next day, we were again in town. Dr. Earl, who was the health department, stopped me in the street and announced he was coming to dinner at Camp that night and what could he bring? "Ice cream!" Anna had wasted no time in telling him about these poor, abused children, and he lost no time following up with an official investigation. He arrived at Camp just in time to see the boy in charge of that night's dinner, taking paternal pride, triumphantly delivering a 'made from scratch' strawberry pie from its womb in our wood-fired oven from the dump. It was slightly lopsided and slightly over-cooked on one side and under-cooked on the other, but it was still beautiful. Someone suggested we eat the pie while it was hot and the ice cream before it melted. The pie tasted even better than it looked. We then pan-fried some ham steaks and heated peas and carrots in a #10 can on the stovetop and ended with fresh lettuce and tomatoes from the Burgess's garden.

Dr. Earl told me why he had come, on official business. After our meal and a peek into our well-stocked larder and seeing obviously happy, healthy kids, he realized what had happened. I explained the arrangement with the Rheinlanders, and he knew them and the Burgesses well. He soon had us in hysterics as he described his conversation with Anna. He became a dear friend and staunch supporter of the Camp.

At the end of the first summer at Mills Farm we had done enough clearing to earn an invitation from the Rheinlanders for another summer and some time off. We pooled all our cash and chartered a small schooner called the *Leila* for a week. We packed up and took the ferry to Rockland, leaving the truck there, packed and ready for the trip home. We picked up the schooner and sailed it back to Vinalhaven, mooring it at my grandmother's. By now she had returned to New York. The house was empty and locked. We were nine miles from town with no phone, with no vehicle except the schooner, when disaster struck.

While loading our meager supplies onto the schooner my wallet went overboard and disappeared. In it was all our cash for food for the week. We had only a few small cans of things like beets and some saltines and two cans of sardines; that was it. I had none of the connections on the island that I would enjoy later on, so we were stuck with a difficult situation. We had a conference to see if we should give it up. The schooner was paid for, and I had wisely put just enough money in the glove compartment of the truck to get us home. The kids had only some small pocket change, maybe $40–50 total. What do we do? It was unanimous that we'd stick it out. We'd manage somehow.

The first day out was a glorious sailing day; fresh, strong, steady wind; clear and sunny and warm. Under way, we dunked kids over the side in the boson's chair; we'd head up into the wind and stop for swimming; we toasted on the deck. Even with these diversions we made good time and by late afternoon were in Buck's Harbor, a favorite scenic stop for the big cruising schooners from Camden. We dropped out hook fairly near the *Adventure*, one of the largest schooners in the fleet.

Our little schooner the *Leila* was modeled after the *Adventure*; we were an exact replica, in miniature. We had finished our saltines and one can of sardines and were getting ready to pack ourselves as tight as sardines to sleep in the tiny cabin. The *Leila* was designed to sleep five, not eight. We were conscious of our plight for the first time all day and feeling hungry and a bit forlorn.

Then, from across the water, I heard someone playing pretty competent chords of an old jazz standard on a guitar! I grabbed my clarinet, got in our tender and rowed toward the sound. It was coming from the bow of the *Adventure*. I hailed the guitarist and got invited aboard. Helmut Vles was the first mate and a pretty good guitar player. I joined him and soon a small crowd of passengers gathered to listen.

After a while a man in a chef's hat came from down below carrying a big pot and headed toward the rail. I called out, "Hey, wait a minute. What's in that pot?" "Left over Chicken a la King," he answered and continued toward the rail. "Wait! Wait! What are you going to do with it?" I asked. "I'm going to give it to the fish." I jumped up, ran over with clarinet in hand and stopped him. I explained our situation; that I had seven, eight counting me, hungry kids on that little schooner. I explained about losing my wallet. I explained about the Camp and what we had been doing all summer. That night we ate so much Chicken a la King, with homemade bread and leftover salad we were totally stuffed, nearly sick.

For the rest of the week we followed the *Adventure* from port to port. Helmut and I played for the passengers every night and David Berry, the cook, made sure we got the leftovers. The kids and I all gorged ourselves on leftover shrimp casserole, steaks and one night, lobster. David Berry became a friend who would help with carpentry projects when I lived in Bowdoinham 30 years later, and his mother became a close friend of my mother's when she lived in Brunswick!

David took good care of us. We returned to Rockland, brown from head to toe, fattened and healthy after a glorious week of sailing, swimming, sunning and high adventure! The cash in the glove compartment for the trip home was exactly enough to buy gas, but we didn't care about eating! All the way we laughed and reminisced about our crazy adventures, and by the time we got home most of the boys had signed up for the next summer!

The second year at the Mills Farm was fun and relatively uneventful. We continued clearing. A few of the older second-year boys were entrusted to use a small chainsaw, and we made a lot of progress—so much so that we took a vacation at the end of the summer having more than satisfied our landlord. The weather was favorable, and we spent more time at the quarry and visiting my parents, who were spending their summer at the Big House. My grandmother became too frail to spend even a short time on the Island, and my parents took the place over. The rest of the clan considered it more than they could cope with. We utilized the waterfront and discovered we could do a lot of the necessary maintenance of the boats and docks.

After a day working on the waterfront we would often linger in the evening for a chowder supper and later, around the fire, bodies lying everywhere, wall to wall on the floor, my mother would read horror stories to the kids, making the drive and hike back to the Mills Farm camp site positively spooky.

Things went smoothly. There were no discipline problems. The Camp ran itself. The kids enjoyed the work and took great pride in giving Mr. Rheinlander the tour of the area we had cleared. The usual quarry trips and excursions by boat were routine, and before it was over, there was a crew signed up for the next summer.

Hopkin's Farm

The following year my parents offered me the use of some family property adjacent to the Big House, known as Hopkin's Farm. My grandfather purchased this property from Capt. Emery Hopkins, who was a direct descendant of Stephen Hopkins. Stephen Hopkins was with my ancestor, William Bradford, on the Mayflower expedition. Now, three hundred and fifty years later, the families had made a complete loop. Vinal Hopkins had worked for my grandparents for many years and late one summer, when Bill Hopkins, Emery's grandson died, I was asked to play some music at the memorial service for him at the cemetery on North Haven.

During the previous winter the New York Jazz scene had deteriorated and I had taken refuge at my parents' home in Stamford and to survive, was driving school busses full time. Al and Rod Meyerhof owned the bus company. I acquired an old Metro Van and built in a few bunks. This, along with a Ford pickup I bought for ten dollars from Al Meyerhof, transported us from Connecticut to Maine. We caravanned up to Rockland with these two questionable vehicles, ferried across to Vinalhaven and set up camp at the new site.

Settling into Hopkin's Farm, we used the foundation of the old main house as our kitchen/dining area. All that was left of the Hopkins farmhouse was a partially filled-up cellar hole and foundation. The first summer at our new location we still had the army tents. We set them up attached together, making one big tent. We dug out the narrow, ell section and made a crude A-frame of birch poles and covered them with tarpaulins. We set up a small gas stove and a Servel gas refrigerator. We built shelves for food storage and tried to keep things dry. There was mosquito netting on the ends that helped some against the organized formations of these unwanted guests. The weather was generally good to us. We swam nearly every day and still washed clothes at the quarry but did the rinsing outside. Because of the bother of washing clothes, as much of the time as possible we didn't wear clothes. It was hot and there was no need to. If you could call it that, 'No Clothes' was the Camp uniform. We took over most of the maintenance of the family waterfront.

Early on each summer we set the moorings, and as soon as the *Anna W* (named after Anna Whittier, of cookie fame) was painted and overboard we placed moorings, hauled around and set up the float and ramp to make the waterfront complete. We scraped, painted and launched the smaller boats and got them ready. This was educational for the kids and helped us pull our weight and return something to my parents for letting us use the land and, most importantly, the boats. Until my parents died their support and enthusiasm for the Camp was boundless and the relationship between the Camp and the Big House was very close. We had no telephone at Camp, but I had bought three old-fashioned crank telephones from the Warren Telephone Company from Sugarbush days in Vermont. The Vinalhaven telephone man, who was a quarry regular, gave us a huge spool of surplus army field phone wire, two-strand and therefore obsolete. We stretched it through the woods from the Camp to the house kitchen and ran an extension upstairs to my mother's room. If a call came in for one of the kids or me on the house phone she'd turn the crank and we'd answer at Camp. If we were at Camp she would tell the caller to call back in five minutes. She'd call us on the hotline and the requested party would sprint to the Big House to get their call. We also used this hotline to alert my parents of our plans. They were aware of every move we made, every expedition and trip downstreet and often joined us. Even after we got an outside phone at Camp we kept the hotline for easy communication with the Big House.

Pops often wandered down to Camp, sometimes before breakfast, to see what we were up to, joining us for coffee and home-fries; and Mother, whose skin couldn't tolerate much direct sun, never missed her annual visit to the quarry to pass her judgment and offer suggestions on diving skills. Someone would call out, "Watch this, Mrs. Terry!" With her huge sun-stopping hat and dark glasses shielding her artist's eyes, she'd peer in the direction of the voice and watch, as the 'someone', naked and unashamed, showed off their latest backflip.

"How was that, Mrs. Terry?" She saw real beauty in this display of young healthy bodies.

The first few years we adventured out by boat when we could; spent time almost every day at the quarry, and acquired a huge Garland commercial hotel-type gas stove from the Finches, whose stone wall I had carried down Cascade Hill in Dumpy. We built a two-hole moveable outhouse. When things got nasty at one location a crew filled up the hole while a second crew simultaneously dug another one. Then the combined crew hoisted the outhouse and placed it over the new hole. Actually it wasn't a 'house' but rather a bench with appropriate openings on a deck with no sides or back. Two number ten cans perched on the space between the two holes. One had lime to sprinkle on deposits and the other paper. It served its purpose! Camp continued this way for several years. The Metro Van was replaced by a 56-passenger school bus I bought from the Meyerhofs. A newer, bigger F350 Ford truck replaced the small Ford. I bought it as a 'cab and chassis', and custom-built a flatbed for it. The bed had a wide channel down the center to accommodate feet and a winch cable. I bolted an Army surplus 20,000-pound winch, also acquired from the Meyerhofs, to the frame just behind the cab. We parked the bus and it became a living room for the Camp and sleeping quarters for myself and one or two staff. The original Army tents sheltered the others. The truck took all of us downstreet and to the quarry. Summers flew by. The custom-made curved paddle hung ceremoniously on the wall, not needed.

In 1966 we decided to try two, five-week sessions instead of one seven-week session. By now I was teaching full-time at Riverdale, and we had more kids wanting to go than we could handle without expanding in numbers, an impossible task which would mean more of everything; bigger truck, more tents, more boats, more staff etc. I didn't have the money to expand but, more importantly, I didn't want to be to be reduced to an administrator, directing a staff. I wanted to be involved with the kids. We could retain the small group and increase the numbers by doubling the sessions, which at first seemed a good idea. I soon realized three things. First, I was going from a year teaching to ten weeks of Camp and immediately back to teaching again with no break; hardly time to change socks. Second, I discovered that it just plain took about five weeks to develop a crew. We'd just get them ready for anything, and then ship them home before we could do any of the crazy, fun things we trained them for. Third, most of the first crew wanted to stay all ten weeks! This idea only lasted two summers, 1967 being the last.

Rules

The Island Camp had been running more than ten years when I first read A.S. Neil's *Summerhill* and found that I agreed almost totally with his philosophy, except about allowing any kids to smoke or using work as a punishment. My ideas, and therefore the camp's philosophy, were not spur-of-the-moment fleeting ideas but all carefully thought out. I insisted on nude swimming, and the 'sneakers only' run around the big field before the mandatory cold shower before breakfast, all for definite reasons. The initiation ceremony was also carefully thought out, with a reason behind it. These ideas became part of the institution, part of an overall philosophy that was the Camp. I wanted to share and teach the kids about these important concepts, so they'd not have to learn it all the hard way. All this still makes sense even after learning about ADD. The very structure and character of the Camp was evolving, long before I had ever heard about ADD. Had I known about it I might have been more aware of things and certainly would have recognized the symptoms in some of the boys but still probably would not have changed things much. Some of the kids, who I now strongly suspect were 'ADDers', were exemplar campers. My system worked very well for them and why not? Look who was driving!

I took the time to interview each prospective camper. If time and logistics permitted I spent time with them and tried to get to know them a little. I often rounded up kids to go to the stock car races in Danbury, and we made Thanksgiving a Camp reunion time; collecting some old campers, mixing them with prospective ones, and going to New York, usually to the Automobile Show at the Coliseum and then Hong Fat's for Chinese food. The old campers were my best salesmen! The Camp's daily schedule, or lack thereof, was carefully explained to the boy and his parents. Emphasis was placed on explaining the rules and the consequences because I wanted everyone to understand things exactly. The rules were the same, carried over from the first summer on Hurricane. First, no boats, waterfront, or swimming without specific permission; second, I expected immediate obedience; and third, no smoking.

These rules were nonnegotiable and pretty clear-cut—not much gray area: either you did or you didn't. The 'no boats' and 'no smoking' rules were really obvious. Immediate obedience was slightly complicated, because I very rarely gave orders and tried never to raise my voice or shout. I would quietly ask whoever was closest something like, "Would you grab that garbage bag and load it on the truck, please? And I'd add a "thank you" as it started to happen. Loosely translated, this meant "You: garbage, on the truck, NOW!" The kids quickly understood the translation. On a boat, if conditions get sticky, shouting commands creates confusion, even panic. I could count on the boys reacting fast, without raising my voice in difficult, even dangerous situations. The rule: react first, ask questions afterwards. After the fact, if they didn't understand, I'd spend as much time as necessary to explain. After the garbage went out, the boy could come to me and say, "Shit Brad! That's the fifth time I've had to take out the garbage!" I would apologize but know I had a good crewmember.

Here again, I disagreed somewhat with A.S. Neil on a third point, the use of physical punishment. He didn't have to deal with the inherent, possibly life-threatening dangers we were exposed to on a daily basis. I had the responsibility of caring for sixteen boys from twelve to fifteen years old. I was dealing with kids, water, boats, quarry swimming, cooking, construction, slippery rocks and a cold, cold, ocean. We were always careful, but the risk was always there. If they broke the rules I couldn't ground them or give them a time out in their room. I never even thought of using work as a punishment and I certainly didn't want to send them home. I wanted something immediate, so as not to slow down or interfere with the rest of the camp's activities and something harsh enough to make a lasting impression.

When the reasonableness of the Camp rules didn't prove to be enough of a deterrent, the consequences would be harsh and immediate: a trip down to the shed, pants off, and ten swats delivered with a paddle. This gave me the final control that I felt I had to have to maintain safety and be able to do the things we wanted to do. This, perhaps old-fashioned, discipline proved very effective. A boy has broken a reasonable rule and fully understands the consequences. Any infraction made me angry. He has put me through the distress of worrying about a lost kid, or a missing rowboat. Ignoring or disobeying directions could be dangerous. I had enough to worry about without this! My anger was vented on his bare behind which sustained no permanent damage. After cooling down and always a long talk, the red behind was usually shown off to the other campers, which served as an additional deterrent for them. The marks faded in a day or two. It was all over quickly; he had paid the price, I wasn't angry, the others saw the results and knew I was serious, and this was all carefully spelled out and agreed to before the application was signed. Harsh? Yes, but I still stand by it.

But I remember one boy who stretched my belief in this system and caused me to have a few days of serious doubts and marathon talks with my staff, all seasoned campers themselves. In late June, interviews over, applications signed, the boys and the parents in agreement on the conditions, the kids would arrive. We'd be ready to start, usually on the first Saturday after the public schools closed.

Every year, the first morning of Camp during a leisurely Sunday breakfast, I'd go over everything again in great detail, all the rules, and the consequences. Every question was answered. Some of the new boys usually inspected the curved walnut paddle which hung ceremoniously, near the old Riverdale School blackboard; some even giving themselves a trial whack, which usually generated considerable respect but no one ever seemed afraid because by just using a modicum of common sense it was difficult to get into trouble.

This particular summer, after the breakfast and the talk, the kids all were eager to go to the waterfront to do their rowing and knot-tying test so they could be cleared to take a boat out by themselves. When I got to the waterfront the kids and staff were all waiting on the dock except for one boy, who was already in a rowboat, cast-off and trying unsuccessfully to row. The discussion about the rules and #1: No boats without permission, was not thirty minutes old! A counselor rescued him and leaving my staff in charge, I took the boy back to Camp and down to the shed. After determining that he understood the rule, I administered the prescribed punishment and we returned to the dock.

Later that afternoon after lunch, we were still testing skills, and he did it again: just hopped into a boat and took off. I was really angry and marched him back to the shed for round two. He could offer no explanation and at this point I should have heard some whistles and bells, but instead I paddled him quite hard. The number of swats was prescribed by the rules. I did have the option of varying the intensity of the swats but this time I really was angry. Even though he still had fading marks from the morning paddling, I made it considerably more uncomfortable this second time.

The following day we were again at the waterfront and he did it a third time! I was really angry and back to the shed we went. He followed me to the shed crying all the way but offered no resistance at all; voluntarily dropped his pants and assumed the position over my knee. There were still marks from the day before but fortunately this time some bells and whistles did go off. Something had to be wrong, and I turned him over, sat him down, and we talked, and talked, and talked.

What became clear was that this boy was so starved for attention that he'd do anything, even get a painful paddling, to get my undivided attention. He knew the rules: "Take a boat. Brad will paddle me, and then we can spend an hour together," he told me. The pain was worth it to him, although this time he admitted he was getting a bit nervous. He knew I was angry the second time and had hit him harder, and was sure I'd be angrier still, the third time. Just to get my attention he was expecting and willing to risk an even worse paddling. I was able to point out there were lots of positive ways for him to get attention. He told me he had been getting into trouble in school for the same reason, and we talked about that. After the talk I gave him the prescribed ten swats. He understood I had to, but I barely touched him with the paddle. I told him to yell a lot and not show his butt to anyone right away; the others would expect to see fire. He became very good at baking bread. The rest of that summer either a staff member or I made a point of keeping him under our wing as much as possible and following summers he was a model camper. I lost touch with him after his third or fourth year at Camp. But after my experience with him I took even more time to check kids out.

My instincts were usually pretty good. I could meet a kid, push a few buttons, and almost every time quickly determine if this was a kid who would do well and contribute at Camp. If I had any doubts about a kid I would arrange a meeting with Jim Gillespie, a parent and Camp board member, and a psychologist. Two of his sons, Craig and Kevin, were long-time campers and counselors. Jim would go after school records if we thought there was any question. Only once did I break my own rule about insisting on an interview with the kid and his parents before signing him up and it created a potential for a disaster.

Camp was three days from starting and I was there with a small crew of old campers getting some basic things ready. We were experimenting with running the two five-week sessions at this time, and more had to be prepared ahead of time. I got a phone call from Jim Gillespie about a neighbor who desperately wanted his son to come to Camp. They knew it was last minute but could pay full tuition and the boy was a good friend of his son, Kevin, by then already a second-year camper. We needed a paying customer. Jim told me the father was a doctor, an ex-Marine and ran a pretty tight ship at home and that his son, Tim, was a great kid. With this endorsement I agreed on the condition that I talk privately with Tim on the phone before we made the final decision. An evening telephone call was planned.

When we spoke I told him in detail about the rules and consequences, the nude run, cold shower and swimming at the quarry. He laughed and seemed to react favorably to all my button pushing, so I said yes. Two days later Tim arrived at Camp.

His parents made reservations on the ferry, drove him up to Camp and rather unceremoniously dumped him off, handed me a check and the signed application. Then, with hardly a goodbye, they left to catch the next ferry back to the mainland, leaving him sitting on his duffel bag. Kevin helped him secure a sleeping space in the loft but when supper rolled around Tim didn't want to come down to eat. I asked Kevin what was up and he then told me Tim had been forced to come. His father told him, "You're going!" and that was that. He was really miserable. I went up and stretched out on the space next to him, and we talked and talked.

Tim told me his father had been listening in on our phone call and had been telling him what to say. The nude run and cold shower sounded 'gung-ho' and fine to dad who saw this as a way to get his son toughened up: "Put some balls on you, son, and become a real man." Tim saw it as torture and more military-like regimentation. I tried but couldn't convince him that I was as far opposed from that line of thinking as possible. I told him how angry I was that our call had been manipulated and even angrier that he was forced to be there. When I suggested he could go home he told me he could never go home and have to face his father for the whole summer. I finally got him to agree to try and hang in for a few days; do everything all the other kids did and see how he felt about it.

For two nights he cried himself to sleep, but he took his run and cold shower, did his kitchen duties and seemed very happy at the quarry. A few days stretched into a week and he was constantly in the middle of everything. Jim was right. He was a great kid. He didn't mention going home again but instead called his parents and got permission to stay for the second session. I still wonder if we had had the usual interview, would he have ended up at Camp in the first place?

I don't mean to dwell on the use of the paddle, but it was part of the Camp policy. The situations were few and far between where it became actually necessary to use it. Parents, staff, board members and the kids themselves accepted it as a viable alternative to more traditional restrictions that, with a small group, were not practical. Ground one kid and the Camp was grounded. The only times it was used were in very clear-cut situations, pretty flagrant violations, where there was no question about anything. A boat had been taken. A direct order ignored, or the few times smokers had been caught. These were dealt with quickly, age and attitude determining the severity. I had little sympathy for second year campers who knew the ropes and still refused to comply.

Control for me was not in any way to restrict but to expand; so I could have, in the shortest possible time, not just a bunch of kids but a well-trained crew. This method definitely paid off. The range of our activities became nearly boundless. With total confidence we could, and did, go anywhere and do anything.

The Camp enjoyed an enviable reputation with the people of Vinalhaven. This reputation was greatly valued. I stressed this. We were constantly on display and the boys' behavior reflected directly on the image of the Camp. The boys understood and enjoyed feeling welcome even in mob formation at any of the stores. If someone was short a quarter for candy, credit was easily obtained. Any kid could charge camp supplies at the hardware store; waves and friendly "hellos" were the rule, not the exception. We were a fixture at the Thursday night church suppers. All the ladies fell over themselves to bring us more pie. Every year we won a prize for our entry in the 4th of July parade. Our 'open house' attracted local fishermen, Police and Fire chiefs, and the sister of a U.S. Senator. Island kids swam at our quarry and went with us on expeditions, and one abandoned eight-year-old, who later became my adopted son, spent a whole summer with us as our mascot. Stan fits in another chapter but can be introduced here.

Routinely, weather permitting, we made a stop at the quarry for a swim, sometimes staying all day if it was nice or for a quick dip if not. Sometimes we went swimming in the rain. One particularly fine starlit

Rolling the boom.

Gift of the artist, Helen (Mather) Handley.

Stress relief. Gift of the artist, Matthew Terry.

night, sitting around the fire, we discussed making the next day a quarry day. We had no other pressing projects, why not? If the weather looked good in the morning we'd do it.

I always was awake early and this morning, seeing the beginnings of a white-hot sunrise, predicted a great quarry day. The kids eagerly started just at dawn and packed the truck with supplies. We drove to the quarry, getting there just as the sun cleared the trees and started to warm away the morning mist. Instead of a run around the field and the cold shower the boys agreed on making a certain number of high-speed quarry crossings. That early in the morning it was colder out of the water than in, and most of the crew kept swimming while breakfast got underway. Eggs to order, pounds of bacon and mounds of home fries were cooked up in a big pan over a small hot fire built in a wedge of granite ledge. The kids all swam around like seals but changed briefly to land mammals when their egg orders were called. They'd pop out of the water, dripping wet, grab a paper plate and load it up. Some kids preferred to lie in the sun and dry off; some kids returned to their swimming immediately, some sat up to their necks in the water while they ate: So much for the idea of waiting twenty minutes after eating to swim.

The sun, now higher, was gradually heating the granite ledges. More glistening, wet, naked bodies would occupy places on the warm rocks and then return to the water leaving behind damp, abstract imprints that quickly evaporated. If there was a lull in our splashing, our shouts and laughter, we'd hear voices of people approaching up the road. At first, shapes only through the alders or maybe a recognizable voice, until they appeared on the stone steps at the entrance of the quarry, then friendly greetings as assorted visitors, mostly old friends, came to enjoy the freedom of our quarry.

With help from my parents I managed to purchase the quarry and thirty-three surrounding acres. The road in was our right-of-way. The property was shaped something like an irregular snow shovel with the road as its handle. The kids kept incredibly active, scrambling up the ledges and jumping and diving off countless times with countless variations of flight and entry into the water. There were group jumps, and the old boom from quarrying days that had been floating in the quarry for years provided hours of fun as people, like log rolling lumberjacks, tried to climb up and stay upright on its slippery, spinning surface. It was a never-ending show. Some kids got really good at keeping their balance and could stay on long enough to get completely dry, Others lost their balance, tried to stay on and then after sometimes long and very funny gyrations, loose it and make an ungainly splash-down.

One boy we nicknamed "Buddha," would start running across the ledge, then quickly sit down, getting into a perfect lotus position. He became a little bouncing Buddha as he slid on his butt across the remainder of the slippery ledge and plopped into the water, maintaining the pose all the way. This brought howls of laughter every time.

Between all these activities we also cut sight lines for the survey. With only a Boy Scout compass and tape measure we surveyed the property. Along the back line of about 1800 feet, we were accurate within a few 'minutes', closer than a degree! We also removed thirty-five junk cars from the property, including seventeen from the quarry itself. One of the older boys, Derek Stavenger, was a really good swimmer and diver, and would be a counselor the next summer. He would swim down and secure a line to anything he could find. We'd use that to pull through and attach a bull rope, which in turn was wrapped around the floating boom. Using it as a winch the boys would all get on one side of the boom and turn it. As soon as the 'catch' got into range we'd connect it to the winch cable on the camp truck and haul it out. Great excitement each time; we never knew what we had 'til it surfaced. Wendell Jones would come by periodically with his backhoe and truck to haul the hulks away

At some point towards the middle of this particular blissful quarry day, a young boy showed up. I hadn't seen him before. With no hesitation he peeled off his clothes and jumped in the water with the others. He was blond and light skinned, very well proportioned and athletic looking, quite obviously pre-adolescent; I guessed nine or ten. He was an excellent swimmer and was balancing easily on the boom and jumping fearlessly off the highest ledges.

As the perfect day wore on I noticed that his very white behind was getting too much sun. I spoke to him about it, put some sun screen on it and suggested he cover up and loaned him a towel since he didn't seem to have one. After a while we left and went back to Camp.

A few days of poor weather kept us at Camp and we skipped the quarry. Instead, we made bread and the kids caught up with summer reading and postcards home. Mattresses were hauled down from the sleeping loft and spread on the floor and the kids staged hilarious tag team wrestling matches. Water fights were another favorite rainy day activity. Someone would find it appropriate, even necessary; to chuck a cup of water at someone else and it would start. "Keep it outside," I'd tell them.

Outside the A-frame after some rain, the grass would quickly become slippery and muddy, washing clothes was still a time-consuming chore, so within seconds all clothes were off and water and mud was everywhere. The rule was to keep it all outside so we'd keep things dry and clean inside. The outside shower was a constant source of fresh water supplies, and the kids would slide in the mud and chuck water and mud at each other, run through the shower, clean off while loading up their buckets and go at it some more. This could last for hours.

Inside would be a roaring fire and eventually the wet and tired combatants would collect around it and toast, noisily, wrapped in dry towels and lots of hot chocolate. Supper would follow.

It was two days before we returned to the quarry. The kids wasted no time getting in the water, but I spotted the little boy with the pink bottom sitting on a ledge on the opposite side the quarry and went to him. He was a mess. He had been crying and the tears had formed deltas through the grime on his face. He was shirtless and considerably sunburned on his shoulders and back. His filthy pants were completely stuck to the major sunburn on his previously lily white mid section. He'd been there since we left two days before. I made a sling with a towel to carry him. He was too sore to walk and cried more when I touched him; it was difficult to even move him, but I rushed him to the Island Medical Center.

I still had no idea who he was, not even a first name, and he was not in any shape to tell me anything. The nurse at the center seemed to know who he was. His name was Stanley and he was known to have had a rough upbringing, on his own a lot of the time.

Doctor Earl, the nurse and I all went immediately to work, carefully soaking and separating his terrible pants from his raw skin. Poor kid, everything was sunburned and stuck to his clothes. As we worked on him, through his sobs, he told us that he wasn't sure if it had been two days or two weeks since he'd seen his dad. We called the police.

At the medical center we finished as well as we could, trying to make Stanley as comfortable as possible. Police Chief Reynold Tibbits came immediately to appraise the situation and through some connections with a judge on the mainland got emergency State custody that afternoon. Stan, with head-to-toe salve and some new clothes that he wouldn't be able to wear for a while, officially became my ward for the summer and the camp mascot.

Mr. Tibbits was the only town cop and as such also the Chief of Police and a good friend of the camp. Occasionally the state would send a trooper over to the island for support but 'Tibbs' was the man. Several times he went out of his way to help avoid possibly uncomfortable situations with my campers.

One year I had a new junior counselor who looked more like twelve than a sixteen-year-old with a valid driver's license. Mid-morning the boy drove the camp truck downstreet to pick up the mail while the rest of us were at the quarry. Tibbs spotted him and really couldn't believe that he was old enough to be driving but knew the camp and knew me so he did nothing. A day or two later he stopped me on the street and said he hadn't wanted to embarrass the kid and even though he was pretty sure it was okay, still wanted to confirm with me that he was really legal to drive.

Another summer two second-year boys asked to spend a night camping out at the quarry. The quarry property was only a short walk to town. I was cautiously optimistic and hoped I could trust them to be on their own.

However, they did stray, went downstreet and managed to find someone to buy them some beer. About 2:00 a.m. Tibbs found them asleep in the doorway of the hardware store on Main St. The state trooper was on the island. To avoid him and avoid the boys being found in such a public spot in the morning, Tibbs picked each boy up and carefully deposited them, still sound asleep, in the cab of the local fuel delivery truck parked in the Vinalhaven Fuel Co.'s lot across the street.

The next day the boys met us at the quarry acting as if nothing had happened. They didn't know that Tibbs had already called me at camp. When we got back to camp after our swim the culprits were quite surprised to see me grab the camp paddle and invite them to come with me to the shed. When they knew that I knew, they weren't too surprised by what happened next.

Rules (again)

Real discipline pays off. One day we were at the quarry when the fire whistle went off. I was only slightly curious when an engine or two went up towards the north end of the Island, but I remembered that for fire protection at camp we had borrowed three 'Indian pumps' from the Fire Dept. I also had a faint underlying worry that it might be us, so I decided to cut short our swim and at least collect the pumps in case they were needed.

As we headed toward camp we saw considerable smoke and a Coast Guard helicopter swooped by, heading to Calderwood's Neck. I knew it wasn't us, but I also knew about the danger of fire on the island and we went quickly, collected the pumps, our two chainsaws with spare gas cans, extra clothes for the kids and some blankets just in case.

When we approached the fire, the State Fire Marshal, freshly on the scene by helicopter, stopped us and quite definitely told me to take my kids, turn around and go away. Then Dick Ely, the Vinalhaven Fire Chief came over and quietly and matter-of-factly said, "Brad, take your truck up and park it next to pumper #2. Take three of your boys and the chainsaw to the end of hose line three and start cutting a fire line, you'll find Louie up there cutting already. The other boys should stay near the truck and we'll find things for them to do". The State Marshal had a puzzled look on his face, like he really wanted to say something but could say nothing; Dick was in charge. As the fire whirled around us, Louie and I spent the next sixteen hours cutting trees as fast as we could. Dodging the fire, the three boys with me took turns lugging gas and oil for the saws, and bringing occasional coffee and sandwiches for us.

The other kids' primary assignment was to keep the hoses wet so they wouldn't burn through and shut down. A few boys patrolled with two-way radios and directed the Indian tank bearers to hot spots along the hose lines. The kids all took turns directing, lugging the Indian tanks, cooling off the hoses, catching a few winks, and after a sandwich and hot chocolate provided by the wives of the volunteer fire department, they would go at it again. The Indian tanks were filled and refilled and lugged away again and again.

One small boy fell down with a full tank strapped on his back and couldn't get up. It was too heavy. He was like a turtle on its back, limbs flailing in the air, helpless. He was relieved of lugging duties and delegated a permanent 'radio man'. Another had fallen asleep leaning against a stump. Dick Ely handed him a two-way radio and told him his mother was on the phone. He was so sleepy that he answered, "Hello Mom?" This got more than a few laughs.

After thirty-six hours the fire was finally controlled and Dick told me we could go home. We headed back to camp, totally exhausted. A huddle formed around the shower as everybody helped everybody scrub everybody down. We were all filthy, crusted with layers of soot and black sludge and all much too tired to eat. I don't remember when we woke up.

A few days later, Dick called and asked me to bring a list of the kid's names around to the fire station. In a few weeks he called again and asked me to bring the kids down. He presented them all with checks from the State for fire fighting. "They all did a man's work and deserve the standard pay!"

It was quite a lot of money, $2 per kid per hour for the thirty-six hours we were on duty! The kids unanimously agreed to give it all to the Fire Department to buy more Indian pumps, which we continued to borrow. Dick overcame the Fire Marshal's objections explaining, "Brad's boys are a trained crew. They'll do what they're told and we need them." The camp's reputation was well known.

Another example of the importance of real discipline working was a situation with a heart attack victim. A few years after acquiring the *Dirigo* to be our camp boat we were coming home late from an expedition. It was dark and foggy. Most of the kids had already headed up to camp so I took the three who happened to be helping me put the *Dirigo* on the mooring, yelled to the staff on shore to explain what we were doing and took off heading to where we thought the person was, on a small sailboat anchored in Perry's Creek. On the way we discussed plans with the Coast Guard by radio. We found the victim through the fog, got him on board and since I was needed to assist him, I simply directed and the kids brought the boat back out to the Thoroughfare, through the fog in the dark by RADAR, to a rendezvous with the Coast Guard. The kids already knew how to do all of it. Camp was in its sixth week and I knew they would follow my directions instantly and exactly. The Coast Guard guys couldn't believe it when twelve-year-old Rick Cash, standing on a stepladder so he could see out the window, deftly landed our 43-foot *Dirigo* alongside their forty-footer. We had saved a precious couple of hours and the man survived. This kind of thing would not have been possible with a 'gang of kids,' but with a trained crew we could and did do almost anything.

Ever since my first skinny swimming experience with my father and his boss, J.V.N. Dorr, in the river at The Dorr Company Mill in Westport, it always seemed totally natural to me. Whenever practical I shed mine and just feel more comfortable. I wasn't brought up to have any special feelings about it.

Often, when sailing with my parents, mother at the helm, Pops and I would strip and swim off the boat. Before I started the camp I really didn't have any thoughts about it one way or another. But what became the camp policy of nude swimming and the nude scramble around the field had definite antecedents. I had been appalled during Boot Camp to witness a 'GI shower' inflicted on a young guy about my age. For some reason, he had never had to take his clothes off in front of other people. He couldn't deal with the zero-privacy, group nudity of the Army showers, so he didn't shower! After a week of not taking a shower he got pretty raunchy. I watched as a group of guys that had the misfortune to bunk near him dragged him into the shower, roughly stripped him naked, and held him down by his arms and legs spread-eagled on the shower room floor. They poured liquid lye soap on him and scrubbed him down with the stiff brush used to clean the toilets. When they finished his backside they flipped him over and did his front. In obvious pain he screamed and pleaded and twisted and turned but they held him tight and they scrubbed and scrubbed. From head to toe he looked like a cat had clawed him. He was first in the shower from then on; I saw the scratches for weeks. Thinking about that, I decided that no kid should have to face something like that. No kid should be ashamed of his body so I insisted that they go without clothes whenever practical. I did it. The staff and all the old campers were completely comfortable with it, and soon the kids all did it naturally, without shame, at an age when boys are most self conscious about their less than equal and less than perfect bodies.

Another reason was that some campers could afford $60 designer bathing suits while other scholarship kids had only ragged underwear for swimming. Naked, they all were the same. Naked in the cold shower they all yelled just the same and all shriveled proportionately. It gave the staff and me ongoing inspection opportunities. We could be sure of clean healthy bodies. The nude run and cold shower were mandatory for everybody, everyday, staff, myself included, everyday except Sunday... but we all ended up doing it for fun on Sundays, too. It just made us feel good. We all turned brown, or in some cases browner, and everybody stayed very healthy.

I allowed no bullying or 'ganging up'. The law was in my hands and I was careful never to allow it to change hands. I had read *Lord of the Flies* and seen the movie. In the Army I had also witnessed a 'blanket party', an appalling situation where justifiably angry guys took the law into their own hands. During Basic Training there was a guy, admittedly a pain in the ass, who was sloppy and constantly doing things that got the rest of us extra duty. He'd leave scuffmarks on the floor by his bunk and this resulted in 3 a.m. wake-up calls for all of us. The drill sergeant would yell at us, "Hit the floor! All I want to see is elbows and ass-holes!" This meant down on our hands and knees. Then in the freezing cold, wearing only jocks or Army issue boxer shorts or nothing at all, we had to scrub the whole damned floor with our toothbrushes. We were cold, we were tired and it happened more than once, caused by the same guy. One night after 'lights out', four of the biggest guys grabbed the four corners of a blanket and held it over his bunk, completely pinning him down under it. The drill was for the rest of us to stand around the bunk and pound the hell out of the blanket with our fists. I must admit I joined in, hit the blanket, but not too hard and in the area of where I hoped his legs were and mostly just pounded the mattress. The beating finally stopped, people returned to their bunks and the four big guys, on cue, let go the blanket and quickly returned to their bunks. There was only quiet moaning from under the blanket. The beating was severe. The next morning his face was a mess, and he had raw bruises everywhere; no part of him had been spared. He managed to half drag himself into the shower. Some of the guys laughed at him and snapped him with their towels. I couldn't look him in the eye. I wanted to tell him it wasn't me. "I was the guy who barely hit your leg." I wanted to say, "I didn't hurt you. I would have protected you but I would have gotten the same if I had tried. I had to go along." In spite of what he had caused I felt sorry for him. It certainly didn't need to go that far. It was near the end of Basic. I had already decided that I would do all I could, without going to jail, to get out of the Army. I never did speak to the guy. He avoided us and we, him. What had I been a part of?

I told the kids both of these Army stories and explained all of it to the kids. I wanted to be sure they never participated in anything like that, so I kept a close watch.

The first few years of camp the older second and third-year campers initiated the new ones during the rowing trials by dumping them in the cold water off the float. This was fine and fun. The new ones got a first hand feel of how cold the water really is and were officially baptized into the camp at the same time. Then one year we had a few rather large and strong first-year campers who decided they didn't particularly want to get thrown in the water. It quickly could have turned ugly, and I stopped it before it began. I had already devised a new initiation and had planned to implement it that summer. It proved very effective and satisfied all the old crew.

We'd load everyone onto the *Dirigo* and with our 4 dories in tow, head out past Hurricane Island to the open bay where the water is even colder. I'd get the boat going full speed and we'd throw a life jacket overboard. Someone would yell, "Man overboard!" and with a stopwatch timing us, we'd stop engine, close haul the dories, rudder hard to port, then, full throttle, make a sharp turn, come around, stop and retrieve the life jacket. It took about a minute, plus or minus a second or two, to complete this maneuver. I would explain that if a boy fell overboard, under these perfect conditions he'd be in the water about that long. Then, to really drive home the point, the new campers had to strip and go overboard for the same length of time it took us to make the 'rescue'. They could have a life jacket if they wanted but most were strong swimmers and declined. They were to tread water and stay near the boat but some would always ask if they could swim around the boat instead. "Sure," I'd say. "No problem, go for it." With an old camper spotting each one, some more bravely than others, they went over the side. What they didn't know was by the time the water reached their crotches they'd stop breathing and their balls would disappear somewhere into their chest cavity. The brave 'round-the-boat' swimmers rarely took more than two strokes and even the life-jacketed ones held on tight to their spotters. There was always a fair amount of pleading but they had to stick it out. As their time was up they were hauled onboard, surrounded by dry towels and given mugs of hot chocolate and warming congratulations from the others. Harsh? Perhaps, but it cemented the relationship with the old campers; no ganging up, no one ever got hurt. They were never in any danger, and a very important lesson was learned: the cold water is no joke; it just plain hurts after thirty seconds. I'd only have to explain once about no roughhousing on the boat. "At night", I'd tell them, "in the fog, it might take five minutes to find you, or longer. Do you understand?" They all understood.

I also didn't tolerate kids ragging at each other. Sometimes two kids (several times brothers) just couldn't get along and would be at each other all the time. "You did!" "I did not!" After a few warnings, I'd give them an ultimatum. "There are three ways to solve this," I'd tell them. "First, you can go out in a boat for a while, spend some time together, talk this out and end it. That's by far the best way." "If you can't do it that way, maybe you need to fight it out. Okay? That can be arranged. No audience, no one taking sides, no one cheering anybody on, just us. We three will go out to the field, you'll strip down; no point in ruining clothes, and you can have a fight. I'll referee so no one gets seriously hurt, but you can fight 'til one of you quits. I won't tell anybody who quit or who won; that's up to you. That's a second way." "If that doesn't work there is a third way I know will work. I'll take you down to the shed and paddle both of you, and keep paddling you 'til you both promise to stop. Guaranteed, one way or another, your bickering is going to stop!"

This all said, most arguments were settled without violence. I did referee a few fights: free form wrestling, slapping, even titty-twisters were allowed; no hair pulling, no spitting and no closed fists. Not much got hurt except sometimes pride, and the combatants ended up showering together, washing the mud and tears out of their ears and admiring their shared marks of battle. "Gotcha a good one there, didn't I?" "Yea, but look where I got you!"

It didn't matter who won anymore, they were friends. The problem was resolved. Harsh? Perhaps, but it worked every time. It never got to the third stage.

Indian Attack and A-Frame

"Tired of being wet? Let's build a building!"

1967 was one of the wettest summers in history and not just the camp's history! The ferry had to use radar sixty-three out of the seventy days we were there. The mosquitoes were monstrous in size and numbers. The constant fog, rain, drizzle, and more fog, combined with warm temperatures, was perfect for them and destroyed everything for us. A freshly opened box of Corn Flakes became a soggy mess by noon. The old stones of the farmhouse foundation were slimy wet with large slugs appearing everywhere. Clothes and particularly socks and sneakers never got dry. Sleeping bags got mildewed as if not already nasty enough; damp and dampness prevailed, everywhere. The school bus provided our only dry space. It had a floor furnace that would dry things out, but it would quickly become a sauna.

We were running two five-week sessions that year, and the first group never saw the mainland. I was hard-pressed to convince them we really were on an island at all. Before camp we had considered, though not too seriously, taking the whole crew in the bus to Montreal for Expo '67. After the first two miserable weeks the decision was easy. Hasty phone calls were made to get parents' permission, and it took less than a day to get ready and hit the road. With everything packed, we spent the night all crammed in the bus in the parking lot downtown to be assured of a spot on the first ferry. Early morning one of the kids strolled out the door, half asleep and naked, heading for the outhouse before realizing it was very public downstreet at the ferry landing and not isolated and private like at the camp. Expo was exciting and a vacation of sorts for John Howard and myself. (John learned to row at camp and went on to a career in the Navy. After first being XO, he was then skipper of an LST with a crew of two hundred. Now retired, his last duty assignment was Base Commander at Little Creek.)

While the kids enjoyed the Expo safely on their own, John and I enjoyed a beer, feeling only moderately negligent and guilty. We were inspired by all the interesting designs surrounding us, started planning and sketching a shelter that would utilize the foundation and would be something that we could build with the kids. We had brought measurements since this was not a completely new idea. The terrible weather had hastened the deterioration of the old Army tents. A careless finger could puncture a hole through the canvas. This had prompted talks with my parents and the Camp's board about the need of a permanent structure. We decided the simplest would be an A-frame.

We camped three nights on an Indian reservation just across the bridge to Montreal, parked the bus and set up two small tents along the St. Lawrence Seaway where we could dash into the water and not be too obvious to the passing supertankers. We were on a small man-made island connected to the shore only by a one-lane concrete bridge.

The Indian kids we met, some riding horses, were friendly and really intrigued by a school bus with beds and a kitchen! We gave them a tour of the bus and gave them hot chocolate, which was also amazing for them, and on our last day we brought about six of them with us to see the Expo. We definitely made some friends. We were all anxious to get started with our building project and hurried home. We had shared the plans with the kids, and they couldn't wait. Everybody was busy drawing their own plans, and John and I built it a dozen times in our heads.

John Moore, an architect, friend and camp parent advised us about correct dimensions for lumber needed to span twenty-four feet. We had wanted a steeper roof. Passmore Lumber could get some 2x8s a bit shorter than we wanted, but could get them now. We settled for the flatter pitch.

We ordered the lumber and spent the day Thursday shoring up the foundation walls and adding nearly level and parallel concrete sills on opposite sides of the hole. While this masonry was setting up, on Friday, we went with my parents' two boats, the ANNA W and the WINNIE M, to Camden and loaded up our lumber: sills, frames, tongue and groove sheathing and roofing paper enough to cover a 24x28 foot building. The sterns of both boats were nearly awash, and the bilge pumps ran constantly. I figured if we lost the load almost all if it would float anyway. We made it back by mid-afternoon and started work. Even before the boats were completely unloaded we had made one of the A-frames to use as a pattern. Subsequent frames were laid out on top, measured and cut and bolted together. As soon as three or four frames were assembled, the whole crew gathered. Using ropes and long poles, lots of hands and straining bodies and tremendous excitement, we hoisted them and held them in place along the sill. Tongue and groove sheathing was next, put on diagonally to triangulate and support the frames. It started taking shape very quickly and seemed much bigger than we expected.

The crews constructing the frames were learning new tricks from each frame they completed and started getting them out faster. Within minutes of getting one frame placed and secured the final bolts would be tightened down on the next one, and it would be ready. Before the frames were halfway done the roofing crew had the sheathing done all the way to the top at one end. The building grew as if someone with a brush was painting it by numbers. We worked furiously.

Eddy McCormac, an old friend, was attending culinary college and had his summers free. He had a summer job cooking for my parents at the Big House and was our culinary advisor. He taught us how to buy supplies economically and cook healthy food for our large hungry group. (We learned that the portion sizes on labels mean nothing when feeding kids.) During the entire construction period he provided wonderful continuous soup and sandwiches.

I'd see a kid hammering away. Then he'd disappear, to return in a while with a sandwich in one hand, hammer in the other and go at it again. We worked all night. The truck headlights and two Coleman lanterns gave us just enough light. People would drop out and catch some sleep and come back.

Charlie Allen, half hanging over the sheathing he was nailing, fell asleep with the hammer in his hand. A roofer would call down to someone with a saw for a certain length of sheathing. The sawing would start and then another call for more staples for the roofing paper. All night Friday the sound of voices, laughter, shouts of encouragement, hammers banging, saws rasping, and staple guns clicking filled the air.

We worked all day Saturday and by nightfall all the frames were in place. Everybody became 'roofers' and the remaining sheathing went up very fast. A layer of heavy roofing paper went over the sheathing and some building plastic was stapled to cover the ends of the 'A'. Sunday morning we moved our kitchen and food supplies in from the old ell through the new mosquito-net door.

By suppertime Sunday we were inside, with my parents as guests, eating lobster. That night the cross beams were covered with plywood and the kids all slept in the newly created and dry sleeping loft. We kept the original construction ladder for going up and put in a fireman's pole for coming down. We were under cover and bug-proof and had done it in three days! The stove kept it dry.

Our trip to Expo with the second group was uneventful until our last night at the reservation. We had camped in the same spot. One of our horseback riders had fallen off his horse and broken his arm. We took him to the Expo a second time along with several new friends. We came back to our campsite late after a full last day and dropped off our young friends with sad goodbyes. The bus had a 6x10 box on the roof that held all the sleeping bags and tents when we traveled. The three kids whose turn it was to sleep up on the roof rack would dispatch sleeping bags and the two small tents for the others. The tents were erected and the kids turned in quickly, tired from a full day.

I was about to climb into my bunk in the bus when a car pulled up. It was a small English car, probably a Hillman. Four people got out and started yelling about what were we doing here. "This is Indian land, white man no welcome here."

It sounded like a script of a really bad movie. I pulled on some shorts and sneakers and went outside. There were two Indian boys and a girl and a white boy, probably in their early twenties, all drunk; the three boys very drunk. I only tried for a moment to explain that we'd been here before and realized talking was futile. Out of curiosity some of my kids had come out of their tents and one of them came over to me and quietly reported that he'd seen a gun in the back of the car. Without raising my voice, and praying that my crew had learned well their lessons about immediate obedience, I quietly told him to tell the kids to all grab their stuff and get on the bus NOW.

Within seconds the tents were down and thrown topsides to the three boys still up there. The boys, dragging unfolded sleeping bags piled quickly into the bus; John started the engine. The drunkest of the group then lurched at me, and I was able to step aside and push him face down on the ground with my full weight on top of him, and I yelled to his buddies that I'd break his neck if any of them moved. They took me seriously, particularly the girl who seemed to be trying to calm the situation. The guy under me was groaning but not much more, I let go and dashed to the bus and John started driving away.

After picking up their buddy, our four friends got in their car and took off towards the bridge. I took over driving from John, made a U-turn, and waited to pick up a straggler who had been taking a pee. The kids quickly secured the stuff on the roof rack and scrambled back in the bus. The gun thing really worried me, so I got the kids to put all the bedding across the back door of the bus and lie on the floor.

Our friends had parked the Hillman in the middle of the bridge and one of the drunken Indian guys got out, picked up a beer bottle, broke it off and headed towards the bus door with the neck in his hand. Our bus door was pretty secure but this was getting nasty fast. I leaned out my side window and told the girl, who was driving, to move the car now, or I'd push it off the bridge. I put the bus in 'low-low' and started inching it ahead. She was the least drunk and I guess it was her car because she moved it out of the way. We squeezed passed it on the narrow bridge and took off as fast as we could.

Before we got out of the reservation they caught up to us. They followed us and tried a few times to pass, but I kept the rear of the bus swaying across the whole road; they finally gave up when we got out to the highway. We reported the incident to a Mounty we saw a few miles down the road. He said they (The Mounties) couldn't do anything, and we had been lucky. He told us about a Mounty who had gone there once to quell some sort of problem. They stripped his car of everything non-essential, so that it still would run, but no doors, no glass, no fenders etc. Then they stripped the Mounty and sent him on his way.

I didn't stop driving until we had crossed the boarder in Vermont. We decided we wouldn't even make hotel reservations 'til we got back into the States!

We stopped somewhere over the border in Vermont and found a spot to get off the road and try and sleep. Everybody was too wired to sleep much. We headed to Sugarbush the next day and Bill Rowgowski, owner of a great restaurant and great friend from my days at the Inn, gave us a deal on a gourmet barbeque dinner for the whole crew. We deserved it.

One summer there was a very serious boy who was always finding ways to hurt himself. He was constantly stepping on things, got his fingers stuck in the wringer of the old Maytag washing machine, etc. He was an absolutely sweet kid and very serious. He examined the paddle very carefully and was ultra cautious and diligent about following the rules.

One day he asked permission to go for a hike on the property across the road, by himself. I told him, " Sure," and that we'd toot the truck horn when it was quarry time. That was the signal to round everybody up for a swim. After a while we tooted, he returned, and we all went for a swim.

For several days afterwards I sensed he was being even more serious and quiet than usual. My counselors had noticed it, too, and we wondered if something was wrong. We decided that the following day I would simply ask him what was bothering him. The next morning, quite early, he brought me a cup of coffee and sat down on the edge of my bunk. None of this was unusual, but he seemed very nervous. After a short silence he volunteered: "Remember a few days ago I told you I was going to take a hike? Well, I didn't just take a hike............. I, I, I had….. an ejaculation!"

From the bunks above, stifled, explosive noises erupted from my two counselors and I nearly bit my tongue in two to keep from exploding myself. I gulped down a burning hot charge of coffee and scalded myself enough to react to my burned tongue and maintain some control. It took a long moment. Then, still partially choked, I explained that this was okay. He had not broken any camp rules. (His prime concern, I think). He had done something perfectly healthy and normal for a boy his age, I was glad he had told me, if he had any questions, etc., etc. I managed with great difficulty, I hope, to not hurt his feelings, but for the rest of the summer if any of the staff or I even went out the door someone would be bound to ask. "Where're ya going, t' take a hike?"

We had a loose rule about language. Generally I let it slide. I told the kids I'd really heard it all before in the Army. I was not impressed and only warned them about 'garbage mouth' being inappropriate at the Big House and Church suppers. We made no big deal about it, the novelty of this form of freedom of speech soon wore off and most of the time there was very little offensive language. If I thought the language was getting out of control and perhaps the boys were doing it unconsciously I'd declare it a 'Sunday,' which could fall on any day of the week.

The loose rule was that any word spoken that even sounded like something that would 'shock my grandmother' would earn the speaker an immediate swat on the bare behind with a special 'Sunday' paddle. Handmade by my brother Peter it had nice buns carved on one side and was flat on the other. It stung like crazy. Whoever was closest to the paddle could administer the swat and no one, myself included, was immune.

One morning I was still in bed drinking my coffee and about half the campers were sitting on my bunk talking, discussing plans. I had just declared it was Sunday, and the rule was in effect. Kevin Gillespie, a counselor that summer, was in his upper bunk and like a naked Tarzan, swung down on a rope suspended from the ceiling and whacked his toe on my bunk. "Ow/shit/fuck," he shouted. One of the boys grabbed the Sunday paddle and I said, "Kevin?" Grinning, he bent over and grabbed his ankles and the kid delivered a resounding swat. "Ow/shit/fuck," Kevin said again, still grinning he bent over again and another swat landed. "Ow/shit/fuck," he said again. He kept quiet after the third swat. The kids loved watching a counselor get whacked and everybody, including Kevin, was in hysterics.

Camp continued to flourish and develop as the years went by. The experiment with double sessions didn't work because it usually took almost five weeks to get the 'crew' working like a crew; then they went home. So after two summers we went back to a single session of seven weeks and limited it to sixteen campers, two junior counselors and one older boy with a driver's license as head counselor for a total of twenty people. I'd come up a week before, usually with one or two older campers and my staff members to get a few things organized. It was nice to have the water and gas hooked up and at least one boat in the water before all the rest of kids showed up.

The seven weeks seemed to go by very quickly and we started adding an eighth week at the end. The idea was to invite a few special younger campers, who were planning to return the next year, or older ones, who would either be next year's staff or would be moving on and wouldn't be back, to stay on the extra week. We always ended up with the whole crew!

For several summers we made an expedition out of going to the drive-in movie in Rockland by boat. It took about an hour and a half to get to a spot, off shore and closest to the drive-in, where we'd anchor, row ashore and then hike about two miles through the woods to the drive-in. We'd been there before with the camper bus, and I had made an arrangement with the manager; we sat in comfortable lawn chairs near the front and watched the movies. It was great!

They didn't start the movies 'til it got dark, usually after 9:00 p.m., so the show ended as late as 2:00 a.m. We'd pick our way back through the woods to our boat and get home in time for a sunrise snack and a marathon sleep.

One Sunday, about 8:00 a.m. after a drive-in movie expedition the night before, I was wakened by the persistent honking of a car horn at the end of the torturous camp driveway. We kept the road that way to deter casual entry by exploring tourists. It was fine for the camp truck and my Bronco, and if you knew exactly the right path, you could, without leaving vital parts on the rocks, navigate it in a Volkswagen. This morning the tactic had successfully stymied whoever was there, so they stayed in their car and honked instead. Bleary eyed, after almost no sleep, I pulled on some shorts and gingerly (I had misplaced my sneakers) picked my way down the driveway to investigate and found three Jehovah's Witnesses sitting in their car. A young man was driving and honking. He and the two young women immediately got out, surrounded me and started barraging me with doctrine and pamphlets.

They finally all took a breath at the same time allowing me to explain: first, we'd been up all night, second, this was boy's camp: I had sixteen kids in my charge, all with very diverse backgrounds and religious persuasions; I had Jewish kids and Catholic kids and a few I didn't know about. (I don't remember if we had our 'Buddha' then or what, if any religious group he aspired to). They finally left, leaving me with an armful of pamphlets, but they were not satisfied and returned the same time the following Sunday.

We had our run and showers and were just sitting down to a leisurely pancake breakfast when the horn started up again. This time I remembered my sneakers and at least was fortified with a mug of good coffee. Almost word-for-word it seemed, the previous conversation was repeated and they finally left again, satisfied I hoped.

The next Sunday, again right at breakfast time, they negotiated the rugged driveway and came right up to, almost into the A-frame, and sat in the car, honking the horn and peering in, only a few feet from the big window of the 'exec A', my staff's and my bedroom, and only yards away from the outside shower! Kids were wandering around inside and out, mostly with no clothes on, still drying off from their showers or starting to get their breakfasts. I saw uninvited strangers barging into my private living quarters; I was furious but didn't know what to do.

We did have a diverse group. Several of my campers were Riverdale students and two of them were black kids from the city; very bright eighth graders, great kids, big boys, second-year campers, both with an irrepressible sense of humor. I casually suggested to them, "Why not go and see what they want?"

They immediately took the situation in hand. As we watched, these two quite tall, very black and very naked young men, strolled nonchalantly outside to say "hello". Our visitors, for some reason, didn't stay very long to talk. The boys candidly stood and watched as the car quickly turned around and sped down the drive, leaving most of its exhaust system behind. When the boys came back they were doubled over with laughter as we all were. Through their laughter they said they wished they'd known ahead so they could paint their bodies with some flour and put some sticks in their hair and find a spear or two. It was funny, but I felt a bit sorry for our visitors. I explained to the kids they were doing their thing as they saw it. I didn't subscribe to any discrimination, but this invasion of privacy was too much for me and the consequences proved too much for them. We were never visited again.

The big fireplace provided a good place to dry towels or clothes after doing laundry. Often, some of the boys would leave their clothes/towels hanging long after they were dry, so I came up with another casual rule, more a plan I was sure would be effective. If something was left abandoned for a day or two it would be picked up and put in a big box under my bunk. To get it back the owner had to give a staff member or me a backrub, the duration loosely depended on the item. One day, after about a week of collecting, it was quarry time. I honked the horn and kids collected to the back of the truck. Two boys emerged from the A-frame stark naked, without a stitch. Everything they owned was under my bunk. After our swim, they had to sit in the cab in borrowed towels while we went downstreet shopping, and there were marathon backrubs that night. I thought my scheme would fix everything but for these boys my brilliant plan didn't work at all. Within a week the same scene happened again, and one of them is still that way to this day. Summers and campers came and went. Many returned for several years in a row and some became counselors, but the basic philosophy remained pretty much the same and I stand by it.

Today The Island Camp wouldn't stand a chance—we'd be shut down in an instant. We rarely started a day wearing clothes. After the shower, clothes would be added only when needed as the day's activities unfolded. It became completely natural for the boys to be without clothes and had no shock factor except for some outsiders. Some of the funniest situations arose when outsiders strayed into our domain. Another story comes to mind.

We had cleared the right of way to the quarry and done minor repairs to the road in. I placed a discreet No Parking sign in the center of the small turn-around at the end of the road nearest the quarry. Without too much jockeying around I could turn the truck around and park it there. I liked having the truck nearby and easily accessible and headed the right way in case someone got hurt and, after all, it was private property. When we arrived my turn around and parking space was blocked by a large gray Mercedes with Massachusetts plates, parked exactly under my sign. I couldn't turn around and we all went in to investigate. Sitting on the rocks were two quite old ladies with white going purple, frilly hair, wearing black, frilly bathing suits that covered them completely. Only their heads, hands and feet were sticking out.

Within seconds they were surrounded by twenty young, naked teenagers. I must admit some of the boys performed inverted cannon-ball/moon-shots that added to the already considerable shock factor and with short inhalations of surprise the ladies scooted across the ledge to their car and left us at top speed, never to be seen again.

Peter Jakobson was an organizer; a Riverdale kid, and first year camper whose voice had not yet started to change. The first day at camp he sat at my desk and organized everything, balanced the checkbook, sorted the bills and even wrote out a few checks for me to sign. I immediately authorized his signature at the bank and put him in charge of all the camp finances. A day or so later he called Rockland Produce and started rattling off our order for about $1,500 worth of groceries to be picked up that afternoon at the public landing in Rockland. At some point the guy taking the order stopped him and asked, "Is your mommy there?"

Our home-designed, homemade septic system worked flawlessly for years but never would have met any current codes. Our do-it-your--self kitchen fed 20 people, 3 meals a day, for 10 weeks for 25 years. That's 105,000 meals, not counting the large parties with invited guests.

No one ever got sick from the food, but I'm sure the water temperature and dishwashing procedure wouldn't pass any current codes. We didn't have a nurse or a rest period after lunch. We used child labor: children preparing meals, children doing the wash and building shelters. Children driving tractors to cut the fields and using chain saws and navigating boats at night in the fog with RADAR. And, and, and, staying up all night to watch a moon landing on television! And, my God! They run around naked and swim naked and leap off cliffs naked and get sunburned bottoms. Sometimes they swim at night and in the rain, and they get a paddling if they break the rules. "Child abuse, child abuse!" I can hear it. The successfulness and value of this abuse was proven by the return rate of campers coming back for more, year after year. We were very careful and probably lucky. The boys sustained only the usual minor cuts and scrapes, a few stitches and only a very few more serious injuries, quickly handled by Dr. Earl at the sophisticated medical center he pioneered. (His official visits to camp

Winter camping at Spring Vacation.

Completed A-Frame.

Ropes course, Island Camp style.

for supper each summer were a high point for the kids.)

The country was fast developing a crazy 'sue everybody' attitude. My board of directors finally felt we had to have some basic liability insurance for the camp; the liability policy on my pick-up truck was not enough. Signed waivers we had from the parents would only be flags, not a real deterrent. Even though it would have to be proved in court that I, or my staff, had been negligent, it was not enough. The staggering cost of this insurance was a prime factor in closing the Camp down. The constant financial crunch was another factor. We didn't charge enough. We felt we couldn't ask parents to spend what other summer camps charged and expect the kids to have cold showers and do everything for themselves and work their asses off all summer. We had no daily swimming or sailing or tennis classes, no art or archery. We didn't offer riflery or basketweaving; underwater or dry. We didn't spend much time sitting around the campfire singing folk songs, and there were no socials with a sister camp. Our facilities were primitive to say the least.

My parents always welcomed the campers and opened the Big House to us as a rainy day refuge. Kids could, and did, ask to come up alone or in small groups to read a book quietly, to have a moment away from camp. My mother was always ready to greet them and loved to talk with them in any formation. A few used the piano and one summer two boys volunteered themselves as models for an artists' retreat group.

After my father died my mother looked for ways to put the Big House to use and hopefully defray the mounting costs of upkeep. She opened the house for a series of summer workshops, organized by an old family friend, Polly Brown. The famous humorist Marshall Dodge, of *Bert & I*, conducted a weeklong serious philosophy workshop, but not so serious as to exclude some stories. The kids were invited. Marshall was at his best.

There were other workshops scheduled too. Dr. James Gillespie, the psychologist, camp board member, and father of two campers who both became counselors, gave a career seminar for a week.

Polly Brown did her own week-long drawing clinic for six or seven serious artists and one day invited me to play my clarinet while they worked. I could comfortably leave my staff in charge at camp and take an hour off. The exercise for Polly's class was for the students to draw quickly what they saw for about a minute or two. Annie, the daughter of my boss from Riverdale, Dr. Gronningsater, served as housekeeper at the Big House for the summer and was of course a quarry regular, tan and healthy. Her older brother Arne was now head counselor and Kenny, a younger brother was a camper. When Polly asked her, she had no problem posing nude for the class. She'd sit on the floor in a relaxed, comfortable pose and I'd study her and play improvisationally on my clarinet, off the top of my head, concentrating on what I saw in the pose. Polly would say, "change". I'd stop playing, Annie would change her pose, the artists would turn to a clean page and start again and I'd try and find something different to play as the artists scratched furiously with their charcoal sticks. Soon two campers looking for me appeared and watched for only a moment before peeling off their clothes and joining Annie on the living room floor for a series of relaxed and beautiful poses. (This activity would not fly at 'Camp Tou-Tou-in-the-Pines,' Summer Camp for Adolescent Boys.)

The night of the moon landing we were invited to the house for a fish chowder supper after which we all spread out our sleeping bags in the attic. As the event unfolded, we watched it all night, on a tiny black and white TV set that offered a slightly wintry looking picture of history in the making.

My parent's support was immeasurable and made the very existence of the camp possible. They bought the *Dirigo* and gave me the Hopkins Farm land and funded the materials for the A-frame and finally made the purchase of the quarry possible. But we were too big to be funded by family alone and too small for big contributors.

Tom Watson of IBM gave us $1000 one year, which was great. We really needed $10,000, too much to ask from him and too little for IBM to bother with. I was slowly going under each year. I never got a salary and figure it cost me about $3,000 a year out of pocket to keep it going.

On paper things looked okay only if everybody was a paying customer, but some years more than half the kids were on scholarship.

The construction of the A-frame and the purchase of the Quarry property were two paramount events that dramatically played in the formation of the camp, especially affecting the scope of our activities. The purchase of the *Dirigo* was the third. My father had expressed interest and agreed with my idea to have a camp-owned boat. Our tax-exempt status was secure and the expenses for a vessel could be legitimately covered. We spent part of a summer searching and at one point, found, a dream for both of us, the schooner *Surprise*. She was

With Coot (Brian Eaton)... Downstreet. Vinalhaven.

A rainy day at the Big House. Fred Garbo
with Alex Terry (below) and with Eddie
McCormac, Jr. (right)

Brother Peter
with campers
launching the
new float.

without masts on a mooring in Camden when we went aboard. She was perfect. Lots of headroom, bunk space for countless kids in sleeping bags, sturdy, not fancy, very seaworthy and manageable with a small crew. That was the problem. That summer I had an older and seasoned crew and we could have managed sailing it very well. But the turnover at camp was such that I couldn't always be sure I'd have a ready crew right away. I couldn't handle the boat alone, which also meant my father would have to rely on either my being there or having someone around to sail it with him. We agonized, and when the reality of the cost of maintenance hit us we reluctantly gave up our dream.

While in Camden the agent who had showed us the *Surprise* suggested we look at the *Dirigo*, also for sale at a very attractive price. I was expecting, from the price, something pretty scruffy and we were amazed when we went aboard. Granted, an old boat, it was sparkling clean and completely ready to go, Coast Guard licensed and approved for forty passengers. (I qualified for my U. S. Coast Guard Captain's License the following year.) The hull weighed fourteen tons, before adding the GMC 471 diesel, 500 gallons of fuel and 150 of water. Massive is the best description. We didn't spend much time deciding and had her at our mooring before the end of the summer. I got enough time to feel very secure with the boat and we arranged to take it to Five Mile River in Darien, Connecticut, to winter at Jenkin's Boat Yard. The owner's son, JJ (John Jenkins) was a camper. We bartered boat storage for camp tuition.

The start of the trip down was uneventful. We relied on John Howard's surgical navigation skills and had no problem finding our way. We did look like a big lobster boat and a little out of place in Rockport, Mass., where we stopped to top off the fuel tanks. We pulled into a dock displaying a large Mobil sign and were summarily told we didn't belong and couldn't buy fuel there. While I argued to no avail, Sandra, my very large and faithful German Shepherd, went ashore and left a mountainous deposit, which she'd been holding for hours, on the little island directly between the two gas pumps. Someone on the way back from a candy run reported it to me and we departed quickly, leaving the deposit as a way of saying thanks and bought our fuel at the fish wharf across the harbor. We decided we didn't like Rockport. We continued through the canal and encountered really rough seas at that end of the sound. We had planned to run all night and get home early the next day, but the weather got worse. John's navigation was frighteningly accurate. At one point, now in the dark and a driving rain, he informed me we should be right about at a buoy marker. I switched on the searchlight and there it was about a hundred feet dead ahead of us. Without the light I couldn't see it at all and might have easily smashed into it. I asked John to put us a boat length to port or to starboard, *please* not dead on! In spite of the pounding we were getting we felt we were in no danger. The automatic bilge pump came on no more frequently than usual; Eddie McCormack was readying lasagna, but we decided we were just tired of bouncing around and John plotted a course to take us in to New Haven, the closest harbor. I came to the new heading and in about ten minutes the storm just stopped.

We could see flashers and the lighthouse at New Haven and lights for 30 miles down the sound. In a few more minutes we saw lights on the shore of Long Island. We quickly decided to continue on to Darien; we could practically see it. I changed back to a slightly adjusted course and headed for a lighted buoy I could see. I had been at the helm during all the rough weather and asked Arne Gronningsater to take over for a while. I stayed with him for a few moments since we were heading directly into still very rough seas. We started going up and up on what seemed to be an endless wave. I grabbed the throttle and pulled down the rpms to an idle, and we kept going up. Fortunately we were nearly stopped when we started down, seemingly straight down, bow first. There was an unbelievable crash and shock, like being dropped on concrete. Dark blue water completely covered the entire pilothouse and poured into the afterdeck. Gallons of seawater with pressure like a fire hose came in through the forward cabin vent and completely soaked Eddy who somehow managed to keep the lasagna dry and upright. We sat in shock wondering if we were going to sink right there. The pump was running full tilt, and I headed us towards New Haven. There was a lot of water in the bilge but the pump handled it and overnight we slept, safely tied up to a big barge. I heard the pump come on twice... about normal! The rest of the trip was uneventful although rough seas made it a bit slow, and we were tired and glad to be on solid ground when we finally got to Five Mile River and the Jenkin's Boat Yard.   Riverdale started almost immediately, and I think I can safely say I'm the only one who ever brought a load of kids to a Riverdale football game by boat. I'm guessing it was around Thanksgiving because it took a few days. I rounded up some campers, mostly Riverdale kids, and brought the *Dirigo* down to New York for

The *Dirigo* and the *Winnie M.* with camp dorys.

The *Dirigo*

the schooner races, tallships, etc. We watched the spectacle of magnificent ships, got up pretty close and personal. Like in Rockport, our over-sized Maine lobsterboat, mixing with skyscrapers and fiberglass luxury yachts looked a bit strange here, too. We got lots of curious looks, but it all felt friendlier than Rockport.

Midday we headed up the Hudson to a small marina just past Riverdale. Dr. G. made two trips in his VW van to get us all to the game. For the kids from Maine it was all amazing. The Riverdale kids went home after the game and a smaller crew spent the night on board and piloted the *Dirigo* back to Jenkin's the next day. We spent one more day getting the boat ready for winter storage, and then, back to school. No more 'yachting' for a while.

Back to the camp

I could chronicle story after story about the camp, perhaps I will in another book. In the years to come we enlarged the A-frame, with first an executive wing and then a kitchen wing. We replaced the portable outhouse with a two-hole flush system, complete with a 1000 gallon steel tank we towed home from Rockland behind the *Dirigo*. We spent the summer lugging truckloads of rocks for the leach field; it all worked beautifully.

I made some mistakes, but I still strongly believe in the whole concept of the camp. It was right and good. My idea was simply to teach the kids everything I could teach them, the best possible way, by hands-on experience. Everything, before they turned sixteen and started dealing with the responsibility of driving the family car. They all were so smart, knew so much and were so sophisticated, yet they hadn't experienced anything. They had only heard about being cold. They'd seen in the movies the sailor standing on the bridge of the destroyer peering through the fog, but they didn't know how scared, in real life, he really was. They told jokes I hadn't understood 'til I got to the Army, and yet they couldn't scramble an egg or boil water. One boy, trying to bake a cake, actually asked about the recipe, did he need a level, or a heaping tablespoon of water? Another kept stirring the spaghetti water so it wouldn't stick to the pot.

Aside from making sure everything was understood there was another reason for the lengthy interview with the kids and their parents. Before I accepted a kid I had to be convinced that the boy would benefit from camp and the camp would benefit from the boy.

We were a small group. The kids came from very diverse backgrounds and had to learn to work together. I needed a team. I recruited with that criteria in mind. The only other qualifications were that the boy really wanted to come, be at least eleven years old, and could swim. Discipline was essential—not at all to dominate, but to allow a freedom that would otherwise be impossible. There was no set plan. The kids planned the program as much as possible. I suggested things and vetoed plans that were really impractical or perhaps dangerous, weather was usually the deciding factor. The main focus however, was Do-it-Yourself. I wanted to teach kids how to *do* things.

I'm most proud of the fact that in twenty-five years I never turned anyone away because they couldn't pay. I just wish I could go back and give each kid one more hug. I miss the camp terribly. If there were a way, I'd do it all again in a heartbeat.

IN FOND MEMORY OF ISLAND CAMPERS:
'Doc' (Argo) Flemming *(Viet Nam)*
Jeff Edgeron *(After Viet Nam)*
Rob Keough *(Drunk driver)*

John 'Terry' Starbuck
Peter Thomas *(Hit and run)*
Jonathan Thomas *(Heart attack)*
Billy Roy *(Hit and run)*
Eddie Graf *(9/11)*
AND
neighborhood friends from N. Stamford,
John Shindow and Jackie Robinson Jr.

15

Diary: First Trip to Poland
(1991)

They went to no great expense to make me comfortable.
—Buddy DeFranco

The summer of 1990 I was still very much involved with the Maine Jazz Camp. At the last minute, one of the trombone teachers had a family emergency and sent as his replacement, Isi Rudink; a wonderful teacher—outgoing, friendly, very energetic and very funny. Everybody liked him immediately, especially the kids. I learned that he had been teaching in Poland and was bringing a group of his Polish students to the States later that summer. I didn't believe it when he said, "Polish Jr. High School kids playing Jazz! Brad, man, Brad, Brad, man, you gotta hear them, Brad!" Isi had arranged a U.S. tour for his Polish Youth Ensemble later in the summer.

In August I had a concert for IAJE in Long Island with John Basile near one of the venues Isi's kids would be playing and arranged to come and hear them. They were wonderful! I loved them all and made a promise to visit them in Poland the next year. A month or two later, with plans in the works to definitely visit Poland in the spring, I got a letter from Darek Zelek, the clarinet player in the group. It read:

> *Dear Bred,*
> *You will stay at my house.*
> *Darek*

Logical, since he was the clarinet player, and I took it to be an invitation. The Diary starts in April 1991.

A note to my friends in Poland:

A year ago I hardly knew where Poland was on a map, and I certainly never expected to travel there. Then, by chance, I met eight of the most wonderful kids, your kids from Krakow playing my music, jazz, in America. As a jazz musician and teacher I don't make much money, but I manage to do what I love. I have now seen much of your country. I have played with great Polish jazz musicians for wonderful audiences and have taught some of your wonderful kids. So, I offer my observations with respect and love and caring. I hope to return soon and stay longer.

Please take care of yourselves and your country. In America we sometimes really do good things. We have many regulations about smoking, stiff penalties for polluting the air and water and littering. Poland has been trampled on for generations, but now it's your country again, and you must take great pride in restoring it. Your country, its people and especially your kids are a great resource. In 35 years of teaching, I have never seen kids who are so eager to learn. The potential is enormous! I'm only one American, and a jazz musician at that, but you have my greatest respect and admiration.

Day One, April 6, 1991

The plane was almost full and left JFK nearly on time. I sat next to a nice lady who sells her artwork to galleries in New York City. She was interested in the Friends of Jazz and the duo for possibilities of a Yugoslavia tour. I will send her a tape and some PR things.

We arrived ahead of schedule in Belgrade. Customs was very interested in my blue bag, which weighs a ton! They offer free use of a sort of modified shopping cart all over the airport, which makes schlepping bags a cinch. Everybody seems to have a cigarette hanging out of their mouths at all times.

As part of the travel deal a bus, owned by the airline, took those who were flying on the next day to the Hotel Slavia. I checked into a comfortable small room in the obviously older section of the hotel. Lots of wood paneling, all very clean, but somewhat worn-looking; a comfortable bed and good meals. Lunch started with an automatic soup and piles of good bread. I wasn't offered a menu. A plate of some sort of goulash arrived as I finished my soup. Bottled water is shared between tables and people seemed to use that as an excuse to start a conversation. They were all milling around. At every table there were a few people standing or sitting backwards on a borrowed chair having animated discussions. Some would drift to another table and start again as if everybody knew everybody. Maybe they did.

After ice cream (the waiter did speak some English) I went up and took a quick hand-held shower, made quicker by running out of hot water. I headed out for about a five-hour walk. I saw a huge new domed church that was being built on the foundation of an earlier one, probably destroyed during World War II, a tremendous project. There is lots of construction in this city. Just half a block from the Hotel is what looked to be the Police Station, and the whole street shows signs of bullet holes and some fairly recent masonry repairs. As I wandered I saw more signs of war damage.

Every major street corner is dotted with little newsstands. In the glass display areas around the booths are toys and Barbie dolls right next to hard-core, graphic, show-all porn magazines whose covers left nothing to the imagination, all right out in the open. I can't figure out the money at all! I bought a cup of Turkish coffee for lunch and gave the waiter $2.00 American and got back 50,000 Yugoslav somethings, worth about 50 cents. Window shopping I saw a flat of eggs for 1.3 somethings, a pair of good-looking shoes for 150.20 somethings and a small pack of four Duracell AA batteries for 43.0 somethings.

Lots of people were out in the parks and streets, all very friendly. They usually make eye contact and smile and offer some sort of a greeting. Some older men tipped their hats, and kids, out in force with bikes and soccer balls, waved and smiled. It was a long walk.

Back for dinner, more soup, bread and some sort of beef stew. No success in finding jazz spots. A wake-up call for six tomorrow morning.

April 7

A comfortable night, but I woke up early. I checked out and had wonderful coffee with hot milk and fresh rolls. We loaded back on the bus at 6:30. I met a guy from Hungary, via California; he now lives in Santa Rosa. He escaped from Hungary in 1956 and now runs a machine shop. My flight left two hours ahead of schedule. I'm wondering how I'll connect with Isi... I guess I'll have to wait and see what happens.

This will only be believable to people who know Isi: it's the end-all airport story. I did arrive more than two hours early. Customs was not interested in me at all and, having not a clue where or how to reach anybody, I sat in a conspicuous place near the main entrance of the arrival building and put my feet up to wait. A least a dozen taxi drivers asked me if I was okay and were disbelieving when I said a friend would meet me. Just as I was having my own doubts, I heard my name over the PA system.

Isi, on the phone, told me to sit tight, he was on the way. I pushed my shopping cart of bags out past a long row of Mercedes taxis, and their disbelieving drivers, and again put my feet up to wait. Isi arrived in a taxi, which for clarity, I'll call Taxi #1. He bounded out with Darek, who I'll be staying with, Lucas and Bartek, all students of the Jazz Ensemble. During the next few moments of hugs, shouts and more hugs, Taxi #1 was paid off and sped away as we hugged and shouted some more. We then tried to find a way for the five of us plus my mountain of luggage to get back to the hotel. One of the taxi drivers who had offered to help me earlier said he could take all of us, so we piled into Taxi #2. And then horror struck.

Isi had left a small bag with all the cash, all the receipts from his tour—his wallet, passport, everything—under the seat of Taxi #1. Really a calamitous situation. We first raced around trying to find Taxi #1, then Darek, Bartak and I took off in Taxi #2 and checked out a few taxi stands near the airport while Isi and Lucas raced back and forth checking with the police and airport security. Taxi #1 was not a regular airport taxi. There was no trace of it, and Warsaw is a big city.

With a pall of real desperation, we headed toward the music academy (Freddy Chopin's no less), ate a rather dismal lunch, and then walked a long way to our hotel. I was hurting from carrying my really loaded bags, even with help. Bartek offered to take the blue one, but only lasted a few yards. After calls to the American Embassy and a few radio stations, Isi and Lucas took off to pay a huge amount (in excess of $100 for ten words) for a public-service-type radio spot. On the way, in the middle of downtown Warsaw, Lucas spotted Taxi #1, sprinted across six lanes of traffic, flagged it down, and discovered Isi's bag, untouched and intact, under the back seat.

I played a concert that night to a somewhat small but eager audience who presented me with two bouquets of flowers. A first for me! The kids are fantastic, all playing very well; I can't wait to show them more right notes! I presented them all with the Jazz T-shirts and gave Anna the flute from Encore. Lots of hugs and tears, a lot of them mine. (Encore was a non-profit organization I started. Based on New Eyes for the Needy, which had been founded by my grandmother Julia Terry, we collected used instruments and got them into the hands of needy kids.)

After the concert we found a deli that was mostly closed and out of bread. We went en masse from counter to counter trying to find anything we could take back to the Hotel and construct a meal. We ended up with monumental blocks of cheese and canned hams. We did finally find some bread and soda and fruit juice. We were all afflicted with the giggles. The deli people were glad for our business, but I suspect gladder to see us go. We got back to the Hotel at last to eat our dinner. I played "Take 6" for the kids who were still listening, bug-eyed, at 11:00 p.m. The kids really seemed to like the jazz T-shirts. They seemed to really like everything. Their English is still very limited, but they are also very shy about trying it. I think I can get them going in time.

Isi is asleep in the bed across the room, having nodded out in mid-sentence. From my room I can see the river and the train bridge. Trains are still running quietly at 12:00 midnight. How could I ask for anything better than this?

Day Three, April 8

We were up and at breakfast by 9:00 a.m. in the Hotel. I'm figuring out the money somewhat. 14,000 whatevers equals about $1.40, so a roll at 400 equals 4 cents. One cent for a piece of bread plus 20 cents for a cup of Turkish coffee. I found out the hard way that you must stir like crazy and then let 1/4 inch of sludge sink to the bottom. It's tasty and strong, and I liked it.

Then we were off to sightsee. We walked and bussed and walked some more to the Old City. I let our kids use the camcorder, which drew stares from all the other kids on the street. I felt somewhat self-conscious as the American with the fancy toy. Our crew all went into a church and were really intrigued by the art and sculpture. They also take their religion seriously. They would cross themselves and kneel at prayer for several minutes. We went through some crypts below and then wandered back toward more Old City, all reconstructed brick-by-brick after World War II.

Back to the hotel after a severe weather change; it suddenly got very cold and rainy. We grabbed our instruments and went to the Academy for lunch. Then I had an hour one-on-one with Derek, and Eva, who plays the oboe. Even without language, I managed to explain the cycle of fourths and then hung on while they whipped around twelve keys! I showed them some blues scales and just started the blues form when our hour was up.

Isi had planned meetings with some jazz big shots at the Jazz Society. We spent some time trying to write down and understand some of the Two Live Crew stuff to our Polish friend, Andrzej. I tried to explain that this was not what America was about! Isi went off to collect the kids and I went with a twenty-three-year-old trumpet player to tour around. Isi met us at the Jazz Club where we played after a spaghetti dinner of sorts. The kids really played well. My lecture on time seemed to work. A saxophone player, Zbigniew Namyslowski, who is number one in Poland, played wonderfully. He's a nice guy and will be in Krakow later. The kids all ended up in my room and were fascinated with my scale chart and more fascinated with the Yahama synth that looks like a funny sax. We ate some bread and cheese at 1:30 a.m. and now (2:30) to bed.

Wednesday, April 9, 1991

Up early and after a bread and coffee breakfast took a long walk to the train station. My bags, somewhat lighter, still left hickeys on my shoulders. The kids wore the Jazz T-shirts with great pride. The train to Krakow was fast, clean and smooth. We went from somewhat flat farmland to much more hilly terrain. Most of the kids took turns with the camcorder. It was hard for me not to keep it running most of the time. Poland is very beautiful!

We got to Krakow about noon and were met by several parents. The kids all said goodbye and disappeared. (In the morning all the kids stand up and shake your hand when they first greet you. They do that for each other, too. You don't sort of slide into the group. Hands are extended, and greetings are exchanged all around. Sort of starts things off on a pleasant note!) Darek's mom is a slightly shorter, slightly wider version of Darek. She met us and we walked several blocks to where she had parked her Mercedes four-door sedan—diesel, like the taxies. It must be a standard bottom line because there seem to be a lot of them around. We drove out to their home a few minutes (10) from the

Centrum. After a quick snack we returned to the Centrum and dropped off Isi. Darek took me on a tour of some castles and churches and all the music stores! I thought it must have been some special day because the streets were packed and the shops were all full. There is an extraordinary rebirth—awakening and excitement. I found out that all this activity is a normal everyday event!

We took the bus back to Darek's and met his sister, Angela, and his brother, Rafal. Angela was very quiet and domestic, doing all sorts of chores, cutting up vegetables into tiny pieces for a salad that was wonderful and hard to describe. I played the synth with Darek, and then he sight-read about five tunes from a Jamie Abersold album. He played one ballad, the first time through, with such passion and feeling that it made me cry; I have it on video.

We had dinner with very little conversation; no one speaks more than a few words of English. The TV set went on as soon as we sat down; a curious Western custom. Supper was soup, then cold cuts and bread and an egg salad with assorted veggies with a smooth-texture sauce. A new sensation! Cakes and coconut cookies followed with hot tea sweetened with grenadine syrup. I tried to help with cleaning up but it seems as if this is woman's work! My kitchen gifts seem to have been put away. I'll have to be sure Darek's mother understands that they are not special but should be used. I gave Wanda, Darek's mother, a tablecloth and some matching potholder mitts.

Isi showed up about 10:30 p.m. to outline plans for me for the next week. He was unable to get a visa for me to go to Russia with the kids. They were all cursing the Russians and their regulations. The kids stayed up late and insisted that I come and say good night to them. Isi brought a young seventeen-year-old trumpet player with him to meet me. His name was Mark Zibeski. His English was quite good. Earlier Darek and Rafal showed me their school English books, which in my opinion are deadly. They are as bad as any French One book I ever remember! Here is maybe a real opportunity; a good "English as a Second Language" program is needed here. Anyway, an elaborate plan involving my leaving at 7:00 tomorrow for Warsaw unfolded. After tucking the kids in and more talk and tape playing, I got to bed about midnight.

The house is hard to describe. I will get pictures of it. It's new and mostly finished. Darek's dad has been living and working in Chicago, sending all his money home. They are much better fixed than most, by my guess. The house has a large entryway next to a garage. All the doors and walls are quality woodwork throughout. There is intricate wood paneling and custom work on the stairs and ceilings. There is a small kitchen and bedroom with a bathroom with shower and a large living-dining room all on the second floor, with a balcony looking out over a fenced-in yard, and across the small street a railroad yard! There is all kinds of activity during the day. I'll get the camcorder going for sure. On the third floor are four more small bedrooms and a large bathroom and another long balcony across the front. My view of the railroad is spectacular!

Wanda woke me early and gave me Kava and some croissants with butter and jam plus rye bread and small cold cuts. I had packed the night before, so I was ready as she hustled me out of the house to the waiting Mercedes. She parked quite a ways from the station and then led me, practically running, to buy my ticket, and we got to the platform with a few minutes to spare. I never found out how much the ticket cost. Wanda insisted on paying. Maybe Isi made some sort of arrangement. I'll have to find out. The train left on the minute and arrived in Warsaw on the minute. It was smooth and very fast, I guess sixty-five mph at times. It was a typical European train with compartments and numbered seats.

At first I landed in the wrong compartment and someone immediately asked in English, "If may I please help you?" It was a young man, maybe a college student, who was very shy, but his English was pretty good. He explained where the seat numbers were on the compartments and on my ticket and directed me down to the next space. My compartment had a young married couple that took turns falling asleep on each other's shoulder, and two middle-aged businessmen. I'm not sure, but they were well dressed and were both reading identical newspapers but both glancing constantly at each other's paper. It was kind of a funny sight gag in real life!

There was an older man who looked like a working class peasant type with blue pants and a light coat. He had a few parcels and a small suitcase and a huge black trench coat. He was sitting in the corner and sort of disappearing into the folded trench coat. He dropped off into a sound sleep for the rest of the trip.

Wanda had warned me about thieves and muggers in the station at Warsaw. (I felt much less apprehensive than soloing in the New York subways!) I walked a few blocks and found my way back to the Jazz club where I sat in the sun feeling pretty foolish waiting for Henryk Majewski. He is the president of the Polish Jazz Society and will be my contact and guide for the next week.

Soon several musicians joined me outside the club (not yet open). We realized that we were all headed the same way. Several of them spoke English and were able to explain the plan somewhat. More people collected, including Henryk, who looks a bit like Al Hirt with hair, also a good mainstream trumpet player. The jazz critic, Andrzej Brodowski that Isi and I translated Two Live Crew with showed up, and I had a real English-speaking companion. He was great, answering questions about everything. The Polish rebirth is truly extraordinary! Visually the countryside still has an oppressive look. But the urgency, the excitement, the new openness is something that I could feel within twelve hours of being in the country, and it grew on me.

The bus ride was uneventful until about two-thirds of the way when the right front tire of the bus exploded! The split rim of the wheel went charging in different directions down the road. One went off to the right, the other crossed the road just missing on-coming traffic, and we sort of slid to a stop. The driver explained that it was a new tire with only 1,000 kilometers on it, but it sure was wasted! All the passengers got out of the bus and sat down on the side of a small hill off the road. I retrieved the rim from across the road and pitched in to help the driver change the tire, working up a sweat and getting pretty grimy. I hope I'm doing my best to dispel any bad vibes these people may have about complaining Americans. Maybe my fellow passengers were confused, but I made a friend of the bus driver. He's here at the festival and greets me warmly about six times a day!

I'll get a rundown of the players, but it's the cream of the crop. The first concert featured several excellent groups, all very interesting. Apparently a Polish tradition, after the concert there was a jam session that started about 11:00 p.m. It was my first chance to play. The vodka kept flowing and personnel changed. I packed up my horn about eight times only to be prodded or motivated on my own to unpack and join in again. I packed up for the bus ride home at 6 a.m.! The sun was coming up as I pulled massive covers over my head and slept without moving until about one p.m.

I got up and showered and had no hangover—I felt fine. Several of the crew were up and having breakfast. I ordered a ham omelet and kava. The omelet was small, somewhat slippery, but very tasty. The coffee was the usual with 1/2 inch of silt/sludge/waste oil type substance that eventually settles to the bottom. You don't drink this stuff to the last drop! That sludge probably makes a good chrome cleaner! I was talking with Andrzej, who is the head of a Polish radio station and a jazz buff. We were joined by Eyrik Kulm, a great guy and fine drummer. He moved back here two years ago after fourteen years as a starving musician in the States. He is heading his own bop/Cannonball type quintet with all super players including the top piano player in Poland and the top bass player. The bass player was mild and apologetic about his playing and his English. He played with warmth and amazing control and technique.

Henryk informed me mid-afternoon during a late lunch that this was to be my rhythm section for a thirty-five minute segment of the concert Friday evening. I was somewhat pleased! Erik's quintet played first. Then I came on and played a few tunes and then invited the two horn players from the quintet to join me. The festival was labeled "Jazz Standards", so I was right at home. They know a lot of tunes but also don't know a lot. I could probably make my nut just teaching new tunes and chord changes to these guys. I'd ask, "do you know such and such?" and if they didn't know it, I played it for them. They seemed very interested. My set went well in spite of losing the monitor for the bass and piano about halfway through.

I think they liked me. Later Erik took me down to a little office and I was paid 1.27 million Polish whatevers; about $140. This is apparently quite a bit more than a Polish family earns in a month. (The trumpet player in Erik's group, Robert Majewski, son of Henryk and an excellent powerful lyrical player, told me at breakfast that he has a day gig at a radio station that pays $80 a month.)

After the concert there was another jam session. It was pretty good at first but it deteriorated as people switched instruments and began singing very bad blues (me included). It only lasted until five a.m. this time and no vodka for me. (I decided it could be hazardous to make a regular thing of it. Even the first night I was careful not to overdo it, but the vodka is extended sort of like a handshake and you more or less have to accept.)

I slept well except for two wake-up calls, both false alarms, one by phone from the front desk wanting to know if "You are ready to bus?" and "When would you please leave the hotel?" Later someone pounded on my door and went away. I got up about 1:00 p.m., showered and

First concert with Andrzej Jagodzinski, Zbigniew Wegehaupt,
and Erik Kulm.

Same night, add the horns.

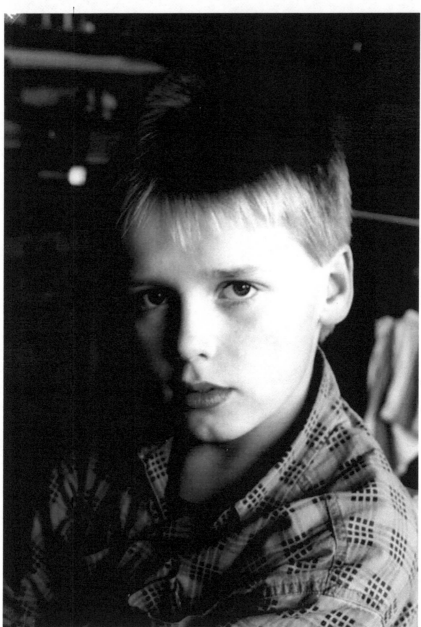

Rafal Zelek 1991.

headed for breakfast. I had muddy coffee, some soup, and a very good schnitzel (chicken fried with batter), some wonderful home fries and some not-so-wonderful canned peas, some shredded carrots and celery roots, which I'd never had before. As I finished Robert and wife joined me. As they get to know me a bit they all seem less shy about trying to speak English and soon jumped right in. It's great! I get them laughing about their mistakes, and it becomes pretty good fun. From time to time they teach me a phrase, which I can hang onto only for a few minutes and then forget. I definitely do not have a knack for languages, especially this one!

Erik joined us and soon we had a full table. The conversation was mostly Polish being spoken with Erik translating. About 3:00 we piled back on the bus to the Centrum of this small, rather dingy, beat up looking town to the auditorium for sound checks and so forth. The concert got under way at 8 p.m. The first group, called Central Heating, is a Keith Jarrett-type trio with very young (early twenties, the oldest is 23) musicians. They had very good 'head' arrangements of some standard tunes and absolute master players. The piano player played with fierce drive and extraordinary Chick Corea, Keith Jarret, Bill Evans-type lines; never going where you expected. He was truly exciting and had quite his own style. The bass player was also mega chops with some really technical stuff with more of a Gomez sound and lots of ideas of his own. The drummer had comparable chops, listening and blending and responding to everything. I talked to them afterward and promised to send them a form for Hennessey and told them to get a demo tape, which they can do. They are all at the Academy at Warsaw where they have access to recording equipment. They want to come to the USA and go to Berklee College of Music. I can't imagine why.

Erik Kulm told me that he had received a scholarship to Berklee. He applied at the suggestion of someone on the Berklee faculty on tour in Poland. He saved and managed to get to Boston to find that the scholarship was $500 in the form of one month's worth of subsidized housing. He didn't have a dime. He went to New York City to teach himself how to play jazz, did odd jobs, a few gigs and lived in the subway; learned pretty good English and eventually went back to Poland.

Things are tough here. My breakfast, a substantial plate of food with fresh bread, a large salad, coffee, and later two cups of tea came to about $2.80, which seems particularly cheap until you realize that $130 a month is considered good wages. Christian Broadacki, associate editor of the Jazz Forum considers himself pretty well up the ladder. He's about my age, plays the piano, and is a nationally known writer and critic and makes about $300 a month. The tiniest Polish-made Fiat costs about $3000. Even though these numbers seem very different, the level of existence seems similar to mine and a lot of musicians I know in the USA.

Enough editorializing and back to the events. The concert continued at a high level of expertise. I am rapidly thinking there is very little Americans can teach Poles about jazz. Their musicianship is startling!

Robert did a duo with a guy with a bass guitar and a synthesizer and really played the synth like an instrument. Very fascinating! They made amazing sounds and very tasty. A second group consisting of bass, flute and violin performed, doing mostly original bits that ended up, to my taste, somewhat repetitious and modal. They were all excellent players, but not quite my bag.

Last was the rhythm section of the night. The same young drummer from Warsaw was sitting in, Zbigniew Wegehaupt (Zbishek) on bass, and Janusz Skowron, a young blind piano player who was a powerhouse. Again, unlimited chops (all of them), but a bit too busy for my taste during other's solos, but this is, I think, a characteristic of many young Polish players. On sax was the number one hot-shot of Poland, Zbigniew Namaswoski.

After the concert Zbishek (the bass player) and I became drinking and talking buddies. First, at the jam session after the concert I played with Zbigniew and Robert and the Trio of kids, then some more with Janusz, the blind piano player, and Zbishek who was painfully shy about his English, and if you can believe it, shy about his playing, too! Every other word was "I'm sorry" or just plain "Sorry". This guy is a monster player, great ear, wonderful time, really impeccable chops; a really sweet, friendly guy and so modest it hurts.

Going back to the jam session. It was held in a large theater, converted to a dance hall. There was a stage with a curtain, then a raised platform for the band and piano. It was one step down to a slightly lower platform for the horn players and singers. There were tables in a horseshoe around a dance floor with a busy bar at the back. There was very little talking during the music, and even the worst of the instrument swapping and dreadful vocals got rounds of applause. The drinks and, to my palate, quite good food (Zbishek did not agree) were served by strikingly gorgeous, very tall, Russian waitresses. They had amazingly long legs that started (as you were sitting down) exactly at eye level and continued forever all the way to the ground. The mini skirts started just above where the legs seemed to start, somewhat distracting! They wore too much makeup but had rather gorgeous bodies. I guess it didn't really matter about the food after all!

Here in Poland there seems to be the same policy about nudity and porn as in Yugoslavia. At Darek's during supper a TV ad warning about breast cancer came on showing a very lovely bare-breasted girl in a shower examining her breasts. Darek and his younger brother really didn't even seem to notice it, much less react to it! The most graphic, legs apart, girlie magazines are on display in public newsstands. According to Andrzej this is new here since the Communists left, two and a half years ago.

Zbishek and I talked about jazz, about being married and not married. He was getting pretty drunk, and his wife was very upset with him. He was being quite funny, judging from the reactions of the others. She was obviously angry. Their conversation became loud and very animated.

Sitting between them in the booth and unable to extricate herself was Robert's wife, who was gorgeous, dark-haired, and could have been a model. She kept glancing at me with a 'how do I get out of this?' look and from the other side of the booth, just with eye contact we both got the giggles and soon, without a word, we were both in hysterics. Without being able to pronounce any of the names, the smiles, nods, body language and total music communication is truly wonderful.

So, after playing some nice things at the 'session', interesting tunes and some ballads, etc., Zbishek and I talked almost non-stop, ending up in his room with a last sip of vodka about 7:30 a.m. The bus back to Warsaw was leaving at nine a.m., so I packed and got some coffee. I had a quick visit with Andrzej and Henryck along with more early morning vodka with a glass of instant coffee! On the bus Zbishek was all curled up, sound asleep in an impossible position sort of wedged under his bass. I managed a nearly full-length stretch across the very back seat with my clarinet as a pillow and managed to sleep some. The road, like most Polish country roads, was bumpy. The seat had a springboard effect propelling me forward at every bump. I didn't actually fall off, but constantly felt I was about to, so sleep was fitful at best.

Back finally to Warsaw. We pulled up in front of the Jazz Club, and I was amazed that people recognized me from the Saturday night performance; apparently broadcast live on national TV! We said goodbyes to the trio and prodded Zbishek out of his seat. He and Erik joined me for a quick lunch, and Erik drove me a few blocks to the station where I bought my ticket (about $2.50 for a 150-mile ride!) and saw me off, first-class to Wodge, where I was to be met by Maciek Pawlowski.

The first-class compartment was slightly more plush than the third-class one but smelled of years of smokers. I tried to sleep but really could not because of the smoke. The other two people in my compartment were chain smokers. One was Arabic, who at the end of the trip told me in pretty good English that I was where I was. The other did not stop smoking long enough to say anything. Just as one would finish a cigarette the other one would start, so I spent much of the trip in the hallway with access to an open window. I saw sections of very poor farm country and sections that except for the architecture could be USA suburbs. A common sight is a man wearing a suit driving a horse-drawn, rubber-tired farm wagon.

Again the train was very fast and exactly on time. Henrick had mentioned two trains to Maciek. I was on the first; he met the second. After I arrived and was obviously not being met, I found a very nice young man in a money exchange office who gave me a token for the telephone, and I tried a few times to call Maciek. I had no idea who I was looking for, had never met him and his phone did not answer. Finally after about half an hour of my standing around and trying to look obvious, a very pretty young lady came up to me. Her name was Anna, and she asked if I was who I was and was glad when I said I was. I said goodbye to my friend from the money exchange office, who was from Kuwait and spoke quite good English.

Anna, Maciek's girlfriend, called out to someone and Maciek came running on the scene. He was a very attractive young man with sideburns shaved way above the ears, wearing a dark suit and tie. Anna's English was pretty good, while Maciek's was halting. We got on a bus for twelve cents per ride and headed to their home.

Their apartment is in a complex of buildings all about fifteen to twenty years old, built by the Communists (Russians) for the masses. They look like low-middle rise versions of the ones in New York City or the approaches to the Bronx. They are clean but the construction is pretty sloppy, and there are lots of them. These things go on forever. We're on the fourth floor and I gather from Maciek that his rent and utilities are about $100 a month. He and Anna share, but he only earns about $130 at his job at the academy. Anna teaches so they get by. We had a quick light supper with a young friend who is a sax player. I had a short nap before dinner and after dinner a half-hour walk with Anna and Maciek and then right to bed. I haven't gone that long without sleep for quite a while!

About 8:00 the next morning I heard them moving around and got up. We had the apparently traditional rolls, dark bread and butter, leftover egg salad from dinner and always cold cuts. There was a good big pot of coffee with no mud; a first! Then Anna left to go to her modern dance class. Maciek and I tried to talk and managed to compare notes about our similar states of poverty, agreeing that we also had made a choice to do what we do. He couldn't quite believe or understand(?) that I had given up a month's work and paid most of my own way here to teach for free. Does sound pretty nuts. Then he whisked me away to 'downtown'.

The city is a mess with a somewhat leftover look of World War II after years of what has amounted to Russian occupation. First we made an aborted attempt to see the modern art museum, which was closed for remodeling, then headed to the Music Academy for some lunch. It was pretty much the same fare as at the Academy in Warsaw—fried chicken leg, mashed potatoes and shredded carrots and a chicken soup with rice and peas and not too much chicken; all quite tasty. There was also a strange-looking loose pudding on a plate. Before we could even taste that, Anna showed up and rushed us out to a studio a short tram ride away. Still wondering about that pudding.

Maciek had recorded a few tunes from his big band on a sixteen-track tape and wanted me to overdub a clarinet solo of "In the Mood" and "Don't be That Way." We were allowed ten minutes of studio time! Then a very attractive lady did a ten-minute radio interview with me and made me whistle some tunes for her. I must send her compact discs. She said she could get them airplay.

Anna now became my official babysitter. Maciek for some reason stayed behind and Anna took me back home to shower and nap and change for the concert at the Jazz Club.

The trams were packed. We squeezed onto one. I was on the step and really got pushed around every time the door opened or closed. I had my hand on my clarinet case one step above and also pressed quite firmly against a very pleasant young girl's bottom. She either didn't notice or didn't care but I was afraid to move. I guess I was somewhat distracted by this because at the last stop as I tried to move to get off, my sneaker got grabbed by the lower travel arm of the door and my foot got really stuck. I tugged away. It was not crushing my foot but it was not letting it go, either. Finally, in desperation, I slid my foot out of the sneaker and then managed to free it. I was relieved because I might have lost a couple of toes. No damage, but Anna was very apologetic about the crowds and my ordeal. I made light of it all, explaining that they were old sneakers, I had all my toes and as far as I was concerned it was just another adventure.

I hit the tub/shower, actually a small tub with a hand-held shower. For me, being only inches narrower than the tub, it was damned near impossible to wash. There are places that I like to use soap that are unreachable in this sort of apparatus; no room for a hand down the side, can't spread to reach between from in front or behind, and I don't do well standing on my head. Hands and knees seemed to work well, but it was impossible to rinse off. I managed finally by backing over the edge with my feet outside, soaping and rinsing. That solved, the armpits were a real challenge. It was soap, rinse, and hold the showerhead. If you let go of anything even for a second you're done! The nozzle takes off like an unattended fire hose; the entire area gets soaked. I managed to spray most of the bathroom. Washing is a three-handed operation; best done with a friend for sure!

After a brief nap I dressed in my suit and went with Anna to the Jazz Club. We rehearsed a few things and waited for the concert. The band, all in tuxes, looked and sounded great—good all around. I did my thing and got a great reception including three red roses from the wife of the conductor of the local symphony. We had a short break and then another set. Anna sang two tunes the first set. She has a good strong voice, right on the money. The second set I played most of the solo parts. The third set was all by the band, which really sounded good. These are mostly once-a-week players with a few full-time pros who periodically have to leave town and play Mickey Mouse cruise ship gigs to earn enough money.

There were some really strong trumpets players who were hitting and popping high Fs and Cs with consistency! There were two good trombones and five saxes, one of which was the young alto player who was at dinner last night. A gorgeous sound! After the band, there was another break, and a jam session developed. I ended up playing a duet with the sax and clarinet player, Jack Delong. Incredible sound and good chops. We had a ball really working off each other and really brought the house down! It's so nice to play quietly and with taste and have an audience go nuts!

This all lasted awhile and finally, after many hugs, goodbyes and a few farewell vodkas we got a ride home in a small Russian car made out of pegboard with no pegs. The wife of the drummer drove us all the way home at about 60 mph. We had a quick snack, brown bread, cheese and cold cuts with an orange drink, and then to bed. I really think I made some friends and probably a few more places to stay. Not bad for a day's work!

I started the next day with a clinic at the Music Academy. The director met me and through an interpreter extended all sorts of greetings, hoping somehow that I was some sort of ambassador and could help him make his musicians world famous. My clarinet players all had impeccable chops. I'd guess maybe in their early twenties, maybe younger. Anna confirmed they're all 21 or 22 and really did understand what I was trying to say, simply what Roger Kellaway told me, "start hearing and playing different scales and different intervals." I showed them a little about getting inside chords; fun. They asked questions, and we played a little back and forth, trading choruses of blues. Maciek at the piano was changing keys to keep our ear training up to snuff. Later I did a radio interview with whistling and all kinds of BS about myself.

Anna and I came back to the apartment without adventure. We made a stop at a food market for some provisions. We bought a large loaf of dark bread. At the shop they have a big hand slicer, somewhat like a radial-arm saw, and Anna indicated to the clerk who cut the loaf where Anna designated, and we took our piece home.

I had my first touch of stomach problems, slight gas pains and loose bowels. I took two green pills. I expect it was the vodka and scotch that was poured in last night more than anything. The people here seemed surprised that I don't drive a Cadillac and have a fancy home. Several seriously asked if I'm related to Clark Terry. They were also surprised when they learned that I paid my own way over here. We're listening to Mingus "Ah, umm" and Anna is making a soup. I will nap and give a concert at the Academy later, with another jam session after.

I have another brief TV interview scheduled before the concert.

It started to snow as Anna and I arrived at the Academy at about 6:00 p.m. The band was all there, somewhat recovered from last night. We had a brief sound check for me. In the band room there was a TV crew waiting to interview me. About eight of the band members simultaneously wanted to interpret for the lady announcer who spoke no English. Finally I realized that I could not sensibly answer unintelligible questions coming from eight directions, so I nodded to the cameraman and started talking for about three minutes about why I was here, etc. Everyone seemed totally pleased when I got through.

The Academy is in a palace that was built by some Count for his girlfriend. It was very dingy and in need of repair but a magnificent building. The concert hall is a sort of drawing-room arrangement. There are many elegant old houses here. They were confiscated by the Communists, but now an effort is being made to get them back to their original owners. Some of the owners are dead, and most of these magnificent houses are in terrible shape. They've been used as army and police barracks and were pretty well trashed, so anyone regaining ownership has to face huge restoration costs. Some of these houses are on a scale with Newport, Rhode Island, truly impressive; many like the up-scale Vaughn Street houses in Portland, ME.

The concert was a huge success and we had several encores, then off to the session. There was a burning rhythm section with a leather-clad violinist playing hard be-bop lines at 100 miles an hour. There was also a very Slavic-looking bass player who soloed faster than anything I've ever heard. Absolutely impossible chops. There were lines all over the place at tempos I can't begin to articulate; almost drum-roll speed. He was a very shy man with no English at all. Most of the musicians do speak a little and are eager to try. One of the clarinet players from the workshop showed up, and I encouraged him to play. Jack Delong was there, too, and again I think I made some friends. These guys all have good-to-excellent classical chops, but are amazed at my ability to construct lines that don't necessarily arpeggiate the chord. It's fun to see their reactions when I go a bit outside. Great time! There were hugs and kisses from total strangers and most of the players.

It was cold and snowy so we sprang for a taxi ride home, where we had beet salad and Polish hot dogs and tea and again that wonderful bread, all served with such style by Anna. She used very simple kitchen dishes but always had a garnish of a leaf of lettuce or a radish and always a candle on their tiny table in their living room/bedroom/dining room/music room.

They are great kids. I plan to leave some money discretely. They will probably be upset but they have spent so much time babysitting me. To bed now, it's 2:15 a.m. I wrote a note to Maciek and Anna and left them $40 U.S., about what the whole band made last night. Maciek's monthly take home pay is about $130 so I guess this is a lot, but my rationale is that I'd probably spend that in four days just on food and gas at home.

I slept in somewhat and when I woke up Anna had already quietly left for her class. Maciek made tea and we left for the station. He seemed surprised when I paid for my ticket. We then met Anna at a pizza place and had more tea and good pizza, a large square with Polish sausage and peppers and canned peas. In Poland you eat everything because that's all there is. It's pretty simple. They waste very little. Bread and groceries are not packaged or wrapped. You bring your own shopping bag. The refrigerator is like the ones college students have in their dorm rooms. Food is bought every day and everything is used up. Toilet paper does exist. So far no need for my emergency supply. It's like sturdy paper towels. You tear off a piece about the size of your hand and use it carefully. None of this bunching up a fist full. First of all it doesn't bunch! I'm sidetracked again; so many impressions! They were both surprised when I insisted on picking up the check.

We had a tearful farewell at the station, and the train is now pushing sixty miles an hour as I write. We left exactly at 12:37! There are manual gates at most crossings, although some are automatic and some are permanently closed; you open them as you go through! We passed some huge glass factories in Radom with six towers looking like a power plant or steel mill spewing horrific smoke. There was a sign next to the track, "Welcome to the Bay Area"? The buildings are all uniform gray brown from fifty years of unchecked pollution. Also there was evident war damage from WWII.

I was joined in my compartment by a young couple that I never did figure out. At first I thought they might be newlyweds. They had a black bag and some really cheap gift-type things. I couldn't be sure if they had just received them or had just bought them to give to someone else. There was a wristwatch and pen set. The back of the watch was chipped and the business end of the pen was stuck in the cap, so when you took the cap off it exposed the plastic ink reservoir. The girl tried with her teeth to make the cap round but it still stuck. Another item was a sort of hair-care manicure kit in a very flimsy plastic case with an assortment of nail files and strange-shaped scissors and a curling iron.

The girl seemed much too young to be married and started reading a comic book. The guy was reading some sort of novel. They lacked the intimacy of a married couple, more like cousins perhaps. The guy was maybe twenty and the girl about fourteen, I'd guess. I looked for clues to their relationship, but found none. They did share some real laughs, so I stayed confused.

One other man, fairly heavy with blue jeans and a gray sweater, apologized for not speaking English. I find that apologizing right back with, "English only, so sorry," seems to be magic. These were the only words we spoke until we got off at Katowice, where I had to change trains. He looked at my ticket and found the information from the schedule and then walked me to the right platform, shook my hand and said, "Goodbye and good luck". I thanked him and had about a fifteen-minute wait. Soon a very modern sign, all computerized, flashed the time and destination, so even I could understand. The nice man in the sweater reappeared just as the train pulled in, came over and pointed me in the right direction. I thanked him again and once I was in my compartment he gave me a final wave and walked back out of the station. He had obviously waited to make sure I was okay. This type of kindness and concern seems to be the rule.

I must learn what went on during and since World War II. The train stations all look like movie sets, and I imagined all sorts of battles and death and destruction crisscrossing this beautiful but battered country. I saw about as many tractors as horses plowing fields. They are mostly new-looking tractors, including one that was stuck, or about to be. It was usually one horse and a man behind the plow with a woman picking and chucking rocks behind him. I saw a whole family out behind one horse with a small boy doing the rock throwing and quite a group, 4 or 5, going over the soil with hand tools. One of the men fell down and was pitched a forkful of hay by one of the girls who he promptly tackled. It looked like hard work, but they were having fun.

I did see one modern manure spreader, but most of that was done by hand. I guess a truck comes by and drops a sizable load (about 1 cubic yard) at intervals of a few yards. Then, with a pitchfork a single man was spreading it into the soil. Along the rail line there seem to be remains of bunkers. Also at some of the gate crossings there were reinforced concrete bunkers attached to the rather tidy shacks that the gatekeepers must live in. They are made like small houses, really, most with gardens. There were chickens and some turkeys in and around everything.

The train left on time but was slower going than the one down from Wodge. It was a local and somewhat noisier and bumpier. I learned that was because the trains ran over the huge network of coalmines in the area, and the vibrations from trains going too fast would cause them to collapse. The rail network is extraordinary! Why our great country isn't smart enough to do something like it is beyond me. I'm sure people would use the trains if they went where you want to go, when you want to go. They could be kept inexpensive if people used them. These super trains are so cheap. My fare from Wodge to Krakow, about a six-hour trip at speeds up to 65 mph, was $3.30. It costs much more to drive. What's Amtrack from Boston to New York these days? How do you get to Boston? Where do you leave your car, etc.?

The schedules are carefully worked out, and since everything is on time you get where you want to go. I had, according to my schedule, fourteen minutes between trains and it worked exactly that way. Anyway, it seemed long toward the end, but right on schedule we pulled into Krakow. Anna said she would call and tell Wanda when to meet me. I hadn't walked more than 30 feet when I heard "Brad, Brad" and was practically attacked by Rafal with Wanda close behind. I had to wait until I got to the house to explain what I meant by saying I felt I was "coming home". It took a while, but they were pleased. The English lessons with Rafal started immediately. We had supper and watched George Bush speaking Polish. Then a Polish/Turkish soccer game which really was something to see. The Polish team won even though I was rooting for the wrong team the whole first half. I tried to translate things like 'near miss' and 'that was close'. Rafal picked it up very fast, so it's fun to find ways to explain everything. He keeps looking up Polish words for me to give him the English. I managed to convince Wanda to let him skip for the day; that he'd learn more English than at school. I told him he was going to 'play hooky' from school and be my guide. Try to explain that line to someone who doesn't speak the language!

After the football (soccer) game they watched Dynasty. The second and third syllables of that title sums up its characters pretty well. I'm shocked to think that millions of Polish people are getting that kind of impression about Americans. It has to be the most revolting display of evil people and money and power at its worst. I tried to find all the words I could in the dictionary to describe how I felt; nasty, evil, disgusting were there. Bitchy, conniving, scheming and manipulative were not. I tried to explain that I wanted to 'smack' them all, but that's not in my dictionary either.

Finally that was over (I'll have to get Isi to explain how upsetting this is!). We had a quick cup of tea and then to bed. Rafal, I think, understands if he wakes up early that he should come and wake me up. 'Waking up' he's got, but 'early' is not too clear. The morning will tell.

A stuffy nose kept me awake more than the sounds of trains, which sort of soothe you to sleep. No whistles blowing, but definite sounds of trains moving about. They are all electric, so no diesel sounds or smells. I remember being lulled to sleep on a few ocean liners. The steady sound of power and moving is very comforting. Rafal is not an early riser. His room is across from mine, and with the doors open we can see each other. He looked up about when I did and soon came bounding in. We talked for a bit, and then he disappeared and got dressed, so I did, too.

Downstairs, breakfast was the usual with coffee and hot milk (all mixed). Then after an impromptu English lesson I explained to Rafal that I wanted to mail a letter and buy some postcards. The letter part was easy and he soon led me out to show me his school (he played hooky) and guided me to the Post Office. He seemed to know all about airmail stamps to America and handled everything. We took a back way along small streets toward home. The corner paper shop didn't have anything except cards with flowers, and I had a hard time explaining picture postcards of buildings, etc.

Along the way we would stop and try to explain things from the Polish/English dictionary. Sometimes we would take the book and while walking try to find a word. Then we'd stop, and Rafal would show the English word to me, with a lot of pointing and sign language. I've managed to tell him a lot, and as he gets to know me his English seems to improve.

He spends less time thinking about the words and is more apt to just start talking. I was going to try and explain that to him but he's doing it on his own. I think it works better to just pop out the words without too much thought; like playing a jazz solo. Do it and analyze it later. I did explain and he understands (I think) that since I was a teacher it was okay to try and okay to make mistakes. Not to worry. He stuck at it all day and well into the evening, talking and never getting far away from our trusty dictionary.

We came home with the letter mailed but no postcards. We ate some more bread and cold cuts, and then with Wanda we all hopped a bus and headed to the Centrum. The neighborhood is surprisingly diversified. There are many private homes and most have fences with garages either attached or underneath. There are some large apartment buildings like those in Wodge, but mostly these are smaller one-family homes. There's lots of stucco and highly-glossed wooden trim.

This house is immaculate. We take shoes off downstairs. There is a sliding glass door to the stairwell and all is very spit and polish (no pun intended). Darek's room, now mine, is about the size of my room in Maine with a comfortable pull-out bed, a table with two synth keyboards and free-standing closet and dresser. The furniture is all good quality with a light oak stain. The floor has a nice parquet design (the real thing) and a soft brown rug. There are a few plants with large green leaves and a door out to the balcony and a view of the railroad yard. The door to the hall has an opaque glass panel that lets in light but diffuses shapes so you can see if someone is there but not really much more than that. The doorknobs, as well as the light switches, are all top quality. There are car posters, etc. on the wall, a typical teenager's room, except for its neatness!

Rafal's room was somewhat smaller with a bed that folds completely into the wall. A huge sheet-covered quilt is lashed down with strips of cloth and he seems to squirm down without untying them and can completely disappear under the mountainous covers. Papa, as I have said, works in Chicago and sends money home. Probably good financially, but particularly rough on Rafal to be without a father. He has not seen him in five years! Darek saw him last fall with Isi on his tour of America. As we walked to the bus stop, Rafal clung to me and delighted in keeping in step. On the bus he put his hand on mine and kept looking up at me and then in the street he kept my hand in place on his shoulder with his own hand and almost strutted with me in tow like he was showing off his American friend.

We found postcards and I bought about sixty that are now almost all written and addressed. We'll make another trip to the Post Office tomorrow and do some more exploring. Rafal now understands 'find' and I want to 'find' some shoes I had seen in a shop on my first day here with Darek. I managed to find the shop again and for about $25 bought a pair of real leather shoes that look Polish. I think people here look at your feet first. My worn-out L.L.Bean suede sneakers sure ain't Polish. Then the glance immediately rises to eye level and I guess I don't look Polish either. I hope the shoes will help. They certainly are comfortable. Leather products seem to be cheap and of excellent quality. Wanda delighted in arguing (or maybe discussing) the size and price of the shoes. I was delighted remembering the last time I bought new shoes was in Austin, Texas, seven years ago. It's Goodwill all the way for me. Wanda and Rafal did not believe these were my first pair of new shoes in years.

Back home there was more food and a very elaborate English lesson interrupted by Darek home from Russia a day early. It was very exciting. He arrived by taxi and had lots of stories to tell about Russia. He spent 22 hours by train each way to play two concerts for audiences. I will try to find out more. He was warned not to take the camcorder due to danger of having it literally ripped off. He took lots of pictures that he will get developed. We had more food, and then Darek and Rafal and I went to telephone Isi at the pay phone. We came back for more food and Isi arrived as I was about ready to go to bed, full of stories about Russia and its lack of plumbing. I read some of this diary to him and I think he liked it. He told me about going to a store in Moscow marked 'Fruit' in Russian and finding a bin with potatoes and one with carrots; and nothing else! Speaking slowly in English the kids understood. A friend came by to get Isi after he had regaled us with stories and given me my schedule for tomorrow.

I again headed for bed to write this and was intrigued by Darek and his sister who sat in her room and talked and laughed together for more than an hour. How nice. These kids really seem to enjoy each other! It's midnight, and finally to bed. There is a dog barking outside but no trains for half an hour!

Friday, April 19

Time is going much too fast. Wanda is off at work early and the kids and I had a jam session. I got Rafal playing Watermelon Man changes. He can really swing and seems to love it. There may be a real possibility of his coming stateside with me for a few months to learn some English in a hurry. At the end of the day, Isi and I discussed plans for bringing the kids over for jazz camp. I'll get dates and start planning. If I can, I'll cover Darek. Hopefully I can get $100 off for jazz camp. Maybe I can plan a few fund-raising concerts after camp. Then Rafal would go home end of August with Darek. We shall see.

Isi was supposed to meet me at 11:00 but showed up at 12:30, allowing Darek, Rafal and me to have quite a jam session lasting several hours. Isi did finally arrive and we bussed off to the Centrum and caught a shuttle bus to the Music Academy. It was swarming with young kids all playing seriously. I did about a half hour for some neat kids who were impressed with my ability to hear a chord and make up a melody. I was able to show them that I heard the basic thing and then tried to get inside it.

Urick and Mark Zibeski, music students of Isi's, came to collect me and rush me off to a workshop for clarinet players, all older, about 17 to 19. There were some pretty good players, but not much jazz knowledge. I had fun trying to explain how one plays by ear. Even with language problems, I can get them grinning and extract a laugh or two. They are such neat kids and so enthusiastic! Two hours went by instantly and Isi showed up to coach his high school jazz band. The kids all play pretty well but have a late start in improvisation. They were playing "Hello Dolly" with the drums 1000 miles away from the forty-foot long grand piano and the bass. The bass player is from Norway, spoke very good English and was here because of the excellent music and cultural opportunities. The time was a bit shaky, so I moved the drummer into the curve of the piano. The bass player's tuning mechanism had a screw missing, so one of the strings kept slipping out of tune. He also had a small amp with a 1/4" speaker (if that big), and the room was a horror of echoes!

Nevertheless, we managed to get a nice groove going. The fourteen-year-old drummer looked older and had terrible equipment. His sticks were taped up, and the ends looked like artist's paint brushes, completely frazzled. It was impossible to get a 'ping'. It was more like a 'slosh' on the cymbals. With all this against him he got a marvelous Jack DeJohnette New Orleans shuffle groove going on "All Blues", with time locked in and a swing like crazy. I spoke to him afterwards and he knew all about Jack DeJohnette. I'd like to do a pop quiz of twelve-to-fourteen-year-old jazz drummers in the USA. "Jack who?"

Mark and Urick, Isi and I all went to Mark's house for dinner. We had chicken and some soft sort of potato ball with a very rubbery texture and later, very tasty coffee. It was a pleasant apartment on a similar scale as Maciek and Anna's, but the building was nicer and they obviously had a higher standard of living. Their mom drove us home.

Darek and Wanda were still up listening to "Take 6". Now I'm done for the day. It's 12:30 and I must mail postcards tomorrow. Can't think of too many reasons to come back home. Hardly anybody stared at me today. Must be the shoes.

April 20

Today Rafal came in about 9:00, and we had a marathon English lesson lasting several hours. Wanda drove me to the Centrum and we met Isi and went to a workshop for some of his older students. We moved from a huge cold room to another building; a music school, and another warmer but tiny room. In one corner was a large coal-burning ceramic furnace that was a few feet wide and went nearly to the ceiling. The lumps of coal were huge, 8"–10" across, and the fire had to be kept going. It was a bear to start.

The kids all need decent equipment. The J.C. Penny drum set literally fell apart during a drum solo. The bass amp looked like something from the 40's. It was a two-piece arrangement with a unit inside that looked like a Sears battery charger. This came out of what was the speaker cabinet, and various weird plugs made the thing work. The kids all played pretty well. The bass player played good notes and really managed to establish a nice groove. I think they had the best 'time feel' so far in a student group.

This lasted an hour or so, and then we walked back to the Zebik's and ate again. Wanda took Isi to a gig and Darek, Mark and Jurek and mom and I all went to hear the Mahler five-part symphony with the Krakow Orchestra. Mark was making his debut with the Symphony and wanted me to record it. We set up the camcorder in the balcony and caught his show. The conductor, a guest from USA, was Charles Bernstein and did the whole thing with no score, and I think made a very good impression. Mark wanted his autograph, so after the concert, at the reception, I went right up to him. He was very nice and was quite amazed that Mark was only a junior in High School. He, too, has fallen in love with Poland and may come to the Ensemble rehearsal tomorrow, and he invited me to call and stop by for a drink tomorrow evening. I think I will! We mingled for a while and got a ride back home. Rafal greeted us at the gate in the rain with his usual mile-wide smile. Wanda is concerned about his coming with me now but thinks six weeks in the summer is okay. Darek is going to try and convince her that I can tutor Rafal and get about four years worth of English done, so I'll keep trying.

April 21

Rafal didn't wake me up early, but he did come in later and we went over the English words he learned yesterday. I forgot to mention that yesterday I showed him blues changes and Watermelon Man. I played the synth and Darek played clarinet, and he started to get it down. More about that later.

After the usual breakfast Wanda, Rafal and I had a long walk to church; Darek went to his Church Youth Group on the other side of town. I don't begin to understand how that kid maintains great grades in school and does all these other things including week-long trips to Russia. The service was not unusual. Thanks to my early Episcopal training I sort of knew what was happening with the Catholic service. I was impressed by the number of people and particularly the number of young people, teenagers, who were apparently alone, not sitting with families in groups, although there were many of those, too. A friend of Rafal's, a kid in his class in school, was standing in front of us. There were seats in the center of the church but both isles were full of standees, including Rafal and myself. Rafal and his friend knew the service and all the responses, all the hymns, which I had never heard before. Even after the Communion and prayer part was over the friend remained on his knees with his eyes shut for several minutes. One would think that two eleven-year-olds standing next to each other for an hour would have some sort of mischievous diversions. Only once did they exchange a few quick comments and shared a quick giggle and were pretty serious about the whole thing. I had a tough time standing and didn't much like kneeling but had to in order not to be obviously standing all alone. Rafal sort of tugged at me at the appropriate times. The service was obviously in Polish and what I thought might have been Latin had a Polish accent, so I didn't get much. The sermon sort of went by me, too. There was some nice chanting by the Priest and supplementing a great-sounding organ was a guitarist and flutist who played with the choir and gave it all a folksy feeling. It was not the usually oppressive (to my taste) Catholic service.

We met outside after the service. Wanda had left Rafal and me to fend for ourselves. I think she was in the choir, but I couldn't see. On the way home we stopped for cheesecake at a little shop. Rafal spotted some gum with racing car playing cards, so I bought two packs and he was really surprised when I gave them to him. His eyes got really wide open, and he had a look of total disbelief that I had bought them for him. Soon after we got back we were joined by Darek, and we ate the cheesecake, made sandwiches and tea and watched television. There were some short cartoon things about pollution which I was glad to see, better than a rather dreadful English lesson by a Polish lady with a heavy accent quizzing some Polish kids in English. It was an attempt, but I suspect not much help.

There are some pretty good English language movies shown, but there is a Polish 'instant translation' drowning out the English completely. The same voice translates all the parts so the heroine sounds just like the hero. They should subtitle the stuff and let the language be heard.

"Sesame Street" is dubbed into Polish, too; not dubbed, translated, even the alphabet stuff. What English there is goes by much too fast for kids to grasp. I didn't have time to explain all the words flashed up on the screen that begin with the letter 'D'. The whole segment was over before Rafal could get even one word. This has to be discouraging! There are areas where American TV could really be helpful.

At noon Wanda and I went and picked up Lucaz, Bartek and Isi at Isi's apartment. We all piled into Wanda's car and went to the Cultural Center in Nowa Huta, built by the communists near the steel mill of the same name. (As I understand it they robbed the poor to give to the rich.) It was an impressive building, but very austere and 1950ish; everything okay except for the piano being a bit out of tune.

We were soon joined by the rest of the ensemble. Rehearsal lasted several hours, and the kids really let go and played pretty well. My job was to listen to each kid play a few choruses of the blues and make comments. They were all sticking pretty close to the blues scales, so I think I loosened things up a bit by trading a lot of '4s' and a long trading bit with Philip, who is a remarkable drummer with great ears; a real 'listener' who has impeccable time. The kids were understanding that the blues form kept going even during the drum solos. Bartek, with the darnedest hair like a giant Afro, grins all the time. He was wearing the huge combat boots he bought in the States. I showed him some walking bass lines on the synth, and soon he got the idea. Isi has them playing "I Got Rhythm" at a crazy tempo; too fast for me, but Bartek and Philip lock in together and swing most of the time.

My comment to all of them was again, thanks to Roger Kellaway, "Listen to and play different intervals and scales." Most of them caught on right away, and the playing soon took on very interesting twists as some of their classical influences filtered into their solos. Greg Berniak plays violin and clarinet both really well. On both instruments he's playing very advanced classical pieces and sight-reads anything. He wants me to give him a clarinet lesson tomorrow after school; don't think I can show him much about the clarinet! These kids are all amazing. Bartek, the bass player, is really a bassoon player. Anna, who now has her flute, plays and sight-reads all sorts of heavy classical piano stuff!

We came home after a huge dinner at Anna's. Her family rolled out the red carpet, not unusual here as I'm finding. Their apartment is similar, almost to a 'T', to the apartment of Anna and Maciek in Wodge but more comfortably furnished. I tried to explain that I was only the carrier of the flute. Anna wrote a letter to the donor, and I enclosed it with mine.

We ate and ate! All the best china was out on a white tablecloth. There was wonderful homemade mushroom soup, then mounds of potatoes, beets in a mush-kind of form, thinly shredded carrots, a salad and an unusual compote of fruit—all made from their own garden. Then we had meat with gravy, I'm guessing pork. It was very good and quite tender. It was pork loin I'm sure. Then we had tea and coffee and two different cakes and sort-of shortbread cookies with jam that was hard to describe, maybe strawberry, maybe date or fig, or a combination, in between two cookies, like the 'end-all' Oreo.

Red champagne followed, imported from Bulgaria. It was sort of sweet but good. Then there was more coffee. Anna's older sister (a knockout) and husband and two adorable but somewhat painful kids of 2 1/2 and 3 1/2 came for dessert, and Thomas, Anna's brother-in-law, gave Isi and me a ride back. He took me to Darek's and then took Isi home. I called Charles Bernstein, and he said he was tied up with his wife's family but please to send him some stuff and he would help any way he could. Isi and I talked again about getting these kids to jazz camp. It's a must-do thing!

Monday I woke up about 7:00 and saw Rafal peering in at me through the door. He really enjoyed the music last night. We did some more English. I got across the concept of 'making a plan' and what are we going to 'do'. Our plan is to go to the Post Office and mail 63 postcards so they get home before I do! He's getting pretty good about telling me he does or does not understand. He knows that "does not" is rewarded with the same laugh and hug as "does" so he's not afraid to let me know. I spent the morning writing out "Groove Yard" for Darek and caught a nap while Wanda went to the dentist. I got good video stuff, I hope, of trains, Rafal going and coming home from school, Darek and Wanda and Angela and the house. They may be boring to everyone else but fun for me. About 1:30 Wanda took me over to the Music School on her way to work, where I met Greg and Darek. Greg had asked for a clarinet lesson. He plays very well but needs to work on his sound in the upper register. I am constantly amazed by these kids. I gave him a ligature and DEG Barrel. I happened to have exactly the right length and type. It was one less thing to lug back home. I spent about an hour with him. He is wonderful. He is very quiet and has great ears. He plays back anything. He was in tears when he realized the barrel and ligature were his to keep. So was I.

Then we went to a tiny storage room with Greg, Darek, and a tiny ten-year-old drummer with a round face and big eyes. He really listened to a few albums Isi had collected from a radio station in Dallas. I had told Darek all about Stan Getz and Bill Evans and found five Bill Evans albums and a great Getz collection. They were impressed that at random I could scat along with most of the solos! I explained how much these players influenced me. I must be sure they really understand that word. Greg had to go for his 'real' clarinet lesson, so the mini drummer and I shuffled around and finally set up in the huge recital hall. The kid was amazing! He had all sorts of independence and solid time. We traded perfect 4's, and we fooled around with me playing free and following him in 3/4 time, bossa novas, funky shuffling type stuff, you name it. He was deadpan throughout but broke into a funny "Yea haw" and a big grin each time we finished! I must find out from Isi who he is. The school has a full-time music program and also is like a magnet school for performing musicians, junior high and younger, too. Kids all over the place are doing recitals, group lessons, and private lessons. It was really active, exciting and fun to see that many kids, that young, going at it with such fervor! It is similar in activity to NOCCA in New Orleans, but the school was the size of a medium-sized U.S. high school. Amazing! I'll try to get some pictures. I taped the ensemble rehearsal there a few days ago. Lucas wandered in and, we played some blues. Isi brought in a new flute player who had never played jazz. I showed him the blues scale and the 12 bar form and C Jam, and within a chorus or two he was playing his ass off. I'd guess he was about 14 with excellent chops and nice ideas, good time and good notes, all in five minutes. These kids all play so damned well that if they grasp the concept; look out! They're all over the place. I guess the hard work pays off. Darek at 15 is playing classical things that are very hard, for me! I tried to play along with Greg on some etude he was playing by ear or memory and it was a handful. The clarinet is his second instrument. His violin playing is really impressive. My little drummer hung in there, swinging like crazy the whole time.

Isi arrived with Mark and his mom. I had the tape of the Mahler concert, and we went to their home again for an incredible meal of soup, a beet broth with dumplings, 'Polish blintzes' Isi called them, and then a main dish of veal and mushrooms in a rolled-up crepe. It melted away. As usual there were beets and mounds of potatoes, a compote, and afterward, a flaky cake (bought on the way home to assure freshness) with lots of custard-type filling and very light layers of crust and powdered sugar on top. It was wonderful! We had coffee afterward and watched the video hooked up with some wire because none of my plugs would fit. Urick managed to record it, but it all came out in black and white and with no sound. I'll try to make them a copy that will work on their system. Isi went to sleep on the couch. We finally moved him, and they took us home. Rafal was still up, and we had a few minutes to go over his growing list of English words. Darek and I were up 'til 11:30 listening to a concert of his, and he went off with the tape recorder and I drifted off about 12:30 with Keith Jarrett still floating in from Darek's room. He's all excited. I'll be interested to see if it affects his playing. I have no doubt it will! The following morning Darek and Angela were off early. Rafal was here 'til 9. I showed him some more opposites and Al Corey's trick with the pencil, a spinning quarter trick, and the fool's knot with a clothesline!

Wanda and I are off to Auschwitz, on a tour. I'm looking forward to this, obviously with mixed feelings. I don't want to see it yet I feel I must. I'll be different when I come home. We got underway about 10:30, and it was very interesting to see the outskirts of Krakow from the road. We soon got onto Route 40, a sort of autobahn. It looks a lot like the Maine Turnpike with very little traffic and no speed limit! We hadn't gone very far when we heard a flapping noise from a rear tire. Part of a retread was coming loose. Wanda got the jack out, was all set to change the tire and seemed amazed when I took over and finished the job. Soon we were on the way again. Auschwitz reactions will have to wait. I need time to let it all sink in. I shot about two hours' of video and a few pictures before the batteries ran out. I'll probably write about this when I see my pictures. We took a scenic route home past all sorts of little villages and then through all of Krakow. I'm impressed with the huge number of new houses. I do wish I could spend more time here!

We had supper and the soda I bought, which seems to be a pretty big deal here. Isi came over to explain my schedule tomorrow and managed to persuade Wanda to let Rafal fly to New York City on May 30. I can meet him and have him for five to six weeks. He should be talking a mile a minute. He seemed very excited about it. I'll go to the American Consul on Thursday to set up visas, etc. I hope this flies! Darek is listening to a big band tape. He did some nice stuff with scales against chords, what great ears and what enthusiasm. I should have planned two more months here.

Thursday

Yesterday started off as usual. The kids went off to school on staggered schedules. Rafal went to school about 11:00 after quite a hassle with Wanda about homework. His math appears to be first-year Algebra with graphs, etc. He is doing so well in very advanced stuff. His writing is much neater than mine. He was behind in his biology and Wanda spent an hour with him in his room going over things. He went off and Wanda took me to the Rotunda; a jazz club where I met Isi and rehearsed with Jarostaw Smietana, a guitar player with impressive chops. He heads his own quartet doing a lot of John Scofield stuff and some originals in that bag. It's real powerhouse stuff and he played very well with not too many clams! These guys all play with real finesse. The swing things we did tended to speed up, and I couldn't get things to quiet down enough so I could hear myself. Polish soundmen seem to be so intrigued with the equipment that they spend all the time fooling around with it. In the middle of a solo I find a three-second reverb on my channel. Things like that are always happening. We ran down some tunes and I got a ride back to the house. Darek, Rafal and I hopped a bus and came downtown to another underground jazz club, downstairs under an art gallery. The gallery was full of paintings of naked American Indian-type people shooting bows and arrows in very photographic style. They were startling realism in abstract settings. For example there was a naked Indian lady whose left side was red and the other was chocolate brown sitting in the woods playing alto sax? We sort of rushed through the gallery. Isi and I did a lecture/demonstration-type thing to a full house of eager kids and parents, maybe 100 people crammed into an underground crypt, all brick and stone with large rooms with arched ceilings. It must have been some type of storage area. It was a good spot. Stone steps led down well below street level; cozy and dry. A central hall led to at least five chambers. One was the college international language club; a sort of grotto. One was a bar and another a small restaurant. We were in one of the larger chambers. Isi and I talked about improvising. I did my bit where the piano player plays a chord and I play the basic notes of the chord then improvise on it, explaining the language business, etc. Then the ensemble played a short set. Greg amazed me showing in three days signs of his recent exposure to Bill Evans. He played very melodically before and I heard all sorts of Bill Evans-type intervals. He seemed thrilled with these discoveries. The kids played well. Then a quartet of older kids played. As usual, all play their instruments extraordinarily well and again particularly the bass player. Form seems to be a universal problem with 'B' sections popping up at strange times. Then the Jorostaw trio, plus myself, played some of the tunes we had run down earlier. Jorostaw is a bit too busy behind solos but plays very well and does some amazing chord solo stuff. He does whole choruses of chords with a lot of drive and nice lines.

After that set we packed up, Darek went home and the older crew went to yet another jazz club, underground. A band was already playing, so Isi and I got a hamburger, actually a Polish cheeseburger. It was ham and melted cheese on a roll, with butter and tomato; very good. After a few warm beers I again played with the quartet. We were joined by Isi about 1:30. After several calls back for encores we all were given roses and champagne by the club owner. That's a switch!

Today Wanda left Rafal and me alone while she went to the Consulate for papers, etc. Rafal has been glued to the dictionary in a so far three-hour English lesson. His willingness and desire to learn is exhausting for me but so rewarding. He really understands the plan to come to America, and now he sticks to me like glue; hardly lets me out of his sight! He is learning rope tricks, all laced with pages of new English words, which I write down as he learns.

I discussed with Wanda the details of getting a visa for Rafal, and as we headed to the bus stop, passports in hand, Isi and Mark drove up in Mark's Fiat. I got a quick drive around the block; fun little car! A new one must be quite nice. His is ten years old and shows it! Isi and Wanda discussed things for a while, and then Wanda and I headed off again.

Surprise, surprise! We got to the U.S. Consul and I encountered the first rude, unhelpful person I've seen in three weeks in Poland in the American Consulate Office! I couldn't believe it and plan to write a scathing letter to Mr. Bigshot at the Consulate after I get the Visas. The woman seemed angry and there was no greeting, no hello, how are you, how do you like Poland, etc. Not even any eye contact. This woman was so rude. She refused to answer any questions and was as unhelpful as I think it is humanly possible to be and still be present. At the end she thrust a card toward my side of the desk, turned away and without a word or a glance in our direction started typing. There was no goodbye, no effort to be pleasant in any way. If that is the way she behaves with a U.S. citizen I hate to think how she treats Poles. It was disgraceful and certainly not the American image I want my Consulate to project. Some letters to follow! I want a handshake and a big smile and some common courtesy. I'm still angry! The only negative experience I've had here in a month, as a stranger in a foreign country, comes from the staff at my own Embassy.

It was a comedy of errors tonight, put together by Isi, I suspect. I thought the plan was to go with Darek to the Jazz Juniors at the Rotunda, meet Eva at 6:30 and go to their home for supper. Darek thought the same but at 6:00. Wanda thought she should take me to Eva's at 6:00. Eva thought I'd meet her at the Music Academy at 6:00. I went with plan A. Darek left me saying he'd be right back, and there I was. I had no address or phone number for Eva and was about to take the train and bus back to Wanda's to find out where I was supposed to go. There was no sign of Isi, nor return of Darek. An older student who I'd met a few days before assisted me with the phone and we called Anna, who gave us Eva's number, who was waiting for me at the Music Academy. I hopped a cab and for $3.00 went all the way across town and found Eva. It was a short walk and a short train ride to her house.

Eva lives in an apartment in a smaller building, but of similar construction as the ones in Wodge. It had bigger rooms and more quality work. Papa, having waited for two hours for his dinner, had done some serious damage to some French cognac and offered me some. Not wanting to be impolite... Delicious dinner with a good fresh salad, no beets or potatoes or soup, veal thin sliced with gravy served over what I think was dark rye bread prepared like French toast. The veal had been breaded and fried, sort of like chicken-fried steak. It was all very good. I found out that Eva's parents are both psychologists. We had more brandy, and, after a few attempts at conversation, Papa retired for a nap that lasted the duration! He did manage to tell me that dyslexia is a common problem in Poland and that Polish is a difficult language, and many Polish people don't speak it correctly. Eva and her mother and I talked more after he retired. We talked some about music equating to language. I related my story of the Embassy. I got a tour of Eva's room full of wonderful plants in window boxes. She's nuts about horses, and collects stamps with flowers and animals, and has a mysterious, classic beauty like Garbo or Eva Gardner. She's really a beautiful girl. Isi arrived with Wanda. We had a short visit and then a ride home. It's been a long day! It's 12:30 and I'm done!

Friday

I had the usual wake-up and English lesson with Rafal. He went off to school at about 9:00. Wanda went off to take Darek to school. I was planning to take the bus and train to the music school where I'm subbing for Isi. He is judging the Jazz Juniors contest. It's a big deal, I guess, with bands from all over Poland competing. I had hoped to hear some of that, so with mixed feelings I took over his three afternoon groups. Wanda insisted on driving me to the school. I bought a dictionary for Rafal and Darek, and met with great bunch of, I'd guess, eight to nine-year-old kids, again all playing well. My hot-shot drummer was there, all smiles, but very disappointed that I wouldn't be able to see him at his home Sunday. I might try to put that together somehow. There was also a really good little violin player with all sorts of chops and good ears. He picked up things very fast and seemed the most on the ball. It's hard to decide since they are all on the ball. The language barrier is pretty tough. The second group was slightly older, and all the same observations apply. I got the bass player playing 4/4 on "All of Me"—cooking! The little blond violin player really played well with such concentration. He was eleven or twelve maybe. Both violin players played well. There was a cello player who was good, too, but shy about soloing. It was kind of confusing with a lot of piano players. The ensemble was next. I showed them "Watermelon Man". They seemed to like it with an A flat vamp at the end of each chorus.

Philip and Bartek cranked up and played unbelievably loud, but with good time. Then we went on to the other tunes for the concert. Bartek was playing 4/4 on a very fast "I Got Rhythm". I got them to play Blue Bossa very slowly and find all the bass notes and tried to explain they must learn to hear all the changes. It was fun for me. They're such great kids!

I went off with Darek to visit Greg, who was not at school or the rehearsal. We took a bus ride to a newer apartment complex with thousands of kids. We found Greg at home. He had been sick, and to add to last night's crazy mix-up, he also had been expecting me for dinner last night!

Greg's parents were considerably older than I had expected. His 19 year-old sister is absolutely lovely and tall. She greeted me with all smiles and then had to go somewhere. Greg's parents seemed very much more 'Old World', more peasant-type. I may be totally wrong. Greg is tall, blond and very good-looking, but so frail and delicate. I gave him my last Basile tape and adjusted his clarinet. I gave him some key oil, and we visited in his room for a while. I've got to get him something decent to play music on. He has a beat up cassette player, monaural, which plays tapes about a third low and very much slower. With his great ears and talent he has got to be able to hear music regularly on good equipment.

We left after many handshakes and thank-you(s) and hugs. It was a short bus ride home. Darek and I decided not to go to Jazz Juniors to hear a band we'd never heard of. Back home we spent some time adjusting Darek's clarinet and putting together an English tape. We also played some duets and ended up playing blues with me on the newly tuned piano downstairs. I finished the tape about midnight. I hope it's not totally boring. If they will listen to it, it should work.

Saturday

It was a busy day, and this is only an outline. My fantastic trip is drawing to a close. We started with the usual English lesson and then off to a rehearsal with a swing band for a concert tonight. It was fun. There were some good players. Then back home to eat, and then off again to set up for the kids. After a sound check I got the ensemble's set on tape. The night went on with impressive performances from the winners' circle of players from the Jazz Juniors; all high school or early college age, incredible players. Later a pro group from Warsaw played, with Zbigniew on sax and Zbysek on bass. My camcorder batteries died, but I got some of it.

Wanda let Darek drive all the way home on a roundabout way. He does pretty well at 15 in Krakow traffic! Quick tea and to bed about 1:00 a.m. Isi told me I have a delay in departure. I'm not going to Warsaw until Thursday, and I'm glad.

Sunday, April 28

I went to Isi's very nice apartment and met his friend, Scott, who went to school in Texas with Isi and just happened to be in Krakow. He had gone to the Rotunda as a place to hear some jazz and saw the kids. He finally saw the poster and realized it was Isi's group of kids. He had no idea Isi was here and hadn't seen him in years. Small world!

Lucas came over to Isi's and had an hour trombone session with Scott. Meanwhile, Isi, Anna (Scott's lady) and I went ahead to Lucas' home for food. It was a similar mass-produced apartment in a complex a few minutes from Isi's. There were all sorts of goodies, cold cuts, cheese, wine, sweets and fruits, etc., all laid out. Lucas' little sister was all dressed up and played the cello for us after our meal and was, as expected, excellent. She had a good big sound and perfect intonation. She played some pretty complicated stuff with a real drive and attack. To only listen you would not believe this was a diminutive seven-year-old girl with long braids and a bright red dress. Lucas arrived with Scott, and we all ate some more. Then his brother, Chris, took us in the family Fiat to Phillip's, the drummer with the first ensemble. Chris, I guess, is in some sort of trade school and is an auto mechanic. He drove fast, but competently.

Once at Phillip's, we ate again. Seems I was making the rounds and visiting all the families of the first group. The table was all set in the living room. There was a beautifully laid-out salad with sliced cucumbers from their own garden. Then there were some sort of dark potato pancakes with veal and gravy on top; a mountain of food, and, imported from France, some warm beer. Phillip's father is a lawyer who worked his way through school as a chef and got the recipes from Bulgaria. I have never seen or tasted anything like the food he prepared; it was all excellent! He now is running his own advertising firm, very on-the-ball, and a truly handsome man. Phillip's older sister is rather large, but very attractive. She was just back from three months in Palestine. She spoke pretty good English (as did Chris Hoder, Luke's older brother). We watched some videos of Stanley Jordon. Philip knew every bit of everybody's solo, every kick, every turn. He is taking lessons on vibes, but has had no training on the drum set. The videotape I have of him is amazing. He's been playing drums for 1-1/2 years. We had cakes and tea, and I felt totally exhausted. We raced to my rehearsal with the Malinowski's Big Band. I played through a few tunes and then did the concert at 6:00. We played some pretty good charts. All strong sections and all very young; most of them in their mid 20's. There was a very good piano player.

After the concert we went to a jazz club, and I sat in all night with the Beal Street Band—a somewhat limited repertoire of older stuff, but fun nevertheless. I made some friends, an English couple on vacation who are jazz fans and two exchange students from Sweden who were all over themselves about my playing. Both want me to come and do festivals with John, so I must send some PR stuff. We had a few vodkas and then a ride home in a 20-year old Deux Chevaux about 2 a.m. It's been a long day!

Isi is going to Germany for five days with the kids on Tuesday. I must go to the travel agency to see if I can find a way to tag along. Plan A will be to go to Germany and fly from there to Belgrade and then home.

Monday, April 29

Darek stayed home to do some piano and clarinet practicing for his recital. You should hear the classical piano stuff this kid is doing!

I took my first solo trip downtown to try and find out about air fare from Nuremburg to Belgrade and went from here to there looking without much success. Finally, I found out that the tourist agency was not for airfare, after wandering through all sorts of gorgeous buildings in the central 'market district'. I bought a tape player for Rafal to listen to his English tapes on. I got home and presented it to him and thought he would eat me up. Then, we went off to the U.S. Consul where there were swarms of people. We finally got our interview consisting of a few words with a council guy who was the only person I've seen in the place with a smile and a twinkle in his eye. Rafal told him in English he was going to the U.S. to "get a job". The permission was granted very quickly and we were to come back in half an hour. We went to the Central Place, and I thought, as did Rafal, that we were to stay put while Wanda did an errand taking only ten minutes, she said. Nearly an hour went by when I dispatched, or rather Rafal suggested, that he go to the Embassy to see if he could find his mom. He raced off and was back in a moment saying his mother was there. We went back and waited with her for a long time to get the passport with the visa. Rafal nearly burst when his named was called. He must have said ten times he was "very, very happy" in loud English, causing people to look at him in amazement. He clung to me with almost a fervor. We made a quick stop for pizza and then home. Isi arrived and had found it impossible to get a visa for me anyway, so I'm back to Plan B. I went to Isi's singing group rehearsal. The kids were doing words to Billy's Bounce. The time was a bit flaky so I laid into them and really got them swinging. It was fun. There were some good voices and one really good girl scat singing lines!

We went back home to discuss travel arrangements for Rafal and the other kids for Jazz Camp. Isi and the crew are away tomorrow morning. I'll see them off. Then Wanda and I will get Rafal's ticket. I'll pay half, I can manage that. I'm as excited as he is. Thinking of all the amazing things we take for granted that he's never seen made me cry! Both he and Darek have made great strides with their English, It's fun to hear! They understand much more. I'm done! It's 12:30 and Darek is still listening to my Basile duo tape!

Tuesday, April 30

We were up early and sped off to see the kids and say goodbye. They were all in their bus, and we had a tearful farewell. I was so tempted to simply bag everything and grab my horn (which I had thought to bring) and get on the bus and go. All sense of responsibility leaves me on occasions like this, so it was a close call. Wanda and I followed the bus back through town. The kids were all waving and off on quite an adventure! Thirty-six hours by bus to Nuremburg! We went back home and then to town to find out about tickets for Rafal. I'm not sure whether it will be Pan Am or LOT, but he will arrive the 24th or 25th. I gave Wanda $300 or half the expected cost. I am out of my mind, but having a full-time kid on my hands will be a treat for me, and this kid is a pistol. We decided to hold off buying the ticket until Isi decides what airline his crew will go on.

Back briefly to last night, Isi and I talked about all the details and scheduling, etc. for these kids to come to Jazz Camp. I must get to John and Steve ASAP. It must happen! Wanda then took me back to the

Academy where I met with Witold and the little kids. I forgot my video. There's a little violin player, about nine years old, and look out! The guy from the big band was very cordial but even with a few hints about my poverty and how much I appreciated getting paid for my gigs, etc. he made no mention of money for my concert with his band.

I took the tram back home, solo. What a gas! I guess not everybody loves trams, but these things are great. They are quite fast and noisy and bumpy, but they give you quite a ride for 12 cents. My trip home, at least ten miles, on the tram and then more on the bus, took less than an hour and cost 24 cents. The bus-tram network covers the entire city. A maximum walk of a few blocks gets you to one of these forms of public transportation. You buy a book of little tickets and then cancel them yourself in a little hole-punch arrangement that perforates your ticket with a coded pattern. It's sort of on the honor system. Most of the time you could get away with not canceling, but there are spot checks and stiff fines if you don't have the correct coded and canceled ticket. When things are wall-to-wall, people don't bother. So, many ride for free. From here I can walk two blocks, and every five minutes two buses, one downtown, the other around to the other side of town, arrive on schedule like clockwork.

I got home, showered, and waited for my ride to God knows where for a jazz jam session recording thing put together by Maciek's uncle. Maciek and I met at the jam session a few nights ago, and he more or less insisted that I do this. Since I've got all day tomorrow with Rafal and Wanda, I said okay.

They arrived about 8:20 and we sped away in the mini Fiat to some small town about half an hour away. We went in through some very imposing gates to the campus of an agricultural college and lab. We had a brief visit with Maciek's family and then a walk up to what must be a school for young kids. The uncle had all sorts of mikes set up and seemed to think things were best when every one was turned to it's peak before feeding back.

I found myself with the piano player from Witold Malinowski's big band who was really pretty good. The guitar player from Isi's vocal group, the singer and Maciek were really trying hard. Everything was painfully too slow to start, and then gradually slowed down even more. Papa Jake would have said, "I wonder if this F___thing is going to stop!" Such enthusiasm!

There were a small group of onlookers who applauded wildly.

Hopefully the tape will be blank! I managed to get a few somewhat happening things going with the piano player. I managed, tactfully I hope, to extricate myself after only one tune with the banjo player. Fortunately, he had a van and was going my way. I explained I had to get up early. It was my last day. I'll be back to visit again soon and so on. Home.

Wednesday

Wanda, Rafal, Angela and I all took off for the mountains. I spent some time adjusting the fan belt on the car, and we got going about 10 a.m. The drive up was great. We started out on a turnpike at first then some small roads through little towns. The terrain reminded me of Big Sur and parts of California. Zakopane, our destination, is a ski resort with several major hotels and all the scenic wonders to go with it. There were big snowfields and snow-capped mountains. There seems to be a network of cable cars that take you to the tops of several mountains, then you ski down to the town of your choice. At the edge of the snow you stop and hike the rest of the way. We met Wanda's brother-in-law who lives with his son who is nearly a ringer for Rafal. They are the same age and are good buddies. It was fun to watch them together. If I had a home, I would have invited him to come with Rafal to the U.S. They run a small grocery store. We met them there and got some supplies and headed for a scenic tour that included one of the biggest hotels. We went to the roof and I took lots of video. We had a snack, overlooking the pool, of French fries and coffee. Then we had a short, impromptu bowling game. The kid's idea of a 'bowling team' was for all three to let fly at the same time. They were great fun to watch and thoroughly confusing for the automatic pinsetter, which finally quit.

From the bowling alley at the hotel we went to a little cabin-type place where we had a goulash and then by car to the home of the Pope and the new church being built there. It was very interesting to see the quality workmanship. We continued, too late for a cable car ride, to the brother-in-law's little apartment for bread and cheese and cold cuts for supper. I drove home. Our final stop was at the station where I bought my ticket to Warsaw. Back home, the kids went to bed early. Wanda presented me with a dozen of the glasses I said I liked, so I packed everything up and got to sleep with very mixed emotions. I really love it here and fell asleep thinking of ways to make it a permanent thing.

I was up early, all packed. Wanda, Rafal, and I rushed to the station and they saw me on board. Rafal was in tears until I explained that in 24 days I'd see him in New York, and even though I was sad to leave I was glad that I'd see him soon. I had more time to think on the train. I arrived and got to the Jazz Club and soon Zbishek and his wife arrived and soon after Eric came. Plans were made for me to stay with Eric since Zbishek and his wife were living with his in-laws, and I guess things are pretty tight. Eric took me home, stopping for four bottles of wine. His brother came over and we talked and talked all night. After four bottles of wine and then two of vodka we were still going strong at 12. Zbishek was supposed to come over but never made it. I slept very well, took one of those contortion showers and waited for Eric and his wife, Elena, to wake up. They have two apartments, one that Eric has and one that belonged to his girlfriend, now wife. They told me an unbelievable story about her daughter being more or less kidnapped by her father.

We had breakfast with strong coffee and beautiful scrambled eggs and we watched Walenza on TV. It was the 200th anniversary of the Polish constitution. Then Eric took me to the airport and left me there after more tearful farewells. During the usual passport control and luggage check-in I was behind a young American girl who had been traveling around Poland with her cat! She was loudly complaining about the long line and the terrible service, complaining about everything in general. I went to the back of the line so as not to be the next with an American passport. We were bused out to where the plane was parked and one by one, were escorted around to the right side of the plane and our checked-through luggage was hand loaded. Security, I found out: no unclaimed luggage would go on the plane.

Then another one-in-a-million experience unfolded. By pure chance, out of 150 passengers, I asked a man standing near me if he spoke English. Not only did he reply yes, but he was American, a classical pianist from Minnesota, a Baha'i and friend of Charlie and Anne Jennison. His name is Mark Ochu. How about that? We teamed up for the duration of the trip to Belgrade and were joined by chance by a very nice Polish mathematician en route to his research gig at Cornell and all became good pals. The most unlikely trio. We walked around Belgrade until quite late, stopping at a little bar for tea and two glasses of wine ($3.00) and elected to travel together today. Ryszard, the Polish gentleman, produced a bottle of Polish vodka. I produced the glasses from Wanda, and Mark had some little crackers from Paris and we had a great evening, talking 'til late at night in my hotel room. The American cat girl was still complaining, even at dinner in Belgrade that night.

Heading Home

Mark had just flown yesterday from Paris to Warsaw to Belgrade only to hear the pilot announce that there was a shortage of fuel in Belgrade and we'd have to go back to Paris to refuel for the hop across the Atlantic. Another adventure for me. Another landing and takeoff. Maybe I'll see the Eiffel Tower.

I did finally say something to the cat girl on the plane. She was sitting a few rows behind me, and when the pilot, in very clear English, announced the refueling plan she really went off, complaining, almost shouting about the delay. She carried on for a while and finally, very uncharacteristic for me, I said in a loud voice, "Why the fuck did you ever leave home?" There was considerable applause; the English needed no translation; she was silent for the rest of the trip.

Len will meet me in New York City. I can't believe this is all nearly over. It seems only minutes ago that I started this novel. We are slowing down now for our approach to Paris. I must continue with reflections.

I have been overwhelmed with such consideration and kindness for the past month. I feel if I possibly can I must repay this somehow. I also find my tolerance for people who are not kind and considerate has dropped. I hope that whatever decisions I make for the remainder of my life can help promote this basic, human decency and concern for others. I heard a few people complain about this, that or the other. For me this whole thing was an incredible adventure. The cat girl moaned and groaned because we would spend an extra hour refueling in Paris; I got to see the Eiffel Tower. The hassles at the ticket counters, the 'airport tax', the delays, etc. are all part of what is! I'm so glad that I can appreciate what is. I could see complaining if I was physically really uncomfortable or deprived of sleep, or had to go long without food. I felt fine; I slept well and was prodded into eating about eight meals a day. I met interesting people and enjoyed literally every minute of my trip. I saw lots of things that need change, things that I'd do a different way. Am I nuts? I liked everything. I was interested in things that didn't work, and fascinated with those that did. Just because things are not to your standards doesn't mean you should complain about it. Except for the incident at the Consulate and Dynasty, I was really proud of being American. I was given respect and pretty special treatment because of that and I'd like to think it's because of my attitude and perhaps my talent as a jazz player. I was certainly treated as a professional and given a salary commensurate with that. A doctor or lawyer is a professional and gets paid for it. In Poland, so do professional musicians!

Making friends, for me, is paramount, and I think I did pretty well. I have free places to stay in three major cities in Poland, which is like money in the bank. I really think I contributed and carried my own weight. I have some wonderful new friends and a family. What more can I ask for? Well, I can think of one thing—a way to get back to Poland, ASAP.

16

Triology
(1997–present)

It was another once-in-a-lifetime event. The chances of ever repeating it have discouraged me from even attempting to attempt it.

I had been in Poland for a while doing a lot of playing and school programs with pianist Joachim Mencel, whom I had met on a previous trip. Joachim and I had been performing as a duo in Poland and in the States and on this trip Jose Torres and his wife Izza had booked us in multiple schools around Bytom and I had gotten to know their son Tomek. He had spent a summer with me the year before.

One of many, we did an early evening workshop at a small music school in Chrozow, half way between Bytom and Katowice.

About fifteen kids showed up. Thirteen-year-old Tomek was there of course because his parents had booked the gig. A small younger kid about eleven from his school played the piano; they knew each other but not as friends. Another thirteen-year-old boy from Zory, about thirty kilometers away, showed up playing electric bass. His mother ran a music school in Zory and had heard about the workshop.

Mateusz Kolakowski could barely reach the pedals of the piano and his idea of jazz was a chorus-and-a-half of 'Body and Soul' played flawlessly from a transcription I'd guess. He was fine as soon as I explained about repeating the form and just playing the chords during solos.

Michal Baranski had been playing electric bass in a school rock group but had six or seven years of classical cello and piano at his mother's school. He instantly picked up the idea of walking bass lines from one chord to the next, and while still playing electric, pretty soon started playing acoustic bass as well.

Tomek Torres also had had six or seven years of classical piano, marimba and percussion, tympani, etc. His father, Jose, (who gave me the nickname 'Bradski') is nationally known for his well-established Cuban band. (His story is a book by itself). Tomek, on his own, was learning the drum set after school and on weekends.

It didn't take long to see this trio was something special and I remember telling Joachim at that first workshop, "I don't know how, but these guys are coming to the States". The rest of the story is history. They did come that first summer. All three with spring birthdays had just turned twelve, fourteen, and fourteen, and astounded audiences all over by their totally adult level of playing.

We recorded a CD that summer. It's fun to play it for musicians and after a few tracks tell them the ages of the kids—they won't believe you!

Multiple summers followed: concerts at the Polish consulates in NYC, Chicago and San Diego, Big Bear Jazz Fest in Vail, and several in Maine.

I'd told Jamie Aebersold about the kids and we visited him on our way back east. We met him and soon he asked, "Who is the bass player?" Michal responded and Jamie directed him to a bass. Michal started 'noodling ' and Jamie grabbed the phone. Within minutes he had lined up two high school workshops and another across the river at DeVry for his college jazz class.

I booked us at a small gallery in Kennebunkport, Maine. We were set up at one end of a long living room. There were openings at either end, to a parallel hall and beyond that an old house full of art treasures.

We always set up in a semi-circle so we could maintain eye contact and during the last tune of our first set I saw Michal's eyes pop open wide as he sort of glanced at the first opening. I followed his gaze and there, standing in the hallway, was former President George H. W. Bush. Michal had recognized him immediately; I wonder how many of our high school sophomores would?

The room was dark and with no fanfare or interruption of any kind the President went down the hall to the second opening and invisibly found a seat at the back of the room. We ended the tune and as the lights came back on I made a few cracks about seeing someone I thought I recognized from a poster in the Post Office, which brought a few laughs. Then a smiling President Bush came up, shook our hands and said kind things about his visits to Poland and amazed the boys by

Michal Baranski, Mateusz Kolakowski and Tomek Torres.

Tomek, Mateusz and Michal.

Triology portrait with me at the beginning of second U.S. tour.

Triology and me with President George H.W. Bush.

U.S. tour set in stone.

With Mateusz at Bowdoin College, Brunswick, Maine.

Willow Street concert.

Michal

On the
road

Triology playing with Buddy DeFranco in his garage.

correctly pronouncing the names of several cities. Then he asked if anyone had a camera and we have the picture of Triology and me with the President. But it gets better. We sent copies to him in Texas and he returned them, each one personalized to each boy by name and autographed, "Best wishes, George H. W. Bush." I had noticed somber men in overcoats outside the windows and several more who had not been at the concert. A once-in-a-lifetime for all of us.

Subsequent summers took us across country to Denver and Boulder, Colorado, via Niagara Falls, Mt. Rushmore, and an amazing visit with Buddy DeFranco in White Fish, Montana. We parked the van at the end of his driveway and spent the night. The next day, wanting to play, we set up in Buddy's garage. After a while Buddy came in to listen. I told him how thrilled the boys would be if he played a tune with them. He went back to the house and in a few minutes came back, clarinet in hand. I don't remember the tune but it was great! Buddy went back in the house, but in just a few minutes was back again and we played and played for an amazing jam session. (*Note from present time: Buddy's recent passing—remembering the magnitude of the man and his talent—highlights the memory of this historic event in my life and the lives of these young musicians.*) We continued west, playing at Starbucks in Seattle, and on to a visit with Doug Ramsey in Yakima. Roger Kellaway and Gene Lees presented us at the Jazz Bakery on two different trips. We parked the camper on Gene's lawn next to the pool. On the second trip we played two nights and the next day went to Roger's for what turned out to be an all day workshop with him. At one point Gene made a phone call and then handed the phone to Tomek, who with a look of total disbelief found himself wishing a "happy birthday" to Adam Makowicz.

There was a lot of sightseeing too. Glacier National Park, watching the Blue Angels in Seattle, and the sights in Monterey, Big Sur, Los Angeles, Universal Studios, and Sea World in San Diego. Las Vegas, Hoover Dam, Grand Canyon, Mesa Verdi and a lot of miles in between. Each summer some time was spent in Maine and Vinalhaven. The second summer, at the Maine Jazz Camp, the trio was jamming with the faculty.

At fifteen Mateusz went to the Berklee Jazz Camp. Surrounded by college age kids he was immediately placed in the top group.

At sixteen Mateusz called to tell me that he'd be competing in The Marshal Solal piano competition in Paris. Within minutes I had contacted Sean Cash and we had made plans to go to Paris to cheer Mateusz on. The final concert would be October 13, 2002. We would be there for a week.

While in Paris I took the opportunity to visit the Selmer Factory Store where I'd purchased my clarinet in 1958. Patrick Selmer was very friendly and offered to overhaul my clarinet; I jumped at it. He loaned me their top of the line "recital" clarinet which had unbelievable action but frankly didn't sound as rich and full as my old "Series 9", which he readily admitted!

A few days went by and I started to panic, remembering the last repair work I'd had done in NYC and the bill I got. I called Patrick several times. Several days had stretched into almost a week when I got the call to pick it up. Selmer technicians had put the horn on all the original 'gigs' and set it up exactly like new. It was spectacular!

Still wondering how I was going to pay for it, if I'd have to abandon my plan to rent a car and continue on to Poland—Patrick said there would be no charge. Thank you Patrick Selmer!

Mateusz triumphed although he experienced some strange competition politics. He played a very strong program, both his solo part and with the assigned rhythm section. The crowd's reaction said it all. They loved him!

At the end, the third place contestant from France was announced. Then second place, also from France. We were then sure Mateusz had placed first! But, another French name was called and he got the prize. There were loud boos from the mostly French audience. It was obvious to everyone that Mateusz should have won it by a landslide, but five of the seven judges were French and as always, competition politics had been considered.

Mateusz took it in his stride. Everybody else was pissed off! More than 30 people walked out! To cover themselves, the judges came up with a special award for "the most promising young pianist" and this was presented to Mateusz.

Mateusz drove back to Poland with his parents, and Sean and I, in our rented Renault, hit the road. Spending a delightful but somewhat forgettable night in a hotel in Amsterdam, we left the leftovers as a tip for the chambermaid. Then on to Poland for a wonderful ten days of visits with all the boys. On the way back to Paris we stayed a night in Germany with an aunt of Michal Baranski's. Her house was within walking distance of a huge health center, which turned out to be mostly

Michal Baranski 2014

Tomek Torres 2014

Mateusz Kolakowski

Studio Koncertowe PR im. W. Lutosławskiego - 8.11.2006

ad LiBiTuM
1st Warsaw Jazz Concert

Mateusz Kołakowski

clothing optional! Pools, saunas, waterfalls, hot tubs, places to sit or stretch out—all spotless and delightful. We didn't want to leave!

The following years there were more visits back and forth, me to Poland and the boys here to the U.S.

In 2007 Mateusz came for the summer on his own and I booked as many gigs as I could. On our way home from Tuesday Jazz Night at the Mt. Washington Hotel we stopped in Bridgton to see my brother Peter. He and Mateusz headed right for the piano and started tearing through a lot of Chopin, Peter on the bass end, and Mateusz on the treble end. Occasionally Peter would get lost and Mateusz would reach around him, take over the left hand and get everything back on track. They were laughing and giggling like school kids.

A year later, Mateusz and I visited again, again on the way home from Mt. Washington. Peter was in the final days of lung cancer and pretty much out of it, but he managed to talk briefly with Mateusz. Mateusz then went into the living room and tore up pages and pages of Chopin from Peter's collection. At one point he played a mazurka first time through straight from the page, and then proceeded to improvise loosely, using the form. The results were emotional and amazing and my sister-in-law Mary Lou said Peter was just lying there with a smile on his face. Peter was gone about ten days later. I'm glad I have that recording.

Now, in 2015, these three kids all are all over Poland and playing internationally. They all have stuff on Youtube. Michal and Tomek are both married. Michal has two children and is a full-time professor in charge of the Jazz Bass Department in Katowice! Both of them are playing everywhere, Michal with all the best players in Poland, and Tomek with his kick-ass-off-the-charts rock group Afromental, and with his brother Filip in their father's renowned Cuban Band. He also joins Michal on occasion, playing with some of the best.

Mateusz is also playing his Chopin Jazz and touring worldwide. He recently toured Poland and recorded an album with Dave Leibman.

I can imagine finding one really amazing player but to find three at once, showing up independently of each other and playing at such a high level. They came up with the name Triology.

That's once-in-a-lifetime again for me—times three at least.

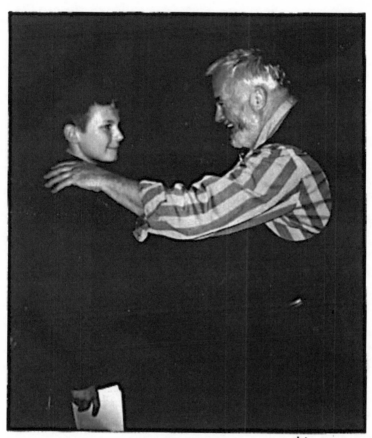

March, 2003

To beloved Brad,
great musician and indefatigable educator,
in token of remembrance of common and
incredible experiences

Mateusz

17

Willow Street
(1991–present)

Back in America I have my own pad on Willow Street in Bath, Maine. I had been looking for something that could be mine but was totally discouraged by the selection and the prices. Everything was for more money down than I could possibly find and higher mortgage payments than I dared assume. For months I searched. There was nothing I could consider until I spotted 36 Willow Street.

From the multiple listings book, at my friend Mike Baribeau's real-estate office I determined that the shell was built in the late fifties as a three bay garage-storage-repair-workshop for a general contractor who used to live across the street. It was a simple 40' x 25' frame building with a low-pitched roof, peak running the long way. There was a dormer on the left two thirds, facing the street. The asking price for the building and its 60' x 120' lot was $27,000. From the multiple listing sheets I got the address and went to have a look. Halfway down the short street the place was easy to spot. I parked and was struck by the quiet, even though it was only a few minutes from the center of Bath. Two little girls on tricycles made a U-turn in the paved area that fronted the building. They looked at me with smiles but not much curiosity and returned to the middle of the street to ride. I pried open one of the overhead doors to get a look inside. It was simple. The bottom of the door was rotted enough that I could stick my hand through and reach the latch. Inside, it was one big space. The owner liked to bring in his trucks and move things around. The place was full of every sort of construction equipment and byproducts; tools, hand tools and old power tools, glass cutter and stocks of glass, broken furniture, broken window frames, and broken screens, piles of assorted rusty nails, bolts, screws and a bucket of plumber's lead, pipe cutters and stocks of assorted pipe. Countless pails of dried up paint, some new, petrified paint brushes, plumbing fixtures and cracked toilets. You name it and it was there except it was mostly all pre-building code and seemed of very little use to me as I contemplated making this disaster into a home.

Mr. Stewart, now the owner of the contractor's house across the street, was pleasantly curious about my breaking and entering, more curious about the insides and joined in with my inspection. He told me it had been on the market and unused for several years. At his suggestion I offered $20,000, which was immediately accepted.

The bank, of course, laughed at me when I applied for a loan. I had been paying my car payments on time and my only credit card, from Sears, showed a zero balance. I didn't owe any money. With $1,000 down I could walk into the Ford agency and drive away a new $30,000 camper van, pack my stuff and flee to Mexico and never make a payment, but I couldn't borrow $20,000 to buy property; a place to live that wasn't going anywhere. A very good friend came to my rescue and simply took out a $20,000 loan in his name, which I 'assumed'. I had made a $4,000 down payment and so now had the borrowed $20,000 to get myself sheltered before the cold set in. When I closed and got started it was November 18th.

The owner had cleared most of the stuff out, and after a few days of cleaning and shoveling I was ready for Portland Insulation Company to insulate the shell, completed in a fraction of the time and at a price of about what it would have cost me just for materials. The three rotted overhead doors came off, one replaced with a good insulated door, complete with one of the few real luxuries I've allowed myself, a remote-controlled garage door opener. The first time I came home late in the pouring rain and didn't have to brave a cold shower to get in my house I realized it was not exactly a luxury. I thought it would be great to drive my car inside and watch TV from the front seat but when the codes officer told me I couldn't keep my car parked inside where I lived, I reluctantly separated the garage area from the living area with a fireproof wall. The other two garage doors, once removed, left a space that became the front wall of the living area with three windows and a front door. I lived inside this space in my pop-top camper 'til the last minute. The original owner had wanted unobstructed space for his trucks and equipment and put in huge cables that were all that held up the main timber spanning the 40 ft. clear area. These came out. With floor jacks straining and rafters creaking I loosened the 3 six foot long turnbuckles, which I've kept as souvenirs. 10x10 posts and a carrying beam with a flat steel core were carefully put in to replace the cables. As I released the pressure on the jacks, I ran back and forth across the street to constantly monitor the visible sag in the roof which slowly disappeared; my calculations were close enough. Water and sewer lines were brought up through the floor, the phone was working and a Toyo kerosene furnace was cooking; my pink plastic-coated cave was ready. I pushed my pop-top camper out through a specially constructed escape hatch, out into the first snow of the winter, quickly sealed off the hatch with a specially constructed cover, and was home. Showering was done across the street at the Stewart's. Washing was done in the kitchen sink, and all toilet activities were done by careful aim into the 4-inch waste pipe sticking out of the floor and flushed with a bucket.

For the first year about all I did was to try and stay warm. The sloping concrete floor (double layers as I discovered putting in the pipes) made for interesting furniture arrangements. I lost 1/2 inch of elevation per linear foot; the floor was designed to drain towards the doors and was 12 inches higher at the back wall. I had bits of scrap wood handy and could level things by feel pretty well. I had found at 'Dot's Deals' some great old carpeting and underlayment that kept the floor somewhat warmer. Coming back from my second trip to Poland, I managed to put in a wood floor. Each floor joist had to be tapered and custom fit to the rather uneven sloping concrete. All had to be laid out, fitted and then all removed again so a plastic vapor barrier could be placed under them. The plastic went down, joists put back and secured; then I placed bag after bag of pouring wool in between and finally put down plywood flooring that would have to suffice for a year or two.

A door from Dot's used stuff shop went in between the garage space and the living area. The plumbing moved from under the kitchen sink onto a small riser where I installed a shower stall, salvaged from a house my friend Mike Baribeau was refurbishing. I had, I thought, a not-too-badly-cracked toilet from my own junk pile. Fitted with new inner workings it worked fine but seemed to seep a bit around the base; I'd have to live with it. The bathroom boasted a nice folding door from Dot's, but it was more than a year before I put in a bathroom wall; it was the best seat in the house for watching TV; fine for me but a bit disconcerting for some visitors.

Little by little the place was becoming more livable. Sheetrock covering the pink, plastic-covered insulation stayed gray for years before I could afford paint. When I thought I could justify spending a few dollars I put tiles on the floor and nearly completed a workable kitchen. I had constant ideas about ways to add an upstairs and expand here and there. The upstairs was a sleeping loft and storage space for bags of things that have been following me around. I haven't a clue what is in some of them. The original decor of pink fiberglass insulation, covered with plastic, remained for a while; I couldn't quite stand up in the center. 'Dot's' rugs moved from downstairs kept it snug.

Downstairs was really almost perfect for me alone, but it's still difficult to entertain much. The whole space with kitchen and now partitioned-off bathroom is only 24' x 24' so it gets cluttered pretty quickly. I have an ancient stereo with huge, bureau-sized 'Voice of the Theater' Altec Lancing speakers. I bought them from Jim Contner, one of the kids in the hot rod club in 1965. I had them in the Emporium, and they still sound warm and wonderful.

I can listen, cook, microwave, toast, sauté, abloute, shower, be wet or dry, dressed or undressed, practice or watch the news. One space fits all. My faithful Ford Festiva is just through another of Dot's doors, warm and out of the weather. Perhaps, best of all, just eighteen feet from my back wall is the railroad track. As the train approaches from either direction it toots its horn at grade crossings. I usually have a few minutes warning before it blasts its horn, right by my house. Streets at both ends of Willow Street cross the tracks. Horn blasting, engine roaring; the whole house shakes. It's great! All my plants and vines dance, the reflections on the glass in the picture frames dance and shimmer, and unless exactly hung straight the pictures shift out of plumb, little points and rings dance across the coffee in my mug. If I'm playing a record the needle jumps off the track. Can't miss it when the train goes by… nothing pianissimo about it.

I'll fast forward to now.

The Willow Street pad, like so many other things in my life, has evolved, to where now it almost looks like a house. Bathroom walls happened early on and a sink from the Vinalhaven dump soon after. After leveling the wood floor, and several years of Vinyl tiles, with great help from my friend Marty Corey, I installed some laminate flooring. I used lots of large rocks for a retaining wall, lugged railroad ties and back-filled to created a nice and reasonably private sunning area between the house and the train tracks; a sliding glass door provides access.

After living downstairs for a few years and only sleeping on a mattress upstairs, with Herculean help from Sean Cash, we added the second floor, and moved the bathroom up to the top of a new central staircase. I reinstalled the vanity salvaged from the piles of stuff I found here. A new shower stall replaced the salvaged one from Mike Baribeau, and my brother Peter gave me a bidet; probably the only one in Bath, Maine.

I now have two bedrooms. Someone can actually stand up straight without bumping their head, and not tread on anybody's mattress on the way to the john.

Sean was instrumental again, installing four skylights with an amazing barrel vault ceiling he designed. I found a wood-burning stove and did all the masonry to install it myself. Rafal (from Poland) helped with the cleaning up.

My constant companion and housemate for the last 8 years is Holly, a Belgian Shepherd rescued from a shelter two hours before she was to be put down. She's seventy pounds of love who would like to live in my pocket. Mankind is not deserving of this kind of devotion but I like to think with Holly it's a two-way street.

I fenced in the 70x60 side lot and installed a pet door for Holly to access her bathroom.

For my bathroom, I replaced the vanity salvaged from the previous owner with a new, colorful, Mexican sink I found in San Antonio and replaced the constantly seeping, smelly, nasty toilet with a new 4.5 second flush gem, from Jacuzzi. For the first time in 17 years my bathroom smelled fresh and clean instead of like the Paris sewers. I'm guessing the old one had been abandoned for a reason.

More recently, after seventeen years of dripping faucets I replaced the old kitchen sink from the dump with a new one with new, no-leak fixtures. This spring I plan to add a new picture window to the west, sunning space side, which will bring in a lot more light. The new fence now offers total privacy even from the windows of the passing trains.

Most recently I've managed to get some dead trees down and remove brambles and burdocks to make Holly's space look less like the rain forest. That brings Willow Street up to Spring 2009. Life is good here.

In March 2011 disaster struck. Near my house is a catch basin. The basin serves only to equalize the high water levels on the street and the back of the property, which would after a fairly heavy rain, occasionally partially flood the street and my yard. Catch basins all over town were cleared in anticipation of heavy rain but for some reason not on Willow St. and, with the basin plugged, the water was eighteen inches higher on the street than in the back. Water rushed in through my garage and rose to five inches over my floor, water mixed with raw sewage complete with pink toilet paper.

From mid-March 'til just two days before leaving for Poland on my latest trip, I had been fighting city hall trying to get the town to accept some responsibility for an estimated $8,000–$10,000 expense, just to get back to where I had been. A rumor got started that I was about to submit a letter to the local newspaper and they reluctantly came through with $3,000 if I agreed not to send the letter; not enough but way better than nothing.

This last bit was added in December 2011 in Poland as I try to finish writing this book.

18

Fast Forward
(1970–2010)

They should have a lottery in Maine so hunters can shoot barns.
—Garry Merrill

I can't and don't want to detail everything that has happened to me in my seventy-three years on this planet. Fast Forward is sort of a "been there, done that" way of connecting various timelines between the chapters where I have gone into more detail.

I've filled in most of the spaces up through my departure from Riverdale, so now I'll fast forward.

Camp continued for a few more years.

I accepted the job offer from the Village School in New Gloucester and started right away after spring vacation. With help from my father I bought a house with a barn right in the center of the tiny town and took in several kids as boarders. Three or four were Penobscot Indians.

I bought a large GMC (TDM-36) city bus and converted it into a camper, famously named the "Blue Lunch". Serious engine rebuilding was needed but it served the camp well and subsequently made three trips to the west coast.

When I first moved to Maine I figured my music days were pretty much over but I heard about 'Sessions' at the Bridgeway Restaurant in Portland and went to have a look. I found Don Doane leading the session. He was a wonderful player and we quickly established a friendship. He'd played with some of the greatest big bands, Maynard Ferguson, Stan Kenton and Woody Herman, to name a few, but gave it all up to be a father and be with his family. He helped me get my first gigs in Maine and I played gigs with him. We enjoyed mutual trust and thanks to Don I began to make some good music connections

The next summer in August, my father died.

To set the record straight: Pops had taken a long row in his much-loved rowing dory, out almost to the Monument, had come back and headed out to Calm Island in the *Anna W* with my mother and brother, Arthur.

They trimmed brush, had lunch, and Pops took a skinny dunk in the ocean and sunned himself for a while in a small sheltered cove. Loading up to come home he thought he poked his chest on a stern cleat while hauling in a rowboat. Once back home he made two trips back down to the dock to bring up various tools and picnic baskets and then told mother he was feeling tired and would lie down for a spell.

Mother made her traditional tea. A short while later she went in to check on Pops and found him lying very still, cold and clammy. She called me on the hotline at camp. We immediately called Dr. Earl who was out to dinner but went to the Island Medical Center, picked up the EKG machine and was there in fifteen minutes. Dr. Earl hooked up an IV. I drove a nail in the wall behind the bed to hook it on.

The summer doctor in North Haven was a heart specialist. Dr. Earle called him and I was dispatched with a few campers in the *Dirigo* to pick him up at the Casino, sort of the central drop-off place on the North Haven waterfront. By now it was dark and very foggy. Seeing nothing but the radar I headed full speed, oblivious to the moored pleasure boats surrounding the Casino, snatched the doctor and had him back to the scene quickly. He conferred with Dr. Earle, looked at the almost dormant EKG, conferred some more; we all knew that there was nothing more to be done.

In a few minutes, with Mother holding his hand, he opened his eyes and said, " I feel very tired," and stopped breathing.

I took the doctor back to North Haven, going much slower.

As school started that fall, with my house full of Village School kids, I fixed a room for my mother. The plan was that she'd stay a week or two before heading back to the house in North Stamford. It almost instantly became clear that she couldn't face the Woodbine Road house all alone, and she stayed with me for the winter. Strangely enough, on the way up to Vinalhaven at the beginning of the summer, my parents had stopped in Brunswick and talked to a real estate guy about finding a house there. They were seriously thinking about making the move to Maine.

A friend alerted Mother about a house, right next door to the real estate man's house; 11 Federal Street. Brother Peter was called to inspect, and the deal was done. With help from some of my boarders and the old blue bus, I moved most of the stuff from Woodbine Road, and Mother moved in.

Meanwhile, after a year the Village School went belly-up, owing me a year's salary. I sold the New Gloucester house and moved into an unfinished shed area behind 11 Federal Street. I put in plumbing, insulation, heat, a tiny galley kitchen and spiral stairs up to a sleeping loft. (Sound familiar?)

The Augusta Jazz Society probably got my name from Don Doane or someone at the Bridgeway sessions. I was paired with Lenny Breau, whom I had never heard of... but some of my friends seemed to know about him. We met at someone's house to run down a few tunes and I was stunned. I'd never heard anything like Lenny's playing. The concert went well and before we parted, plans were in the works to meet at my mother's house in Brunswick and do some recording. *The Living Room Tapes* resulted.

I would live there and care-take for my mother until she died December 19th, 1978. She had experienced short blackouts when she would briefly loose consciousness and wake up very confused. She'd lose track of time, that my father had died, where she was, etc. But in fifteen minutes to half an hour she had everything back on track.

In the early evening of December 19th she was resting, reading upstairs in bed. From the bottom of the stairs I called up and told her I'd go out to get something for dinner. She cheerfully responded she'd take a bath and come down when she heard me come home.

When she didn't appear I called up to her and got no response. I went up, heard the water running in the bathroom, knocked on the door and called to her. No response. I peeked in and saw that she was completely under the water, not moving. I went in and pulled her head up to try some CPR, but there was nothing happening.

I pulled the plug to drain the tub, covered her with a towel and called 911.

The eventual autopsy revealed a tumor, which had caused all those problems with her eye. The official cause of death was 'accidental drowning'. She loved soaking in a hot bath. She slipped away quietly. The tub was full, within inches of the brim, yet there wasn't a drop on the floor.

Carole Simons, whose son Jeff had been at Camp the summer before, and some other family friends descended. My friend Al Miller took me and several of my foster kids in for Christmas.

Due to really bad financial planning the house had to be distress-sold to pay the taxes. I would soon be homeless.

The following spring, with a much smaller than expected inheritance, I was still able to put a small down payment on a house in Brunswick and asked Carole and her two younger sons to move in with me. Her son Jeff had been living with me and going to the local high school. In August we were married in Vinalhaven.

The Island Camp finally closed down when my board of directors thought we absolutely had to have comprehensive insurance coverage. The best estimate we got was $1,000 per kid, per season. With half the kids on scholarship the camp closed down due to financial duress and the prohibitive projected cost.

I sold the land back to members of the family and the A-frame was torn down. The *Dirigo* had to be sold too, the end of an era.

We lived in three places near Brunswick. I adopted Carole's two younger boys, and we hosted a swarm of foster kids; Stan, from the quarry was one of them. When my gigs and Carole's job both hit dead ends we packed up the whole crew and, at the urging of my old friend Helen Mather, moved to Austin, Texas. We were told by the state that Stan, who had been with me for eight years, couldn't go with us to Texas as a foster kid, so we adopted him. His parents with whom he'd had no contact with in all this time—eight years... both hired lawyers to block the adoption, but we prevailed.

We had a house with a pool and a big mortgage. Carole had a good job, and I was playing four to six nights a week; we were okay.

Then, the drinking age was changed from 18 to 21, which affected about 40,000 U.T. students and shut down most of the small clubs I had been working in. All I had was a Sunday happy hour for $25.00 and all the pasta I could eat. I did a stint as a teacher's aid at the Adolescent Day School at the State Hospital. Given no opportunity to use any of my skills, I was a 'go-fer' and bodyguard. It gave me nightmares. At night I pedaled solar hot water systems door-to-door, with little success. I eventually went back to driving school buses.

On my way to work one morning a car suddenly pulled out of a convenience store directly in front of me. I was driving my jeep, and to avoid hitting him opted for the shoulder, which became a six-foot hole with a culvert at the bottom. I stopped real fast. The steering wheel was bent around like a croissant, and I could feel my beard on the inside. Thirty-six stitches (in three layers) later, I was told that another sixth of an inch would have left me with a flap instead of a lip. Not so great for a clarinet player.

I made a proclamation that "I was a clarinet player". It cost me a job, a car, a house, and a wife, in rapid succession. After the divorce I left Texas for Maine with a trailer behind my eleven-year-old station wagon and $600. I spent the winter watching the snow fly at my brother Peter's.

I won the Hennessey Cognac Jazz Search in New York with John Basile. I moved to Monterey, California for a year and a half to play with Jake Stock and The Abalone Stompers. I came back to Maine, parking my trailer at the Cash's, found Izi Runick at Jazz Camp which led to the Polish adventure that started in 1991 and which continues to evolve.

I could go on. Three wonderful cross-country trips in the Blue Lunch camper bus. Multiple cross-country tours with Mateusz, Michal and Tomek (Triology). Nineteen trips to Poland. The last, fall of 2009 for a whirlwind, nineteen concert promotion tour of the "Live at Fort Andros" CD with Joachim Mencel. Everything first class, and planning another in the fall of 2010.

Along the way I've taken advantage of Poland's wonderful healthcare services twice... actually, four times. Twice I went to Joachim's dentist and had eight ancient fillings replaced or repaired costing eight dollars a tooth. And twice I went for a serious fifty-thousand-mile check up. Whole enchilada.

The night before the first of those events, a nurse showed up at the Zieba's house and administered an enema. She retuned and did it again in the morning.

Then for a day and a half I was poked, prodded, treadmilled, cardiogramed, stressed-tested, x-rayed, and had my backside invaded by a camera crew. Tomek Torres was my translator and said that watching the exploration of my innards on TV was much more interesting than the Biology class he was missing. A day and a half later, with before and after visits with the doctor included, the bill was one hundred- sixty-five dollars.

Mateusz was my translator five years later, same deal. But this time things got confused in the translations and returning home I went to my 'family doctor' and was specifically asked for blood tests; never suggested by my doctor before.

This doctor didn't seem interested in my ADD at all, choosing to dismiss it. A week after the tests he simply informed me I had Diabetes. Period. In shock, I may or may not have heard anything he said after that. I had no idea; Type I- Type II; no clue. All I had was visions of Ella Fitzgerald with no feet and I panicked. As I left his office in a daze, his secretary berated me about a bill I'd forgotten to pay. I didn't want to go back and ask him to clarify the situation and had to wait for ten days for a consultation with a dietitian who explained it was Type II.

Fortunately, I found a wonderful local doctor in Bath who now knows me well and has me totally under control.

I had back surgery to install an X-Stop, which gave me some relief, but two years later it was removed and I had a laminectomy. The relief after that was short-lived too. Fifteen minutes on my feet is about it. Airports present new problems.

Not as bothersome and with better results, two knee operations, bursar removed on one, and torn meniscus on the other

I am noticing a general diminishment of energy. I'll be seventy-eight soon and like those old 78 rpm records, I'm feeling a bit obsolete

But now, as we began back in Epilogue One: June 5th, 2010, I'm shutting this down. Seems to me, I've reached that certain point... to finish this while I can, rather than have someone else do it.

Almost anyone, given enough time in a studio, can come up with a perfect album. Individual notes can be corrected and timing can be tweaked to within a millisecond. In my personal record collection the live performances captured, as was, are by far the most exciting and interesting. What you hear is totally honest; the way it happened. The same holds for this book. I'm sure I could arrange for a dozen qualified proofreaders to fine tune this so every comma is in the right place, every metaphor mixed perfectly, no loose hanging participles, or muddled metaphors.

Hey! That wouldn't be quite honest. Much to the chagrin of those who have helped me I've only altered things when they told me what I had written was really confusing. Don't look too closely. If it matters to you, you can surely find mistakes. Please just remember who was writing this!

I've decided, as my seventy-third birthday rapidly approaches, that its time to finish this project. There are more stories to tell and someday

I might, or might not get around to putting them down on paper.

My nephew Bern Terry and his companion/partner Katie Shepherd have graciously given me a place to stay here in Lincoln. Back in April, I invited myself to visit Bern and he introduced me to Jamie Masefield. He told me on the phone that he had a neighbor on the next farm over who played the mandolin. My reaction was pretty much, "Sure, okay, tell me about it, sounds great..." I'm sure when he told Jamie he had an uncle in Maine who played the clarinet and whistled, Jamie's reaction was about the same.

Before we actually met, Bern played some of Jamie's CDs to me and some of my stuff with Lenny Breau for Jamie. When we met in Bern's living room we only played four tunes but the communication was seamless, total, almost telepathic. Only a few days later Jamie called me in Maine and told me he had landed us a spot in the Burlington Discover Jazz Festival, June 7th. This had given me a perfect excuse to visit here again.

The concert Monday was a great success and from all accounts we made friends and have gotten rave reviews. My nephew Matthew, Bern's brother, said it was like a non-competitive tennis game. You have to get the ball over the net but the point is to place it so the other guy can return it. This therefore is my newest project and a joyful one.

My goal is to finish up this writing project as soon as possible. I'm sitting at a big kitchen table with a view of fields and almost mountains. My wonderful dog Holly is next to me and will bark only at any visitors coming so I'll have plenty of time to slip on some shorts and be 'street legal'.

No barking dog, just a faithful snoozing one at my feet but my costume is about the same as when I started writing this fourteen years ago in Krakow, Poland. Much to the amusement of my Polish friends I often added 'ski' to English words so they would become Polish. Jose Torres gave me the nickname Bradski... I'll keep it.

Washington Square, NYC. 1980 Photo by Al Miller

19

Brad Terry (So far.)

Jeff really ceases to amaze me.
— John Basile

Editor's note:

Though music written as notes on a page holds little relevance for him, it seems only right in sharing the timeline of Brad's life, to place his milestones along a music staff symbolizing the constant presence of music through out his life. From his early youth to his present day musical collaborations, Brad has improvised all along the way, looking, it seems, for balance and harmony and inevitably finding excitement and adventure.

Brad is always learning, always teaching, always inspiring with his clear expression, sweet sound, and extraordinary ear, which, entirely unfettered by reading notes from a page, allows for his engaging sense of humor and collaboration in making music with others.

Enjoy the journey!

1937 June 9th. Born,
I'm told, in The Hague,
Holland.

1944 Lived briefly
in Washington,
D.C.

1939–1944 Stamford, CT Played
recorder by ear. Heard my first
music teacher (piano) tell my
mother I was "without musical
talent" and "un-teachable."

First girlfriend, Nancy.
First vehicle, Dumpy.

1945–1946 London.
4th grade, cold and
wet.

1946–1953 Started at
Bement, and then various
New England boarding
schools. (Rapid succession)

Brad, learning to walk.

Second vehicle replacing Dumpy built by brother Peter

1950 Benny Goodman convinced parents to purchase first clarinet from Connecticut Music Exchange, Stamford, CT. Clarinet came with three free lessons from Ray Taranto.

1952 First band: 9th grade, St. Paul's School. Befriended and mentored by choir director, Dr. Channing Lefebvre. (Still got kicked out, midway through 10th grade.)

1952 First gig: New Year's Eve Party with Fred Fischer, New Canaan, CT.

1952–1955 Played whenever, wherever. In and out of Salisbury School (and others). Played Mozart Clarinet Quintet by ear—only ever attempt to play classical.

First tracks in Connecticut

Nancy Lounsbury, Ted Mather with Helen Mather, Marianna Mather, and Sue Lounsbury. Home from Bement for Xmas 1947.

1956 First Jazz concert: Darien High School, re-creating Benny Goodman trio; Fred Fischer (p), Micky Earnshaw (dr), and myself. Benny and Alice Goodman were in the audience with my parents.

1957 Recruited as "ringer" (driver) with Yale Bull-pups, Dixieland band with Steve Swallow playing bass. Three lessons with Benny Goodman.

1957 Started sitting in regularly at Eddie Condon's on 4th St. NYC. Picked up gigs with Wild Bill Davison, George Wetling and others.

1957 U.S. Army Feb 4th—August 4th (180 days).

1957–1958 Started sitting in with Buddy Tate's Celebrity Club Orchestra NYC. Soon became a regular and started playing with: Buddy, Buck Clayton, Dickie Wells, Eli Robinson, Rudy Rutherford, Major Holly, Sadik Hakim, Sir Charles Thompson, Bobby Pratt, Herb Gardiner, Vic Dickinson, Doc Cheatham, Roy Eldridge, Rex Stewart, Joe Jones, Dave Frishberg.

1958 Moved to NYC with Steve Swallow. (Next door to Roswell Rudd.)

1958 Bert Stern's *Jazz On A Summer's Day*. (Clarinet player in the old car with the straw hat!).

Steve Swallow
bass

Chuck Folds
piano

Brad Terry
clarinet

Charlie Keil
drums

⸗ / 1958

1958 **Started** The Island Camp for boys, which I ran for the next 23 years. (Vinalhaven, ME.)

1958 Summer tour of Europe with Steve Swallow, Chuck Folds, Charlie Keil, and Pat Williams. Played two weeks at Blue Note in Paris opposite Chet Baker, Kenny Clark, Pierre Michalot and Al Haig. Started studies with Joe Allard, NYC.

1958–1960 Struggled in NYC as Rock and Roll took over.

With Don Elliot of Jazz Doctors. Westport, CT 1958

1966–1969 Landed trio gig at the Sugarbush Inn, in Vermont with Don Coates (p) and Howard Kadison (dr). There for three winters. Visiting guests, Buddy Tate and Buck Clayton.

1960 Moved to garage apartment (the Emporium) at parents' and drove school buses. Booked whatever, whenever. Gigs with Steve Swallow, Wayne Wright, Sam Brown, Ahmed Abdul Malik, Percy Brice, Ray McKinny.

With Jim Gillespie. Vinalhaven, Maine 1958–60.

1960s More gigs with Buddy Tate, Buck Clayton and trios with Wayne Wright, Sam Brown, and Steve Swallow but generally a lull. Became a regular with "The Jazz Doctors" Westport, CT Played with Thad Jones, Gay Mehegan, Don Elliott, Bernie Leighton, Joe Corsello, and Rick Petrone.

1972 Recorded *Eddie and Me,* Live at Odyssey House benefit in NYC. With Eddie Thompson (p) and Lyn Christie (b) (Brad Terry, Livingroom Records.)

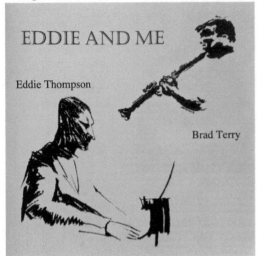

EDDIE AND ME

Eddie Thompson

Brad Terry

Continued the Island Camp on Vinalhaven. When it closed in 1980 I joined the staff at Maine Jazz Camp.

1973 Second Odyssey House benefit concert with Chuck Wayne and Joe Puma.

1969 Started teaching at Riverdale School, NYC. Met Eddie Thompson. Played regularly with him and Major Holly, also Lance Heywood and Bobby Jones.

With Eddie Thompson. Freeport, Maine. 1975.

The following kind words are from Doug Ramsey, winner of the 2008 Lifetime Achievement Award of the Jazz Journalists Association and a contributor to Jazz Times for 35 years.
"The whole created by two gifted musicians willing or able to subsume their egos and really listen to one another can be larger by several magnitudes than both or all of their parts. That is what developed here between Brad Terry and Eddie Thompson. This music, recorded thirty-four years ago is as fresh and surprising as a sudden spring shower."

1974–1978 Moved to Maine. I'd already been playing with Dick Cash, Les Richards, Sonny Cardilli, Bobby Giasson, Claude Noel, Don Nelson, Willie Maiden, and Roswell Rudd. Started playing with: Don Doane, Jaxon Stock, Gerry Wright, Joe Laflamme, Billy and Dominic Moio, Roy Frazee, Steve Grover, Ben Street, Les Harris, (Sr. and Jr.) Tommy Gallant, Jim Howe. Weekly *Sessions at the Warehouse* in Lewiston, ME. Trio with Jaxon Stock and Tom Bucci. Concerts with Eddie Thompson, Buddy Tate and Grey Sargent.

1976 Appointed by Marshall Dodge (and Al Miller) as Jazz Director for first Maine Festival, Bowdoin College. Collaborated for many years with Al Miller on *Music & Mime* shows at schools, The Theater Project, and The Young People's Theater.

1978–1981 Started recording sessions with Lenny Breau. The original album, *The Living Room Tapes, Vol. 1,* was released in 1986 on the Musical Heritage Society Records label , shortly after Lenny's death, and was reviewed by Gene Lees in his *Jazzletter*. *The Living Room Tapes, Vol. 2* was released in 1990. Leonard Feather gave it four stars in the L.A. Times. *The Complete Living Room Tapes* (both Vols.) was re-released as a CD in 2002 by Art of Life Records. A DVD, also with Lenny Breau, *Live at the Maine Festival*, was released by Paul Kohler, Art of Life Records)
(*One Long Tune*, a fascinating biography by Ron Forbes-Roberts, details his visits to Maine and these recording sessions.)

With Chris Neville, John Lockwood, Steve Grover. Friends of Jazz. Bowdoinham, Maine. 1981

1981 Started The Mid-Coast Jazz Society. (Became Maine Jazz Alliance)

1981 Received a National Endowment for the Arts grant and brought Dizzy Gillespie to Maine for a week of performances ending at Merrill Auditorium in Portland. Invited by Dizzy Gillespie to play "Cuban music" at the Village Gate in NYC.

1981 Started Friends of Jazz with Steve Grover, presenting Jazz clinics and workshops to Maine schools statewide. Members included Mark Perry, Charlie Jennison, John Hunter, Chris Neville, John Lockwood, Tony Gaboury, Tim Sessions, Ben Street, Greg Cohen, Dan Hall, and Tom Bucci.

With Mark Perry and Lenny Breau.
Sebago Lake, Maine. 1981

With Dizzy Gillespie
Merrill Auditorium,
Portland. Maine. 1981

With Aaron Terry and Dizzy. Bowdoinham, Maine. 1981

1982 Concert with Friends of Jazz and
Portland Symphony Orchestra (with
Director Bruce Hangen) with Tim Sample
and Gary Merrill.

Screen printing the Friends of Jazz shirts. 1982

Back when the world was young (about 1958), I found myself playing at a private party with a Dixieland band up in New Canaan, Connecticut. We went way past quitting time - our host was mellow, the band was hot, and no one wanted to stop. Jam session.

Well after sunrise, when we were down to playing duets on African thumb pianos, a tall guy built like a lumberjack and carrying a naked clarinet wandered in. Some of our crew seemed to know him. The blues in 'F' was called, and I got my first listen to Brad Terry. I was bowled over.

At age 18, Brad was already one of the fastest clarinetists around and well into bebop, which is a rarity on clarinet even now. What do critics say about Brad and this album 30 years later? Gene Lees reviewed it in his *Jazzletter.*

I had to get past Brad Terry's playing to listen to Breau. He comes as a total surprise. I had in my head an unformulated image of some local semi-amateur musician whom Lenny probably indulged out of kindness, and perhaps too because his home offered Lenny a retreat, a place to hide from troubles. Wrong. Brad Terry is a wonderfully warm, fluid, responsive, inventive player, far and away the most attractive clarinetist I have heard in years.

"Brad Terry is my favorite kind of musician: One who explores music - guided by a childlike curiosity and enthusiasm." - Roger Kellaway

"Brad Terry is such a happy sounding player.... and whistler; remarkable, really inventive. It's infectious." - Jim Hall

Doug Ramsey in *Jazz Times: "[Brad] is one of the well-hidden clarinet secrets of our time."* And we'll let Chet Atkins have the last word - overheard to Willie Nelson at the Austin, Texas Opera House: *"I've heard this album. It's the best Lenny Breau ever recorded."*

Leroy Parkins

AL1004-2

Liner notes, *The Complete Living Room Tapes.* 1982 Photo from Maine Festival, *Jazz at the Fountain*

leonard g. feather

13833 RIVERSIDE DRIVE
SHERMAN OAKS, CALIF. 91423

•

(818) 995-1333

September 3, 1986

Dear Brad:

Thought you would like to see that I did manage to get a review of the album in the Los Angeles Times. This column was syndicated. I hope you will get some sales out of it.

Sincerely,

Leonard Feather

Note from Leonard Feather acknowledging his review of the Living Room Tapes in 1986. (Volume I on vinyl)

1983 Denver, CO with William Galison, Dale Bruning, Art Landy and others.

1987 Recorded whistling track with Roger Kellaway and Red Mitchell (50/50 Stash Records).

Duo with John Basile 1989   (Art of Life Records)

1989 Won Hennessey Cognac Jazz Search in New York with John Basile. (First duo to ever apply.) Recorded *Duo* album with John Basile.

1984 Moved to Austin, Texas. Played with Paul Glasse, Gene Ramey, Al Manion, Spencer Starnes, Clay Moore, Susie Stern, and Mitch Watkins. Found nearly full-time music work 'til a change in the drinking age shut down many Jazz venues.

1987 Moved back to Maine.

1989 *Whistling Demo* with Howard Levy and Jon Webber. (not published)

Recorded soundtrack for Sesame Street segment, *First Steps*.

1990 Concert with John Basile for International Association of Jazz Educators (IAJE) conference on Long Island.

John Basile and me. Gift of the artist, Joe Whitten.

1991 First trip to Poland—Polish National TV on third night. First Polish Students visit for the summer.

With Joachim Mencel. Poland. 1994

1991–2013 Annual
trips to Poland.
Touring with: Andrzej
Jagodzinski, Byszek
Wigahaupt, Erik
Kulm, Leszek
Mozdzer, Emil
Kowalski, Peter Baron,
Jose Torres, Joachim
Mencel, Jarek
Smietana, Andrzej
Cudzich, Andrzej
Dabrowski, Adam
Czerwinski, Jacek
Niedziela, Henryk and
Robert Miskiewicz.

With Buddy De Franco. Poland 1995

Concerts with Bob Winter
(p)and others: WGBH
Boston, Harvard University
and Mast Cove Gallery.
1994 *All About Spring* with
Joachim Mencel
(Art of Life Records)

1995 Diagnosed with major
league ADD. Ummmm.

1993–2001 co-director (with
Krzysztof Klima) of the
International Clarinet Festival,
Krakow, Poland. With Alan
Hacker, Guy Depuis, Phillip
Cuper, David Campbell.
Personal performances with
Buddy De Franco.

With Marietta Atwood. In Bath, Maine 1995.
A Streetcar Named Desire.

Germany: Performed Phil
Wilson's *Jazz Face of Stephen
Foster* with live audience for
live broadcast on National
Radio with Phil Wilson and
the Frankfurt Radio Big
Band.

With Szymon Klima and David Campbell. Poland. 1996

1996 *Brad Terry Plays Gershwin* with Jarek Smietana (Quartet)

1997 *Brad Terry Plays Ellington* with Jarek Smietana ("little big band").

With Lesek Mozdzer, Buddy De Franco, and Emil Kowalski. International Jazz Festival, Krackow, Poland. 1995 or 1996

1997 "Discovered" Triology at a workshop with Joachim Mencel. Mateusz Kolakowski (piano), Michal Baranski (bass), and Tomek Torres (drums). (www.triologyjazz.com)

1997 January: Presentation at IAJE (International Association for Jazz Education) convention, Chicago, with Joachim Mencel and that same winter, The Theater Project's *Winter Cabaret*, Bath, ME, and concerts at St. Paul's School and UNH.

The Steve Grover Quartet
featuring Brad Terry

Remember

1998 *Remember* with Steve Grover, Frank Carlberg, and Chris Van Vorst Van Beest (Steve Grover, Young Grover Music)

1998 January: Week-long workshops and concert tour, Polish Embassy, Moscow, Russia, with Joachim Mencel.

BRAD TERRY & JOACHIM MENCEL QUARTET

COLORADO

Darbyterr 2

1997 *Colorado* with Joachim Mencel, Paul Romaine, and Dwight Kilian
(Brad Terry, darbyterr/Livingroom Records)
Original artwork, Matthew Terry 1977

1997–2004 Continued visits to Poland. Summer tours of the U.S. with Triology: Performed at the Polish consulate in NYC (Guest appearance, Adam Makowicz), and at the Knitting Factory, NYC. Presented at the Jazz Bakery, L.A. by Roger Kellaway and Gene Lees.
Performed at the Polish Consulate, Chicago.

2000 "Presence" with Triology: Mateusz, Michal, and Tomek (Brad Terry, Livingroom Records)

2002 England and Wales: First week of clinics at Aberystwyth, Wales with Joachim Mencel, joined by Tomek Torres and Michal Baranski.
Second week by myself: improvisation workshops with wind players from the National Youth Orchestra under the direction of David Campbell.

2004 Performed at tribute concert for Tony Montanaro. Pickard Theater, Brunswick, ME.

2001 Triology: Second performance, Jazz Bakery, L.A. Featured at the Annual Labor Day Jazz Festival (Vail, CO). Triology takes 4th place at International Combo Competition, Hoeliaart, Belgium, September 29th. (Youngest group ever to apply.)

2001 Sept 12: Opening concert at International Clarinet Festival, Krakow, Poland. Duo with Joachim Mencel.

Brad Terry & Joachim Mencel
LIVE IN FORT ANDROSS

INSPIRAFON

2006 *Live in Fort Andros* with Joachim Mencel (Joachim Mencel, INSPIRAFON, Poland)

Favorites for Liza... with William Galison. Bridgton, Maine. 2007

Music credit on 2007 film by Huey: *Theater and Inspiration,* with Tony Montanaro.

2007 UNH workshops and clinics. Piano master class with Mateusz Kolakowski.

2006 Live recording with Larry Garland: *Jazz al la Carte* CD, Maine Sound Stage, Brunswick, ME.

2006 Live recording with Joachim Mencel at the Maine Sound Stage, Brunswick, ME.

With Steve Grover. WBT 70th Birthday. 2007

Fred Fischer with my brother Peter.
Bridgton, Maine. 2007

2010 September played live on Warsaw Radio 3 with Joachim Mencel, Dima Gorelik (g) Maciej Adamczak (b).

With Jamie Masefield. 2010

With Paul Sullivan. 2013 *Jazz Jukebox* duo: audience chooses the program from our list of 200 tunes.

2013–present: Ongoing duo with Peter Herman.

With Peter Herman at The Theater Project. Brunswick, Maine

Throughout all these years there have been countless and un-dateable performances and both learning and teaching opportunities along the way.

From the three private lessons with my first clarinet from Connecticut Music, with Ray Taranto and later, private lessons with Benny Goodman and two and a half years of studies with Joe Allard—to the attempts early on to learn to read music—at the London Conservatory, at Mozarteum in Salzburg, Austria, extension classes at Julliard, and finally, three private lessons with Keith Wilson, Yale Music Department, at which point I gave up trying to read music—my path into improvisation was surely influenced by these early attempts at formal studies.

From random assorted gigs, interviews, workshops, clinics, and private lessons (teaching) in New Jersey with Fred Fischer, Texas, and California, *Jazz at Noon* in NYC, a concert with Eli Newberger and Butch Thompson in PA—and including the cross-country adventures with Triology—to decades of performances and associations with organizations in Maine and New England: Maine Festival, Maine Jazz Camp, Starbird Music in Portland, ME, the Chocolate Church in Bath, ME, improv clinics at Maine High Schools and Junior High Schools, Deertrees Theatre in Harrison, ME, WCSH TV's *207*, LRTV in Bridgton, on Rich Tozier's *Live Show* on MPBN Maine Public Radio, and on MPBN's *True North* and *Maine Concert Series*—solo, and with Triology, at The Top of the Hub in Boston with Chris Taylor Trio, a decades-long run at The Press Room in Portsmouth, NH, with Jim Howe, Les Harris Jr, and Tommy Gallant, and with Bob Winter, Marchal Wood, Bob Gullotti, and Paul Verrettte, and with many others in many places over the years—to me now, these have all become one long tune.

Recent turns have reinforced my feelings about getting out of the music business. It's emotionally and spiritually draining. There is the euphoria of the performance and then the letdown, and always the frustration of things getting fouled up... rarely our fault, but rather things happening out of our control and always affecting our pockets.

Joachim and I went to Germany, where we were supposed to do three days of workshops at a University and an evening concert at a local Jazz club. The University part was organized by a saxophone teacher there, who said everything was all set. The club offered us a guarantee of $150 that would cover some expenses, plus 80% of the "door". We drove fourteen hours to Wurtzburg. Well, never trust a saxophone player. He neglected to tell us that the University was on Spring break. So, no workshops and the expected "door" we would have generated when the University was in session obviously didn't materialize either. We came back with just the $150 (50% of our expenses!). I was counting on this income to get me through the month, and now had to be even more careful about money for the summer, thanks to another screw-up, this one with LOT airlines.

I had reserved and charged to my VISA the three ($760 each) tickets for the kids' (Triology) USA visit the up-coming summer; Bath/Brunswick Rotary money all safely in place in my "Island Camp Scholarship Fund". Two weeks later LOT informed my travel agent that there was a computer error, admitted it was their fault, but said, "Sorry Charlie, the tickets are $1,080 each now." So I'm down $960, and I've budgeted pretty close to the vest. That would buy a lot of miles for the van... even a few trips to McDonald's. They gave us 24 hours to decide. I'm stuck with it... LOT won't budge. I hope for some good gigs/concerts in October and beyond, not just some remote chance of a gig in some smoky club. I doubt I will stop playing, but it sure would be nice to be really selective about where and when I play. NO MORE weddings, bank-openings, car-shows, polo games, political rallies, whale-watching-cruises, dinner-dances, strip-joints (well, maybe) and NO NEW YEARS EVE PARTIES EVER AGAIN!

Before I fenced in my side yard I had a trolley arrangement for Holly. A cable stretched crosswise from the railroad side to a willow tree very near the street. Another cable with a pulley at the end intersected it and ran to the front door. It gave Holly a lot more scope that just a straight cable.

I was up in the willow adjusting the tension on the cable when the piano player who was renting the house just across the street pulled into his driveway. Very reminiscent of my special tree at Woodbine Road, I was completely hidden. He and his brother were talking as they got out of the car and his brother was asking who's who about the neighbors. When they got to my house I was quite flattered by very complimentary things my neighbor told his brother about my reputation as a musician.

The brother then asked, "Why doesn't he have a big fancy house and fancy car?" "Because he plays jazz."

61 years on the bandstand. (Whew)

For a taste of the music profiled in this timeline we invite you to go to: https://soundcloud.com/bradterry for a free download.

Currently I'm playing with and being challenged by a new young friend, guitarist Peter Herman. An opportunity to perform with him for a Lenny Breau Scholarship Fund concert in November 2013 pulled me out of Doldrums St., Retirementville, South Depression 101-01. (I was all set to call it a day and officially retire.)

We play tunes I've known for fifty to sixty years that he is hearing for the first time. He brings with him a fountain of new and different ideas about the tunes and I keep asking myself, "Damn! Why didn't I think of that years ago?"

He keeps me on my toes and keeps me going. So thank you Peter.

With Peter Herman. 2015

Brad Terry (So far.)

20

Characters
(1947–present)

This chapter presents sketches of a few of the people who have been most instrumental in my life. They were steadying hands on the tiller, showing me non-judgmental support along the way.

Chap Chap

Immediately after we returned from England, Leila Chapin-Hundley came to Woodbine Road to help my parents cope with the steady flow of Dorr Company visitors that started arriving as my father tried to re-start the war-torn European branches.

I was in the fifth grade at boarding school in Deerfield, Massachusetts, and during Christmas break, Leila entered the scene. She became my best friend and the only adult in my life who was not judgmental but took me for who I was.

She lived in an apartment in Stamford and was recommended by a woman named Qupie who worked for my grandparents.

It was snowing and Leila had trudged the mile and a half to our house from the end of the bus line, Saunder's Store in North Stamford. She had on a red hat and bright red boots. She explained she was part Black and part Cherokee Indian. She had a lovely smooth almost honey-colored complexion, very black hair and a wide smile.

She had several last names from several husbands who were all "bums" (her favorite expression). She was warm and friendly, and I immediately felt totally at ease with her. I felt I could tell her anything and she'd be okay with it. She became "Chap Chap" and I was "you old bum". My brother Peter was around and he became "Boss," and an "old bum" too. She put up with all my shenanigans with never a cross word or hint of disapproval. She'd help me clean up my room, and never scolded me for the ongoing messes I created. If I said something funny or naughty she had a way of putting her hand to the side of her face and with a slight crooked smile, roll her eyes to the sky and say, "Oh Braddie, you old bum!"

She told me my first dirty joke when I was about ten. She asked me, "Do you know what I'd buy if I had a million dollars?"

"No," I said.

"I'd buy me a new ass, 'cause this one has a crack in it!"

As time went on she became part of the family. She lived with us, still helped out, but made more money working for several well-to-do families in the area. My father carefully got her started with Social Security and kept her account in his ledger. She was always there for Thanksgiving and Christmas as well as any kind of family gatherings. She always put extra places at the table and was un-phased if six more showed up at the last minute for dinner.

I remember she bought a new Chevy, which we joked about because it was much fancier than Dad's 1941 Ford.

After she retired, she moved to an adult apartment complex in Akron, Ohio, to be near her sister. I visited her several times on my way home from various western trips.

The first time there, when I asked for her at the desk, everybody knew her and seemed to know that I was coming. Her apartment was tiny and very neat. She made me a sandwich and we sat out on her small balcony. She told me each time, the story of the night she volunteered to take three or four of the Woodbine Road Gang to the movies. We all wanted to see different movies so she dropped one or two in New Canaan, then took the others to Springdale and Stamford then reversed the route and picked us all up. She thought it was a riot!

Then, the story of driving my brother Arthur's Ford sedan. She came to Cascade Hill (Where I had careened down in rock-laden Dumpy), and lost the breaks. She gained speed and finally went off the road through a fence and down a steep embankment at the last sharp turn to the right, near the bottom of the hill. Doug Nash, grandfather of my friend Charlie Nash from public school, saw her go by, very fast, and heard the crash. He rushed down, saw the hole in the fence, no car visible and naturally assumed the worst. As he approached, Leila all covered with dust and grime crawled out through the hole in the fence and on to the road. Doug told us later he was terrified and sure he was seeing a ghost.

These stories were all told with huge smiles and laughter. And every time I tried to add a detail I'd get that wonderful smile and Leila would say, "Oh Braddie. You old bum!" "No, you're the old bum," I'd tell her, and she'd laugh and smile again.

Her unconditional support for me was so important.

About 2005 I was heading west and tried to contact her for a visit but couldn't find her. No one answered her phone. No one would have known to tell me.

Another special friend indeed.

Benny Goodman

If I ever knew, I don't remember what the occasion was when my mother met Benny Goodman. I know she was not shy about talking to anyone, and she posed a question to the great man: what to do with her thirteen-year-old son who was flunking all his classes and doing nothing except constantly playing the recorder by ear. Benny said, "Get him a clarinet." Soon after that I got my first clarinet with its three free lessons.

When I was just starting with the clarinet, Benny gave my mother some reeds in an autographed box that she sent to me. I was still at boarding school in Deerfield, Mass. I was in awe!

Later, during my bus driving days, I was taking Benny's daughter Benje to Lo Heywood, a private school, and in some round about way finagled an invitation to actually meet her famous father, my idol. I managed a few lessons with him that were unproductive but started casually dating his older daughter Rachel. Benny negotiated with George Avakian to get us on the sound track of *Jazz On A Summer's Day*. I saw him on and off in Stamford.

Once, he was rehearsing a quartet in his studio. Benny played so close to the horn I couldn't see what he was doing so I sat on the piano bench next to Hank Jones. Roy Burns, only a few years older than I was, was the drummer; I don't remember the bass player... Arvell Shaw?

The Reverend Jim Morton was a classmate of my brother Jim's at Harvard, and before he became Dean of the Cathedral of St. John The Divine in New York he had a parish, Grace Episcopal Church, in a pretty rough area of Jersey City. I'd known him since my brother's wedding and we kept in touch. He invited me to visit his church and sit in on a Boy Scout meeting. Soon afterward I negotiated with my boss at the bus company to borrow a bus during a long weekend in the spring. I drove to Jersey City and picked up about fifteen very black, very excited, young Scouts who loaded piles of borrowed sleeping bags and gear into the bus.

Benny had bought a small farm in Stamford as an investment. It had an abandoned house, a barn, and a small pond and he had given me permission to bring my busload of kids to camp out on the property. It started to get dark soon after we got there Friday night. We quickly set up tents and organized a sort of mess hall in the barn with a few coolers and a Coleman camp stove, cooked some hot dogs and went to sleep early. In the morning I made coffee and the kids didn't seem surprised when I walked down, in the buff of course, and dunked in the pond. Only a few of them could actually swim but within a few minutes they had all shed their clothes and were romping around in the water.

Benny was notorious for being a cheapskate. There are terrible stories about him. However, about noon Saturday he showed up to see what we were up to. He opened the back of his new and cherished Mercedes Kombi. The car was packed to the roof with more groceries than these kids or I had ever seen, really hundreds and hundreds of dollars worth. Everything imaginable: fruits and vegetables, assorted soda, milk, and fruit juice, chicken, steaks and hamburger all ready for the grill. There were some pies and cakes for desert. I know these kids had never seen anything like it and they were in awe of meeting Benny himself because in those days, kids that age knew who he was! His generosity was amazing.

I had already lost touch with him before moving to Maine. I went to hear him play a few years before he died and was disappointed that he was playing pretty much the same way he had in 1937 at the famous Carnegie Hall concert. He was still living at his apartment at 200 E 66th Street, NYC, in the same complex where my 'Little Granny' Trafford lived. This story is getting a bit convoluted, but the concierge, Lou Belgradier, became a friend after he drove my grandmother out to Stamford for Thanksgiving. He was somewhat taken aback when he was given a place at the table with the family—not just the hired driver!

Lou kept me up to date on Benny, whose health was deteriorating. One day I found out from Lou that Benny was there and decided to go see him. I wanted to show him my album with Lenny Breau and some PR things including a nice drawing on the cover of *Audience* from a

Sunday newspaper in Maine. Benny greeted me but refused to even look at material I brought. I was proud of it and wanted to share it with him. After a few minutes he ended the visit and simply said, "Why don't you take that to someone who can help you?" and showed me the door.

Buddy DeFranco told me a Benny story, which I re-told in the liner notes of my own Gershwin album.

> Years ago Toscanini decided to do the Rhapsody In Blue on his radio show and the logical choice to play the introduction was Benny Goodman. Benny practiced for weeks and the event was widely publicized. Half way up the famous "glissando" on worldwide radio Benny squeaked; really squeaked. The critics were quite kind about it, saying it showed Benny was human. Later, Eddie Sauter, who was arranging for Goodman at the time, presented him with a tune he'd written called, "The Squeak Heard Round The World." Finding it not at all amusing Benny fired him.

Benny Goodman obviously was a great influence on me but I have mixed feelings about my relationship with him.

Leonard Coppold

Len Len Len!

My friendship with this amazing ex-Canadian started when I was about seventeen or eighteen years old. We met somehow at a jam session at a castle in Westport, CT, owned by a strange lady who loved jazz. It was a castle even with a moat I think. I was going to tell this story here, but he beat me to it with his contribution to Second Stories, so I am including this here in Characters!

> Hi Brad. Well here goes. If you don't like the content just scrub it ok?
>
> My musical association with Brad has been very long and so memorable and GAD, what an inspiration he brought forth in our close friendship for over some fifty-five years. He was always full of surprises musically and otherwise. This is just one of very many that I recall at this time:
>
> Picture Brad and Len sitting in his very little Fiesta automobile in the middle of Queens, New York in the parking lot of

White Castle on a Saturday morning at eleven a.m. (to beat the usual crowd) eating out of a box of six (each) and downing them at very high speed (which Brad was very good at) and then he said, "Len, I want you to hear this new cd release." Namely, TAKE SIX, which was a group I had no knowledge of. We sat in total silence except for our duo munching of remaining bits of the fine burgers. WHAT a glorious album with such unique voicings and exciting moving musical themes—and without any musical instruments! I was really startled with the superb talent of these fine gentlemen.

Away back in 1993 I recall Brad calling me at my Long Island home asking if I might be interested in joining him along with about twelve other young musicians from Maine and elsewhere to visit Poland for a month to do jazz workshops in various part of the country. He mentioned he would like to know my decision within a week or so.

Len forgets to mention here that it was a group of high school kids and that he'd have to pay all his own expenses: airfare, everything.

I called Brad back within thirty minutes saying I was packed! What a tremendous experience it was and yes, I joined him and a group again the following year. YEP, Brad was always full of surprises. What A GREAT GREAT GUY—YES you are Brad! Skoal Len

And SKOAL right back Len! We shared a lot of great adventures, way too many to recount them all. Of course two Poland trips, but way before that, a crazy, snowy, winter trip to Bement School in the Griffith to do a concert. The original MG heater never really worked and burst from the pressure of the high capacity water pump of the Griffith's Cobra engine. Extremely over-powered, the car broke loose on any wet road—forget it in the snow. A crazy move from Long Island to Florida with a Ryder van and my Chevy van loaded to the roof. It was snowing hard as we packed up in Stonybrook. We left early in the morning. It was still snowing, but we got to Washington, D.C. that night. The weather was balmy when we took off in the morning and I opened the window of the Ryder van to enjoy the fresh air. At the bottom of a slight incline I had to stop for a red light and the snow that was still piled high on the roof of the van slid off and came crashing in, covering me about a foot deep.

And then there were the trips on Dr. Haughwout's sailboat, the *Melody*. One year we picked up the boat in Rockland, or maybe

Len Coppold. Vinalhaven, Maine.

Vinalhaven, and sailed down to Pemaquid. We tied up to the public landing and after some dinner started playing some tunes. There was at least one big sailing cruise boat in the harbor and soon several skiff-loads of passengers and some rowboats with spectators were clustered around us.

The next morning weather was iffy. We stayed put, but late afternoon it had cleared enough that we decided to venture out and find a more private anchorage. A few miles out it started to get a bit rough and the weather seemed to be closing in again so we anchored in the lee of an island and went to sleep. About midnight I woke up. The boat was heaving and pulling on the anchor. The tide had come up and what had been our breakwater to windward was now under water and big waves were coming over it and thrashing us. But it was also crystal clear with a bright full moon. We pulled anchor and set sails. As soon as we cleared the island we went wing and wing, boiling along all the way to Harpswell before dawn. This is not all that much about Len except to point out he was literally up for anything.

He knows every tune. We once recorded a tune where we change keys six or seven times one time through the tune. He is a world class accompanist playing only rhythm guitar but fascinating chord voicings moving all the time, and a sense of humor that never quits. His switch from collecting huge Lincoln town cars, Chryslers and giant Cadillacs, to MGs... puzzles me a bit but nothing really surprises me about this wonderful friend.

Skoal Again, Len.

Joe Allard

Shortly after leaving New York with my musical tail between my legs I enrolled in an extension division class at Julliard in what would prove to be yet another futile attempt to learn to read music. I was frustrated almost from the beginning because I could play my instrument considerably better than my classmates yet they could read the music and the whole situation just made me feel stupid, again.

I heard through the grapevine about Joe Allard who was well respected as one of the leading reed instrument teachers anywhere. I applied and had to wait almost a year for an audition to find out if he would even take me on as a student.

The great day finally arrived and I found my way to his studio on the second floor of the tiny building right across the street from Radio City Music Hall. (The building is still there.) A very pleasant secretary greeted me and introduced me to Joe. He looked much more like a family doctor than a music teacher; not very tall, gray hair, very distinguished and well dressed in a suit and tie. He was immediately friendly and with a smile asked me to "play something." At that point I could play almost everything I knew how to play in about five minutes. A few moments into this, the phone rang and his secretary called in and said, " It's for you Mr. Allard, long-distance."

He excused himself and started talking on the phone in the next room. His voice got louder and he started calling the caller all sorts of nasty names, language I hadn't heard since the Army. He sounded really angry and slammed down the phone. Then, as he passed his secretary he said, "If that asshole Stan Getz calls again I'm not here."

I was in shock. I had just recently started listening to a lot of Bill Evans, Sonny Rollins and had been a huge fan of Stan Getz for several years and here was my teacher talking to "God" that way. I would later find out that Getz was in Sweden and had called the day before asking all the same questions; he was obviously high on something. Joe was furious. He came back in, apologized to me and then said, "Put your horn away." I figured I had completely blown my audition but then he said, "Were going out to lunch."

For the next two and a half years, as often as I could, I took Joe out to lunch; it was infinitely cheaper than lessons. He told me I had a big round fat sound and not to change it. We spent a lot of time talking about all aspects of being a musician and performer and he shared valuable information with me that I've tried to share with any students I've come in contact with. We did occasionally go back to the studio where he showed me some really technical stuff about adjusting the clarinet and working on reeds.

One of his bits of advice, which very few teachers will ever pass on to their students, is that the creative process comes in waves. It's normal to have a slump and it's healthy to try and ignore it and do something else for a while. For the first four or five years I ran the camp, I left my clarinet at home and would be itchy to play when I got back in September. I headed to Joe as soon as possible.

Joe told me the best way to learn something is to try and teach it to someone else. He said, "There are two 'must be' conditions for playing music, equally important, so not necessarily in order. #1. Plan to give 100%. #2. Plan to have fun." I add, practice fifteen minutes every day.... no days off, no excuses. Broken arm or fat lip from fighting; okay to take a break for a day or two. I explain that you don't grow two inches the day before you go to the doctor for your physical; it's been a slow growth, impossible to even measure on a day-by-day basis. Day by day you'll not see results from practicing but you are growing and it does take time. If you get really discouraged, maybe take a break. If it's important to you you'll come back. It has to be important.

I still pass on what I learned from Joe Allard; about the urge and creative inspiration coming in waves. It's okay to have a down spell, and okay to give it a rest. He also told me to imagine two ascending parallel lines, the top line representing what I could hear and the bottom line, what I could actually play on my instrument. The idea was that as my technique improved so would my ideas—parallel lines. He told me about "fooling people with your playing". (A better word than 'impressing'.) "At the beginning you can fool people who don't know anything about music. Then you can fool people who do know something about music. Third stage is when you start fooling yourself which is total bullshit."

He told me if I ever got to the point where I could play everything I heard it could only mean one thing; that the top line had flattened out and I wasn't hearing anything new. That was the best time to go and run the camp for eight weeks in the summer.

When I came back from France in 1958 with my new Selmer Series 9 clarinet, I eagerly showed it off to Joe. He played one scale on it and immediately offered me ten times what I paid for it. I told him that was a guarantee that I would never part with it. I still have it, and play it all the time fifty-six years later.

After Joe retired he moved to Connecticut to be near his daughter and I managed to see him a few times, but towards the end it was difficult, Alzheimer's I'd guess.

I'm sure he inspired many more than just me, but I'll never forget.

Dick Cash

About a year after the chance meeting with Helmut Vles on the deck of the Adventure during that first summer of Camp at Mill's Farm, Helmut hired me for a few gigs and introduced me to Dick Cash. I was immediately drawn to him by his humor and musicianship. He knew thousands of songs from every genre, all the words and all the outrageously altered words to everything, encyclopedic. We rapidly became life-long friends. We played when we could, here and there during the fall after Camp. If I were headed to Vinalhaven I'd park my car at his house in Rockland. I ate many a family meal at their big picnic table; the only way to seat six kids and friends. The wall-to-wall welcome mat was always extended and a few summers later both his older sons, Rick and Jeff, came to Camp. The musical and family relationships grew. I think during the second summer Rick and Jeff were at Camp, Dick and his wife Jannine, brought their youngest son, Sean, out for a weekend; they were welcome guests of my parents in the Big House. But Sean, age eight, preferred the Camp. Immediately comfortable without clothes around Camp, he was like a fish in the quarry and totally at home with sixteen older 'brothers'. His parents went home and Sean became sort of a mascot and stayed for the rest of the summer. Dick and I managed a few gigs in Maine before and after Camp for several years, and one year at my parents' invitation he drove his whole family down to Stamford through a blizzard for Thanksgiving. As I remember they drove all night arriving in the morning on Thursday. That might have been the year his son Jeff attended Riverdale and lived with me for the winter. When I moved permanently to Maine we played more often and the friendship grew. Sean graduated from Rockland High School a year early, attended the Ringling Bros. Clown College and toured with the Circus for two years.

I had been living in Maine for a while after my divorce, when I got an offer to play with a band in Monterey and so drove out to California. Soon after arriving I got the news that my dear friend Dick had been diagnosed with Lou Gehrig's disease. I was living in an eighteen-foot trailer at a mobile home park in Sea Side, just north of Monterey. Work was spotty, but I managed to get back to Maine for a visit and pick up a few gigs. Dick and Jannine showed up at one of them, and I was shocked to see my friend. During the break we talked, and I suggested they should come out to California and visit me. I had negotiated to 'yacht sit' on a 40-foot sail boat at the Monterey Marina on my return. They had never been to California. "Why not?" said Jannine. They both showed up a week later at another gig, and Jannine came up to me waving plane tickets. They flew out and we spent a week exploring the sights in my Olds station wagon. Dick was getting frail, but his spirit and enthusiasm never wavered. A wheelchair was welcome touring the Queen Mary, but he made few concessions to his illness. With help from Jannine, I plotted a surprise for Dick.

I had been playing with a wonderful young pianist, Smith Dobson. I had told him about Dick, explaining that not only was he a close friend but also my all-time favorite singer, and I wanted to get him recorded with a really good trio. Smith contacted a studio and rounded up a drummer and bass player. They all volunteered their time. I had asked Jannine to give me a list of twelve tunes Dick really liked to sing, which I gave to Smith. I told Dick that I had been asked to record a quick jingle with a great trio. It was a beautiful drive and he could come along if he liked... he took the bait. The studio was tiny, and as we got set up the only place for Dick to sit was on a stool next to me. Jannine was crammed in the control room but could see everything through the soundproof glass. We did a quick sound check, and then I moved the mic over in front of Dick, gave him the list of tunes and asked, "What would you like to sing first?"

He did one of his classic moves, thumping his forehead with the heel of his hand, and saying, "I'll be Dick," and we went at it. In about as long as it takes to play the CD we recorded the album. I called it *First Take*. Jannine was laughing and crying in the booth. (Smith Dobson was killed in a car accident on the way home from a gig, April 2001)

My gigs in Monterey soon fizzled to zero, and I decided to come back to Maine. I had no work, but Dick and Jannine offered me a free place for my trailer, which I lugged back across country. The Olds wagon made it, but it was slow going. I parked my rig a few hundred feet from the house and connected an extension cord for power and a garden hose for water. With salvaged lumber I added a lean-to shed arrangement that doubled my sheltered space.

Earlier in the year his boys had built him a deck with a ramp. We spent some daytime there but as fall approached Dick was fading fast and stayed in bed almost all the time. At least I was there to keep him company and give Jannine a break and some small comfort. Soon, as the weather got colder, and even with a wood stove in my lean-to, I had to abandon it all, winterize my trailer, and move inside to the basement of the house.

Christmas approached and a benefit concert was planned for Dick at the Waldo Theater. Musicians, fans, and friends, all of whom loved Dick, converged, and the small hall was packed. Everybody played. At one point Dick, who was in the audience in a wheelchair, said he

With Joe Laflamme, Phil Verrill, Dick Cash, Billy Moio, Mark Perry.
Maine Festival.

wanted a mic, and one with a long cord was brought to him. His voice was steady but strangely quiet coming from someone who used to sing with such power and command.

"I've written a poem," he said, as the room hushed.

"This dying by inches has been kind-a hard. My boys built me a deck so I could die by the yard."

There was stunned silence… Dick Cash at his worst and his best. People moaned, some laughed, some cried. Nobody knew how to react. To be honest I don't remember what happened next… at all.

I could tell you more about his humor, but all of it was clever, outrageously funny, outrageous jokes, and most not suitable for a family show.

Dick died a few days after the first of the year. He was determined to not die during the holidays and "screw up everybody's New Year's Eve." Sheer willpower kept him going those last few days.

At the memorial a week or so after he died, a minister who Dick and Jannine didn't really like very much, had asked to speak. Since he was associated with the church they had occasionally gone to, Jannine, to be politically correct, reluctantly agreed to allow him to say a few words. Several other people had spoken briefly about Dick, but this guy started in and went on and on and on, thirty minutes or more. When he finally finished Jannine said, in quite a loud voice, "Cash, you bastard, you always get the last laugh." The place went into hysterical laughter! I guess that's part of his humor, too.

Jannine is gone now too after a long bout with lung cancer.

Two friends sorely missed, and never forgotten.

Eddie Thompson

Shortly after starting at Riverdale in 1969, Wayne Wright, my old guitarist friend from early New York days invited me to a Sunday session at a little club on Bleeker Street called Jacques's. The man in charge was pianist Eddie Thompson. The bass player was Major Holley who remembered me from the Celebrity Club, sitting in with Buddy Tate, so getting invited to play was a given. I arranged to stay at school in a dorm room so I wouldn't have to drive back to Connecticut Sunday night. Soon I was making a habit of the Sunday gatherings and started going down town on weeknights to play duo(s) with Eddie. We quickly became good friends and I soon discovered that he knew more tunes than anyone I'd ever met. Before Christmas that year I had booked him to play a concert with me at school. He and his wife Mary spent some time at my parent's house in Stamford during school vacations and I got to know him better. He was a wonderful warm outgoing guy, great sport, ready for anything. He refused to consider the fact that being blind since birth was any sort of a handicap. He traveled all over New York on the subways with his guide dog Maeda. He was independent and fearless.

One summer I invited Eddie and his wife Mary to visit me at Camp. My parents were delighted to welcome them at the Big House and they stayed about ten days. We did some boat trips on the *Dirigo* and Eddie used his quality reel-to-reel tape recorder the way sighted people use a camera, recording everything. Several times he went with us to the quarry and had no problem losing his clothes and swimming around. He joked that since he had no way of knowing if anybody was looking at him, he didn't care. He'd feel his way down the ledges to the water and with kids clearing a path would launch himself. The kids all cooperated by being really quiet and letting someone on shore be the only one talking and guide him back to a safe landing place. At one point he asked to be guided to the sunning rock so he could jump off. Gingerly I took him up to the top. He felt the edge of the ledge with his toes and after an "All clear" from the kids below, jumped off. He went up again, this time setting his recorder and yelling out, "Eddie Thompson jumping off the cliff, take twooooo", and leapt into space into the water below. Fearless, he made several 'takes'.

One night my parents sponsored a lobster dinner in his honor at Camp. It was a gala affair with all the fixin's. Eddie had never encountered a lobster so I sat next to him with my eyes closed and talked him through it. He was delighted; so pleased that he didn't have to worry about trying to keep from spilling his food everywhere and keeping it neat and tidy on his plate The whole point was he was supposed to get it all over himself. Back at school in the fall I went downtown as often as I could. One of the funniest scenes I ever witnessed was Eddie helping Lance Heywood (Another blind pianist) eat a lobster at Jacque's. Lance had ordered the lobster and Eddie kept telling him how to deal with it and reassuring him it was okay, he was supposed to get it all over himself!

During Thanksgiving break I rounded up five or six campers from the previous summer, took them to the Auto Show at the Coliseum and then downtown to see Eddie at Jacque's. I hadn't warned Eddie, we just showed up. I told the kids, "One at a time, go up to Eddie and just say, 'Hi Eddie'. That's all. Nothing more." At the end of a tune one of the boys went up and said, "Hi Eddie" and Eddie immediately said, "Hi Jeff, man, how are you. It's great to see you!" I never got used to Eddie's amazing abilities to function normally. After a late night at Jacque's and no school on Monday, Eddie invited me to stay at his house in Queens. I had my old 356 Porsche and was again amazed as Eddie gave me flawless driving directions all the way, ending with, "Turn left at the next light and find a parking space halfway down the block if you can." After I told him exactly where we parked he led the way to his building, and we took the elevator to his floor. He opened the door, we went in, and as soon as the door closed Eddie disappeared into the apartment and I was left standing in the hall in total darkness. It was about 4:00 a.m., I heard the toilet flush and then the sounds of the refrigerator door and a beer being opened, then some music from the stereo. I fumbled around looking for a light switch and finally called out, "Eddie, man, I can't see a thing". "Funny," he answered. "Neither can I." He knew where everything he needed was, but since he had no need of any lights couldn't be of help to me. I fumbled around and eventually found the switch. After a few beers I stretched out on the couch and Eddie started to read out loud from a Braille book he held on his lap. The words came out at a completely normal speed with all the right inflections and pauses for punctuation. At some point he said I could turn out the light, and he continued to read in the total darkness 'til I fell asleep. The only time I saw him get angry about being blind was when I took him, Mary, and his sister-in-law Sue, to Coney Island and the guy running the bumper car concession wouldn't let Eddie drive a car by himself. In his wonderful clipped British accent he said something like, "For Christ's sake mate, the whole point is to bump into people." The guy wouldn't budge so I offered to drive and then let Eddie take over and do the driving. With almost surgical skill he threaded his way through traffic and unerringly bumped Mary and Sue.

Eddie also had a relentless sense of humor and had no patience with blind people who considered it a handicap. Some stories and a few of my favorite jokes come to mind. Once we were walking somewhere in New York and came across a blind guy chanting something about, "Buy a pencil, support the blind." Eddie headed us toward the voice and then said, "Bug off man. This is my corner." Later he told me this story about a blind guy selling pencils in the subway.

Every day a commuter gets off the train, puts ten cents in the tray, but never takes a pencil. This goes on for months. Finally one day the commuter puts his dime in the tray and the blind guy asks, "Are you the man who puts ten cents in the tray but never takes a pencil?" The man admitted he was and the blind guy said, "I just wanted to let you know, the pencils are fifteen cents now."

Another of his one-liners, "God said, 'Let there be light.' And you know what? You could see for fucking miles!"

I learned a lot from Eddie and a lot about him too. I learned when we were walking somewhere to let him take my arm and not slow down or change my pace for curbs or stairs—always full speed ahead!

The restroom and pay phone at Jacque's where we played were down in the bowels, well below street level, the lights were completely out. I felt foolish trying to negotiate the simple process I went down there for and then Eddie told me something I've remembered since. He always washed his hands before he went to pee. He explained he knew exactly where his pecker had been since he left home but had no idea where his hands had been. He only washed afterwards if he peed on himself. Still makes sense to me!

I needed to make a phone call and was fishing for change for the pay phone in the dark. I handed him a fist full of change, which he immediately sorted, then he dialed the number I gave him and then put the appropriate coins in the appropriate slots. I was amazed; he took it for granted.

Eddie told me many stories about his childhood... mostly how difficult it had been for his parents to watch him playing or riding a tricycle, heading for a tree or a stairwell and not calling, "watch out!" He had to find out for himself and had multiple scars to prove it but it also made him fearless and independent.

He told me of a tour he did through the Midwest traveling from town to town on a small commercial plane. At one layover for fuel the dozen or so passengers got off for a short break to stretch. Eddie elected to stay on board and the pilot asked if he would like anything. Eddie said he was fine but maybe Maeda his guide dog needed to go out. The pilot obliged but when the passengers saw the pilot walking up and down the tarmac with a guide dog no one would get back on the plane. There was unmistakable joy in his voice when he told that story.

Just when I thought I'd heard every Eddie story I came across this

Eddie and Me.
Freeport Middle School. 1975

in Bill Crow's book, *Jazz Anecdotes*. Eddie was playing solo in a small club. People up front were listening but there were talkers at a table in the back. Someone from a front table turned around and loudly 'shushed' the talkers where upon Eddie from the piano in his wonderful clipped British accent said, "Sorry mate. I'm playing as quietly as I can."

Eddie loved his Dewar's and Pall-Mall cigarettes. I tried to slow down his smoking and drinking by hiding his cigarettes and glass on the piano. He'd ask for them and threaten to play everything in 'E' if I held out. We were walking somewhere in New York on a blustery day, he had my arm. He asked me to stop in some sheltered doorway so he could light up. After my deliberately passing a few he pulled me to a stop and said, "This one will do."

He moved back to England and a few years later died of emphysema. I thought I knew a lot of tunes until I met Eddie. I learned so much from him about playing, dealing with and overcoming blindness and about spirit and the joy of living. He's gone, terribly missed and never forgotten.

Don Doane

The unmistakable, instantly recognizable gruff voice sounded angry. "Hey Brad. It's Don. They said I can't play this Friday." The emphasis was on the 'they' and anger directed at 'them', the staff at the VA home. Don had a stroke twelve years ago and moved to the Veterans Administration Home in Scarborough three years ago, when his care become to much for his wife Barbra to handle. Peter Herman and I have been twice to 'sit in' with Don who practices his trombone every day from 1:00–2:00 in the afternoon. They had told him since he had been sick in bed for several days that he'd have to give up our session. His reaction sounded 100% like Don Doane.

When I first moved permanently to Maine I thought pursuing music was probably not in the cards but soon found out about weekly jam sessions at the Bridgeway Restaurant in Portland, run by legendary trombonist Don Doane. Don had played with Maynard Ferguson, Woody Herman, Stan Kenton, all over, but gave it up, and returned to Maine to teach and be with his family.

Knowing a bit about jam session etiquette I ventured in, put my name on the list and waited patiently for my turn to play. I think Don appreciated my more professional attitude and that I was okay with whatever tune was called. He was very pleasant with me afterwards and invited me back. I returned as often as I could.

It was only a few months later that he called me to play with him and some real pros at a gig in New Hampshire. Tommy Gallant, Les Harris Sr., Phil Wilson, and Herb Pomeroy were four that I remember. We stopped on the way home at the HoJo's on the Maine Turnpike. We ordered some food and my drink came with a cherry with a stem. I couldn't resist and while the waitress watched I tied the stem into a knot in my mouth. The waitress asked Don if he could do that. He answered, "No. But I can do a tongue stand."

He set me up with other gigs and once after a Bridgeway session he asked if I could stick around and play the evening gig in the dining room with Tom Bucci Sr. "Sure," I said. The gig started off well and we had some people up front asking for tunes; the music was fun. But soon

Don and me at the Bridgeway Restaurant, Portland, Maine. 1970s.

the owner Tony Notis came up to me and said, "Stop playing jazz. I don't want any jazz in here." I looked at Tom—he looked at me. I packed up and went home. When I called Don to tell him what happened he laughed his head off, thought it was hysterical. Our friendship was already pretty secure.

We had a nice thing going about money: we never talked about it. If Don called me he'd tell me the details: where, when, what to wear, who was playing, etc. but never how much. At the end of the gig he'd hand me a check or a wad of money. I'd shove it in my wallet; never counted it or looked at the check 'til I got home; I knew it was right. He did the same with me; just put the money in his wallet with a, "Thank you".

When Peter and I saw him in November of 2013 he excitedly told me that he had been walking for the first time in twelve years. He was a super basketball player and was trim like a Marine, known to have been a bit of a brawler, an avid athlete and powerhouse trombone player; so much energy! So I understand his frustration and anger being told by anyone he couldn't play. What a trooper and wonderful friend.

Thanks for everything Don.

Marshall Dodge

Marshall was two years ahead of me and four years behind my brother at St. Paul's School, although our paths didn't really cross until we met years later when piano player Mark Perry and I auditioned for the Maine Touring Program. Marshall was on the selection panel. After the audition at the Brunswick Library he asked me if I had any recordings, and I told him of the homemade vinyls of my duo with Eddie Thompson. He invited himself to my apartment at the back of my mother's house on Federal Street, sat down and listened. After a few minutes he got up and headed for the door, saying as he went, "This is outrageous." And disappeared.

The following morning he appeared in his beat-up Ford station wagon and presented me with a top-of-the line Tandberg reel-to-reel tape recorder, two quality microphones with stands and a shopping bag with a dozen 10-inch reels of tape. He told me he was upset with the poor quality of the pretty much raw recording but loved the music. "From now on," he said, "record everything you play." He set up an account at Eastern Music for me to buy more tape as needed, and his interest and generosity made all the *Living Room Tapes* with Lenny Breau, a reality.

Soon after this Marshall started the Maine Festival at the campus of Bowdoin College. He recruited Al Miller to be Artistic Director and I was tapped to be Jazz Director and during the next few years I saw a lot of Marshall. I felt, along with Al and many others, honored to call him a friend.

As the festival grew, Marshall got more and more aggravated by the red tape and political wrangling; he was not happy at the board meetings!

One late afternoon after a particularly difficult meeting he appeared at my house on River Road. My wife and I and two or three of our kids were sitting on our waterbed watching an episode of *Roots* on TV. Marshall came into the bedroom and, without a word, kicked off his shoes, sandwiched a spot on the side of the bed and watched the show. When it was over he put his shoes back on and left. He didn't say one word. He knew that at my house he didn't have to perform or be funny or speak at all if he didn't want to. The kids loved him.

One Thanksgiving Al arranged a New York trip with YPT kids and Marshall drove all the way down to Greenwich, Connecticut to do a benefit concert for my Island Camp Scholarship Fund.

When Mother opened the Vinalhaven house to several workshops, Marshall taught a Philosophy workshop. He was always great with the kids from Camp.

For several years I was lucky enough to perform with Marietta Attwood, a marvelous singer/piano player transplanted from New York. We played live at the Chocolate Church Arts Center in Bath for numerous concerts and a production of *A Street Car Named Desire*, directed by Chuto Chapin, Marlon Brando's acting teacher! Marietta, too, became a good friend of the family and me. It was a real shock when Marietta died suddenly. I took our whole family to the funeral parlor in Bath for a memorial service. To try and distract everybody on the way home I turned on the local radio and heard the bulletin that Marshall had been killed in a hit and run accident while riding his bicycle in Hawaii.

Still more, much-missed friends. Wow.

Al Miller

For my 70th birthday recording-concert-party I asked Al Miller to emcee the event. As the audience quieted Al took to the stage, turned his back and for five minutes had everybody shouting with laughter as he demonstrated all the things you didn't want to see from the people sitting in front of you. Only at the end did he face the audience to start the introductions.

Al Miller. Master of Ceremonies at my 70th. Brunswick, Maine.

Marshall Dodge had picked Al Miller to be in charge of the Childrens' Area at the first Maine Festival to be held on the Bowdoin College campus in August of 1976. The following year Al took over as Artistic Director for the Festival and asked me to be the Jazz Director. "Jazz at the Fountain" provided almost non-stop music from the best Maine musicians from the opening gate 'til closing every day and included evening concerts in more formal settings. The video with Lenny Breau comes from one of those concerts.

There are too many stories, all of which have cemented a solid, and most wonderful friendship. He has been there for me on so many occasions. He arranged a CETA grant, finding me work at a time when I was unemployed and in real financial trouble. When my mother died six days before Christmas he welcomed me, along with an assortment of foster kids in my charge, to Christmas dinner at his home. He let me camp out in the theater when I was homeless for a while. He has helped me to become comfortable and at ease talking to an audience, to be my own emcee at concerts, and generally have the confidence to do what I do as a performer. He has opened a lot of doors for me, completely understandable because he's done that non-stop for countless kids and adults through the Theater Project for over forty years.

I'm glad to say I've known him almost that long.

Lenny Breau

A lot has been written about Lenny Breau. He is still revered by guitar players of all genres, even now, long after he has gone. The Internet is full of information and Ron Forbs-Robert's book, *One Long Tune* covers his amazing story best.

I can only add that once again blessed with incredible good fortune, I was able to spend time with Lenny, learn from him and be a small part of his amazing legacy.

The best way to sum it up is with the following liner notes I wrote for our *Live at the Maine Festival* DVD:

The Thesaurus has been no help finding adequate words to describe my feelings about having the opportunity to have known Lenny Breau. "Gentle genius," "gifted player," "superb and totally supportive accompanist," and, "revered friend," all come to mind, and none seems strong enough. After a gig with Lenny I felt like my ears had been in traction. I felt in awe, but he never intimidated me, though he easily could have. He always listened and supported—but also pushed me to do my best.

This short DVD illustrates this amazing empathy and gives a glimpse of Lenny's genius. We had such fun.

I'm honored to have been a small part of his amazing legacy. I miss him and will never forget him.

Thanks so much, Lenny.

Brad Terry

With Lenny at the Maine Festival.

Hi Brad
miss playing with
you
Lenny

Miss you too, Lenny.

Randy Bean

McBean's Books and its proprietor, Randy Bean were an immediate magnet for my mother who was an avid reader. She discovered the shop on the corner of Maine Street, in downtown Brunswick, only a few blocks from her house on Federal Street, before she even bought the house. When I moved from New Gloucester into the shed I converted at the back of her house she had already established a friendship with Randy, admiring his vast knowledge and willingness to find any book she was looking for.

Of course I got to know him and was also impressed with his knowledge of Jazz and his ability to find rare recordings for me.

I landed a gig at the Bowdoin Steak House every Saturday night. Randy had hinted he used to be the 'Boy Singer' with a big band 'back in the day'. And one night I invited him to sing a few with my trio.

As Randy explained it, singing with us re-kindled still another career and he soon started booking weddings and concerts and helping a lot of musicians including me by finding work!

I have to say he wasn't Sinatra but there was an honesty about what he did and any flaws were pretty much forgiven because of the obvious joy he had when he performed. To me weddings are intolerable but he always got the best players and did the best he could to take care of business and do things right.

When I was homeless he put me up for a while and for several years his shop, now McBean's Music, was my only mailing address.

We established a real friendship. His knowledge of tunes was right up there with Eddie Thompson and several times, from Poland, I tapped into it. This was before e-mail. With no concern about the time I called him, a sleepy voice would answer—it might have been three in the morning. "I'm stuck," I'd say. "I can't remember the bridge to . . ." I'd whistle or sing the first part of some tune and he'd answer by singing the bridge. Then, "Thanks. Good night, Randy". End!

I heard from spies he'd tell everybody about those calls for weeks afterwards.

It's never easy to say goodbye and traveling as much as I have it seems I'm always leaving some friends somewhere as I head off somewhere else.

I remember all too well saying goodbye to Randy. I was heading off for a several months' stay in Poland. After a few hugs I still see him standing in the doorway of the shop smiling gallantly. He had been diagnosed with terminal prostate cancer. We both knew we'd never see each other again.

Dr. Peter Haughwout

A pleasant voice on the phone was asking for Mr. Terry. I answered that I was Brad Terry and she said my old friend Randy Bean, owner of McBean's Music had given her my number; she was looking for some musicians to play for a surprise birthday party for her husband. Randy had told her I was a clarinet player and could probably come up with something. She told me her name was "Maryann something something." It was months before I really figured out the last name, Haughwout.

She asked if I could do it and if I could bring a piano player. I told her I'd be glad to do it but at the moment didn't have a piano player, but had a guitar player staying with me, Lenny Breau. There was a long pause. I almost thought she had hung up before she asked in a somewhat faltering voice, "You mean, *the* Lenny Breau?" The conversation went on and she explained that her husband Peter was huge Lenny fan, thought he was the greatest ever, etc. etc. The deal was made and the date confirmed.

While Peter was away, distracted by friends, Lenny and I set up in their living room and were playing quietly when he arrived. The whole party was a surprise and this was definitely a moment when I wish pictures had been taken. I'll never forget the look of disbelief that said, "Lenny Breau in *my* living room?"

That was the start of a thirty-five-year friendship that was still going strong when another Peter (Herman) gifted guitarist and Lenny fan played with me at Peter's memorial service in 2013.

Dr. Haughwout was E.N.T (Ear, nose and throat) doctor and he became involved treating some of my foster kids. Because of the music connection he started coming to all the concerts I did with Lenny and we became family friends.

Both he and Marianne had a flair for wonderful off-beat events; and an almost bottomless sense of humor.

One annual event at their house was Derby Day. Friends showed up appropriately dressed. As bets were placed, mint juleps were served; lots of enthusiasm as the race came on the TV.

I was living in Bowdoinham, married and had a house full of foster kids. For some reason we had rescued and adopted a donkey. The white goat in the Dizzy Gillespie picture left the farm after it ate the temporary license plate on our newly acquired Jeep. We also had a Ford van . . . Can you see where this is going? We loaded the donkey into the van and headed to the Derby Day gathering and for a few hours gave 'round-the-block' donkey rides to all the kids and most of the costumed guests: fancy clothes, giant hats and all. The whole neighborhood was buzzing.

Later, possibly around Thanksgiving, while eating some turkey I managed to get something lodged in my throat. I couldn't dislodge it even with big chunks of bread. Late at night after trying to sleep I decided I'd better check in at the hospital. If it got worse there was no way my wife could get me there if I was in trouble. Peter was on call and met me about 3:00 a.m. He took a look and told me to stay there, he'd take care of it in the morning. As they were wheeling me in to the O.R., I jokingly said I'd like a doggy bag, wanted to see what it was. They put me under and apparently the anesthetic alone had done the

Dr. Peter Haughwout on board the *Melody*.

trick—nothing there except signs of abrasion. When I came around in the recovery room there was a gaggle of nurses standing around talking and laughing. Around my neck in my doggy bag was a turkey drumstick. In the hospital that story buzz lasted for months.

The *Melody* is a lovely sloop, about 22 feet long with a small outboard. It sailed beautifully. Moored in Harpswell, it was a bit of a sail to get to open ocean. After taking me out a few times, Peter let me borrow it on my own. Peter and Maryanne usually had a week to go sailing every summer but were restricted because it was a long sail to get anywhere. A plan immerged and for several summers I would round up a kid or two, an old camper or friend, and sail the boat from Harpswell down east to Rockland, Castine, to Buck Harbor. Peter and Maryanne would meet me there, get on board and I'd drive the car back home. A week later we'd rendezvous; they'd drive home and I'd sail home. We did this for several summers.

In 2001 I found my place in Bath, made an offer and to my amazement it was accepted. I barely had enough for the down payment; both the bank and VA turned me down for a loan. Out of the blue Peter offered to take out a loan on his own and give it to me.

I did the bulk of the moving when they went from Brunswick to Bowdoinham. I lived with them in Bowdoinham during some homeless time. I helped as much as I could moving back to Brunswick. Peter invited me to lunch every few weeks and I was there for Christmases, Thanksgivings and many Sunday dinners.

As his health deteriorated I visited more often and near the end Peter Herman joined me for a few informal concerts up to the day before he died.

Maryanne asked me to play at the memorial service and I invited Peter Herman to join me. She gave me a list of seven of the doctor's favorite tunes and I decided to collect them and play them as a medley. John Basile promoted the idea of playing tunes in ascending keys; C to D-flat, to D, then to E-flat, etc. Each tune in a higher key. Maryanne had no idea but her random list followed that criteria exactly.

The question lingers: How have I been lucky enough to have friends like this?

Thank you Peter and Maryanne.

Dizzy Gillespie

> (Playing Cuban music) *Where the f*** is 'one'?*
> —*Dizzy Gillespie*

Volumes have been written about this man and his music. His recordings, his exuberant character and originality have influenced almost everyone who plays this music today. I feel forever grateful that I was able to share a moment of history with one of the nicest people I ever met.

The Friends of Jazz was a group I started with Steve Grover in 1981. We played concerts and put together a Jazz Improvisation workshop program we took to schools all over Maine. We attracted the attention of the National Endowment for the Arts and received a grant to help put Friends of Jazz programs in schools.

Part of this money went to co-sponsor with Colby College Dizzy Gillespie's visit to Maine. Here for a week, in-between concerts, he joined us for some of our workshops for kids. He stayed at a local motel but spent some of his free time with us in Bowdoinham. We fed him and he entertained us non-stop. I had a house full of adopted and foster kids. Everybody had a ball. Saturday we played a concert at

Dizzy. Bowdoinham, Maine.

Merrill Hall in Portland. We arrived and were playing Monk's *Well You Needn't* as a sound check. Back in the dressing room Dizzy said, "You know, you're playing the bridge wrong. It starts a third higher." We had already shared enough jokes and spent enough time together, so I sort of sarcastically joked, "Well thanks a lot. Now you tell me." "That's okay," he said, "That's the way I play it, too."

Dizzy had worked with the big band from Colby College during the day. They were pretty shaky and tentative and not nearly up to Dizzy's expectations. They were to go on first, featuring Dizzy. Our quartet would go last and maybe Dizzy would play the last few tunes with us. The Colby band really faltered and Dizzy gave up on them after the third tune. After intermission we came on. We played our first two or three tunes and then suddenly there was Dizzy, horn in hand. He sort of strolled onstage and finished the set with us. On one tune he made some extraordinary sounds and rhythms with a Jew's Harp and invited me to whistle with him; too much fun. On the way home he insisted on sitting in the back of my van on a milk crate, the only thing to sit on in the back, so my wife could have the front seat. He put his hand on her shoulder and was explaining alternate trumpet fingerings. About 12:30 a.m. we stopped at L. L. Bean's so he could buy a new pocketknife. He spent Sunday with us. I took the classic picture of him riding our white goat. We sent him a copy. His wife told me he'd had it framed and kept it on his mantle at home. The tour was a success, and we parted with hugs and promises to keep in touch. Dizzy told me to call him anytime if I was coming to New York.

I don't remember the date, but I made a trip to New York and called Dizzy at his home to say hello. He told me he was playing at the Village Gate, to come on down and bring my horn; he'd leave my name at the door. I pushed my way through the crowd waiting to get in. A huge guy at the door almost pulled me inside when I told him my name, and I went down into the dungeon-like bowels of the club and found Dizzy, who was dressed in his long African robe. He greeted me with a hug and said, "We're playing Cuban music." I panicked. "I don't know a thing about Cuban music," I told him. "No problem," he said, "Just vamp on F 7th. Next tune, vamp on B Flat. That's all there is to it."

After listening to him vamp and hearing a bit I realized that harmonically it really was that simple, but I had no clue about the rhythms, which seemed to go everywhere. So I played and whistled a bit. Every time Dizzy started playing the dozen or so drummers went wild. At one point Dizzy started one of his fantastic convoluted descending lines. Starting way up high, the intricate line came cascading down. About mid-way he stopped, looked over at me with a twinkle in his eyes said, "Where the fuck is 'one'?" and kept right on playing. During the break we talked about doing a jazz album with all natural instruments. Diz made some amazing drum sounds just with his mouth and fingers. He mentioned some guy who sang authentic-sounding bass lines and thought he could interest Bobby McFerrin. I didn't follow up. I was in Chicago temporarily working for Rafal's father when I saw a newspaper with a headline that Dizzy had died. Just to have been a tiny part of that history was a gift.

Jarek Smietana

"My father wants you to play the Rhapsody in Blue clarinet glissando as introduction for the album." Even on the phone Jarek's voice, instantly recognizable, was full of authority and I realized protesting was useless.

I had never attempted to do it and tried a few times before heading down to the studio were we were to check the final mix for the Gershwin CD we recorded the day before. And now to attempt the impossible. I tried it most unsuccessfully several times and then, really by accident it worked; smooth as silk all the way up. Fortunately the tape was running. Jarek was poised with just the right chords and we pulled it off. I made him promise that if it got on the CD he'd never ask me to try it again. My one and only.

I met Jarek on my first trip to Poland at the Standards Festival in Sedelce and the following year he invited me to tour with him and a quartet. Through Jarek I met Jose Torres and Joachim Mencel and established a good reputation with Polish musicians and the venues we played.

Aside being a formidable player Jarek was a warm friendly giant of a man and I was lucky to have spent a lot of time with him. I think that first trip he introduced me to the famous sausage place in Krakow and we went there many times after.

I remember one dark night hurtling along in Erik Kulm's VW through a forest with no noticeable landmarks and Jarek suddenly calling out, "Stop, stop," many, many times. With no sign of a sign we turned into a small dirt road that in about twenty feet opened up into

Jarek Smietana. Poland.

a small clearing. There was a small wooden cart/ lunch wagon attached to a small car. We were really in the middle of nowhere. We all piled out for some Zurek, a great Polish potato soup with kielbasa, salads and always fresh bread. Apparently the woman who ran the concession had been a classmate of Jarek's in grade school. I have no idea how he found the place. Back in Krakow on multiple occasions I'd go to his apartment early in the morning. We'd take the tram down town to some markets he liked and he'd buy all sorts of goodies most of which I didn't recognize. We'd head back and he'd cook up a fantastic breakfast always with good coffee and that Polish bread to die for.

He told me that once, when he was hosting American sax player Carter Jefferson, after the gig he took him to the main square to hear the famous trumpet player in the church tower. Carter didn't believe that he played every hour on the hour 24/7 but Jarek dragged him to the square anyway. The hour came but no trumpet player. This reinforced Carter's disbelief and infuriated Jarek. A police car was parked across the square and they went to complain and found the trumpet player passed out in the back seat.

Lots of good times. He organized the quartet for 'Brad Terry Plays Gershwin' CD and wrote arrangements for 'Brad Terry Plays Ellington', which was recorded with a ten piece 'little big band'.

In 2012 Jarek developed a brain tumor that, after surgery left his left arm paralyzed. About six months later he died, leaving a legacy of wonderful music and hundreds of fans and friends. I was both. He took me to places that most Polish tourists don't know about.

Holly

Someone asked me, "Is that your dog?"
I answered, "No. She's my friend."
It has nothing to do with ownership.

Old Bro and me.

21

Old Bro
(1937–2008)

I wrote this for my brother Peter's memorial service/gathering, in Bridgton, Maine, Sept. 20, 2008:

For all of my seventy-one years on this planet my Old Bro Peter has been my anchor to windward.

The photo of him pushing me in the wooden truck he built for me sums up my relationship with him better than any words... but I'd still like to say a few words anyway.

Somehow he always managed to find time for me. Early on, he made a point of taking me on camping trips for my birthday. Once we borrowed a canoe from my father's boss, Mr. Dorr. Leila, my only non-judgmental adult friend, dropped us off way upstream on the Housatonic River, up beyond Newtown, and picked us up downstream a few days later, wet and cold. We had a tent and it rained constantly. (It always rained when we went camping.) It would have been early June, and I remember swimming briefly and really hurting from the cold water. We spent the nights in our tent reading stories and trying to stump each other with spelling words.

One summer when I was nine or ten we took a four-day cruise around Vinalhaven in one of the family's 16-foot sailing dinghies. We spent a night in Vinalhaven Harbor and for warmth headed for the movie theater. I was too scared by the movie so we returned to the dinghy and cooked spam over a candle in the rain. We went on to Calm Island, spent the night and got close to dry in the little house.

But in the early morning I woke up and noticed the dinghy was gone. It had broken loose and drifted well out to sea on the out-going tide, only to return on the incoming tide but to Leadbetter's, another island. We could see it about half a mile away. We were stuck. Peter decided he had to do something. Clutching a driftwood board he swam across to retrieve the boat and keep it from being smashed on the shore. When he got back he was so cold he couldn't get out of the boat. I managed to half carry, half drag him to the house where I had a fire going and a hot kettle for tea.

At an early age I was sent off to boarding school. Peter came to see me in several spring plays. One year I was typecast. I had the lead in Peter Pan. My flying was spectacular, and I really was Peter Pan. I've never really given up that role.

Back home in Connecticut, Peter and his friend Allen Pratt, both probably in their twenties, got a border collie and named him Tamper because he chewed everything; destroyed socks and skivvies and anything else lying around.

I came home from school for the summer and quickly informed them that he was, in fact, a female. I was eleven or twelve. With considerable embarrassment she was re-named Tammy. Later, Peter and Mary Lou shipped Tammy to me in Connecticut because she was not doing well in the heat at Fort Sill, Oklahoma. Tammy was my best friend for many years to come. It was the beginning of my love for a series of wonderful non-judgmental canine friends.

When I was sixteen, Peter was being shot at and experiencing the horrors of his time in Korea. I managed, with my license of three days, to totally destroy his Hillman Minx convertible. I guess he got the insurance, but he never said a word about it.

At one point I remember talking with him at length about my disappointment in not having any kids of my own. He finally told me, "Having kids is no big deal; even slugs reproduce." It made me ever grateful for my wonderful extended family, which numbers in the hundreds and spans at least fifty years.

Finally, I was in Poland on 9/11. I heard on the radio something about "Lotinski", "Nowa York" and "World Trade Center." Mateusz's grandfather's face turned ashen as he tried to translate. We rushed to a friend's house and were watching CNN as the plane hit the second tower.

The next night, 9/12, was the opening concert of the International Clarinet Festival in Krakow. England's premier clarinetist, David Campbell, would play first and present a duo of classical pieces. Joachim and I were to play the second half. With my whole world upside down, I didn't know what, or how I was to concentrate, or do, anything. Peter was the one person I felt I had to talk to and, amazingly, just after we watched the second tower fall, I got through. (There was no phone service to the USA for the next two weeks.) I explained my dilemma and my fears, and he simply said I had to go through with the concert. "If not," he said, "They will have claimed another victim." As usual his calm and wise words comforted me and helped me get through.

My life has been full of rough seas, a lot of fog banks, and a few major storms along the way. Peter was always my anchor to windward.

Please have a good look at that picture, it really says it all.

I miss you, Old Bro.

22

Second Stories
(1938–2014)

Brad invited people to send him stories they remembered about him. This chapter is that collection of "second stories".

The beginning: Letters from Brad's mother in Holland to her mother in New York, 1937–1938.

"Braddy is gaining alarmingly. We have reduced him almost entirely to fruit and vegetables, butter almost eliminated and a dash of honey substituted for sugar. But he still puts on weight He is slow and lazy chiefly because he is perfectly happy wherever he is on what ever he is doing. There is no incentive to move because he likes whatever toy he has and if he has none he just laughs for amusement. He is very responsive and his apple cheeks and black eyes are very beguiling but he would be better looking if he had more hair.

Braddy has been promoted to three meals (plus orange juice twice) and the schedule works beautifully Orange juice at 7 A.M, bath at 8:30 (when the boys are at school) , breakfast (bread and milk and prunes) at 9, sleep until 11, out in pram until 12:30 lunch (vegetables, potato, broth, etc.)Sleep until 4 (orange juice), playing and visiting until 5:30 supper Bread and milk and applesauce), bed and not a sound until 7 in the morning. It firs in well for Mme. Roger and he seems to thrive on anything. He has three teeth and doesn't sit up firmly alone yet and we don't push him. Very responsive and unbelievably good.

Jim's birthday was a success in spite of our overwhelming difficulties. (1)

Mr. Watson (2) arrived in The Hague for that one day and the telephone rang all day—people trying to locate him and he was moving so fast he wasn't anywhere. I had a talk with him between his massage and his conference with the Prime minister of Holland and he regaled me with tales of his visits to six kings, two dictators and all other potentates—absolutely fantastic. He managed to come to see Peter and the baby and pressed money on them. (3) Brady who had been all smiles, howled when he was given the note and hurled it on the ground! It was funny and I fear a bad omen. I hope he has many talents and a strong back to make up for his inability to cope with money."

1. Peter was recovering from a severely infected knee; in and out of the hospital, high fever etc.
2. Tom Watson, IBM
3. Years later mother would tell me it was a one hundred dollar bill.

An email from sister-in-law Perrine Terry.

BRAD, you are my 'small' brother, and the unique man who made me spend a night (alone) in his tree house, I was 19 and you 14. I asked you to remove the ladder because I was afraid to be visited by the cows, below. We both did this AGAINST the will of your mother!

To this day, I am grateful to you. NOT because you brought me pears for breakfast, NOT because you thought of French girls liking freshly pressed sheets. BUT because IN a corner, when it was quite dark and I had a flicker of unromantic panic (ladder missing) = I discovered an empty yoghurt jar and a box of Kleenex and sighed with double relief, "How thoughtful of him!"

Brad, we do need to upscale our souvenirs:
OK, 58 years ago !
BEST/LOVE TO ALL Perrine

From niece Lucia Terry,

On Dec 6, 2011, at 7:19 AM, Lucia Terry wrote:
My earliest memories of Woodbine were all very wrapped up in you and what your mother and then my mother would call your billybollys; always something going on. As little girls, Liza and me, days spent watching the comings and goings; I think you were doing tree work or landscaping of some kind at the time, like 1963,4,5,6ish; evenings spent under the piano, jazz imprinting my mind and spirit. One time, Liza and me, left in your care, in our beds in the pink room over the kitchen. We're supposed to be sleeping, but we're watching out

the window the happenings in the yard below: cars and boys and music and noise, exciting then to us, at our young ages, a harbinger of the interest in the same kinds of things to come later in our teenage years; and scaring ourselves with games of alligators in the water under the beds. Hearing you come into the house below to check on us, we jump into bed and fall quickly asleep; you sitting on the edge of my bed which is the closest to the doorway and telling me how you can tell if someone's really asleep by how they breathe. I don't remember, but imagine that I could not have stayed asleep under this scrutiny and at this point must have 'woken', laughing... and probably gone right back to the window when you left.

My first ever ride on a motorcycle was with you on the windy, that's wine-dy, not win-dy, roads of New Canaan; I did not have the opportunity to be on a motorcycle again for many decades, but when I was, that visceral memory was there, in the seat of my pants. We went for a ride in the Griffith as well... musta been... a feeling I will never forget. These were one-of-a-kind experiences which led I am sure along some kind of sensory-memory timeline directly to my short and so sweet stint of helicopter pilot training.

The Village Gate in NYC circa 1969: I am 14 ish and I am there with you, in a favorite haunt of my parents, they are probably there to, and I hear for the first time a piece of musical theatre magic called Jacques Brel is Alive and Well and Living in Paris. This visual musical experience made an impression on me that would haunt me my entire life... still does I think. I made friends with what the piece meant to me when I performed it at Deertrees Theater in the early 90s. Sending 'If we only have love' up to the rafters and out into the night was a release of some sort for me, after years of harboring the energy of that experience. You brought me there and introduced me to JB, and, maybe even that same night, to the curly-headed boy William Galison, who would be a lifelong friend.

All of these are examples of the power of early formative memories, rich sensory moments spinning threads into the fabric of what will be.

Finally, you were there with Dad when his last breath left him. You got me from the other room and together you and I handed him off to the Great Wherever. Your presence and care those last days and weeks, bringing Mateusz to play for him, even though he was already in another place and could not respond in a way we could see, this was very touching and helpful to me. Your love for him helped to carry me for sure in a way I'm not sure I can explain.

All of these I will try to write properly about... just wanted you to know my thoughts.

Love you,
Lucia

From that boy, William Galison:

I first met Brad in my seventh grade year at Riverdale, where Brad was the new "shop" teacher. I was a misfit, the youngest kid in the class by half a year and an aspiring hippie in a serious academic school that had only just discontinued their "jacket and tie" dress code.

Lost in my own world, (then as now,) I was totally at sea in my classes and didn't seem to fit into any of the social groups to which it seemed everybody else belonged. Circulating around Brad at that time was a group of kids with whom I felt entirely unworthy to associate. They were all top students and good athletes, and with Brad they were performing godlike feats like taking apart and rebuilding go-karts, and speaking casually of impossibly complicated things like carburetors and camshafts. I could only admire them from afar.

Brad himself, however, the mysterious Peter Pan around whom these prodigies collected, seemed more accessible to me than his acolytes, and I did have one connection with him that they did not. I was deeply into music, albeit folk guitar in the style of Doc Watson, and while Brad was not enthralled with that particular genre, I think he recognized me as a fellow musician, and ironically, a fellow misfit. As for me, though I knew nothing about jazz, the sound of Brad's clarinet and his apparent utter mastery of the instrument transcended style, and mesmerized me.

One day Brad invited me to see him play at "Jacques's", a jazz bar in Greenwich Village. For an eleven-year-old hippie kid, born into the age of Beatles albums, Peter Max posters and anti-war demonstrations, this place was another universe. Dark, smoke-filled, wallpapered with red velour, and populated by guys wearing hair tonic and sipping Martini's, I was a little disoriented at first. But I went there with Brad on many occasions, and there I sat, under the grand piano I am told, absorbing some of the best jazz music in the world: Eddie Thompson on piano, Major Holly on bass, Brad on clarinet of course, and God knows what other masters who came by to sit in. Jazz may have been considered "dead" in 1969, but the masters of Jazz were not dead by a long shot, and I can imagine that any number of Basie and Ellington veterans sat in at those sessions at Jacques's. Even without knowing the tunes, or appreciating the caliber of the players I was exposed to, my young mind absorbed the values of the music; swing, tone, melody, syncopation, communication, interplay and FUN.

To make a very long story short, 46 years later I identify myself as a Jazz musician, and playing this music has certainly been the primary passion of my life. Reaching the level on my instrument at which I could play confidently

with Brad was a major impetus to practice, and playing with him is one of my greatest pleasures. So when people ask me who were my influences in Jazz, I tell them about an amazing clarinetist they may not have heard of, who lives up in Maine, still a dear friend, still a mentor, and always an inspiration.
William

From grand-niece Melinda:

A bunny tale.

My earliest childhood memories of Uncle Brad are auditory. The knowledge of his presence, on a visit to Pond Road, always carried over the wafting air, up the hill to my small ears. That whistling of a tune, so merry, so rich, was unique to only one person. I was in awe, you see, I couldn't and I still can't whistle. Uncle Brad's jolly face puckered in a melody conveyed so much life energy, the essential moment, creation of music with only a breath.

One of these visits, I must have been about eight-years-old, my brother William six, I remember us trundling up the steep stairs of Grammy and Grampy's house to that bright guest room awash with summer light. I don't know why, or where we were to be going, but I remember that two lessons were given one to my brother, on how to tie his little shoes, and one attempting to teach me to whistle. I can see my small brother, enveloped in Brad's generous lap, watching carefully as Brad relayed the tale that would guide his shoelaces home. "Make two loops like bunny ears" it started, and here's where it diverges from that classic rhyme told by many a parent. You see our story was accompanied by a soundtrack, when the bunny ran around the tree, we could see his trail traced on notes hung in the air. As Brad whistled along with the story, my brother learned to tie his shoes, but despite his best efforts, and all of my breath, I never learned to whistle despite being great-niece of one of the greatest jazz whistlers.
Xoxo Meli

An email exchange with nephew Jimbo Terry.

Hey ho Brad,
One of my fondest memories is a bit hazy from age so you might be able to fill in a gap or two but I recall being taken to the auto show at I think the Prudential Center in what must have been the 60's by you, and I remember the

Batmobile and an Adam West autograph and some buxom car babes followed by a ride home down Storrow Drive traveling at speeds the Batman would have been envious of in what I think must have been your Ford Bronco? My fondest memory ever has to be the time you took me to see George Benson at the Jazz Workshop {opposite the Pru Center} at about age 12 when he was still pretty much an unknown. Getting me in to that club would never have happened in the company of any other person I knew at the time and my chances of attending either event with my parents would have been dead zero evah!

I've told you before how you've influenced me both in music in general and in my playing in particular but that trip to see George was a major contributing factor to my interest in guitar which began at about the same time. That and of course seeing Lenny in the living room in VH as a duo with you, which was life changing to see him up close and intimate like that though the George concert occurred at a more impressionable time for me as a guitarist. I fear if I'd seen Lenny at age 12 I might have; a] been so depressed I never would have picked up a guitar again or worse b] I would not have been capable of comprehending what he was doing. As it turned out I was accomplished enough when I did see him and meet him that I completely did understand what he was doing and how. As a result of the timing of those two events I now find it easy to sound like George if I wish and I can do what Lenny did, albeit at maybe 1/10 of the speed and fluidity... Once again, I owe my playfulness and open mindedness as a musician and in no small part as a human being to you and your unbiased influence and personal generosity.

Jimbo

ps viva la book

Brad:

Hmmmm. I remember seeing G. Benson somewhere but didn't remember with whom or when. Also, and I could easily be wrong, but I know I took kids to the automobile show at the Coliseum in NYC in the 60s and by 1962-3 had the Cobra. Before the Cobra was an Alfa Romero I had as a second car, with the "Green Bitch" as primary transportation. It was a '54 Ford station wagon which I bought second hand and customized by giving it a 350 hp V8 out of a wrecked police car; faster than the same era Corvettes!

Two Broncos followed over several years were some time after the Cobra. Could we have seen Benson in NYC?

bt

I still think I should keep your 2nd story as is.

Bt

Jimbo:

The Batman was when it was current so 1966 to 1968. The speed was in a non speedy vehicle, hence my guess about the Bronco. Speaking of the Bronco there is also the memory of after Xmas before New Years when we went to the Groningsater's in Vermont or NY, Lake Champlain for a big New Years eve party via Vinalhaven. You, me Willy and Matt all piled into the Bronco for that I am sure. Best "story" component of that trip was us sleeping in the smoky loft of the main A frame where the best heat from the smoky fire was and your shepherd of the moment {Sandra?) Duchess?} pulling us on the thick, thick ice on the quarry as we held her tail. It was friggin cold!

George Benson was much later {2–3 years} than Batman but I know I was under age to drink, which for me then was less than 18, I started playing guitar in 6th grade at age 13–14 and I'm sure Benson was at Paul's Mall/The Jazz Workshop in Boston before I was in High School, my freshman year at Salisbury. George's White Rabbit record came out in 1971 so I think it was close to that time.

Remember sharing your Salisbury experience before I went there?

Keep, add or edit what you like funky unc.

Jimbo

Hey B

I left you a phone message of this one too;

I recall you and my Dad being mischievous one October day as you, Dad, myself, and Tim, the camper with a broken leg brought the Anna W. from the Thoroughfare to Carvers Harbor and there was quite a wind blowin'. You decided it would be fun to see if you could bury the bow in the big swells off Carvers Harbor with Tim and I clinging to the cleats. You succeeded of course. I also remember it taking a nice fire at the Big House to warm us up after we had driven back to the house...

Jimbo

From cousin Bonnie Trafford:

One of the nicest things you need to know about Brad Terry is his enthusiastic willingness to help someone out. In 2008, I was faced with the prospect of relocating from Colorado, where I had lived and worked for 36 years, to Maine to retire near family. My original plan was to rent a U-Haul truck with a car *dolly to haul all my stuff, my autistic brother, Brad, and my little dog, Tenzing. The prospect of driving over 2000 miles was daunting, and diesel fuel was almost $5 a gallon! A cousin suggested I call Brad Terry (who is my first cousin) to see if he would help drive across the country. So I called Brad with my proposed trip, and without hesitating or putting me off so he could think about it, he responded enthusiastically," I'd LOVE to do it, just tell me when and I'll come!" Now, who in their right mind would offer to do such a thing? 2000 miles on a bench seat with 3 big people and a dog in a truck, hauling a car didn't appeal to me at all!*

I changed my plan and shipped my stuff in a pod. 3 adults and a dog in a Saturn for 2000+ miles was tough enough for me. We met Brad Terry at the Denver airport and headed east. And you know we laughed. Besides driving 99% of the way, he entertained us with stories and jokes. We arrived 4 1/2 days later safe and sane. If it were up to me, we would still be in Ohio!

THANK YOU, BRAD TERRY.

From cousin Perry Boyden via Lucia:

Lucia.........We're off to the Island tomorrow and one of the first (well, almost first) things we'll do is to try and locate that photo of Lindy and Arthur... know it well as I took the pic... trouble is that we had prints made from the negative/slide for the Terry boys and I'm not sure where I "filed" it... someplace clever, I'm sure !!

About Brad........ he was/is a couple of years older so it wasn't until our late teens that we became friends as well as cousins. Vivid memories of him playing, note for note, along with Benny Goodman on wax... a short while later Benny was in the living room with him !! I missed that but the story is a good one ! "Is it Ok if I bring my friend Teddy along?" His influence was obvious: I was surrounded with piano players... Mom, Dad, Linc, Candace... so I tootled on a recorder briefly and then went off to Boston for clarinet lessons (more stories there but non-Bradski). Talent will out and it was clear that I was no threat to challenge anyone with a reed in his mouth! Mid 1950's... Brad and I go into NYC to meet up with Han who was working as a translator at the UN. He gave us a tour, walking through "no admittance" doors and giving us insights to that incredible building that few teenagers were ever privileged to see... then off to a jazz bar or two when kids were OK, not carded.

Whenever we meet the hugs are intense and we both wonder why we haven't spent more time together. It could be a sad thought but neither one of us is into that as we are thankful for the moment. We share a history but don't talk about it lot until we remember Peter, the glue.

That kinda undoes me... Perry

Transcribed phone call with Les Leiber, of Jazz at Noon, May 15, 2008.

"Hello Les, Hello, It's Brad Terry calling. How are you feeling?"

"Well, you know I had pneumonia?"

"Yes, Edie told me. Hey, You're smart enough not to get pneumonia; what's wrong with you?"

(Laughs) "That's right, I have no right to do it! But I'm ready to do your thing."

"OK. Please tell me the story about me you told at Jazz At Noon when I was there with Fred Fischer."

"In the history of Jazz at noon; we're going back to about 1973; that was about eight years after we started. Jazz at Noon is about businessmen who love to play jazz and get together every Friday at noon. They are good players but went on to other jobs. We were at the Roosevelt Hotel doing Jazz at Noon in the "Rough Rider Room", they called it, and we were filling it every Friday and, lo and behold, we had begun to pay; and I say, "pay" in quotes. In those days the great guest stars would play at Jazz at Noon and get $65.00.

So we were going on with Jazz at Noon, and along the way one of the "businessmen" that came to my attention was a young man named Brad Terry who was a wonderful clarinet player and a great whistler. I was particularly charmed by anybody who could whistle great jazz because of my own involvement with the penny whistle, which put me up in that treble clef. I admired this teacher who was supposed to be teaching woodworking at a swank school in the Bronx. He had dropped in a few times at Jazz at Noon.

There came a time when I had the honor to invite Toots Thielemans from Belgium. Not only was he the greatest performer on the harmonica, jazz with all the modern harmonies and jazz feeling, but he was also considered the greatest jazz whistler.

Well, I had this secret up my sleeve of Brad Terry, and on the day that Toots Thielemans was to be our guest star I told Brad to come down to introduce him to the greatest whistler of them all at that time, or at least the most well known, Toots Thielemans. So Brad Terry came down, but we didn't tell Toots about it and, lo and behold, not only was Toots Thielemans our guest star but John Wilson, the jazz critic of the NY Times was there, and I said to myself, "Oh, boy, this is going to be great." I was sure he had never heard two of the greatest whistlers in Jazz, and he was going to have a great story. OK. Then I saw Toots sitting with John Wilson, and I knew he was going to get a great story; so he came up and he did his shtick and whistled beautifully and played harmonica, and when he was finished he took a bow and started back to his seat next to John Wilson.

I said, "Wait a minute Toots, I have a little surprise here I think you'd like it very much. I'd like to present a fellow named Brad Terry who's really a teacher that plays great clarinet and I'd like you to hear him whistle."

So Brad went into one of his wonderful virtuoso whistling things, and then I motioned to Toots Thielemans to come up.

"Boy, it would be wonderful; let's hear a duet between the two greatest whistlers in the world."

Well, I think I detected a start of a frown on Toots's face, but he had to go through with it, so he came up and he whistled a few choruses. Then Brad did his, and then Toots, uh, well, sort of slunk back to his seat next to John Wilson.

Well, it wasn't 'til later that I learned what a jazz faux pas I had made, because my Belgian friend, the greatest whistler in the world, Toots Thielemans, wasn't exactly pleased to share the glory of the day—and, sure enough, there was no story in next day's NY Times because the jazz editor John Wilson had the good sense to know he shouldn't undermine Toots Thielemans by pointing out how great Brad Terry was. That was the end of Toots Theilaman's involvement in the life of Les Leiber and Jazz at Noon.

I still have great respect and liking for Toots who went back to Belgium; I don't think that that situation had anything to do with his leaving our country.

So then time went along and Brad Terry became a guest artist at Jazz at Noon, and I'm very happy to be talking to him on the telephone and relating this story. That's about all I have to say."

"Les, that's fabulous, that's wonderful. Many many thanks. I will write that down. At some point it will go into a special chapter of stories that other people can tell about me but I can't tell about myself."

From: Dean Langadas
Subject: An old RCS friend
To: "Brad Terry"
Date: Thursday, February 12, 2009, 9:57 PM

Hi Brad:
    Dean Langadas, from your RCS days. You may or may not remember I

was one of the hot rod buffs intrigued by the Griffith stories. I was the guy who showed up with Dean Fochios to take the Bronco off your hands, ran the go-karts for Frank Bertino during RCS summer camp and ended up living with Roy Coe out in California when we were both motorcycle maniacs. All that stuff goes back a ways.

Here's some quick trivia I remember, and a story that you'll probably appreciate:

You were teaching shop in the old dormitory building, and Wilson Alling came in with a broken watch to see if you could do anything about it. You said, "Let's have a look", put it on the bench and smashed it into a million pieces with a 5 lb. hand sledgehammer. You picked up a tiny piece of the wreckage and said, "I think I see the problem right here." That was hilarious.

This next story takes a bit of set-up: not long after getting the Bronco, we had pulled off the top, put in a roll-bar with lights along the top, swapped out the wheels and tires for big knobbies, and, for some reason, always rode around wearing matching blue mechanic's overalls. One afternoon Dean Fochios and I were driving the Bronco in front of the UN building in downtown Manhattan, us vs. the stretch limos parked along the street. Traffic forced us on to the Queensboro Bridge exit, and we weren't going there. So Dean drove the Bronco up onto the merge island, knocking down all the signs and reflectors, and waited for a chance to back down towards Manhattan. Of course, this was 200 feet from the UN, so these antics were witnessed by about half a dozen police cars. One of them screeched up, siren and lights blaring... the cop walks over, calmly surveys the scene of us, teetering on the elevated island in our matching jumpsuits, and says "What are we doing here today, boys, playing tank commandos?" I shared that so you'd know that we put the old girl to good and appropriate use. (He was so amused, he let us go...) We had a lot of fun with that car.

Roy and I were friends forever, too, starting with bicycles in Riverdale, go-karts with you, and seven unbelievable years in California building and racing motorcycles. He was a motocrosser and I was a road racer; he was jumping cars on his Maico during the half time show at the sprint car races, and I held the 600cc lap record at Willow Springs. That's when we were twenty and still bulletproof. I was best man at his first wedding, and we ran a very successful Yamaha shop during the fuel crunch in the early 80's. Roy was lead tuner, and I was the service manager. I've had 36 motorcycles and there will probably be more... We've all grown up despite our desire to the contrary. Roy is a family man with a slew of kids, Dean Fochios is an orthopedic surgeon, and I am the president of a railroad, of all things. Seems if it has wheels or tits, I've always been interested. I play music, too, and always enjoyed your clarinet playing and whistling—saw you on YouTube. You're still terrific.

Anyway, just a hello after too many years, and thanks, Brad, you impacted a lot of people's lives in a great way, and I wanted you to know that we all still think about you. I hope you are doing well and would like to think that our paths may cross again someday. Stay well.

Dean
Tucson, AZ

From Island Camper, Roy Coe:

Hello Brad hope all is well, We are still racing sailboats and doing well, thanx for teaching me how to sail, and how to appreciate the fine lines of a beautiful sailboat, one summer in Maine changed my life, Again Thank You

Big Sur:
A second story from New Gloucester student and Blue Lunch traveler Stewart Wurtz. January 2015

"I'm sitting in the bus here in Big Sur at Jaxon's brother's ranch about to dash through the rain into their house" reads my diary entry from March 13th, 1975.

There were nine of us on this adventure, the first of Brad's bus trips from winter in Maine to California, and back. Brad, Jaxon and Tommy were the jazz trio and the rest of us, pulled from school for a two month "educational" road trip, were from age 17 (me) to about 9. We set out on February 17th, gleefully leaving behind Maine snow and cold, with sights set firmly on New Orleans before taking a southern route to the West Coast. Three bicycles and a motorcycle were strapped on the back bumper as magnets for diesel particulate, and after much scrubbing, short trips around town. The sight of the blue bus solicited plenty of impromptu conversations along the way, as people witnessed this 1950's era intercity bus chug and roll through town.

Driving to Big Sur from Monterrey earlier that day the beauty of this coast really began to sink in. The fog was nestled into the Pacific redwoods and pines, broken here and there by grassy fields and rocky ridges that rolled down to the water's edge, painting the landscape in a surreal misty atmosphere. Upon arrival the fog had turned to full on rain and everyone was in a "wait and see"

326

mode for the day's activities. As the rain tapered off midday we eagerly set out to see the view, a bluff overlook to the mighty Pacific that lay 1000' below. The view was spectacular, intoxicating really, and blue skies were beginning to prevail. Standing there on the bluff the momentum was becoming too much. We gazed down this winding road leading to the ocean, and a beach, and then temptation gave way. Without a word spoken we were off in a heartbeat, racing downhill with full intensity. We were just a bunch of loose cannons really, traits we easily gleaned from hanging out with Brad. It was a stroke of luck we would survive our crazy unsupervised exploits. Trouble was, being spontaneous often meant have fun now and pay later, as we were soon to find out.

The road is a good 3 miles zigzagging down the hillside. Scotti looks at me as we set off, smiles mischievously, and jumps right off the road trampling through the brush, sliding over the rocks as he decides a straight line is way faster than thousands of steps on a long gravel road. Without hesitation, I'm right there with him. The others are quick to follow. We're immediately soaked from waist down from wet bushes as the rains had stopped only moments earlier, but we remained undeterred. The beach and ocean were gorgeous; private, secluded and ready for us to jump in the water bare-naked. Yes, the Pacific isn't too warm in March or perhaps warm ever, so submersion was short lived.

Next morning, the previous day's thrash down the hill is repeated with gusto. Added to the excitement this time is an abalone hunt. Unfortunately the tide was a bit high when we arrive and being too impatient to wait it out, we forge ahead with enthusiasm. What else would you expect, we were green.

The idea behind the hunt was to quickly insert a knife between the rock and the abalone when the waves had receded, while the abalone was still unaware. Any hesitation and the abalone would clamp itself back onto the rock with herculean force letting the rock become one with the crustacean. In a moment's hesitation, partly due to still being dressed in dry clothes and thinking I was about to get doused, my Swiss army knife stops mid movement and the abalone clamps so tight it's not coming free. I hold on tight, get completely soaked from waist down by the breaking waves and struggle with this wily creature for my knife. At this point I'm fine to surrender the abalone, but he has a different plan. Much struggling ensues then I hear a snap. Knife is now in hand but the blade is tucked nicely beneath the abalone clamped with mega force to the rock and a bigger breaker is on its way in. You've got to choose your battles and I knew in an instant that I'd lost this one. I scamper quickly over the rock past starfish and barnacles that are not so tenderly cutting into my hands to escape the next big wave, this time getting wetter shoes for a soggy walk back up the road.

A week later after much agony we head out to the Burbank Medical Center trying to find out what was up with 13 year old Erika. Her rash appeared beyond control. Scotti and the others had some serious rash symptoms too but nothing like the basket case for Erika. It had spread all over her face and arms. Scotti's neck took the brunt of his plague. We're informed it's poison oak and not your average dose or reaction. A week after our Big Sur bushwhacking adventure, now all payment is coming due. The prescription was simple, sort of. Everyone got to bend over and take a shot in the butt to hopefully quell the spread further and maybe reduce the irritation. In no uncertain terms could anyone scratch their pox at will. Up to this point trying to keep this group from scratching would have required a straightjacket and probably a gag too. Now, the threat of a second shot in the butt would work wonders.

A shortcut down a beautiful slope of the Big Sur ranch felt like a benign decision at the time, only in hindsight did we realize our fatal error. On our return to Big Sur two days later the beach beckoned again. This time the road looked like the perfect route.

Stewart Wurtz

An email message From Island Camper Scott Therriault:

Brad,
I don't have a story for your book but I would like to thank you for everything you did for us grubby little kids oh so many years ago (42). The time I spent with you at camp, on the bus trip around the country, tagging along on your gigs and all the other times exposed me to a whole other world outside my pitiful existence. By "whole other world" I don't mean strictly in a geographical sense. I am also referring to a world so different from my "norm" with respect to how other people live, their families, social and economical status and activities. You not only gave me the opportunity to observe those other worlds but also the opportunity to occupy and experience them, to become part of them for a time. What that did for me is make me realize what is out there and that it was available to anyone, no matter where they came from.

What I am saying is not profound but the impact that you and those experiences had on my life were. That has been one of the major forces that

motivated me to try and make a better life for myself all these years.
I can't thank you enough for all you have done.

Sincerely,
Scott Therriault

From Island Camper Jonathan Jenkins:

Lo Brad! What a cruise! Your original Island Camp helped launch a boatload of hearts, but needing safe harbors.

You'll remember this story about your other "Boat!"

At the helm of the "Blue Lunch" was a contented, albeit passionate gentleman. Yes, after my little in-tow Toyota was able to nudge his nearly clutch-less, ancient city bus up and over a little known Mt. pass. Paradise Forest in So. California found us all, including the skipper, Brad Terry, breathing easier. All, meaning "The Band" and a funny assortment of "band-width" campers from hither and yon!

The otherwise known "Blew Lunch's" safe-landing seemed like a crucial crux towards my personal growth. Sailing down the winding road back to the Coast, "The Old Lady" held tight and smelly all the way, before a much needed drink. Brad usually has good expectations.

Out-come, faltering at times means less to him, because his intentions include all his friends and his love of Jazz. Ere-long, wherever Life leads, I'm still glad I landed on the "Artist's" pallet so to speak. Our friend Brad enriches so many lives; colorfully mentoring love for Life.

Coming about now, but thanks for clearing my scuppers Skipper! Jonathan Jay

An 2004 email "outa the blue" from Island Camper, Peter Jakobson:

I cannot tell you how many moments in my life are filled with images of you and all of the wonderful experiences you provided me with. In retrospect I realize that although I was blessed with much family support as a child, my life is inexorably informed by my years with you. You exposed a rather fortunate kid to a different world and you allowed me to develop interests and skills and talents that otherwise would have gone completely unformed.

I know that for you to think about me being a 45-year-old father and businessman living in a house in Mt. Kisco seems rather mundane but when you couple those rather simple characteristics with a guy whose interests in building and boating, automobiles and machinery, music, community and an endless desire to learn... your place in that firmament is exquisite.

22 years ago I joined my father in our business which had been around since 1880 and I grew it into a substantial owner/manager of real estate throughout NYC. Dad still works one-hour days at 78 and my brother Tom and I continue to buy, build and renovate. We are now converting a 40,000 square foot 150 bed nursing home in Astoria, Queens, into an apartment house. Little did I know that our days building Coot's cabin on Vinalhaven would teach me skills that today allow me to share an understanding of construction with my crews, commanding their respect and cooperation. Without such an experience, without being able to frame and plumb as well as they, there would be a wall between us and the "job" would be no fun.

Little did I dream that when you told me to "deal' with your personal checkbook and the Camp's, that I was learning skills that would permit me to deal with all the financial vagaries of multiple operating companies and all of the family members I am responsible for.

These are just a few thoughts about me that I share with you.

And more recently from Peter:

Lo' Bradford!

It has been eons and I keep thinking about you and the stories about you fill my heart and soul.

Whatever I wrote in 2004 I no longer recall but I am sure I have ten better stories about you.

Here is a short list:

Grilling Spam in the shop at RCD
Stuffed into a Porsche en route to Stamford
How to organize a slob
Walnuts and pecans at cocktail hour at the Terry residence
Chatting with Melinda Trafford Terry as a fourteen year old "adult"
Dirigo tales
Buying a Honda

Buying a bulldozer
Building a bowsprit
Breaking a bowsprit
Red Lead on Wades's Head
Going "bouncing"
Sitting with Terry, Liebisch and Gillespie
Bronco tales
Building "Coot's" house
"A dyke from Milan"
Blue Lunch
Blueberry picking, bee bites and an esophageal airway
Almaden exploration
Cocktails in a camper
Yanking the boom out of the quarry, drying it, returning it and
using it as a winch to pull junk from the bottom
Buying the biggest towels in the world
A ketch and a yawl to Jonesport
Cargo nets
Buying the Quarry
For the love of Richard Cash
For the friendship of Wilson Alling
The "new" kid (Peter Herman) is amazing and you are and always have
been.

Bradford, my parents and siblings still ask for you and tell me how
wonderful an influence you were on me and I reflect upon this always but most
especially when I see the confidence I have about myself for which you were
instrumental.

My daughter Haley is 19 and at the School of Theatre at BU and I am 53
and happy with my wife Lisa and two dogs in Mt. Kisco and a continuing and
wonderful career.

When Wilson told me to go "talk to Brad in the shop" forty years ago, he
forever changed my life.

I would love to see you and talk to you.

"Shakes"

From Al Miller:

Brad, deah,

Marshall asked me to direct the children's area the first year and suggested I come over to the Chocolate Church to do some improv with a fantastic trombone player, Brad Terry. So Nat and I joined Fateh, then "Victor", to do some improv with you and... I don't remember Tony's being there, but he may have been. The next year, the Festival's second year, Marshall asked me to head the whole festival and I asked you to be in charge of the jazz program. And so we did and away we went!

   There are many stories, but one of my favorites occurred when we were in the "Blue Lunch," returning to Brunswick after a program in Bowdoin or Bowdoinham: you, a few of the YPT kids and I. We were cruising along at a mild speed when a couple of kids egged the bus. A small price to pay for fame, thought I, but you pulled the bus over, opened the door and took off after the two boys like an angry rhino. The boys were, I think, startled, thinking they had egged us with impunity—well, with eggs, but also impunity. Suddenly, the bus door opens, and out flies this imposing fellow and he's going to catch them and make them clean the egg off the bus. I don't think I've seen lads flee as fast since a friend and I, age thirteen, which was about the age of those two boys, fled the Halloween scene when a police car pulled up after we had taken down a street sign. You, my friend, were running like an Olympic sprinter. The boys got away, and I don't think you minded. You were smiling when you got back to the bus. I doubt the boys egged another bus that year, if ever.

   How's that?

   See you Friday, if not before. Thanks for the first weekend. It mellowed into a complementary groove and worked well.

   Happy days,

   Al

An email exchange with Lee:

From: Brad Terry [mailto:brad@triologyjazz.com]
Sent: Sunday, March 16, 2014 12:34 PM
To: Leland Faulkner

Subject: Re: Hey Brad

Hey... 'tis fun and would be more fun if some night you guys popped in the door! Denny Breau (Lenny's younger brother) said Peter is the best player he's heard since his brother died.. (I told him that a year ago.) He's right up there with my Polish whiz kids.

The place is expensive but you can get by with an appetizer and one over priced (but very good) glass of wine and still retain ownership of most of your extremities. The place is small; only room for 15 at tables. (Need reservations) We play acoustically and, as I said you gotta hear this guitar player!

I was all set to give up on playing last winter, 2012. I wasn't playing at all. Zero gigs and for all purposes retired and came close to declaring retirement and putting my clarinet on the shelf for good.

Peter comes along.. Wow. We're playing tunes I've known for 50–60 years that he's hearing for the first time; he has very interesting different ideas about them. I keep asking myself, "Damn why didn't I think for that 40 years ago?" He throws curve balls at me all the time and kicks my ass!

I hope you can bite the financial bullet and come hear us some time soon.

Other than Thursdays I have almost unlimited free time. A sauna sandwiched between some good wine and cheer would float my boat almost any time.

I'm almost finished writing my book; 360 pages; lots of stories; really final stages. It's called, I Feel More Like I Do Now Than I Did Yesterday."

I have a chapter called "Second Stories." These are stories people can tell about me that I sort of can't tell about myself. They should be true, preferably funny, but not necessarily complimentary. Any ideas? ASAP if you think of something, OK?

Love to catch up one way or another.
brad

Dear Brad,
Well...here goes.....don't get too puffed up.   I remember the first time you improvised with me and, for me. I was about 17 years old, Marshall Dodge and Tony were on the bill with you. Tony had brought along all his students from his workshop that summer, and had us do some bits for the crowd. You said you'd play for my juggling routine. Boy, was I green. I was juggling a top hat, a pair of gloves and a cane, a good trick. I was all about the simple class of it. It was all going great until I dropped. Until that moment, I was all about

making things perfect, never missing a trick, making every catch...that's what juggling was all about. That was my folly, I didn't practice my mistakes, and when the hat trick missed, and my hat hit the floor, I thought it was all over. Until you made my hat/your clarinet laugh at me. The audience laughed, and I was saved. You taught me about comedy in that second of time. You really taught me that "mistakes" can be your friends if you embrace them. The ability to improvise has since become an important part of my theatrical repertoire, as it's always been part of your music. What a beautiful lesson.

I remember listening to you play in the Old Port when a boat gave a big whistle/honk, and you matched the note and honked back. Irrepressibly, the audience erupted with laughter. That's what separates you from the others, timing...and a sense of fun. You don't ignore realities, you embrace them. It's a great thing for artists of all kinds to learn.

I recently brought back the Cages pantomime for an important show I did in Castleton, VA. It's the first time since Tony's memorial at Bowdoin.

It brought back memories of us, performing on stage together, at Dartmouth College. It was a bitter mid-January. I had asked you to come and do the gig with me, remember? I felt amazing when you said yes. I felt like an artist.

I don't think I've ever driven in worse weather for just a few bucks. The show went great, the audience loved your solos, and your accompaniment to my mime sketch was wonderful. I remember that I rode in your old station wagon on the way back, and Karen drove our van. I guess we met up at Dartmouth and caravanned home. During the show, the snow started, and it was heavy, it dropped like cotton. After we packed and headed home, it seemed like we had to plow our own way through the snow on those back roads, bouncing and sailing along the frost heaves, all the way back to Maine. Talking about everything under the sun. As I recall, the tail of that station wagon swished back and forth more than a few times, making us catch our breath. Sometimes the gigs are hard, and the road cold, but sometimes we get salad days. The best days are the ones we remember.

I was feeling low recently, because of the scarcity of gigs, but suddenly I've gotten a few really good offers. So I know how you feel when you say you were going to hang up the clarinet. Somehow, when we're on the edge, the universe throws us a bone. I know I'd never be happy doing anything else, and neither would you.

You're brilliant Brad, and I really love you. Thanks for improvising.

Brad Terry Story #1 from Steve Grover:

Brad had booked a series of gigs over a weekend at The Samoset Hotel on the coast of Maine in Rockland—I think it was in the summer of 1983. We were to provide primarily background music, where the band would play light jazz while people mingled, that kind of thing. He hired a nice group with Tony Boffa on guitar, Tim Sessions on trombone, and a young Ben Street on bass, plus myself on drums. It was a State Treasurers convention, so it wasn't the hippest crowd, but everything was going as expected. At one point after one of the events Brad told us we were playing for some "singer" on Saturday night, and that we would back up whoever this was. I had to leave to play a daytime gig in Portland and on the way out I noticed a 'Now Appearing' sign that had a photo of a group called "The Winged Victory Singers" that was to perform that evening. That seemed intriguing to me, but I split to play my gig and came back and found the band in the lounge downstairs with a very distraught guy who was the director of The Winged Victory Singers. He was expecting a full band, a big band, to back him up. He had shown up with full band arrangements and here was this jazz quintet with a clarinet player who couldn't read.

Tony Boffa assured the guy that he was a good reader, and to give him the piano part so he could figure things out. There were no chord changes, just a full piano part with cues and so forth. Tim took the lead trumpet part, and Ben and I had our parts. Of course we were dressed very casually because of what we had been doing, no formal attire; The Winged Victory Singers were black tie, and here we were with shorts and tee shirts. Anyway, we all squeezed onto this stage in the main room with an attentive audience of state treasurers and their wives/husbands, and somehow we played this gig. No music stands; the music was on chairs, the floor. I may have brought a music stand. I have to say that the director of this outfit was lucky that Boffa and Tim Sessions were there, because they were totally professional. Tim sight-read the trumpet part on trombone and Boffa played beautifully. Brad kind of improvised in the cracks I think, and was somehow trying to keep it together; it was a pretty funny scene. The music was very old school, George M. Cohan stuff, very cornball, with hand choreography and all of that, for which there was little room on stage. The director's blood pressure was at a climax by the time we finished the concert; he was directing with great violence. It was really too much. I think we laughed about that gig for a couple of hours after we finished, at the incongruity of it. Steve Grover

An exchange with Mike McGinnis:

Brad,

As I'm sure you'll agree... the term "know" also has many levels and meanings. I saw this Lester Young quote that said something to the effect of... he didn't like knowing what the changes were because it made him stop listening and start thinking about what he played. I think you're one of the few people I know that really learned to play jazz in the old school way of all the greats. What your ears know and speak when you play is so much deeper than any music school knowledge. It's really like magic to me to hear those melodies flow from your horn. I think it takes much longer and more practice to really be able to play by ear. All the knowing can easily get in the way and I'm constantly working to know less and hear more. I put you up there with my favorites like Getz, Desmond, Chet Baker. None of those guys were considered master sight-readers or classical concerto playing types and that didn't matter. Why would I ever want to hear Paul Desmond sight read or play Mozart when I can hear him play Paul Desmond .
M

Brad's reply:

Thanks Mike,

I have to tell you I feel taken aback by accolades from the likes of you and Barry about my playing. During time shared with Joe Allard he told me there are three levels. First, when you can impress (he said 'fool') people with your playing who don't know anything about music. Second, when you can fool people who do know music, and third, when you start fooling yourself which is total bullshit. I haven't been fooling myself but think I may have been fooling people at level 2.

I appreciate the kind words. Most of the people I know know more than me.

I look forward to any stories you can collect and welcome any opportunity to come to NYC and fool people.
Brad

More from Mike:

My two accounts of Brad Terry come from the late 1980's when I was an aspiring high school saxophonist. Both are examples of his being a tolerant and encouraging mentor amongst other older musicians who were not as nice.

As I was always looking for any opportunity to play with real musicians instead of Aebersold playalongs, I would frequently attend local jam sessions at places like Verillo's and the Cafe No.

1) *Verillo's jam session.*

At these sessions held on Sunday afternoons, the house band would play first and then invite younger players up for a tune or two. On this day after the house band played, I was standing beside the bandstand with my tenor saxophone while some of the local established professionals were also preparing to play. While no one else would invite me to play, Brad was the one who saw me and asked me if I wanted to play and what tune I wanted to play. I said "Scapple from the Apple" and I was able to play it with him and it was very special to be playing with the "pros". Unfortunately, some of the other "pros" felt that I shouldn't have been up there and decided to cut me down to size. They called rhythm changes really fast. Fortunately for me, bassist Ben Street was on my side and managed to thwart the main soloist from cutting me down by playing in a way that made him lose the form. The big "pro" ended up having to stop in the middle of his solo while the bass line under my solo was very clear and made me sound better than I could play at the time. I'll always appreciate Brad's encouragement in the company of so many other not so encouraging folks. Brad made you feel like you could play and were worthy.

2) *Cafe No*

At one of the Cafe No jam sessions, Brad was playing the tune "All The Things You Are" with two beginner musicians who did not really know the tune and were even having trouble reading the melody from the Real Book. As the three of them attempted to play the melody together it was so uncoordinated that a friend sitting with me exclaimed, "I didn't know this was a fugue". All the while, not only did Brad maintain his sunny composure, but, he somehow managed to play in a way that made the musical madness surrounding him almost work. It made me realize how a great player isn't just a great soloist but also can take a bad musical situation and make it better if they are generous enough to choose that instead of giving up in frustration.

M

From David Libby:

Hi Brad,

My story for your book is below. The text in blue could be deleted if it's a little too much information!

In the late 1980s, I booked a regular gig solo piano gig in the lounge of a restaurant called "Prime Plus One" in Lewiston. Formerly known as The Warehouse, it had been a frequent venue for veteran Maine jazz players, including Brad. After a few weeks of playing solo gigs, I asked the manager if he'd be willing to let me book other musicians to play duo with me. Happily, he agreed, and my first call was to Brad. I was excited that he agreed to join me because I loved his playing, of course, but also because I knew that I would learn a lot musically by playing with him.

One night Brad came to the gig looking a little uneasy and not quite his usual cheerful self. The reason for his uneasiness, he said, was that he had undergone outpatient surgery for a hernia that same day. The doctor who performed the surgery told him not to play for a while, but of course that didn't stop Brad. During our first set, Brad kept reaching to his abdomen to stop something related to the surgery from popping out! I was pretty alarmed for the guy, but Brad and I both couldn't help but chuckle about it too.

Steve Grover came to hear us that night, and between sets he asked Brad how he was feeling.

Brad answered, "It only hurts when I stop playing!"

David Libby

From Eli Gilbert:

For my Peabody Conservatory Application, I had to write an essay about my most meaningful musical experience, and this is what I wrote:

During the summer of 2008, I heard a recording of Lenny Breau for the first time. New to the world of jazz, I had never heard anyone play with such facility, as well as beauty. He was able to make the guitar sound like a piano if he wanted, or two guitars playing at once. I found this music irresistible and it has become a staple in my listening ever since. On one occasion, I came across a record called The Living Room Tapes with a clarinetist named Brad

Terry. I had never heard before a clarinet with such a soft warm sound, much less as such a beautiful improvisational instrument. It was later that I found out that the album itself was recorded in Brad Terry's living room in Maine, my home state. I was even more surprised to find that Brad was still living in Maine, a mere forty minutes from my home.

That year I had the opportunity to meet Brad after a performance with saxophonist Jeff Coffin. I was eager to tell him of my adoration for The Living Room Tapes, wanted to ask him so many questions about his time with Lenny Breau. I quickly found that Brad was one of the friendliest people you will ever meet. Within ten minutes of our first meeting, he offered to spend time with me and my friends to talk about his experiences with music, and listen to his expansive collection of jazz records. It was many months when we finally met again, this time the intention being to play music together for a recital that I was putting together at my local high school. After spending some time playing the few standards that I had memorized by that time, I spent hours listening to Brad's account of his life as a musician. I was so completely enthralled in each of his stories regarding some of my favorite jazz musicians, and all the while astounded that I was in the presence of such a great musician myself. From Buck Clayton to Dizzy Gillespie, Buddy Tate to Steve Swallow, Brad is the personification of some of the most important developments in jazz music since the middle of the twentieth century.

Since that day I have played with Brad on numerous occasions, including a recital that I organized at my former high school. Each experience has been more valuable than the one before it, and has always inspired me to continue practicing and developing my own individual sound, as Brad has done. One such session stands out from the rest however. Approximately one week before I left Maine for the Interlochen Arts Academy, I had the chance to sit down and play with Brad again in a duo setting. Unlike the other times we had played together, this session was recorded. The general trend whenever we spent time together is that we spend some time playing, and a lot of time talking. In a span of two or three hours, we might only play three tunes, but each tune feels like an eternity with Brad.

One of the most amazing aspects of Brad's playing is his ability to pick out and play back phrases note for note, after hearing them only once. He is hands down the most attentive musician that I have ever met, let alone had the pleasure to play with. Regardless of the musical situation, Brad is determined to make it a conversation. That is what strikes me most when I listen to the recordings we did that day. The distance in terms of musicality and experience between he and myself is so great, and yet there is no impact on the genuine quality of his playing. To hear Brad answer a phrase that I play is one of the most uplifting feelings I think I can ever feel. It made me feel as if my contribution to the music was worth repeating or continuing.

Playing has never felt as comfortable as it did that day. There were no lead sheets to read off of, no discussions of the form, and often no one counting off each tune. The experience was a culmination of the time that Brad and I had spent together, and was wholly representative of the strong friendship that we had built. It was after this day that I fully realized that Brad is and will always be one of my greatest friends, and is a man that I have a great deal of respect for.

From Sean Cash:

Brad Terry is my second father. Some people aren't lucky enough to have one, so I have some concept as to how fortunate I am to have two. I have had many experiences and adventures that I can directly attribute to Brad; having spent many years at the island camp and being the only person other than Brad and Maeda to have made all three California trips in the "blue lunch".

As much as I appreciate all that Brad has done for me and my family, I am the most grateful for the people that he has introduced me to. There are far too many to mention for my short contribution, but let me share a few.

Helen Handley at the age of 85 gave me a wonderful hug having not seen her since the previous summer. She grabbed one of my "cheeks" in each hand and gave them both a squeeze and with an impish grin said " I've wanted to do that for years !" I made a set of wind chimes for Helen and her husband Ollie in Austin, Texas from bamboo that we stole from some of their neighbors. We were visited by the police. Ollie told me twenty years later that they still had the wind chimes, though he had to repair them over the years. Helen and Ollie were two very dear and wonderful souls that I have been blessed to call my friends and I would never have met them if it had not been for Brad.

I used to head to Vinalhaven the day after school let out and I would come home the day before school started again. I remember missing my dog about an hour before I got home.

Jim Brown taught me how to do magic and how to juggle. Fred Garver showed me how to ride a unicycle and Tony Montanaro connected me with clown college. So as you can see, it is largely Brad's fault that I became a clown with Ringling Brother's circus; I was hired partly because of my log rolling skills that I learned at the quarry. Turns out that globe walking is a very similar skill. We never had elephants at camp, perhaps the living room wasn't large enough.

Kevin Gillespie and Jeff Simons are two of my all time favorite people and closest friends. We have known each other for nearly 40 years. Yep, that's Brad's fault again.

All of my Vinalhaven friends have come from my relationship with Brad. I know most of his family members nearly as well as my own and hold them all as dearly. I have known Brad for nearly one half of a century and have met a large majority of his friends and fellow musicians.

All of them have affected me; some in large ways and some in small, and far too many for me to recall; but all of them positively.

There seems to be a kind of magic about Brad that attracts wonderfully talented and intelligent, friendly people. Just the kind of folks you would naturally want to be with, sharing a glass of wine around a fire or a baby grand piano or both if you happen to be at the big house.

When I was five, I thought that Brad was a god. When I was fifteen, my illusion was shattered and I felt as if Brad had lied to me about who he was. When I was twenty-five, I realized that Brad had not changed at all, but I had.

Brad is one of the most giving people that I know. We were having a conversation during the last decade or so and he told me that his greatest regret was that he never had any children. I don't know exactly how many kids went through the island camp or how many have been affected by Brad in such a positive manner as I; but for myself, I couldn't ask for a better second dad and I doubt that I am alone in my gratitude. Thank you for everything.

Sean

From Jose Torres (on Facebook, after hearing from Brad of his duo with Peter Herman):

COngratulations Brad. You are like Christof Columb becouse you still find the new "Lands" around you. I always will remember the Quartet with Baranski, Kołakowski and Tomek. Young people without experence and how many thinkgs have learned from you. You are a special person for as. Again CONGRATULATIONS

23

Poland: Last Diary
(16 November 2011—5 January 2012)

This is a collection of diary entries from my most recent trip to Poland, e-mailed with many thanks to Marty Corey, and included here with minimum editing. Some of the personal messages to her remain.

I was dealing with a lot of back pain, having had to postpone surgery because of not enough healing time before the trip. I was warned that things would get worse, but it was not dangerous to wait for surgery, which was scheduled for two days after I was to get home.

The scene shifts around to several locations and even for me it's hard to put things in order because my computer died and writing was from all over the place.

So.... Locations:

> Arrive in Warsaw 11/16/ 2011
> Krakow with Joachim.
> Slawek Lach's house in the country; 45 minutes from Krakow.
> Bytom for a few days with Kolakowski family.
> Amazing 5 days in Ukraine.
> Zory with Michal Baranski family.
> Back to Bytom for Christmas.
> New Years in Wroclaw with Tomek Torres and family.
> Krakow with Joachim.
> Home Jan. 5th.

Nov. 18th (?)

I have a few minutes of Internet time so I will try to catch up with the news. The flight from O'Hare via Paris to Warsaw was seamless, very smooth and comfortable. Andre, Joachim's manager met me at the Warsaw airport and we drove about an hour to a monastery where we were greeted by about 80 -100 eager students ranging in age from about 6 years old to 60. I had an ensemble of flute and saxophone players most of whom had never improvised. I was able to loosen them up and then coordinated efforts with Joachim's piano students. We performed for the rest of the group Saturday night. It went well and we were wildly received.

It was great getting to work immediately after getting off the airplane because I didn't have time to worry about jet lag; just went right at it.

I just discovered today that there is a room downstairs with Wi-Fi connections. I'm waiting now for Joachim to do some paperwork and collect some money and then we face a really long drive back to Kraków I'm guessing 6 or 7 hours at least. Fortunately I am wide-awake and will be able to do a lot of the driving. He will drop me off at Slawek's, about an hour this side of Kraków.

I hear things moving in the hall. I think I will have Internet where I will be staying so I'll try to keep writing as much as possible.

B

Wow, I'm with Slawek in his state of the arts house he built himself. I'm wireless on line 24/7 so tomorrow I'll dictate a longer up-date.

It's 8:15 a.m. here now, 2:15 a.m. U.S. time. I doubt you're playing Scrabble.

For some reason I've had problems off loading pictures from my camera but I'm sure Slawek will be able to fix that and I will send you pictures of his house.

He also is getting me a new phone card for my cell phone so I'll have all my Polish contacts.

I have to be careful because I've already noticed I have shorter time on my feet before I have to stop and pain wakes me up at night too; uncomfortable sort of dull ache almost all the time.

I hope you will take my car out for some exercise once in a while; it's good for it!.

Details later after everybody goes off to school/work; kinda strange to sit here and be talking to myself.

Later, bt.

P.S.

Years and years ago when I communicated with my parents with very cryptic 'cables', the family sign-off, indicating everything was all right, was "smooth".

I like it still, so,

Smooth,

Bt

Hitting early tonight but I will get some writing going tomorrow.

I am heading out very early tomorrow morning to meet up with Joachim, sit in on some of his classes and play a few tunes at a birthday party/concert in Kraków. I'll be back here probably around 10 or 11 p.m.

Thanksgiving, 2011

First, a quick update on my adventures so far. The trip over with Swiss Air on one of those huge Airbuses was smooth and comfortable. The food was quite good and there was an endless supply of little bottles of very good red wine. I landed in Warsaw after about 30 hours since leaving Boston; botched connections due to food servers strike in France. Big plane from Boston to Paris flight couldn't get food service in Paris for the round trip and apparently couldn't re-stock in Boston either. So first to O'Hare, Paris and Connection (on time!) to Warsaw. Went directly to a concert / lecture demonstration / workshop with Joachim. Transportation went smoothly in newer vehicles, but I remember a different situation a few years ago.

The Sunday after I arrived in Poland, Joachim and I went to Gorzow (pronounced Goes-ouff) for a week and did school programs and four concerts. We are definitely transportationally challenged. Amazingly, his nineteen-year-old Mercedes made it: 1,000 miles to and from Gorzow without problems, except the rear door keeps freezing shut, and we had to replace a tire, and the heater quit about halfway home, and it only starts if I open the hood and short out some wires on the starter with a tire iron, and anything put in the back gets wet because the floor is full of holes but the holes let us hear and smell the broken exhaust much better, and the extensive body rot will prevent us from crossing the border into Germany in May, so we'll probably go by train. My older Fiat, borrowed from Joachim, might get me to Krakow city limits, anything over 50 mph is very exciting. One night it was stolen but was soon recovered with considerable body damage. I felt obligated to get the repairs done. It cost less than $100 at the body shop but caught fire on the way home. Right now it has no brakes, but only one flat tire!

Joachim told me that when he was in college they were not allowed to do any kind of cooking in their rooms, not even a hot plate or a coffee pot. He taped together two old fashioned metal Gillette razors and hitched each one to a wire connected to a plug. Handles down the razors were placed in a glass of water and when it was plugged in the water almost exploded. Talk about instant coffee; 220 volts heats things up in a hurry.

Krakow 2 days later

Last night I played at a concert/birthday party for Janusz Muniak, a prominent Polish saxophone player who I've known for 20 years. There were lots of very accomplished musicians; old friends, including a really wonderful alto saxophone player who told me he got his start in jazz at a workshop with me 19 years ago!

Now. . . . some free days to catch up with E-mails and maybe even dig into working on the book.

My friend Slawek, where I'm staying, was one of the first kids I met in 1991, an excellent drummer now in the Army band. He visited me in Maine the summer of 1992. His house that he built himself is quite substantial and all high-tech and high quality; superior craftsmanship everywhere. It even has radiant heat in the floor of the bathroom and the kitchen; how nice is that! It sits on a fairly large parcel of land with a beautiful view across the valley to farms and rolling fields and woods. I am wireless / online anytime I want it. We're about 45 min. away from Kraków and he goes into town almost every day for his work so it's easy to hitch a ride. His wife teaches at a music school and is gone most of the day so I have the place to myself; his daughter is in kindergarten and adorable and they have another one on the way, due this summer.

The bicycle I gave him 19 years ago sits in the garage, clean as a whistle looking like it just came out of the showroom!

I still don't know what my schedule will be, where or when I will be going anywhere. At some point Joachim will tell me; I like it that way.

Nothing done yet with the book . . . tomorrow maybe?

Not sure of date

Sorry I was out of this universe last night. My crazy clarinet genius friend Krzysztof Klima picked me up with his son Szymon, also a clarinet genius and we went to Krakow for late birthday supper for Krz's mother. We imbibed a little wine and more generous amounts of rare Cognac from France. Just Krz, Szy and a distant niece of Krz's. Mama lives with her boyfriend; been living with her as a 'renter' for 25 years; she's 78!

Quite late back to Krz's place with Szy and niece. Nice girl, through with college but not sure of her age, almost zero English. When she was 6 her mother was killed in some sort of an accident and a few months later her father hanged himself, leaving her alone. Krz and his then wife took her in. The house is some how hers but it's very old and in terrible shape; an ancient coal furnace that needs almost hourly attention and only recently, running water.

Kitchen: Two-burner propane stove sits on top of the old, non-functioning coal stove. There's a non-functional fridge and plastic tubs in the sink for washing dishes; almost no heat. We listened to Jazz 'til very late but only, once in bed, did I get warm.

In the a.m. the chill was off a bit and we had a pretty good breakfast. Krz's ancient Renault is rusting away with its engine all apart. He is almost completely broke and one of the best clarinet players I've ever known. He could be first chair in any symphony in the world but somehow always seems behind the 8 ball, always looking for work and rarely successful. His son is doing a little better. For several years he had a successful duo with a great classical guitar player who unfortunately fell in love with a psychologist who has turned him completely away from playing music. I didn't catch what she turned him into but, whatever, the duo is finished. Szymon has CDs of the duo with no way of performing / presenting it live. So he's not much better off either. Artists on this level shouldn't have to live this way. (I can't make this stuff up!)

About 11:00 a.m. they dropped me off back at Slawek's

I have to jump around a bit now because Krzysztof Klima has intertwined with me for the last twenty years (my readers should be used to this by now):

It was 1992, my second trip to Poland when I first met Krz and his son, Szymon.

Krz was the clarinet teacher at the Nova Huta Music School. We instantly became friends. Aside from being one of the most phenomenal clarinet players I've ever met, he was a good guy; we had many 'Good Hangs.'

Within a week I'd been invited to his home, a tiny apartment where he lived with his wife and two sons; two small rooms and mini kitchen, bunk beds in the closet-sized bedroom. The living room, not much bigger, was the bedroom for Krz and his wife. No bed. Just a thin mattress pad and blankets on the floor.

Krz's youngest son Szymon was playing the clarinet too and we hit it off right away. The first English word he learned was 'belly-button'. His older brother Lucasz was more into sports and was a ranking Karate belt-holder in his age group; much more than a beginner.

My second trip, the friendship grew. Szymon played with us in a Jazz club in Krakow, with Joachim and the bass player Zibgniew Wegehaupt, now a close friend of Michal Baranski.

I became a partner with Krz and helped organize The International Clarinet Festival in Krakow. Over the years it attracted world-class players from all over and there were lots of amazing concerts. Heavy hitters came from France and Holland. David Campbell came from England and played one year with the Orchestra of St Martin in the Fields in a large cathedral in Krakow.

Krz convinced Buddy DeFranco to come from the U.S.!
I was given the wrong time and flight number. Buddy DeFranco and his wife Joyce had been waiting at the Warsaw airport for several hours by the time I got there. They were tired but not complaining at all and remarkably resilient. I had instructions from Krz. some cash and train tickets to Krakow. The first class seats were better than coach where I usually traveled and they slept some of the way on the two and a half hour ride.

After some down time at their hotel Buddy came to where Joachim and I were working on some of his new tunes and listened for a while. I guess he was curious about who he was going to be paired up with at the concert in Philharmonic Hall the next night.

The concert went very well. Buddy and I sparred but we didn't compete. It was fun.

A day or two later I borrowed Joachim's tiny Fiat 500. Joyce, Buddy, Adam Adamczyk, a clarinet student of mine and a translator too, all squeezed into the Fiat. With its 500cc motorcycle engine it was slow going on the hills but got us to our destination, Auschwitz. I had warned Buddy and Joyce the experience would change them. We didn't talk much on the way home.

Buddy and Joyce were great sports through everything. I put them on the plane home as friends.

With Szymon Klima, clarinet, and Zbigniew Wegehaupt, bass, in Poland.

I was in awe of all of them and got a chance to play with Buddy; I'll not forget.

For the first half of the opening concert of the 2001 Festival, David Campbell played Mozart with a piano player: I sat fascinated, watching David play. The second half was Joachim and me. It was 9/12/2001.

There were too many adventures to detail now: A frantic twenty-three hour bus trip to Paris, buying his ancient Fiat, trips to the mountains to visit family, good hangs and of course watching Szymon become a clarinet player, now perhaps surpassing his father. Why not? He had the best teachers.

Now, return to the diary.

Up early, but have to be quiet for a while; I'll be able to talk to the new dictation machine later. Major wind storms last night. The wind around Slawek's house was going 120 km/h. but his house is all reinforced concrete and all I heard was occasional wind noises near the windows. I heard there were 4 deaths in northern Poland, mostly from trees falling on cars.

I have just hitched up the dictation program again and I hope it works better than it did before, Hey it's working.

I'm really almost finished with the book just waiting now for 2nd stories. I keep thinking of more things to write about, more stories, more snippets but I got to put a stop to this someplace.

I'll keep writing either tomorrow morning from here or tomorrow night at Slawek's. No, more likely Monday when everybody will be at work and I'll have the house alone by myself and can talk freely into this silly machine.

Dec. 1st

Off to Bytom for a few days with Mateusz's family

Next day, Dec 2nd at Kolakowski's

Last night Mateusz had his Diploma Recital at the Katowice Music Academy. His parents, and grand parents, both brothers, his girl friend, Katrina and a dozen or college friends along with the judges from the faculty all assembled in a small second floor studio / concert hall; very nice Steinway piano. Right on time Mateusz came in looking great in a suit with a vest and tie. He took off his jacket sat at the piano bench and sat still for a moment and then roared in to a Ravel piano concerto / sonata? It was the most technically challenging thing I've ever heard or seen... I really couldn't quite believe it. When he finished after only a few minutes off stage he came back in and, with equal skill roared through another amazing, challenging piece by Rachmaninoff.

After brief congratulations from the audience and highest marks from the faculty he was graduated, for sure.

We had a sort of celebratory dinner here with grandparents and both brothers. Even though I don't understand more than an occasional word of the conversation the dynamics of this family is really wonderful.

I'll go into more detail tomorrow or some point soon.

As predicted, my endurance seems to diminish on a daily basis. I'm OK on my feet for about five minutes, then have to find a place to sit or at least lean against something. The pain starts slowly but builds up to a point where I can't control my balance; nothing supporting my 'trunk' and falling over doesn't seem a good option and, as much as possible I've tried to avoid taking these rather lethal medications; may have to start in soon.

The entire family and I went to the movies last night and saw some very strange English spy movie. I don't think anybody really understood what was going on even though it was in English and Polish subtitles. Katrina joined the group. She's bright as hell speaks fluent French and English and is a total delight. I think they are very much in love and I certainly think she's a keeper. What's been fun the last 2 days is how the family seems to really love having her around; everybody seems to love everybody; it's wonderful.

The TV is a bit loud and interfering with the microphone so I'm going to shut this down for tonight and start again, soon as I can.

Ankle?

After the recital yesterday and a bit too much wine I suppose, I slipped on the bottom step of the stairs going down to my room. I didn't notice anything 'til later the next day when I saw my ankle in the mirror sporting a pretty good raspberry, which got redder and quite painful by bedtime. I think I just got a good bone bruise but it still is very tender to the touch tonight. The stairs are smooth polished wood and very slippery. I slipped again to day but not badly and their now older dog has a rough time. They are just plain dangerous. I finally took a little white pill and knocked off 'til about 6:30. My ankle was quite sore and I hope not getting infected. I feel wide-awake now so here goes . . .

Next day pretty full. We had a late dinner and Krzysztof, (Matt's dad) and youngest brother Tomek watched international boxing championships on TV 'til much too late. Dad went to bed around 1:30 and T and I watched some more and folded. His plan was to wake up (me too) at 3:00 a.m. and watch some international Volleyball. Fortunately that fizzled out but I still was wide-awake at 3:00 a.m.

Now back to today and last night:

I spent several hours with Tomek going over chord changes and their relevance to melody and improvising, etc. and think he really is starting to get it. He was playing pretty random stuff and was hearing things differently after the session.

Then last night . . . Mateusz's grandparents came over for dinner and had a little ceremony celebrating Matt's graduation and afterwards, with his father, presented him with a statue of Chopin. "Big deal?" As a matter of fact, yes. . It was miniature model for a statue by a very well known Polish sculpture from the early 50s, commissioned by some Polish city but it was never finalized in full scale due to some Communist pressure. As I said, the artist was a big shot and this is the only existing casting of the statue. It is very avant-guard, one of a kind and worth a fortune! Matt could sell it and buy a house or two.

That ceremony over, we played some tunes, Grandparents went home, Matt and Katrina went partying and we went into boxing mode which is where this all started.

Today, I was supposed to go to Krakow about 4:30–5;00 to meet up with Joachim for a rehearsal with some guys who are going to meet us in Ukraine later this week. Katrina's mom went to another town last night and was to return with her mom in time to get me to the rehearsal. Okay . . .. She got lost and was late. Then there was the obligatory, tea, cake and cookies and we finally got underway almost in good time. Matt and Katrina, with me driving M's car, took off to Katowice with 'moms' following. The idea was to leave Matt's car at the music school so he could return tomorrow by train and pick it up. I was driving very conservatively but you guessed it; the 'moms' lost us, and got lost finding the school. Mateusz and Katrina and I, with me driving her lovely 25 year old immaculate Mercedes went to Krakow.

I made it just in time to help Joachim pack things up. He was off almost immediately for a gig with New Live M. at noon tomorrow somewhere about a seven-hour drive from Krakow. Slawek, dear guy, came into Krakow to bring me home and after some leftover but quite good Pizza, some rare Italian brandy and Slawek's skillful wrapping up my foot, I went up to bed.

I know this much: We train to Ukraine, noon, from Krakow on Wednesday. We play 6 concerts; 4 just duo and 2 with Joachim's wild contemporary quintet. Several duo concerts are in Philharmonic Hall, which Joachim says has wonderful acoustics, a super piano and the best, most attentive audiences he's ever played for. Sounds like fun to me. I might not bring the computer so might be out of touch 'til we return to Krakow some time Monday the 12th.

Das it for now.. Still astounded by Matt's back-to-back powerhouse performances of Ravel and Rachmaninoff. (No surprise I guess but still astounding!)

Here at Slawek's 'til Wednesday a.m. early.

Not surprising that this is going around in circles is it?

Slawek with his excellent military training just wrapped my ankle after I put on some sort of goo from Mateusz's mom; looks like I broke my leg or something.

My ankle is still sore and a bit red around the abrasions. Standing/walking no problem but sitting and more sleeping I get rather strong sort of electrical tingling that usually goes away in 15–20 seconds. But when I try and put my foot crossed over the other knee to put on some goop or rewind the Ace bandage Slawek gave me, the pain is sharp and really severe; sill extremely tender to touch. For that reason I'm having trouble falling asleep so here I am, typing because dictating will wake people up.

I am taking the computer with me but we have a crazy schedule. Leaving here shortly, about 12:30 for a 13-hour train ride to whatever town we're going to. The next day a 300km ride by car to the first concert tomorrow night. Then, each day, another 3–400 km to the next one. We get home some time Monday.

I'll get on line whenever I can and hope I can keep this charged up so I can write details every day.

Ukraine:

Now 3:40 a.m. our time.

Bt

Wow… so much to tell. I'm writing this after the first half of the concert, 125 minutes of duo with Joachim. Then a break and now his very modern band with a vocalist, great drummer from Austria and Polish bass player; all really strong players. There is also a guy who has all sorts of electronic stuff making amazing sounds all very hi tech and fascinating

OK. Here's the scoop. After the concert we'll go out for the usual late dinner and even though I'll be on line I might not get to much writing tonight. We're not off 'til noon tomorrow so I'll try and get writing going in the a.m.

Quickly about our first half of the concert. The 300+ seat Philharmonic Hall was sold out 10 days ago. We did our thing including the 5-note bit, which drew perhaps the biggest response from the audience. But . . . After every tune we got that amazing applause when the audience starts clapping in unison and three standing Os during the segment!' I think Joachim and I are reaching for higher places and getting there! What fun.

I'll be back on for the last 2 tunes to end things tonight. I'll file this for now. When I get back to the hotel tonight there's no guarantee when I'll be doing anything but sleeping.

Next a.m..

I'm not sure how much time I have before we have to head to our next city for a concert tonight so I'll try and catch up in bits. I have notes from the first few days so I'll start with them.

Trip: Krakow to Ukraine

Maciek (sort of J's manager/organizer) met Joachim and me at the station in Krakow and with a little time to spare I bought a toothbrush before we got on the train.

Our compartment was tiny but served its purpose. It was only a bit over 5 feet wide and a bit over 6ft long with a sliding door that went out to the "hallway". The 3 possible full-length bunks were comfortable but complicated. If one person wanted to sleep fine; hit the top bunk. But if 2 wanted sleep, the middle bunk, when in place didn't allow enough space to sit on the lower bunk so it was all or nothing. Maciek went topsides and fortunately J and I were ready to fold at the same time. Sleep was fitful at best. Beata had packed some sandwiches and we sort of rumbled along into the night (it got dark early) 'til we hit the Polish border. We were all awake by then and had to show passports etc.

Then . . . I guess some people know this and Slawek had told me about it but seeing is believing.

Three things from Poland do not work in Ukraine; Polish money, electrical connections and the trains. The gauge in Ukraine is about 8–10 inches wider than the Polish. After the border guys were done we moved a bit and I watched, as both cars of the 'sleepers' were carefully positioned next to 4 synchronized huge jacks like the ones they use at Sears for an oil change. They slowly picked up the cars, slid the Polish wheels out and replaced them with wider Ukrainian wheels. The correct term is 'trucks'.

This really interesting operation took about 45 minutes and we were off. Well not really. 'Crawling' would be better for about 20 minutes. I soon saw ominous concrete barriers with barbed wire on top, guards with nasty looking rifles; kind of spooky; WWII movie set type stuff.

The Polish/Ukraine border

We stopped and some very unhappy looking border patrol guys with ominous looking probably automatic weapons slung over their shoulders came on board. First they wanted passports, took a look and disappeared with the passports; made me a bit apprehensive. Then a patrol guy ordered us out of the compartment and searched it. He asked Joachim what was in the obviously recognizable as clothes hanger bag. Joachim said, "Clothes". He seemed satisfied and didn't ask to see anything else. Then, while we were standing in the hallway another guy came in with a cordless screw driver and removed a ceiling panel, looked around with a flash light, then searched in and under the trash bin and left. We were told we could return to the compartment. After about 1/2 hour a few more burly guys came through with two drug sniffing dogs, one a Holly look alike and the other, a tiny silly looking toy dog. Finally a new guy with the most gold and by far the biggest cap came in holding our passports. He looked at the passport, looked at me and asked," William?" I nodded, 'yes' and he handed it to me. Same with M. and J.

As we finally, slowly got underway a funny sight: I saw the big guy with the "Holly dog" on a leash followed by an equally burly guy with the toy dog on a leash. He must have been feeling foolish.

About eleven-and-a-half hours after our departure from Krakow we arrived in Konstantin. We were met at the station by Olana who hustled us into a big Nissan van. We went first to a great restaurant for dinner; the mandatory soup and then great smaller perogies with salad followed; all the trimmings. Olana had explained to us that she was our Guide. After dinner we were deposited in front of the hotel and Olana quickly hopped in the van and disappeared. The hotel knew we were coming and I checked into a 1st class room, everything spotless, and found out later the hotel was only 2 years old but built inside the shell of a building 200 years old.

In my room after a long luxurious shower I discovered that the Polish adapter Slawek had loaned me did not quite fit the wall receptacles here.

My battery was getting tired and was down quickly to 60%. The front desk was enthusiastic but couldn't find something that worked so I took longhand notes for the next 2 days.

After a good sleep and minimum back problems I met J and M and enjoyed a really good buffet breakfast; everything fresh and beautiful! The discussion was that this was the last frontier in Europe that had not been invaded by the western 'bulge' of fast food and plastic containers. Everything was real. Milk tasted like it came directly from a farm. Things were made locally. Only small Dannone yogurts were packaged.

Our next city and first concert was in Rivne, about 4 hours by van. Most of the roads are terrible with sections of modern highway separated by vast amounts of poorly paved or bumpy, noisy cobble stones.

OK I have to stop now. I'll add more when I get plugged in somewhere.

I sent you a bit about the concert last night, back here in Konstantin. The two concerts in between pretty much the same reception; 6 hours in the van yesterday.

Writing again from Slawek's tonight after an 11-hour drive from Ukraine to Krakow. Joachim drove me here and went back to town to do some more work for a recording thing he's doing tomorrow. I'll do more writing as soon as I recover.

Back to Ukraine

Ukraine broke away from the Soviet Union in 1991. It was once part of Austria and the centers of the cities are very grand with huge parks and gardens all of which looks a lot like Vienna. There are huge ornate churches with immaculate grounds, some sporting 3 or more gold domes and only a few blocks away, real run down depressing houses; blocks and blocks of distressed homes, some small shops, and narrow, mostly dirty streets.

Then, just out of town, amazing contrasts between the 'haves' and 'don'ts'. Evidence of real poverty, some small houses with obviously no electricity and some with concrete block out-houses: IE no running water. Right next door might be a new modern home with landscaped grounds, satellite TV dishes and a Mercedes in the drive. On the road we saw lots of horse drawn wagons with big rubber tires carrying wood or hay; single driver, or perhaps a man and his wife, sometimes a whole family on board. In the parking lot of our hotel there was a Bentley and a Maserati.

Back was bothering me more and more of the time. I was relying on a little pill to help with sleeping only; now I need a boost, or even two during the day. I'm glad I'm doing the surgery thing right off.

I have the next few days free and will do a chunk more writing.

Dec 13th

For some reason my computer quit this morning; plays the nice chord, the apple shows up, then the pinwheel, then -o-o-o-; nothing; worked fine last night. Slawek will take it to a shop near his work this morning and hopefully I'll get it back later today or tomorrow. I'm on line with his computer but I can't use my dictation program 'til I get mine back; I have pages of notes ready to go. So . . .it may be a day or two; whatever ASAP.

Grrrr. I won't know tomorrow if, 1, they know what the problem is, 2, if and when they can repair it. So, I'm planning for the worst; that I'll be off line 'til I get home and can get it to Ralph Lewis.

Yahoo on Slawek's computer works fine and fortunately all book, up-dates, are saved on USP drives. I hope I haven't crashed and lost my addresses and speech recognition program.

I'll try and catch up although I'm not sure what is on my computer.

This will be slow going. I type slowly but sure make a lot of mistakes. Not that I'm any kind of a keyboard connoisseur this one feels different and makes it even slower. Also spell check comes up with Polish approximations.

Back to Ukraine from hand written notes

At the first two concerts, we, the duo, played an 80–90 minute first half. It flew by and I think I wrote about the amazing response of the audiences. For me still hard to believe that somewhere, what Joachim and I do is appreciated by that large an audience. Unison applause and often standing up in between tunes and we held them for 90 minutes. (!) (Sorry but I still can't quite grasp that what I do, in some people's minds is a bit more than just okay. "OK" is the way I rate it.)

Rivne

The hall was what you'd imagine from a movie set of the perfect opera house.

The second half was a piano trio from Russia. The met us for breakfast the first morning in Konstantin after a 23-hour train ride from St. Petersburg. They all spoke pretty good English but were shy about practicing it on me. (They probably spell better than I do)

As I said, our half flew by and after a 15–20 minute intermission they came on. All three obviously had serious classical training and displayed top-level technique but their tunes, all originals, were pretty basic. Nice melodies but simple 2-5-1 chords or obvious descending bass lines. They were rhythmically tricky, all carefully rehearsed and limited improvisation. During the sound check the piano player played some great jazz lines, really fast and smooth but his solos during the concert were mostly blues scale oriented with a lot of major 7ths; nothing harmonically interesting. I really wanted to tell him to listen to some Bill Evans.

Drummer too had great chops but played mostly the annoying backbeat; what Les Harris calls, "A sneaker in a drier." They were well received but secretly I think the audience was more interested in our stuff.

We had a huge dinner after the concert and a pretty early start in the morning; 6 1/2 hours to the next stop, Lviv: A not fancy hotel; quite a downgrade from the first two nights but it was clean and I found out, not too sound proof. As we unloaded after the concert a young couple who were obviously having some severe differences of opinion came out of the front door, passed us in the parking lot and headed out through the gate to the sidewalk. I didn't need to know what they were saying; body language said it all. They would stand face to face and then the guy would start walking away. She would stand there talking a blue streak. He would stop, turn around, she would take a few steps toward him still talking; he'd turn around and start walking away again. It went on and on like a loop.

The rooms at the hotel were all on one long hallway; about 20 rooms. We all had separate rooms, sparse but clean and I hit the shower and went to bed.

Soon I could clearly hear our young couple at the end of the hall; their discussion definitely not over. They must have had a room at the end of the hall because it got quiet but soon, within minutes, one of them, (I'm guessing the guy) came down the hall followed by the other, both talking. I'm guessing again that they went down to the lobby but soon they were back. At one point one of them sprinted the length of the hall in stocking feet; talking in the distance but the footsteps were clear through the thin door, which did nothing to abate the sound. This loop continued until after 3:00 a.m. Several times I was tempted to stick my head out the door and yell, "Stop!" figuring almost anybody would understand the meaning if not the word. I was sitting up about to put on my robe when it got quiet again. Of course I stayed wide-awake waiting for the racket to start again; it was a short night.

At the concert we met Roman Ros who looked a lot like my Polish guitar-playing friend Jarek Smietana. He was very gregarious, speaking faltering but fearless English along with Ukrainian, Russian and Polish.

We got to talking about our lives and interests and somehow boats and sailing came up. Then like a bomb he told me that he had built a 20-meter sailboat! He has sailed it all over the Black Sea and Mediterranean. His plan; in May to take it by truck from Ukraine to Gdansk PL and sail it around to somewhere in Germany. He invited me to come along!

He met us the next morning and gave me a DVD of the boat during construction and in action on the water. It's for real! There has to be some serious $$ somewhere. He was driving a well-groomed newer BMW.

A so-so breakfast; over cooked fried eggs, over, not so easy, good coffee and as always bread to dream about. The drive was much shorter. Along the road I saw a big sign welcoming us to a small town that said:

Opala

1441

We played in another impressive opera house, same routine, upon arrival, lavish lunch, sound check, and well received concert, followed by a huge, late dinner.

The last concert, Sunday night after another long drive we did the best we could with a really inept sound guy with limited equipment; strange because everything from the hotel to the elegant concert hall was really first class.

I was to do my sound check first; just one mic, set EQ, and we're done—simple, quick and easy? Not so. Joachim went to the guy at the board, fine tuned the settings and explicitly explained NOT to change anything. Then his group did their sound check. I was supposed to walk back to the hotel, get changed and walk back but everything took much longer and I was hurting so the director of the festival drove me over and waited while I got ready.

During the sound check all sorts of people sort of wandered on stage armed with cameras, video cameras and notebooks. Someone pushed a small boy, clarinet in hand to stand next to me for a photo shoot. Another guy with a clarinet wanted to see mine and just barged in without asking. Joachim and I were trying to get some results from the sound guy. I'm sure they all were well intentioned but they had no concept that we were on the job, trying to get things ready and needed some space. I would have been glad to spend some time with them, but...

Joachim finally got quite angry and told them all to leave.

During the concert the soundman constantly changed things. When I backed away from the mic just a bit to play something really soft he cranked up the volume to feed back levels and fiddled around with the piano settings too.

Several times we were irrupted by a loud hum that he seemed to ignore. I sort of stopped, matched the pitch, played it and motioned to turn it down. The audience got a laugh and he finally sort of got the message; still kept changing things; tough to concentrate.

As I said, it seemed nobody understood that we needed just a little space. Dressing rooms are called that because that's one of the things that happens there.

After the concert the army of camera-tote-ers swarmed in and I had to keep closing the door while band members changed back into 'civvies'. I was interviewed by two different newspapers both wanting to know my life story; all 258 pages of it.

There was a very pushy flute player who bombarded me with questions about how he could learn to improvise jazz. Hell, I don't know . . . but I tried to explain that, because I can't read music I had no choice. I had to find another way.

He followed me around ending up in the dressing room; going on and on.

My back was hurting and I didn't want another late dinner in a smoky jazz club. The smoke from the night before made me pretty sick and sleepless for several hours. (Noisy fighting couple didn't help.)

The rest of the crew went to the club and came back pretty annoyed. After dinner they were urged to play which would have been okay except there was nothing there; a bare drum set with no cymbals, no bass, and a kid-sized keyboard. They were asked to go back to the hotel and lug their equipment to play for free in a small smoky room.

The people were angry, even rude when they refused. The very unusual incident was a topic of conversation on the long drive home the next day.

Imagine, for instance, going to a dentist for a check up and cleaning. Then you invite him for dinner and get upset when he won't go back to his office, collect his tools and come back to check and clean your kid's teeth.

The next morning the flute guy showed up where we were having breakfast and wanted me to leave our group and sit with him for more questions. I stayed put... we were in the middle of ordering. He got a chair and pulled in along side. I managed to get the order, as Marshall Dodge would say, "squeezed in with a shoe horn" between his questions.

He did give me a cassette of his stuff with an orchestra. Probably a good classical player but pushy to say the least.

I tried to remain all smiles and not hurt any feelings.

I think I have written what happens next; the long drive home and finally getting back to Slawek not too late Monday night.

(After 53 years the zipper on my case is falling apart, left side useless. From the middle almost to the end on the right is okay but it comes apart if I forget and open it all the way. A shoe/luggage repair shop couldn't fix it so maybe I'll email Patrick Selmer and see what they can do at the factory. I like the case; original equipment with the clarinet in 1958.)

So . . . this, I think brings me up to date, written Dec 14
A plan is sort of in place for a visit here tonight from Lukasz Zygmunt; amazing 6'5" skinny bass player who came to the states with Slawek.

Then a few days in Zory with Michal Baranski's family; Mateusz a few days before and after Christmas and then to Tomek's for what sounds like a pretty wild New Year's Eve.

I'm sure there will be another few entries but I think from now on all pretty much things I've seen and enjoyed before.

I'm hoping I'll have a floor when I get back home.

Slawek reports the shop is running a test of my 'systems' and will tell us more later but it sounds fixable...

Joachim called and we have a workshop and concert(s) Jan. 3rd and 4th.

Plans developing ahead....

Slawek is going to Rome to visit his sister for Christmas and has offered me the use of his VW. That means I can drive myself to Zory Sat a.m. to visit Michal's family, then the 22nd to Bytom with Mat and family and then to Wroclaw and Tomek's family the 28-29-30. Jose's band with Tomek and Filip (playing bass!) is playing a big Cuban New Years Eve party. I already know about the Polish party attitudes and saw the same in Cuba when I was there. The combination should be explosive; the Torres clan is a party unto itself!

It's about 3 hours from Wrotslaw back here so I'll have the car back in plenty of time for Slawek's wife Magda to get to her teaching gig at her music school. Last two nights in Poland I'll stay with Joachim.

My computer has crashed and I'll have to wait 'til I get it home. Grr.

Well another lazy day at Slawek's and I got some writing done. I could go to town tonight and sit in at Muniac club but as of now just don't feel up to it. I'd also have to wait again 'til 2:00 a.m. to get a ride back with Slawek after his gig. Nah, don't think so.

Only 9:45 but I'll sleep through.

Baranski's tomorrow.

High pressure or something is sapping my energy; No signs of dawn 'til 7:30 a.m. and pitch dark at 4:00 might have something to do with it. Also I'm taking a few more little pills to keep on top of pain; now uncomfortable most of the day and bad enough at night to keep me awake or wake me up. Pills helped me sleep 10 hours last night and had naps yesterday and today but still feel wiped out. I didn't feel like writing today so I didn't write.

Still no news about anything happening at #36. If I have a non-toxic space, even with no floor that would be nice.

I'm looking forward to driving around for the next 16 days. Hopefully I will, in the next few days, have time and energy to write about some reflections on this amazing 20-year affair with Poland. I've obviously learned a lot and treasure the experience. More importantly, I am pleased that I've made a difference for some of these wonderful kids, now adults; some young husbands, and fathers. Slawek has a daughter and Lucasz is expecting twins in June. Michal's a father, Tomek is married, Mateusz perhaps close behind. And of course, Rafal, and Darek, Adam and David, Kuba, another Michal, younger brothers who also visited me in the U.S. Why me? How can anyone be so lucky?

Slawek lends me his car and as I said, it's great fun driving in Poland. Even though there are a lot of new roads and re-designed intersections I found my way to Michal Baranski's parents in Zory with only one wrong turn. I saw where I was and made a few adjustments on some small roads and a few minutes later was back on track. This includes threading my way around Krakow on a lot of new loop roads since I last was driving here.

I wrote before about Lucasz (Tall bass player) coming out to Slawek's for dinner and spending the night to see me. He is in the process of moving. He's sold his flat and has to get out this weekend and can't get into his new place for 6 weeks so he and his wife, due with twins in June are homeless, He was very funny about it, joking about at least Joseph and Mary found a stable and weren't having twins. We spent the evening and again in the morning reminiscing.

They remembered: 2 weeks camping at the quarry in my old pop-top camper and that Rafal and his brother were with us; all 4 at jazz camp for 2 weeks. They were younger than the High school group the first week but in all the highest bands; playing with Tommy Gallant at Percey's store/restaurant and a boat trip on Casco Bay Lines again with Tommy, then playing with Eli Newberger and Jimmy Massey on Ilesboro and camping out at Willow Street before the second floor was on! Both of them telling me it was an experience they'll treasure; they have told all their friends about it. Slawek had pictures and videos from when I visited here. One video I played a solo clarinet thing and must say it had a good percentage of nice notes but most startling is that I was wearing a suit and tie!

So. The drive to Zory, a little over two hours was fun and easy. Michal's parents and youngest brother Adam were here to greet me and we immediately had something to eat. Mom (Jadwiga) makes amazing dishes in the world's smallest kitchen. I took my usual spot in the corner at the small kitchen table; felt right at home. Middle brother Wacek showed up and we had more to eat. He reminded me of his summer; camping on Vinalhaven, fishing off Popham Beach and eating lobster, being very impressed by the Mt. Washington Hotel when I did "Jazz night" and he tagged along. Then his amazing adventures staying up much too late exploring Greenwich Village with William Galison, when his flight got screwed up. I'd put him on the plane in Boston headed for Newark. When he got there he discovered that they had booked his connecting flight to Munich from Kennedy and he had two hours to get there and of course missed the connection. He had William's number and a friendly stranger let him use their cell phone. William explained to the stranger which of multiple subway choices to chose and the stranger sent Wacek on his way. They found each other! William saved the day and Wacek got a flight home the next day.

After dinner I was set up in an upstairs room and shown this computer. I finally found out how to get Yahoo in English. Their code to access the wireless is, "brad". Really!

I folded early with the old back needing some medicinal help to get to sleep.

Slept long but woke up kinda sore and had a little pill with coffee. They all went to church and later Wacek's tall slender lovely fiancé showed up. She takes classes on the weekends in Katowice and stays with Wacek's grandma who loves the company. She is obviously adored by Wacek's family. After a late lunch she went back to her parent's house where she and Wacek live during the week. Wedding planned in April. I told Wacek I would open the bottle of wine he gave me last year when he came to hear Joachim and me play at the famous salt mine near Krakow.

I got totally dark by 3:45 and I took a short nap only to be woken up by Jadwiga tearing up some Chopin on the piano down stairs. I came down and listened; Chopin, Brahms, and a wonderful Prokofiev piece I hadn't heard, and then two Gershwin preludes: She is way more than accomplished!

Then Marek, Michal's father who had been hand making reeds for his bassoon came in for a final test and the two of them went through some piano and bassoon duo things that brought me to another "why me?" moment.

Marek is principal bassoonist for the Katowice Radio Symphony Orchestra; one of the best in Poland. They play live every Friday accompanying a variety of world-class soloists. They have to be on top; short rehearsal time; be ready for anything.

So, here I am, sitting in the living room enjoying a private concert of really world-class players. "Why Me"?

There have been a few times in my life that I experienced something so special I would have been okay to step off the curb at that moment and be run over by a bus.

One was coming home from Detroit through Canada in my Cobra about 2:00 a.m. There I was driving one of the most exotic automobiles in the world. My faithful friend Duchess was curled up on the seat next to me, the top was down and I was going fast; the Cobra made that easy. Through my headphones I picked up an uninterrupted Andres Segovia concert and there was a display of Northern Lights that made the front page of the New York Times the next day.

Another not quite so dramatic was after meeting Roger Kellaway in New York and playing a few tracks of the original *Living Room Tapes* recorded with Lenny Breau.

Roger asked me to play something and, since neither one of could come up with a tune we played an introduction that lasted about half an hour.

Then he told me that he and Red Mitchell were playing at Bradley's the following week; that I should come sit in and bring my horn. I played every night and at the end was invited to whistle a track on their album *50/50* which I did. I would have been okay stepping off the curb anywhere along the line. (After a bit of whistling I opened my eyes and saw Freddy Hubbard at the bar looking at me with a smile on his face.)

So. Why Me?

I still have two more weeks to go.

I've decided not to rush anything at Willow Street but take my time and get what ever is done, done right.

It's still on the early side but I'm hurting a bit and will get flat pretty soon.

Okay... I promise I'll look both ways before crossing the street.

Observation from Zory

(It is interesting that in only a day or two after the rumor started that I'd go public the town made their 2nd offer. The facts are clear. Even if the public works guy doesn't know enough physics to understand that water flows down hill I can explain what happened.

Even after the facts became clear the guy kept basically lying saying it was all caused by 'flooding". That was just not the case! So yes, except for the one really supportive guy with Community Development I have little love or respect for officialdom in Bath.

Also, I really don't want to be there anymore anyway; I'd rather be homeless for a while, find some place to go and not spend time and energy re-establishing myself at #36.

Whatever, I'm thinking to go slow and see what happens.)

Gotta shower and get ready to front the big band... will be fun. I think Jadwiga has some master classes / workshops for tomorrow. So, probably more later.

Lazy day spent mostly sitting or lying down to seek a comfortable moment with not much success. Did revive to coach a small contingent of the big band, the teacher was sick and called off the rehearsal but 5–6 kids heard I was coming and showed up anyway. In short order I explained to them the importance of dynamics, listening, and showed them the Lenny blues head, "Minors Allowed", nailed down the blues form and some tempo problems. Fun for me and I think the kids learned something and had fun too. Now little pills are kicking in and I'm off to la-la land.

Another rather quiet day. Watched some CNN and BBC news and did a fair amount of sitting and snoozing; back still a problem but slightly better tonight.

Mateusz called from Paris en route from Cuba and I had a great long Skype call with Michal. His 7-month-old daughter seems a sweetie!

Still need a pill to get to sleep and I'm going there ASAP.

Dec 20th, Still in Zory

Michal's mom (Jadwiga) and I made gingerbread from scratch after a short trip to the local big supermarket that puts a Walmart Super Store to shame not just in size but variety. I've never seen so many different brands of similar products anywhere. Just the coffee isle was about 50 feet long with every imaginable coffee available from Nestles instant to 10 varieties of Espresso from different countries, beans and ground; endless choices. Jawiga picked out some things for the next 2 days meals and our gingerbread. I stopped for gas on the way back and was shocked even though I knew I would be. Filling Slawek's VW; 4l.2 liters, 220.5 Zlote. I think translated that's about 10 gallons and about $70.00. Even so the traffic is as heavy as ever and lots of people are going places fast.

The gingerbread project netted four 18" x 18" squares of thin cookie like sheets. They were made into two, two-layered square cakes with jam in the middle and chocolate on top; to be consumed tomorrow. Cleaning up was delicious.

I'll go to the school X-mas concert tonight and head for Bytom tomorrow. Mateusz's mom called: Tomek will greet me at 4:00 p.m.

Me Gawd. I'm still awake but a 2nd round of pills should do the trick. Bonnie has offered me sanctuary as long as needed 'til I have a working kitchen. I told her I had accumulated over $500. in food credits so I could contribute. That's all for now so lights out, TV off and now, no discomfort and hopefully sleep.

December 21, 2011 10:53 p.m.

Trying to sleep. Observations:

A bunch of years ago I got a $14,000 grant to do jazz in schools through the National Endowment. It was a crazy deal with practically no strings attached. They just asked me where to send the $$$; I didn't even have to tell anyone what I was doing or account for any of it. At the end I had to write a brief report on what I'd been doing and attach a few letters from a few schools; das all!

I've never been busier and as I remember put 35k miles on my car, all in Maine. Some kids from Presque Isle high school band called me. They wanted to know if I could come up and do a workshop. They had had a bake sale and could offer me $75 plus a place to stay. I said, "Sure", and went up for a week. For that one wonderful year, which included a trip to Poland I didn't have to put a price tag on my time. I could happily be busy 60 hours a week if I could find that again! It was several years before my S.S. kicked in; don't remember exactly.

That guy in Ukraine wants me for a year and I'm guessing I could teach there for a year. I'd offer it free; just room and board and some expenses. I'd want a small car and a place for Holly. S.S. would continue.

On the flip side, since I moved to Bath, every year I've offered to do free workshops at the high school and junior high with no response. I gave up offering about 5–6 years ago.

Anyway, just some random thoughts that are keeping me awake.

I need to write quick messages to Bonnie and Sean c/o Rafal.

Wednesday, December 21, 2011 8:49 p.m.

Back from a delightful Christmas concert at the music school. The piano guy and coral director had written some really nice arrangements really well sung by a bevy of lovely smiling girls, mostly American carols in English; very interesting changes. I was asked to play, "Have Yourself a Merry Little Xmas" which was fun because I had to wing it with his interesting altered chord changes. Piece of cake for me; that's all I do anyway. I just followed him around but the kids were very impressed that I could do it first time with no run through or rehearsal.

I told Jadwiga I wish I could come and spend a few months with these kids showing them stuff about improvising. She agreed.

I'm a bit better back-wise today but tired too early. If I crash now as I'd like to my pills will take me only to about 4:00 a.m.

Off to Bytom tomorrow afternoon. I do like it here!

Might or might not crash now...

Had to stop the last part fast. Jadwiga asked for a ride to her school because she was running late. We're getting the first snow today. I'll be interested to see if there's any improvement with snow removal from roads; used to be minimal at best. Slawek's VW handles predictably so I'll have fun.

Quick easy drive to Mat's (Bytom) on a new highway that cut the time in half; like Rt. 1 vs. the turnpike. Slawek's car is great. Dinner serving started before I got all the way in the door. After dinner Tomek and I went to the new shopping mall downtown, which was under construction last year.

They want to eat more now and I'll fold immediately afterwards.

Dec 23rd

Good sleep in a cold, cold room but wrapped up in a big quilt and stayed warm. The house is huge and I'm the only resident on the ground floor so they don't bother to heat it all just for my room; not as cold as my room at #36 anyway.

Back to the mall last night:

I was instructed by Mat's mom, Elina, that I absolutely was not to buy any Christmas presents for any of the Kolakowski Family. The English was limited but the message was clear. They have a big oval table in the kitchen where most of the meals are served and I want to find them a big lazy susan which would be very useful when 5-6-7 of us are sitting around constantly reaching for and passing things.

The mall: All new and shiny with Christmas lights everywhere. Modern atrium five stories high with glass elevators and escalators and stationary stairs floating, suspended on cables going every which way like an Escher drawing. There were some young girls dressed as angels handing out some religious material; funny because they didn't smile even when they made eye contact. They all looked really unhappy.

There were lots of shoppers and again I was struck by the huge variety of goods offered. One level was all clothes and there were about 25 shops with everything from Levi, Faded Glory and Gap to fancy places with tuxes and wedding dresses; at least 10 shops selling shoes, 3 huge shops selling sports equipment, an electronic shop that had 20 or more laptops on display, endless fancy stereo systems, at least 20 canister vacuum cleaners; different styles from different manufactures. If you combined all our big box stores you might have as much selection.

We came back home for more food (of course) and after some sports TV I folded and slept in 'til almost 9:00 a.m.

Tomek was going to come down and wake me up but he was still sleeping when I came up. He's off to the local shop, a hundred meters away for fresh bread and breakfast fixings.

Bartek was here briefly and headed off to his job and Mateusz will be here sometime this afternoon.

Tomek and Elina invited me to go to their private English lesson this afternoon. According to Tomek, the teacher is very nice and a fan of mine; been to many of my concerts. Should be fun. Tomek is getting more fearless about just blurting things out, right or wrong but Elina starts and then seeks the right grammar and stops, way too soon to, "get it right".

Breakfast is imminent. Coffee smells drifting in and I know there's more fresh bread to die for.

Later.

Just back home from a sauna with papa and the 3 brothers to an amazing cake Mateusz picked up in Paris. Feeling squeaky clean and drained and heading momentarily for almost guaranteed good sleep.

This afternoon the visit with the English teacher was just Tomek and me. She spoke fluently but with so strong an accent I had to really strain to understand her. I can see why it's slow going for T and his mom; heavy Polish accent. English even with some Polish I could handle. She speaks fast and runs the words together zero enunciation and, seems to me, Polish phonetics mixed in. They need to find someone who just speaks good old fashioned, 'Ammurrican'. I'll talk to Mateusz today.

She's very nice, treated us to tea and fresh baked cakes and lives about 100 yards from the house; all that's great but . . .

I have to move. Tomek, having just vacuumed, is scrubbing the floor here in the living room and I'm in the way.

Christmas Eve dinner preparations started yesterday with Elina and Krzysztof's mother working in the kitchen almost all day. The Baranski's keep the tradition of Carp served today and kept fresh, swimming overnight in the bathtub. Here the Carp was whole but hadn't been swimming recently. Every room in the house has been scrubbed and vacuumed and places for 10 with all the best china and real silverware are set up in the living room. The tree barely fits; almost touching the ceiling and has multiple tiny flashing lights and a mixed bag of ornaments ranging from intricate antique glass spheres to cartoon-like Santas. Both sets of grandparents will be here at 5:00 and I think, presents after dinner. I think I mentioned Elina made it clear, with limited English that I was not to buy anything in the way of Christmas presents.

Krzysztof and I were trying to remember how many Christmases I've shared with them. We're thinking this is #4 at least. I know there was at least one with Michal's family because I remember getting up in the middle of the night to use the john and being quite startled when I turned on the light to see those 4 large Carp swimming around in the bath tub. This visit I asked Jadwiga (Michal's mom) where that tradition came from expecting to hear it was something centuries old. She told me not at all old. It came during Communism because the more traditional smoked or salted codfish was in very short supply but there were many small independent carp 'farms' and that was what was available. I went with her and Marek to get theirs a few days ago. A few minutes from their house was a small pond surrounded by a high wire fence. Through a hole in the ice a man, presumably the owner of the pond was pulling out the fish with a net. A small crowd had gathered and a steady flow of people with various containers came, waited their turn, paid the man and got their fish. Except for the cars, it could have been a century old scene.

I'm learning to write down my thoughts instantly or I'll lose them. This next has nothing to do with this current flow of things except I happened to remember it now.

Grandparents arriving soon so I'll get a nicer shirt and the vest Mateusz gave me a few years ago.

More later I suspect.

Christmas Eve

Dinner lasted from 5:30 (Grandparents were a bit late) 'til 10:00 after all presents and last round of cakes were distributed. It started out with a wonderful Polish tradition. I'm not sure if this is done in other countries but I've seen it always here. Elina passed around small, thin tasteless wafers about twice the size of a playing card. Then, one by one everybody has a moment, one on one with everybody else. You look them in the eye and as you wish them whatever good wishes, they break off a small bit of your wafer and you take a small bit of theirs while sharing some private personal thoughts. Then a handshake and hug, three kisses on the cheek and in my case, being such a sentimental old fool, a face full of tears. Every one told me, "Thank-you." I tried to control myself but kept steaming up my glasses. The longest moments were with the boys, particularly Mateusz but Bartek and Tomek too. In between my private encounters I watched the faces and responses of the brothers to each other, their parents and grandparents. This took about 10 minutes, all very quiet, just a murmur of mixed conversations.

A soup bowl was at each place setting. In it, a scoop or two of smaller that usual meat filled pirogues. Then, a thin borscht beet broth was added, salty and sweet at the same time; seconds on the soup was expected. Then chunks of carp breaded and fried in olive oil. Very tasty but had to watch for bones; salad of peas, corn, diced carrots and cabbage, celery and maybe turnips. An interesting mixture of cooked cabbage and mushrooms was a side dish; everything in ample supply. Seconds and thirds were constantly passed around along with some nice dry white wine. The wine switched to red as a variety of meat dishes, cold, mixed with salad trimmings and one meat and veggies dish in a gelatin mold. Big plates were replaced with small ones as a parade of home made desert cakes arrived along with tea, fruit compote and more wine.

Another tradition, new to me. Under each plate Mateusz had put a dollar bill and a small bit of dry fish scale. He told me, "Keep the fish scale in your wallet and you will always have money there." Sounds okay to me. Not sure what to do with the dollar.

At the end, Tomek, being the youngest, was delegated to pass out the presents. Colorful shopping bags with gifts were first given to the grandparents, then the parents, then to the brothers; he took his time, nothing was hurried. The gifts were small useful things; skin lotion, shaving cream, little household items, socks and underwear for the boys, and even though sternly warned I was not to buy anything I was given a really high quality leather bag for 'toilet articles'. The one I have is too small to contain my necessary prescribed drugs and a toothbrush at the same time. 'Toilet articles' sounds a bit one-sided.

At the very end Tomek handed me an envelope. In it was a framed photo of the 3 brothers looking me right in the eye; great photo. It was signed by all three on the back; another meltdown moment for me.

We adjourned into Tomek's room where he has Mateusz's old upright piano. Reading from a small book of carols Tomek played some Polish Christmas songs as Mateusz effortlessly transposed them to E-flat for Tomek's alto sax; I played along with some harmony here and there. A few times M. would take off and I would follow, often into a jazz standard; "Summertime" and "Willow Weep For Me" both crept in. The audience, all adoring family, reacted well to every note!

After about an hour of this the grandparents left, clean up started and I folded about when Tomek went across the street to the church to sing carols at midnight.

Krzysztof told me that with the closing of the coal mines a few years ago there has been an exodus of people from the city. Bytom has the lowest housing prices in Poland. There are numerous apartments for sale in the $20,000 to $30,000 range and nice places to rent from $200–$300 a month. (?)

I could handle another Christmas here.

Now 10:30 Christmas morning

Not a creature is stirring not even... A-ha! The annoying electronic church bells rang for a while at 6:00 a.m. and just started again so someone must be awake.

Now I'll go for another coffee and bread-to-die-for with sweet butter and real French Brie; cheaper than Kraft American slices in the supermarket. Wines from France, Germany, Bulgaria, Spain and Italy are all less pricy than Gallo.

If I'm going to rot my brain and ruin my kidneys I might as well do it with the good stuff.

Slow lazy day; not much motion 'til early afternoon. Cell phone calls from Slawek in Rome, Filip Torres about New Years plans, Joachim saying hello and Michal about a visit there with Mateusz tomorrow. Tomek Bartek and I went to the movies and saw a 3D extravaganza with way too much blood, flying heroes and flying miscellaneous body parts but spectacular special effects. No plot but the good guys won.

I'm bringing home 350 Euros more than expected and so far have spent almost $0. I'll use up Zlotys for gas and get a much needed oil change for Slawek's VW.

Sean has expressed interest in having my big old "Voice of the Theater' speakers and I've told him he could take them now. I'll spend some 'box dollars' to get a Bose system which can travel easily to wherever I end up. I have to have quality sounds but it doesn't have to take up half the room.

Mateusz would like the record collection so I have to figure the logistics of that. It makes no sense to move them anywhere again except to their permanent home. I want to unload the place as much as possible and get it ready to rent or sell when the time is right. Look out Goodwill.

Is it just me or does this kind of stuff happen to everyone?

Yesterday I had a lazy morning because in Poland the 2nd day of

Christmas is also a holiday; stores closed, not much happening. Tomek proclaimed that for sure he'd be down to wake me up but I had typed all of the last segment before he showed up in the living room around noon The plan was that at about 4:00 p.m. Mateusz and I would drive to Zory to visit with Michal and his family. Mateusz's lovely girlfriend Katrina would drive back to Krakow from here to be at work early Tuesday morning. This plan in place, I spent several hours with Tomek getting him to really understand the relationship of chords to scales, arpeggios and eventually to improvise lines and he's really starting to get it. I think his progress will come quickly.

Mateusz and Katrina showed up a bit after 4:00 and after a few words and hugs she went her way, driving her grandmother's gorgeous 25-year-old red Mercedes and we went ours. About 40 minutes later Mateusz got a call from Katrina that she was stuck; she couldn't shift gears but she had managed to coast into a safe parking spot behind a McDonald's. I prompted Mateusz to ask certain questions and learned the clutch pedal had suddenly gone right down to the floor and it was impossible to shift gears. I asked if it shifted alright with the engine off; the answer was "yes", and I guessed it was the clutch linkage, which would require a trip to the shop. Now what?

Katrina insisted we continue on to see Michal; she was okay and had a book and a warm place to stay... take our time; time to do what?

At this point we didn't know just how we could rescue Katrina and cope with the car. But, pat-pat on the back please, the old man here remembered I had mastered the technique of driving a 'shift' car without using the clutch. I drove the Cobra that way from Stamford to Samoset, Long Island when it had the same problem and I got used to it retrieving disabled Meyerhoff school buses.

We cut the visit with Michal short. Everyone was disappointed, but we did spent some time with his wife and really great little daughter, traditional tea and cakes with everyone, and I did get to play several tunes with the duo. Either one alone is a powerhouse; together, oh my!

Michal told me he's going to Italy, Sicily and Paris with Benny Moten and later to Turkey with Tomasz Stanko. Big time!

Everybody understood that we had to rescue Katrina so M and I headed back to find her. I was pleased because I knew the new and much faster road; new to Mateusz! I was able to get the car going and with Katrina as co pilot and M. right behind in the VW we made it back to her house in Krakow. A full stop requires turning off the engine, starting it up in gear and shifting, oh so gently, when the rpms are just right for each gear. As long as the starter holds out you're okay but I tried to avoid full stops as much as possible. We managed to inch around a really horrific accident with two totally demolished cars; guessing caused by high speed and head on; people gathered and police everywhere. Somebody got a terrible Christmas present.

Close to Krakow Mateusz called and wanted to switch places with Katrina so he could see how I was doing the shifting.

I've told you about this house before, right next door to Pandereski's considerable digs in the most affluent part of Krakow. I got to see more of it this time and also met Katrina's father and somewhat younger brother. He was embroiled in a video game where you have controls in each hand and do battle with the nasties on the screen. Lots of exercise; he said a few words in very good English but stuck to his battle.

We were treated to a regal dinner with all similar Christmas goodies including a home made goose liver pate, which tops anything I've had so far (Uncle goes hunting and provides the goose). Several bottles of very good wine went down before Mama produced some home-made fruit vodkas amply spiked with Spirytus, which is the high octane, 98% alcohol—the fuel of choice.

Sleeping well was not in question. In the morning the house is quiet. I found a shower and used it a while ago and now will get dressed, investigate the kitchen and see if I can find and roust Mateusz. He must be somewhere. I'm using Katrina's computer and panicked a few times when I lost everything so I hope this sends with no glitches.

Merry 2nd day of Christmas.

My expertise was more than compensated for by the great visit with Katrina's parents and seeing more of their house. One thing I forgot to mention, I finally found out why all the light switches to the bathrooms were just below waist high. The reason? Simple... kids were potty trained long before they could reach a standard height switch. Learn new tricks all the time around here.

We got home to Bytom about 3:00. Mateusz insisted on topping off the gas and made a few calls making an appointment tomorrow for an oil change and general check up on Slawek's car; the least I can do. Then Tomek and I went to Katowice to the biggest mall in Poland.

Packed-people watching was fun and since we had an hour to wait before our movie we ate at a pretty classy Italian place. His pizza took forever but we were right on time for the movie; he chose a Kevin Costner flick about crooked Wall Street guys; not at all what I translated from the poster that it was about but we both were interested and T really enjoyed it.

Word is out all over town that I can drive a car without using the clutch. Some music seems to be next on the schedule.

Dec 29

Long lesson with Tomek; got him arpeggiating chords and I think understanding the relationship of chords as they go by to the necessary scales, i.e. the right notes called for. After a dinner visit to Grandfather, Mateusz joined us and I think we got a lot done. I think Tomek is right on the edge of really taking off and I've urged Mateusz to follow up. A bit of wine has hastened desire for bed.

Dec 30

A bit after midnight now after a great day.

Early hugs and good byes at Mateusz's around 9:00 and an easy drive over mostly super high ways and much upgraded rural roads to Nysa where I met Adam Fudali at his ice making operation. He's been at it for 7 years starting out with a small insulated truck and delivering about 7,000 kg of ice his first year. He now has 2 much larger refrigerator trucks and a full time driver. He still delivers in one of the trucks. In a pretty small place he has 4 ice-making machines. They are stacked two high and the ice cubes are collected in a bin at the bottom of each stack then hand scooped to 4 waiting freezers. Any 'snow' is separated from the ice by a hand stirring method, then the clean ice is carefully bagged in 1, 2.5, and 3kg bags, put in shipping boxes and then into a storage freezer. All this is still done by hand, mostly by Adam. He plugs in the trucks overnight and onboard compressors drop the temperature to -40c. Early in the morning he fills the trucks with ice from the storage freezer and he and his driver take off. Last year he was up to 100,000 kg. He's going back to college to get a PHD in business management. I told him he should teach the course.

Writing started again with lightning fast Internet at Torres house, Wroclaw.
In a few minutes a basketball game comes on that Filip wants to watch

so I'll continue late tonight or in the a.m..

The drive from Nysa to Wroclaw was easy; some much-improved secondary roads and some highway with only one traffic snarl as I got close to the city. I had printed a map, which clearly showed road #8 going through the center and out the other side. I saw signs for the center and then signs for #8 then signs showing I was on #5 going completely the wrong direction. Adam called to see if I had arrived. I explained I was lost and he got busy looking at a map and trying to direct me. I found E8, the super highway to Warsaw and got on it hoping to find a landmark and soon knew I was way too far out of town. I got off and tried to get back on going back toward Wroclaw but lost it when all the signs disappeared again. This last wrong turn took me about 1km and suddenly there was, #8, but well northwest of my target. I had an idea where things were but even before it got dark it was overcast to the point that there was no difference in the light from the east to the west; I had no help determining what direction was heading. I called Filip who managed to direct me from a recognizable big shopping mall to their house.

A cousin from Cuba got here last week and since nobody else was home, Filip, the cousin and I went to the Mall and grabbed some dinner. The cousin is just 18 and somehow Jose got him a visa and spared him from the Army at least for a while. He speaks no Polish or English but smiles a lot and seems to be drinking everything in. Filip did a masterful job of 3-way communication.

Jose, Izza, Tomek and his wife Arina were here when we got back.

Lots of hugs but pretty early to bed (about 1:00 a.m.).

Dec 31st

Tomek and Filip and cousin took off at 4:30 to take equipment to the Cuban club where they play tonight. They were back home by 6:00 and everybody got a nap. At 9:00 p.m. we all went into town for a sound check.

The cousin, who had been playing bass and guitar at home plays the piano really well and Tomek and Filip really lock in together; Tomek the driving force, and Filip playing really well too; lots of chops and great ideas.

I have pictures of the huge stage in the center square where some bands will be playing for the masses, expected to draw 20–25,000 people.

I'll take advantage now of some horizontal downtime like everyone else in the house.

I suspect tonight will be loud and late. Tomorrow I return the car to Slawek and probably won't have time to write much more before the last 3 days with Joachim.

Well, I guess we made it! Yes. It's 5:30 a.m.; Home about 5 minutes and too wired to sleep so here goes; quite the night.

After the sound check we returned home and quite intelligently all got a few hours of naptime. We dressed for the evening; I had what I had but was at least as well dressed as some of the guests. Shirts with small black and white checkers seem to be in fashion for the guys and low cut tops and short skirts was the code for the girls. As I remembered from my trip to Cuba the dancing is very suggestive with a lot of close contact gyrating.

Back to the wardrobe list. Jose was in a white suit with a vest. I think the tie was red but I'll have to check my photos; the shoes were red. The crease in his pants could be used to slice bread. The cousin, Fernando (I found out his name later) was wearing a red suit and Filip in a canary yellow suit and vest. Tomek looked like a banker in a conservative grey suit and tie but with shiny silver shoes. They looked great on the bandstand.

Some things I didn't understand. I know Jose and Isa are high up in the organization behind the club; suspect they might even own a piece of it. I know Isa had a lot to do with the decor which Tomek explained to me was really authentic, "Could be in Havana;" Pictures everywhere of the famous old cars, street scenes and lots of photos of famous Cuban artists, writers and musicians. Ernest Hemingway looked like he'd been there.

We caravanned in two taxies. The main square was completely sealed off and there was no parking anywhere near so we left all the vehicles at home. Adam had arrived about 6;00 and the reunion with Tomek was fun to watch. They had been together with Darek and Rafal Zelek. (Marcin Kosofski was the piano player from Poland that summer) All went to Maine Jazz Camp, and Vinalhaven.

The caravan got us to the square about 8:00. The square and club were empty but soon started filling up. Jose didn't start 'til 10:00. Here's what I don't understand: the club is modeled in great detail after a Cuban bar/restaurant but from the start they were playing relentless thump thump thump disco. The thump was so loud rather than hearing it you really felt it, sort of hit you in the chest. (Isn't playing loud non-stop music now identified as torture? I longed for even a few moments of silence.)

When they finally came on, Jose's band was, for me almost painfully loud but wildly exciting. The father and two sons played so tightly together it seemed like there was one mind directing all three of them. Tomek and Filip were side by side in the back and were constantly looking at each other grinning as they anticipated the unusual 'hits' and were obviously having a ball. Filip would play absolutely consistent, solid rhythmic bass lines and, from time to time throw in flurries of 16th notes. All night Tomek reacted with a look of, "Wow, where the hell did that come from!" Filip, with only a year and a half playing bass, was amazing and surprised Tomek and his dad and me all night.

Another cousin (I think) was the lead singer and his wife and Jose provided the tight harmony parts. A young trombone player, new to the band did well keeping up and Fernando in his red suit played really well obviously knowing the music inside out.

As I said, for me it was way too loud and I would have enjoyed it more with about 30% less volume but the excitement is undeniable. Unfortunately within seconds of the end of the set the canned thumping started off again, if anything louder. I tried in vain to find a place a bit quieter but there were speakers everywhere including the men's room. Although everything was new and squeaky clean they had a stainless steel trough urinal—I'm sorry but even new and squeaky they are nasty. Interesting, though a bit disconcerting because instead of a blank wall in front of you there was a one way, the other way, mirror so you could see the band and what was going on the dance floor.

At midnight champagne was served and even though we were two stories below ground we could hear the fireworks outside in the square. Estimate of 50,000 people.

There was a huge stage set up; about 60 feet high and wider across than my property at Willow Street. Jose played two more sets with the same intense energy throughout. Relentless thumping in between which continues after the last set until well after 3:00 a.m.. The bar/restaurant upstairs hosted a disc jockey who was just as loud as downstairs but finally he packed it up and I was able to find a comfortable armchair and some pain relief.

I stayed downstairs way too long and tried to find a place as far away as possible from the multiple sound sources. Even so it was fun because Tomek, then Filip, then Isa or Jose or Adam would come to where I was sitting and ask if I was okay, did I want something to eat, or another drink. The hors d'oeuvres were delicious, huge variety, all photogenic.

After a long wait and after not connecting with a 'radio taxi' we regrouped in front of the club in the now empty main square and hiked a few blocks to some waiting, more expensive but welcome taxies. Filip went to his girlfriend's in one and the rest of us in two more, back home and almost immediately to bed.

Slept, out like a light, 'til 10:30 a.m. Jose got up and cooked breakfast for Adam and me and I followed Adam around the Ring Road to the A4 and scooted home to Slawek's. A nap was in order. A toasted cheese sandwich followed and now I'm finishing this episode of *"Travels With Bradski"*.

Happy 2012. Everybody needs it!

Jan. 3, From Joachim's in Krakow

Sorry I missed last night but Joachim needed his computer as he and Veronika worked 'til after 2:00 a.m. on his upcoming exam toward his music PhD. I stayed up but things got silent and I didn't want to wake him up to get online.

So... first things first. I guess it's okay sometimes to be wrong but if I'm going to be wrong I want to be really wrong. New Years Eve, through the front windows of the Cuban Club I could see a portion of the square to the right side of the stage; not the larger part at the front. I told you the estimate was 50,000 people but that's wrong. Joachim confirmed that both the Radio and Polish TV had the crowd at 200,000. I'll spell it out: Two hundred thousand!

OK. Yesterday:

Joachim met Slawek and me at our usual meeting place near the army base entrance. Slawek has been so generous, not allowing me to contribute for food or anything else. At least I was able to get the oil and filters changed in his VW and leave it washed and with a full tank. And I left a few liters of special oil in the trunk.

I went with Joachim first home and then to sit in with two of his piano students. A big part of playing is learning how to accompany, so I was the bouncing ball; had a ball doing it. The students had to "comp" while I played the tune and improvised; fun for me; good practical practice for them.

Then back home for dinner and somehow it got to be very late. At 3 a.m. I was still reading a thriller that Mateusz had loaned me, highly recommended.

This morning I slept through the 3 kids getting off to school and woke about 8:30 to see breakfast on the table. Joachim was asking if I'd like to go to sit in with more students. I said, "Of course"; we had to leave in 15 minutes. When we got back it was time to pack up and head for a small town about 150 km away for a concert. Beata fed us some Zupa and we headed off, planning for a leisurely drive and time for promised dinner before we played.

Last year, on the way home from the Radio 3 show in Warsaw I was driving the Mazda. About two hours shy of Krakow it started losing power, the turbo started making strange whining noises and started to smoke; we were stopped. Today, I was driving and about 20 minutes outside of town guess what . . . no power, strange whining and smoke from the turbo.

We were lucky both times. As we pulled over, (the first turbo melt down was in the middle of the night) a guy driving a special truck designed for carrying cars just happened to be behind us. He was on his way to pick up a car the far side of Krakow and put us on board; took us right to our door at no charge.

This time Joachim's insurance provided a similar truck, which brought us back home. Beata fed us some potato pancakes and we hustled into a taxi, picked up Beata's sisters car and made it to the gig with 45 minutes to spare. I do like to brag and keep my reputation intact. In all the years I've been blowing air through a clarinet I've never missed a gig and have only been late once; not really my fault. I drove both ways. Fun. It was a small Ford with the full sized Mondeo engine; plenty of zip and I had to watch it as, almost on its own it crept up to 160 km. Gig was fun. Small funky bar with worn everything but a full house of listeners. We played one long set, 3 encores and got a standing O at the end. I drove home; late at night I could go faster... we reversed the car swap and now, 2:30 a.m., I'm going to stop writing and go to bed. 8:30 departure time for 3 combo classes and a workshop at a music school in the afternoon. Can't believe tomorrow is my last day here.

I've had apprehensive moments thinking about getting chunks of my spine removed. I know it's considered almost routine, and I know it does no good to worry, but can't help worrying a bit.

I know we have a concert and a workshop Tuesday and Wednesday but no info, what goes when or where.

Joachim needs his laptop so this has to be quick. Another fun day with combo workshops in the a.m. and a 4:00 p.m. concert/clinic/workshop for about 40 junior high and high school kids; lots of blues scales but we got a lot of them improvising and making the changes on Blue Bossa. After explaining the importance of listening Joachim and I ended with a free thing that went all over the place. They turned out the lights and it really was special; the kids were mouse quiet. Damn, I want to keep this going.

So this regrettably is the final post from Poland, Jan 5th 2012 but hopefully not my final time here.

24

End, Finally

The following is an email I wrote mid-October 2005 at Willow St. concerning my still on-going battle with ADD. I'm not sure who I sent it to. (My dear friend Marty Corey, while proof reading, said I sent it to her)

Well, just about everything that could get screwed up did! I'll try to get it all down. I misplaced the address of the woman who wants the Dixie recording. I finally found it and then mis-addressed the envelope twice and finally had to glue a postcard to the front for the address. I did find stamps and finally got it in the mail. Then I decided to finish the frame for the mirror. I got a new one to replace the big one in my room that came crashing down a few weeks ago. I had three sides done but ran out of material for the 4th. I ripped out two before I got one that worked. Then I couldn't find the wire and hook I bought to hang it up. I also couldn't find the corner clamps I needed to put the frame together (I found them after I was finished). I looked for hours for the birdseed I bought yesterday; I just found it now. I couldn't find my camera and finally found it and took the chip to CVS for some prints of the flood and raw sewage bubbling out of the manhole cover into the street and onto my submerged property. I selected about ten that I wanted, specified three copies of some, and then somehow tripped the "print all" mode and ended up with 65 prints. By the time I finally found the wire and hooks (right next to the birdseed) I was too angry and too tired to do any more. This is pretty typical and so frustrating.

As of September 23rd 2005 I'm back on a substantial dose of ADD medication.

After finding the above I seemed to remember something I had written before and looked for it in my files of ramblings. The following "Bad ADD Day" was written in Poland about nine years earlier. Seems that not much has changed.

A Bad ADD Day?

Today, I hope, is just a 'bad ADD day', and has nothing (I hope) to do with the fact that I'm down to 1/4 of my original 'meds'. My friend Jerry said ADD meds are like wearing glasses for reading; she can read without them but she has to squint, gets a headache and doesn't enjoy what she's reading. ADD doesn't provide such tangible symptoms. A headache would be great... I'd know in an instant. "Wow, better take something."

I started the day by over-sleeping and woke up realizing that my small room is a total mess. I decided after coffee to at least try to organize some papers on my desk but couldn't find my glasses. After about an hour of searching I realized they were dangling from the corner of my mouth. A second hour was spent trying to find my return plane ticket home. I remembered stashing it somewhere because I didn't want to take it with me on a tour. I sifted through piles of papers (which all need to be filed) and finally discovered the ticket tucked away in my checkbook. I have no idea what triggered me to select that as a hiding place. Just now, before I sat down to write, I got some new coffee and discovered that I had cleaned up the kitchen and washed all the dishes! I have no recollection of doing that. I don't see that the meds, per-say, prevent these 'bad days'. A negative side effect of being aware is being aware; I know what's going on, and it pisses me off, particularly when it wastes my time. I will find a filing cabinet and hope it doesn't take me 6 months to sort out these papers. At least I know where most of them are; somewhere in several huge stacks. This is the constant day-after-day frustration of this crazy disorder. I am getting more things done now, but it does drive me to distraction and takes a huge amount of concentration, and therefore effort. Playing a Duo concert requires the most intense concentration, and I can do it without the slightest difficulty. Afterwards, I feel tired but in a most relaxed way. The usual hour-and-a-half set that we play goes by in an instant. But try to sort and file papers and I feel exhausted just thinking about it! I'm too wiped out to start most of the time... so I don't, and the piles of papers get higher. I have to learn to follow through on things so that family, and others can perceive the possibility of something happening; that I might succeed. (I need a lot of help from my friends.) I've been reluctant to ask for more help from the family and friends because I've asked a lot, sensed the reluctance and felt uncomfortable.

I'm totally secure in my ability as a musician. Buddy De Franco for decades has been and remains the most significant modern jazz clarinetist in the world. He recorded duos with Art Tatum when he was 17. He is now 72 and still out there. We shared the final concert of last year's Clarinet festival with a top Polish rhythm section and two clarinets. I had no problems 'sparring' with him, not even sweaty palms beforehand. So, I know I can play with the big boys on any stage. But getting there, all the BS, is where I get bogged down and really have problems. It seems ironic to be able to reach such pinnacles on one hand and be such a klutz on the other. It's called ADD. I have to accept that even though my actions have not always been perceived as good, that this does not make me a 'bad person'. It has taken me 59 years to realize this as a thesis, and only in the last few months am I starting to understand the implications and accept that it might apply to me. "It ain't easy". The use of drugs and/or alcohol is usually a rather desperate attempt at self-medication; sometimes it's the only damned thing that seems to help. There are other ways to cope that are not so destructive. Also, as 'The Book' explains, ADD-ers are notoriously poor 'self-observers'. I never had a clue that anything was wrong. I just "felt the draft".

After re-reading this perhaps I've come to grips with the seriousness of my situation. Few of my friends, and I'm sure none of my family, know all the details. I am not making it, and am seriously considering giving up here and moving to Poland, but I'm truly afraid about doing it alone.

I'm disillusioned and upset thinking that all the camp years and last fifteen years with Polish kids has apparently only been of value to me and no one seems willing to help me continue. There is nothing in the Scholarship Fund to allow me to go looking for some more gifted kids or follow through if I found them. I still have the energy but simply can't take the financial heat; I guess that project must come to an end.

I'm not looking or asking for anything. This is just my reality.

I'd like to keep on playing as long as I keep learning and can stay on top of my game; I think I'll know when to stop. If not, I hope a friend will tell me.

I'd like to play my best concert ever and at the end the emcee comes out and says, "Brad won't be coming out for the encore."

Epilogue Two (again)

Hopefully this will be the final attempt to complete this story that seems to get longer as it takes longer. Now, it's November 29th 2011, my mother's 110th birthday.

Back in Poland now, with a disappointing lack of concerts but enjoying the free time. Seeing many good friends without being always in a rush to get somewhere.

Epilogue Three (again, actually and finally)

Jazz players often 'vamp' or play a 'tag' to end a tune. "And here comes grand-ma, swinging on the outhouse door... and here comes grand-ma... etc., etc." Everybody thinks, maybe hopes, it's the end, but it keeps on going, and going.

I've been playing a tag on this project much too long.

I've been working with Lucia, as usual so supportive and instrumental in helping me draw this to a close. So with nothing else to do except play the final chord, hopefully, here comes grand-ma for the last time.

But we'll see. *"The song has ended but the melody lingers on."*

January of 2015—now.

Special thanks to Lucia for really getting this going; and then, finally, stopping.

The final push is on. Last edits, last looks, book cover, and it's done.
But then, you know—you've already read it.
Time now for you to put down this book and get some rest.
Smooth.

Night night.
bt

Pops and Mom. Vinalhaven.